Lessons on Foreign Aid and Economic Development

"This edited volume brings together 12 different chapters that each address important aspects of the political economy of foreign aid. The contributions are wide-ranging, covering everything from the impact of aid on political institutions and health outcomes to recipient-donor relationships and the political motives of aid allocation. These chapters deepen our understanding of how to evaluate and assess various aid practices, and as such are an impressive contribution to the field."
—Emily Skarbek, Political Theory Project, *Brown University*

"Providing foreign aid to developing countries influences international relations. For example, many industrialized countries have experienced increasing immigration since the early 2000s. Does foreign aid help to promote economic development in recipient countries which, in turn, will give rise to less migration from developing countries? Donor countries pursue strategic objectives when providing foreign aid. Do these objectives relate to changes in government ideology such as from Barack Obama to Donald Trump? This book deals with political-economic determinants and consequences of foreign aid. Experts portray the extent to which aid helps to fulfill its intended purposes. Clearly, political-economic determinants and consequences of foreign aid have been examined for a long time. During changing international relations, this book is published at the right time."
—Niklas Potrafke, Professor of Economics, *University of Munich, Ifo Institute*

"Development policy has become a tensely discussed, politically contested and often misunderstood policy area; in particular the debate around development aid is confusing. This book provides a timely, concise and comprehensive analysis of this urgent issue. It asks important questions and helps to understand successes and failures of development aid."
—Andreas Freytag, Professor of Economics, *Friedrich Schiller Universität Jena*

Nabamita Dutta • Claudia R. Williamson
Editors

Lessons on Foreign Aid and Economic Development

Micro and Macro Perspectives

palgrave
macmillan

Editors
Nabamita Dutta
University of Wisconsin-La Crosse
La Crosse, WI, USA

Claudia R. Williamson
Mississippi State University
Mississippi, MS, USA

ISBN 978-3-030-22120-1 ISBN 978-3-030-22121-8 (eBook)
https://doi.org/10.1007/978-3-030-22121-8

This Palgrave Macmillan imprint is published by the registered company Springer Nature Switzerland AG
The registered company address is: Gewerbestrasse 11, 6330 Cham, Switzerland

Preface

A distinguishing feature of this book is that it deepens the reader's understanding of the impact of foreign aid on development outcomes based on the latest findings in the literature over the past decade. A strong viewpoint that has been existing in the economics literature, especially with regard to economic development, polarizes the perception of foreign aid as being either beneficial or damaging, as a blessing or a curse. As an unfortunate consequence, many readers perceive aid's impact based on the work of scholars who are assessing the impact of aid in light of such polarities.

This book sheds light on the recent studies that have tried to deepen our understanding of the ambiguous relationship between aid and its aftereffects. It highlights the work of scholars who have developed more layered and nuanced findings with regard to aid's impact on a variety of development outcomes, for example, donor characteristics, political motives behind aid giving, evaluation of aid projects, and their effectiveness including the differential impact based on type of aid.

La Crosse, WI, USA — Nabamita Dutta
Mississippi, MS, USA — Claudia R. Williamson

Contents

Notes on Contributors

Faisal Z. Ahmed is an assistant professor at Princeton University. His research and teaching interests focus on political economy and international economics. Some of his work has been published in the *American Political Science Review, American Economic Journal – Macroeconomics, Review of Economics and Statistics, and the Journal of Law, Economics, and Organization*. Prior to joining the faculty at Princeton, Faisal was a Prize Research Fellow at Nuffield College, Oxford University. He spent the 2016–2017 academic year as the William C. Bark National Fellow at the Hoover Institute. Before transitioning to academia, he spent a few years as an international and macroeconomist at the White House Council of Economic Advisers and the Federal Reserve Bank of Chicago.

Christian Bjørnskov is Professor of Economics at Aarhus University in Denmark, and also affiliated researcher at the Research Institute of Industrial Economics in Stockholm, Sweden. As a guest professor, he has also taught Development Economics at the University of Göttingen and the University of Heidelberg. Bjørnskov's research on development economics, political economy and foreign aid has appeared in numerous journals including the *American Journal of Political Science*, the *Journal of Development Economics* and the *Journal of Comparative Economics*. He is a regular columnist at the Danish financial newspaper *Børsen* and editor of the prize-winning economics blog punditokraterne.dk.

Scott A. Burns is Assistant Professor of Economics at Ursinus College, where he is co-director of the Economics Ambassadors program. His research focuses on the intersection of monetary and development economics as well as Austrian economics, public choice economics, and entrepreneurship. He received his BS in Economics from Louisiana State University in 2011 and his MA and PhD in Economics from George Mason University in 2016.

Carrie B. Dolan is an assistant professor in the Department of Kinesiology and Health Sciences. Her research examines the allocation of health aid within the context of effectiveness, efficiency, and equity. Through combining household panels with geographically referenced data, Dolan's research determines the contribution of health aid on key health outcomes. She earned an MPH in Epidemiology from Tulane University and a PhD in Healthcare Policy and Research from the Virginia Commonwealth University School of Medicine.

Thomas K. Duncan is Assistant Professor of Economics in the Davis College of Business and Economics at Radford University. His articles have appeared in journals such as the *Independent Review*, the *Review of Austrian Economics*, the *Journal of Private Enterprise and Peace Economics*, *Peace Science and Public Policy*, and he has been a contributor to the *Oxford Handbook of Austrian Economics.* Duncan received his PhD from George Mason University in 2013. He received his MA in Economics from San Jose State University in 2008 and a BA in Economics from Hampden-Sydney College in 2005.

Nabamita Dutta is Associate Professor of Economics at University of Wisconsin-La Crosse, USA. Her articles have appeared in the *European Journal of Political Economy*, *Kyklos*, *Industrial Relations: A Journal of Economy and Society*, *Journal of Institutional Economics*, *Small Business Economics*, *International Review of Economics and Finance*, and *Economic Modelling and the Review of International Economics.* She has been a visiting research scholar at various institutions in India, Australia, and Germany. Her research has also been covered by the media, in particular by the BBC, *New York Magazine*, and Ideas for India.

Michael A. Fakutiju is a second year PhD candidate in Economics at Mississippi State University. In 2015, he received his MA in Economics at New Mexico State University. His research interests include applied microeconomics, development economics, and public economics. His work has appeared in the *Journal of Economics and Sustainable Development* and *Environmental Management and Sustainable Development.*

Stefanie Haeffele is a senior research fellow, the Deputy Director of Academic and Student Programs, and a senior fellow with the F. A. Hayek Program for Advanced Study in Philosophy, Politics, and Economics at the Mercatus Center at George Mason University. She is the co-author of *Community Revival in the Wake of Disaster: Lessons in Local Entrepreneurship* (Palgrave Macmillan) with Virgil Henry Storr and Laura E. Grube, and the editor of *Knowledge and Incentives in Policy: Using Public Choice and Market Process Theory to Analyze Public Policy Issues*. She previously worked for the Federal Emergency Management Agency and the US Forest Service.

Anne Lynn Hobson is a program manager for Academic and Student Programs at the Mercatus Center at George Mason University as well as a PhD student in economics at George Mason University. She previously worked with Facebook and the R Street Institute. Her writing, focusing on technology policy and resiliency, has appeared in the *Wall Street Journal*, *Reason*, *The Hill*, and other publications.

Shaomeng Jia is Visiting Assistant Professor of Economics at Muskingum University. He received his PhD in Economics from Mississippi State University in 2018. His research focuses on international development, including examining growth policies, entrepreneurship, regulation and foreign aid, in particular. Jia's work has appeared in *Contemporary Economic Policy* and the *Journal of Entrepreneurship and Public Policy*. It is his hope that his research can help people in developing countries, especially those 1.3 billion living in extreme poverty.

Christopher Kilby is a professor in the Economics Department at the Villanova School of Business at Villanova University. His focus within economics is on the political economy of foreign aid, a topic at the intersection of economics and political science. He does empirical research on this topic as well. His work includes statistical analysis that examines the influence of the US and other major donors on the behavior of international financial institutions such as the World Bank and the Asian Development Bank, the domestic politics of US bilateral aid, and the impact of aid on developing countries. Kilby serves on the program committee of an annual international conference called The Political Economy of International Organizations and on the editorial board of the journal *The Review of International Organizations* (edited by Axel Dreher). He is the book review editor.

Katharina Michaelowa studied Economics at the Universities of Mannheim and Delhi (Delhi School of Economics, India). In 1998, she received her PhD in Economics at Hamburg University/Hamburg Institute of International Economics. From 1997–2000, she was an administrator at the OECD, Paris (development research, co-ordination of donor policies, education policy and educational indicators); from 2000–2006, she was a researcher at the Hamburg Institute of International Economics. Since December 2001, she has served as head of the research group "Trade and Development". Since September 2006, she has been a professor at the Institute for Political Science (IPZ), University of Zurich, and from January 2009 to December 2011, she has been the Director of the Center for International and Comparative Studies (CIS). Since July 2011, Michaelowa has served as chair of the Research Committee on Development Economics of the German Economic Association, and since January 2013, she has been a member of the National Research Council of the Swiss National Science Foundation.

Olga Nicoara is Assistant Professor of Economics at Ursinus College. She specializes in political economy, economies in transition, economic development, entrepreneurship, and social research. She earned her doctorate in Economics from George Mason University after graduating from the Academy of Economic Studies in Bucharest, Romania.

Estefania Lujan Padilla earned her BA in Economics with a minor in Finance from the Universidad Francisco Marroquín (UFM, Guatemala) in Spring 2016. Prior to joining Texas Tech University, she taught Managerial Economics at the School of Economic Sciences at UFM. Padilla provided research assistance at the think tank UFM Market Trends and some projects focused on issues in Guatemala (such as, sugar price models and public investment on biodiversity).

Liya Palagashvili is an assistant professor of economics at State University of New York, Purchase, and a Research Fellow at New York University School of Law. Palagashvili's academic papers on topics of economic development, institutions, and foreign aid, as well as on comparative governance, transition economies, and entrepreneurship have appeared in journals such as *Public Choice, Supreme Court Economic Review, History of Political Economy, Journal of Institutional Economics, University of Chicago Legal Forum, Journal of Law, Economics, and Policy*, among others. In addition to academic writing, Palagashvili's articles have appeared in media outlets such as *the Wall Street Journal, Forbes, U.S. News and World Report, Yahoo Finance, Newsday, Philadelphia Inquirer*, among many others. Palagashvili was recently named one of Forbes 2016′30 under 30′ in Law & Policy and has access to promote her work on Forbes.

Claudia R. Williamson is Associate Professor of Economics and the Drew Allen Endowed Fellow at Mississippi State University, USA. Her research focuses on applied microeconomics, the role of culture in development, and the political economy of development policies, such as foreign aid. She currently serves as an editor for the *Journal of Institutional Economics*. Claudia's work has appeared in the *Journal of Law and Economics*, *World Development*, *Journal of Comparative Economics*, *Public Choice*, *Journal of Corporate Finance*, and *Journal of Institutional Economics*. Her research has also appeared in the *Economist* and the BBC.

Andrew T. Young was born and raised in New England. He graduated from the College of the Holy Cross with a BA in Economics and then received his PhD in Economics from Emory University. He has since worked at the University of Mississippi, West Virginia University, and, now, Texas Tech University. He is an author on over 50 peer-reviewed articles in economics journals. His research has been recently focused on historical political economy and, in particular, constitutional economics in Europe of late antiquity and the medieval era.

List of Figures

List of Tables

CHAPTER 1

Introduction

Nabamita Dutta and Claudia R. Williamson

Foreign aid has been a much explored topic in both the economics and political science literature. While the extensive strands of studies have helped us understand the role of foreign aid and the impact that it might have, ambiguous conclusions remain in the literature. This edited volume is an attempt to pull together the relatively recent established findings related to foreign aid.

Perhaps the greatest debate in the literature in this context is the impact foreign aid can have on development outcomes of recipient nations, including economic growth. An extensive set of studies have argued that aid boosts economic growth for recipient nations by helping them escape poverty traps and promoting development (Sachs et al. 2004; Sachs 2005a, b). Yet, the dominant argument in the literature is aid has been ineffective in promoting growth (Easterly 2007a, b; Rajan and Subramanian 2008). Earlier strands of studies disagreed on the impact of foreign aid as they categorized the outcome as black or white, that is, the impact being

N. Dutta (✉)
University of Wisconsin-La Crosse, La Crosse, WI, USA
e-mail: ndutta@uwlax.edu

C. R. Williamson
Mississippi State University, Mississippi, MS, USA
e-mail: claudia.williamson@msstate.edu

N. Dutta, C. R. Williamson (eds.), *Lessons on Foreign Aid and Economic Development*, https://doi.org/10.1007/978-3-030-22121-8_1

'always good' or 'always bad' for recipient nations. More recent studies have explored wide areas of gray, suggesting that aid effectiveness can be very much dependent on the macro and institutional environment of recipient nations and, thus, the notion of categorizing the outcomes in absolute terms of 'good' or 'bad' may not be correct.

Another extensive literature has explored aid's impact on economic and political institutions, sparking another debate as the conclusions have been ambiguous. In the context of political institutions, studies emphasizing the optimistic view of aid argue that foreign aid can have a positive effect on developing countries' political institutions by making them more democratic (see, for instance, Dunning 2004; Goldsmith 2001). The alternative view stresses that aid is not only unable to promote democracy, but it can actually degrade it (see, for instance, Bueno de Mesquita and Smith 2010; Smith 2008; Djankov et al. 2008; Rajan and Subramanian 2007; Bräutigam and Knack 2004; Bauer 2000).

Evidence in the context of foreign aid's effectiveness on economic institutions is similar. Studies concluding that aid does not increase economic freedom are plenty (Young and Sheehan 2014; Knack 2001). In fact, these studies find that aid decreases economic freedom. Heckelman and Knack (2008) find that aid decreases freedom in the 1980s, but aid does not significantly impact economic freedom in the 1990s. IMF involvement may also reduce economic freedom (Dreher and Rupprecht 2007; Knedlik and Kronthaler 2007). Yet, studies like Boockmann and Dreher (2003) show that the number of World Bank projects increases economic freedom.

Other than institutions and economic growth, foreign aid can also have a significant impact on specific development outcomes like health, education, and sanitation. Both micro and macro studies document the success and failure stories of foreign aid with regard to specific development outcomes.

Aid effectiveness is also dependent on donor motives of nations providing aid. In both the economics and political science literature, the significance of politics and leaders in molding development policies for their countries has moved to prominence (see, e.g., Jones and Olken 2005, 2009; McGillivray and Smith 2004; Dreher and Jensen 2013; Potrafke 2009, among others). Yet, until recent times, literature on development aid has ignored the important role that politics can play in shaping aid allocation to recipient nations. Studies assumed motives of donors to be unitary and did not account for differences of ideologies of governments, political and economic incentives, and how political leadership can shape allocation of aid. Recently, a vast number of studies have explored donor motives for aid allocation and have found factors like political and economic motivations, political favoritism, and donors' ideology to be playing crucial roles in such allocations. The type of aid allocated matters a lot in this context and has a direct impact on development outcomes.

This volume not only summarizes the conclusions in the literature about aid's impact on specific development outcomes but also highlights the role of donor motivations, importantly, political preferences and incentives, in aid allocation as well as the role of private aid in affecting development outcomes. A distinguishing feature of this book is that it deepens the reader's understanding of the impact of foreign aid on development outcomes based on the latest findings in the research literature over the past decade. A strong viewpoint that has been existing in the economics literature, especially with regard to economic development, polarizes the perception of foreign aid as being either beneficial or damaging, as a blessing or a curse. As an unfortunate consequence, many readers perceive aid's impact based on the work of scholars who are assessing the impact of aid in light of such polarities.

This book sheds light on the recent studies that have tried to deepen our understanding of the ambiguous relationship between aid and its aftereffects. It highlights the work of scholars who have developed more layered and nuanced findings with regard to aid's impact on a variety of development outcomes, for example, donor characteristics, political motives behind aid giving, evaluation of aid projects, and their effectiveness including the differential impact based on type of aid.

The edited volume is divided into four sections. Section I summarizes some specific development outcomes with regard to foreign aid in the micro and macro context as well different types of aid that can be donated for different purposes. Chapters in this section discuss aid's conditional impact on growth, how types of aid affect outcomes, and how examining health aid at a sub-national level can help us find answers with regard to aid's effectiveness, efficiency, and equity.

In Section II, chapters discuss the role of politics in aid allocation, especially with regard to aid agencies and their motivations in donating aid. One such chapter included evaluates aid agencies, compares them in terms of best practices, and talks about their challenges. Another chapter explores factors that affect World Bank Project evaluations. The final chapter under Section II summarizes donor motives for aid allocation to recipient nations.

Section III discusses foreign aid's impact on institutional quality of recipient nations. The included chapters document aid's impact on political rights of nations, summarizes the inconclusive findings in the literature about aid's impact on economic and political institutions, and also talks about the relationship between state capacity and foreign aid inflows.

Section IV summarizes the role of private aid like remittances and the effect such capital inflows can have on development outcomes. This section further makes the readers aware of how to think about private aid and the limitations they can have.

Section I: Foreign Aid and Macro and Micro Development Outcomes

Chapter 2 by Jia is titled "Foreign Aid Conditionality and Economic Growth." Burnside and Dollar (2000), one of the most influential papers in the 'conditional' aid effectiveness research agenda, concludes that aid can positively influence growth in healthy policy environments, sparking one of the most debated topics in development economics and among policymakers. Easterly et al. (2004), using the exact methodology over a larger dataset, overturn BD's findings, weakening the significance of the aid-policy-growth association. This chapter summarizes, compares, and contrasts the academic work debating whether foreign aid's effective is conditional on the policy and institutional environment. Overall, the chapter sheds light on the aid-policy-growth debate by empirically demonstrating how both sides can be 'right'.

Chapter 3, "Types of Foreign Aid," explores the types of aid that can be donated with different intent and purposes. This chapter by Bjørnskov stresses that foreign aid is given for many purposes and different intentions, yet most studies treat aid flows as a unitary concept. The author relies on factor analysis to yield a statistically valid separation of aid flows into different types. The main types can be interpreted as aid for economic purposes, aid for social purposes (health, education), and aid for reconstruction purposes after wars and disasters; a residual category captures the remaining purposes. Estimating the growth effects of the four separable types of aid suggests that most aid has no effects while reconstruction aid has direct positive effects. The latter type has become more prevalent in recent years. However, as it only applies in special circumstances, it does not provide information on how to improve general flows of aid.

The final chapter included in Section I by Dolan summarizes work with Aid Data examining sub-national health aid flows using a combination of 25 spatially referenced data sets and geospatial impact evaluations. This research answers questions using targeted aid and approaches the aid debate from the perspectives of effectiveness and equity. The general approach is to focus on how the availability of sub-national data allows researchers to address different types of policy questions within the context of effectiveness, efficiency, and equity. Chapter 4 is titled "An Effectiveness, Efficiency, and Equity Approach to Examining Subnational Health Aid."

Section II: The Political Economy of Donor Behavior

In Chap. 5 titled "Evaluating Aid Agencies: Challenges, Comparisons, and Causes of Best Aid Practices," Palagashvili discusses the effectiveness of foreign aid by evaluating performance of aid agencies. The development community has looked to one such answer: they have jump started a movement to identify best aid practices, and to monitor, evaluate, and rank the performance of different foreign aid donors along these measures. There are several main principles guiding best aid practices. Some of these include donors providing transparency in aid, as well as eliminating food and tied aid, minimizing overhead costs, utilizing the recipient countries' institutions, specializing aid, and allocating aid to countries that are both low income and democratically free. Although foreign aid donors have committed to implementing these best aid practices, the research on donor performance and rankings show that donors are still not reaching their stated goals. This chapter summarizes the findings in the literature on donor performance and rankings, including the comparison of bilateral and multilateral aid institutions. Lastly, this chapter examines the literature surrounding the factors that influence donors' decisions to engage in best aid practices. Questions of donor motivation and the political economy of donor strategies and performance have come under scrutiny for influencing ineffective aid strategies.

Chapter 6 by Kilby and Michaelowa explores factors that influence World Bank Project Evaluations. In July 2011, the World Bank's Independent Evaluation Group (IEG) made the World Bank Project Performance database available to the public. With global coverage and spanning the range of sectors important for economic development, this data are a valuable resource for research about development effectiveness, what works and what does not. The chapter first provides a brief overview of the IEG's rating process and the classifications used by the World Bank that may help scholars interested in evaluations, but unfamiliar with World Bank terminology, to use and interpret the database. Second, this chapter examines whether geopolitical or institutional factors influence project performance assessments. The authors focus on how the IEF selects projects for performance assessment and what factors affect project ratings in those assessments. They find some evidence that bureaucratic factors influence selection but only one geopolitical variable—UNSC non-permanent membership—influences IEG ratings.

An important source of capital for developing is undeniably foreign aid in spite of its mixed success and failure stories. Yet, as Tingley (2010) points out this source can be very volatile as donors, while allocating aid, can weigh historical, strategic, geographical, and such factors as perceived by them differently. Chapter 7 by Dutta and Williamson titled "Aid Allocation and Outcomes: What Role Do Political Motives Play?" summarizes the growing literature on donor motives for aid allocation to recipient nations.

Section III: Foreign Aid's Effect on Institutional Quality

Section III summarizes aid's impact on institutional quality. These chapters talk about whether state capacity is affected by foreign aid inflows, the deteriorating impact that aid from the United States has on political rights and how it can strengthen the durability of authoritarian governance, and if foreign aid has the power to affect political and economic institutions.

Young and Padilla explore the relationship between state capacity and foreign aid allocation in Chap. 8, which is titled "Foreign Aid and Recipient State Capacity." A number of researchers have observed that wealthy countries have large states. This observation has been the initial basis for the *state capacity hypothesis*: a critical (if not necessary) condition for sustained economic growth is a state possessing the infrastructure to collect sufficient revenues (*fiscal capacity*) and provide rule of law (*legal capacity*). Poor countries often notably lack such state capacity: revenues as a share of GDP are small; their legal systems are corrupt and/or otherwise dysfunctional. An interesting question, then, is whether foreign aid flows tend to be associated with improvement or deterioration in state capacities. The chapter assembles cross-country data on foreign aid flows and dimensions of state capacity to address this question empirically.

In Chap. 9 titled "Foreign Aid and Repression," Ahmed investigates if aid given by the largest bilateral donor actually harms political rights of recipient nations. For many developing countries, foreign aid comprises a nontrivial share of state revenue that can shape a recipient's governance. For some governments, aid may be a means to repress their populations. This article presents evidence that aid from the world's largest bilateral donor—namely, the United States—harms political rights in recipient countries and strengthens the durability of authoritarian governance. US aid does so by weakening government accountability via the taxation channel. These findings run counter to the stated intentions of the US government—and other bilateral donors—to foster political liberalization abroad via bilateral economic assistance.

In the final chapter of Section III, Chap. 10, Dutta, Fakutiju and Williamson summarize the findings in the literature about aid's impact on recipients' institutional quality. Foreign aid's impact on recipients' institutions is a much-researched topic. Many studies have characterized aid's impact on institutional quality as being detrimental; however, there are counter arguments and evidence suggesting that aid can positively increase political and economic freedom under certain institutional or macro arrangements. The main purpose of this chapter is to summarize the recent studies in this area.

Section IV: The Political Economy of Privately Provided Aid

The final chapters explore privately provided aid and the related development outcomes for nations that receive such allocation. Chapter 11, "Potential Pitfalls in Private Aid: A Cautionary Note for Non-Governmental Assistance" by Duncan stresses that while there is a broad appeal for using private development assistance over official development, assistance, limitations to effectiveness do remain. Those who view private aid as a cure-all for development and humanitarian projects may assume too much. Private aid faces many of the same or similar issues as official aid. An understanding of these particular challenges is important for those who desire to improve the condition of those abroad, and a cautious approach is advised.

Chapter 12 elaborates on the role of personal remittances and Foreign Direct Investment (FDI) as the forms of international private aid most compatible with sustainable economic growth and development. The chapter stresses that remittances and FDI are not only the most prevalent forms of private aid, but also the most effective forms at improving standards of living, market complexity, and the institutional prospects in poor nations. Globalization has led to increased flow of remittances and FDI from developed to developing economies. The increased flow of funds across borders helped stimulate the emergence of alternative payment technologies and microfinance institutions. These private initiatives are better suited to address the specific needs of local communities than foreign aid and other top-down state-led measures.

Lastly, in Chap. 13, Haeffele and Hobson examine remittances between the United States and Cuba since 1993 and finds that remittance senders, recipients, and aid providers act as entrepreneurs by leveraging local, context-specific knowledge and social connections to identify needs and invent new, creative ways to provide aid.

References

Bauer, Peter T. 2000. From Subsistence to Exchange and Other Essays. Princeton: Princeton University Press.

Boockmann, Bernhard and Axel Dreher. 2003. The contribution of the IMF and the World Bank to economic freedom. European Journal of Political Economy, 19 (3): 633–649.

Bräutigam, Deborah A., and Stephen Knack. 2004. Foreign Aid, Institutions and Governance in Sub-Saharan Africa, Economic Development and Cultural Change. 52: 255–285.

Bruce Bueno de Mesquita, and Alastair Smith. 2010. Leader Survival, Revolutions and the Nature of Government Finance, American Journal of Political Science. 54: 936–950.

Burnside, Craig, and David Dollar. 2000. Aid, policies and growth. American Economic Review, 90(4): 847–869.

Djankov, Simeon, Jose G. Montalvo, and Marta Reynal-Querol. 2008. The curse of aid. Journal of Economic Growth 13, 169–194.

Dreher, Axel and Nathan M. Jensen. 2013. "Country or Leader? Political Change and UN General Assembly Voting." European Journal of Political Economy 29 (3): 183–196.

Dreher, Axel., and Sarah M. Rupprecht. 2007. IMF programs and reforms – inhibition or encouragement? Economics Letters 95 (3): 320–326.

Dunning, Thad. 2004. Conditioning the Effects of Aid: Cold War Politics, Donor Credibility, and Democracy in Africa, International Organization, 58: 409–423.

Easterly, W. 2007a. Are aid agencies improving? Economic Policy, 22(52): 633–678.

Easterly, W. 2007b. Was development assistance a mistake? American Economic Review Papers and Proceedings, 97(2): 328–332.

Easterly, W., R. Levine, and D. Roodman. 2004. New Data, New Doubts: A Comment on Burnside and Dollar's 'Aid, Policies, and Growth' (2000), American Economic Review, 94(3): 774–80.

Goldsmith, Arthur A. 2001. Foreign Aid and Statehood in Africa, International Organization 55: 123–148.

Heckelman, Jac C., and Stephen Knack. 2008. Foreign aid and market-liberalizing reform. Economica, 75: 524–548.

Jones, Benjamin F. and Benjamin A. Olken. 2009. Hit or miss? The effect of assassinations on institutions and war. American Economic Journal: Macroeconomics 1: 55–87.

Jones, Benjamin F. and Benjamin A. Olken. 2005, Do leaders matter? National leadership and growth since World War II. Quarterly Journal of Economics 120: 835–864.

Knack, Stephen. 2001. Aid dependence and the quality of governance: cross-country empirical tests. Southern Economic Journal, 68 (2), 310–329.

Knedlik, Tobias, and Franz Kronthaler. 2007. Aid and economic freedom: an empirical investigation using the heritage index. Journal of Development Perspectives 3 (1): 116–135.

McGillivray, F., and A. Smith. 2004. The impact of leadership turnover on trading relations between states, International Organization, 58: 567–600.

Potrafke, Niklas. 2009. Does government ideology influence political alignment with the US? An empirical analysis of voting in the UN General Assembly. Review of International Organizations 4: 245–268.

Rajan, Raghuram, and Arvind Subramanian. 2008. Aid and growth. Review of Economics and Statistics, 90 (4): 643–665.

Rajan, Raghuram, and Arvind Subramanian. 2007. Does aid affect governance? American Economic Review, 97(2): 322–327.

Sachs, Jeffrey D. 2005a. The end of poverty: Economic possibilities of our time. New York: Penguin.

Sachs, Jeffrey D. 2005b. Investing in development: A practical plan to achieve the millennium development goals (UN Millennium Project). London: Earthscan.

Sachs, J.D., J.W. McArthur, G. Schimdt-Traub, M. Kruk, C. Bahadur, M. Faye and G. McCord. 2004. Ending Africa's poverty trap. Brookings Papers on Economic Activity, 1: 117–240 (Washington: The Brookings Institution).

Smith, Alastair. 2008. The Perils of Unearned Income, Journal of Politics, 70: 780–793.

Tingley, D. 2010. Donors and domestic politics: Political influences on foreign aid effort. The Quarterly Review of Economics and Finance, 50(1): 40–49.

Young, Andrew T. and Kathleen M. Sheehan. 2014. Foreign aid, institutional quality, and growth. European Journal of Political Economy, 36: 195–208.

SECTION I

Foreign Aid and Macro and Micro Development Outcomes

CHAPTER 2

Foreign Aid Conditionality and Economic Growth

Shaomeng Jia

Introduction

For the past 50 years, there have been numerous studies assessing the effectiveness of foreign aid. The conflicting empirical evidence keeps this area a highly controversial one in development studies. Although the academic literature has revealed some basic facts about what aid can do versus what aid cannot do, it also leaves us with more questions to answer. As outcomes of aid may require a long time frame, evaluating aid usefulness and advancing our knowledge on aid may also need long-run analysis. Some scholars consider the debate over foreign aid's effectiveness to be over; however, we should expect the debate of aid effectiveness to continue as long as there is allocation of developmental aid.

Among the multi-generations of foreign aid research, a large body of literature considers the aid-growth nexus. As one of the most important targets of foreign aid, economic growth serves as the principal role in guiding the distribution of aid dollars. For example, the most widely accepted definition and measure of foreign aid, official development assistance (ODA) of the Organisation for Economic Co-operation and Development (OECD) Development Assistance Committee (DAC),

S. Jia (✉)
Muskingum University, New Concord, OH, USA

N. Dutta, C. R. Williamson (eds.), *Lessons on Foreign Aid and Economic Development*, https://doi.org/10.1007/978-3-030-22121-8_2

focuses on promoting economic development and poverty reduction. Other types of aid from non-DAC donors are also given in line with similar goals.

Economic growth, hence, is one of the most important outcome measures of development assistance effectiveness. Mainly, this outcome measure has concerned aid researchers and policymakers for decades when they were trying to capture any significance of the 'aid-growth' relation. Recent papers illustrate aid effectiveness at the micro level or project level (Skarbek and Leeson 2009; Kimura et al. 2012; Miyamoto and Chiofalo 2015; Riddell and Niño-Zarazúa 2016; United Nations 2015). However, the evidence at the micro level disappears when economists aggregate into macro-level measures, especially economic growth rates (Guillaumont and Chauvet 2001; Hudson and Mosley 2001; Hansen and Tarp 2001; Lensink and White 2001; Lu and Ram 2001; Easterly 2003; Islam 2005; Rajan and Subramanian 2008; Doucouliagos and Paldam 2010; Yusuf 2012; Chatelain and Ralf 2014; Dreher and Langlotz 2017).

The evaporation of macro-level evidence on aid effectiveness is referred to as the micro-macro paradox of aid (Mosley 1986). The long debate of aid effectiveness consists of two sides—either making efforts to defend or challenge the micro-macro paradox of aid. Evidence indicating aid can positively affect economic outcomes is mostly found at the project level, where aid targets a specific outcome rather than attempting to impact the overall economy (Skarbek and Leeson 2009). Indeed, research in estimating the complexities of aid effectiveness at the cross-country level is fragile, which can be attributed to many reasons. Apart from the common technical problems, such as shortcomings in data availability, imperfect methodologies, and dealing with endogeneity (Hansen and Tarp 2001; Lu and Ram 2001; Roodman 2007; Rajan and Subramanian 2008; Tan 2009; Clemens et al. 2012; Juselius et al. 2014; Qian 2015; Dreher and Langlotz 2017), debates in development theories regarding aid effectiveness remain unsettled.

Foreign Aid and the Poverty Trap

Why are poor countries poor? According to classical economics, subject to the dilemma between exponential growth in population and restrictions of land and other capital resources (Malthus 1789; Ricardo 1817), without technological improvement, income per capita stays around the subsistence level in the long run. However, this theory mainly describes the situation in the pre-industrial society, not the late twentieth and twenty-first centuries. Neoclassical growth theory, on the other hand, attributes poverty to insufficient physical capital (Harrod 1939; Domar 1946; Solow 1956), human capital (Mincer 1958; Schultz 1961; Becker 1962), or lack of technology (Romer 1990; Grossman and Helpman 1990). Regardless, inputs, especially capital, is considered the key to development.

Following this mindset, there is a strand of literature that views underdevelopment as the result of a shortage of capital accumulation. For example, Jeffrey D. Sachs (2005) in his book *The End of Poverty: Economic Possibilities for Our Time*,[1] argues that poor countries are poor because they do not have enough income to save and thus invest. Hence, without enough investment, growth does not happen, and these countries are stuck in a 'poverty trap'. Foreign aid is seen as a cure for poverty since it can be channeled to poor countries without enough income to save and grow. According to Sach's 'big push' theory, once we fill the development "financial gap" with foreign aid dollars, an underdeveloped country would be pulled out of the poverty trap and start to grow by itself.

For some of the least developed countries (LDCs) in the South of Sahara African region, foreign aid has been financing development since their independence during the 1960s and 1970s. Measured as a percentage of a recipient country's Gross Domestic Products (GDP), aid dollars make up no less than ten percent of GDP for countries, including but not limited to, Malawi, Sierra Leon, Liberia, Zambia, and Tanzania. Aid received by some of the least developed countries, especially fragile states, can exceed their GDP. For example, Liberia, one of the most heavily aid-reliant countries, received aid accounting for 176 percent of its GDP in 2010.

A tremendous amount of development assistant aid dollars has been distributed for decades. According to OECD's data, donor countries have devoted about 3900 billion US Dollars (2015 prices and exchange rates) ODA to the top 50 recipient countries during 1970–2016, with 15.8 billion US Dollars (2015 prices and exchange rates) allocated in 2016 alone. The number has been climbing steadily since 1970, with a leap in aid dollars distribution for every decade, except for the 1980s and 1990s (OECD 2018). However, many aid recipient countries remain at the same level of income.

If a country started receiving aid in 1960 and managed to keep a minimum annual GDP growth rate of 1.4 percent, we should observe its national income being doubled in 50 years. This means income for that country should have increased twofold by now. Unfortunately, this is not observed in many aid recipient countries, especially LDCs. For instance, Sierra Leon has been receiving foreign aid since the 1960s, but GDP per capita has been stagnant around 400 dollars (in 2010 constant dollars). Worse, GDP per capita of Liberia, another aid-dependent country, went from over 1000 dollars in 1960 to about 300 dollars today (in 2010 constant dollars). This indicates that development aid could accompany negative growth (ELR 2004; Jia and Williamson 2019).

In the past half a century, we are short of strong evidence supporting sustainable growth with the assistance of foreign aid. Although foreign aid may have worked in certain cases—ignited growth in a few countries for a period, it is not the way out of the 'poverty trap'. The fact that many LDCs do not even grow at one to two percent annually for decades challenges us to investigate more fundamental reasons than merely "not having enough savings".

Apparently, what sustainable growth requires are incentives to be productive. Many growth theories more or less follow the 'factor accumulation' mindset—more inputs transform to more outputs. One thing they fail to explain is why some countries cannot accumulate these factors to begin with. Having more inputs may increase a particular output, but this does not assure that a recipient country knows how to utilize the additional resources, thus solving economic problems (Skarbek and Leeson 2009). Indeed, economic growth is about increasing productivity. If more aid resources and other inputs do not contribute to improvement in "know how", they would not transform to improvement in productivity. Thus, an aid recipient country would not grow no matter how much aid it receives. As a result, examining the incentives to be productive and the ability to best utilize resources is critical in understanding economic growth in general, and aid's ability to influence living standards.

Foreign Aid-Policy-Growth

Triggered by the debt crisis in the developing countries during 1980s, the international community realized that policy reform is necessary for aid recipient countries. Agreed upon by the IMF, World Bank, and the US Department of the Treasury, in the 1990s the Washington Consensus (Williamson 1990) became the guiding light of policy recommendations for developing countries. The policy recommendations of the Washington Consensus intended to add more free market reform conditions to aid distribution. Specifically, it targets stabilizing inflation, reducing government deficit, and promoting trade and privatization. Ideally, these policy goals are achieved through allocating aid to recipient countries based on their commitment of policy reform.

Since the Washington Consensus and the focus on reforming policy, scholars began to think that policy could be the missing link in explaining the aid-growth connection. This idea evoked one of the biggest debates in the foreign aid literature.

As one the most influential empirical papers responding to the Washington Consensus, Burnside and Dollar (2000, henceforth "BD") attribute the reason we do not observe aid raising growth (Boone 1994, 1996) to the distortions of policies in recipient countries. With a modified neoclassical framework, this original aid conditionality paper argues that due to imperfections in the international capital markets, the effectiveness of foreign aid depends on how aid is used. If aid is delivered to investment in recipient countries with "good" policies, it will increase the growth rate. If aid is given to a poor policy country, it will fail to significantly impact growth. According to BD, a country with "good" policies distinguishes from those with "bad" policies by having a higher budget surplus, lower inflation, and higher trade openness. Aid dollars should work better in a country with better policies. Thus, good policy is the necessary intermediate for aid to work, but "up through the mid-1990s…donors were not favoring good policy environment" (BD 2000, p. 848).

Based on their sample of 56 recipient countries during 1970–1993, BD find that there exists a positive relationship between economic growth and the interaction term of aid and policy quality. This pattern is especially obvious in their low-income country sample. Hence, BD call for a change of the aid allocation rule and recommends using policy quality as the guidance for aid distribution.

Logically, a recipient country's policy is not irrelevant to the effectiveness of aid. As a type of between governments transfer, a recipient government with better policies is supposed to "know better" about how to make use of aid dollars than does a country with a less efficient government or worse policy environment. However, this logic does not hold against additional empirical testing.

Easterly, Levine and Roodman (2004, henceforth "ELR") update BD's sample by one period and six additional countries. By doing so, they overturn the conclusion of BD. They find that not only does the positive interaction term of aid × policy vanish, but in some of the samples, the sign even changes to negative. ELR add to the aid-policy literature by demonstrating that even for a country with a good policy environment, aid does not promote economic growth. Thus, we should be cautious when using the policy rule in practice.

Led by these two studies, the aid-policy-growth literature splits into two teams, among which, there are a number of articles supporting BD that find evidence of aid promoting economic growth in recipient countries with a good policy environment (Collier and Dehn 2001; Burnside and Dollar 2004; Ali and Isse 2005; Verschoor and Kalwij 2006; Alvi et al. 2008). However, more evidence seems to be in line with ELR in the literature. For example, BD's result might be data driven by excluding five outliers (Dalgaard and Hansen 2001; Hansen and Tarp 2001). Later research also finds no robust evidence that positive economic growth is policy quality pertinent (Brumm 2003; Dalgaard et al. 2004). In fact, aid can either negatively impact growth under good policies or promote growth with bad policies. Aid and policy interaction may "lead to lower growth in the long-run" (Tan 2009, p. 5). In addition to these debates, there is research with mixed conclusions that contribute to the literature (Dayton-Johnson and Hoddinott 2003; Kohama et al. 2003; Ram 2003).

In an effort to investigate the divergence and confusion in the aid-policy-growth debate, Jia and Williamson (2019) re-evaluate the aid conditionality theory using the original BD framework and an updated dataset spanning 52 years. They find that the confusion in the current aid-policy-growth literature is associated with the data sensitive nature of cross-country aid effectiveness research. Aid effectiveness depends on the selection of country-year pairs in sample, choice of methodology, and measurement of institutional quality and growth rate.

As a response to the imperfectness in earlier research, Jia and Williamson include a longer time span (1962–2013), better quality data, multiple advanced estimation techniques (like System Generalized Method of Moments, Pooled Mean Group estimator, and Dynamic Fixed Effects), but they utilize the same framework as BD in order to compare across studies. Consistent with ELR's finding 15 years ago, evidence supporting a positive role of aid in promoting growth in the presence of a good policy environment is weak. The conclusion holds when testing with different sample periods, methods, or with different measurements of growth and institutions. For example, aid does not promote growth during the 1970–1990 period, the post 1990 period, or the 1962–2013 period, even though the policy environment was improving. Particularly, for the post-1990 period, aid may have harmed growth in some recipient countries, regardless of policy quality!

The results from the Pooled Mean Group estimator (1984–2012) further indicate that looking at each of the recipient countries separately, except for Indonesia and Tunisia, policy is irrelevant to aid effectiveness among all other 67 recipient countries in the sample. Aid is detrimental to growth via the channel of policy in eight countries, including some of those with strongest growth like China.

Basically, research supporting the positive role of good policy in the aid-growth relation, including BD, simply assumes the exogeneity of policy. However, this assumption overlooks the complexity of the impact of aid. Aid is more than merely an extra lump sum resource added to a recipient government's budget. Aid also changes the recipient countries in multifold dimensions. For example, amongst other research on the unintended consequences of foreign aid, aid induces corruption (Svensson 2000; Alesina and Weder 2002). Corruption could erode or offset the effects of aid and its intermediate "good policy", which may be attributed to the evaporation of the macro level significance of aid. Jia and Williamson's (2019) finding that aid can decrease growth at any level of policy supports the notion that aid may undermine positive effects from policy. Thus, aid conditional on policy is an ineffective policy recommendation in the long run.

Policy Conditionality and Aid Allocation

To investigate the role good policy plays in bridging foreign aid and economic growth, we may want to examine changes in policy quality and aid allocation since BD (1970–1993). After the 1990s, many recipient countries improved their policies, such as by becoming more open to free trade. The enhanced policy environment provides us with a good natural experiment to observe if the effectiveness of aid on economic growth has improved accordingly. Figure 2.1, replicated from Jia and Williamson (2019), allows us to contrast the quantile plot of policy index defined by BD during 1970–1993 (in Panel a) and 1990–2013 (in Panel b).[2]

As Fig. 2.1 indicates, about 75 percent of observations in the BD policy index are scored below two during 1970–1993; however, close to 75 percent of observations in the BD policy index in the post-1990 sample are scored over two. According to BD's good policy argument, improved policies over time should be accompanied by a positive impact of aid on

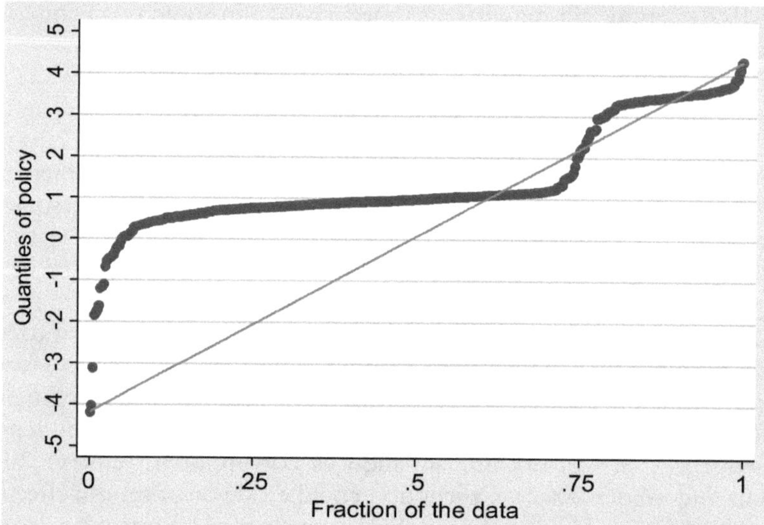

Fig. 2.1 Quantile plot of policy, BD specification, 1970–1993 full sample. (Source: Author's calculation based on data collected from World Bank (1978), Sachs and Warner (1995), Wacziarg and Welch (2008), and Clemens et al. (2012))

growth. However, improved policies seem to have not been facilitating aid, as growth is not observed in many of the recipient countries. As a policy recommendation, good policy has not helped make aid effective. Possibly and partially, this could be attributed to the current aid allocation patterns.

Are countries with better policy awarded with more aid dollars? The answer to this question may explain the ineffectiveness of aid on growth with a better policy environment. Table 2.1 selects the country and period pairs on the tail of the plots from Fig. 2.2 and separates them into two groups—one group with the bottom five percent policy scores and the other group from the top five percent in policy scores.

Indicated in Table 2.1, during 1990–2013, on average, countries with the bottom five percent policy scores received 85 percent more aid compared with how much the top five percent received, as a percentage of their GDP. Based on the policy index ranging between negative five to positive five, the mean policy score for the latter group is 2.77, while the

Table 2.1 Recipient countries with bottom five percent and top five percent policy scores

Countries with bottom five percent policy scores—Mean policy score = −0.91, mean aid/GDP = 2.17

Country	*Periods*			
D.R. Congo	1990–1993	1994–1997	1998–2001	
Peru	1990–1993			
Brazil	1990–1993	1994–1997		
Argentina	1990–1993			
Sierra Leone	1990–1993			
Zambia	1990–1993			
Nigeria	1990–1993	1994–1997		
Venezuela	1990–1993			2002–2005

Countries with top five percent policy scores—Mean policy score = 2.77, mean aid/GDP = 1.17

Country	*Periods*			
Thailand		1998–2001		
El Salvador			2002–2005	2010–2013
Tunisia			2002–2005	
Panama		1998–2001	2002–2005	
Argentina	1994–1997	1998–2001		
Morocco			2002–2005	2010–2013
Mali		1998–2001		
Ethiopia		1998–2001		
Ecuador		1998–2001		

Source: Author's calculation based on data collected from World Bank (1978), Sachs and Warner (1995), Wacziarg and Welch (2008), and Clemens et al. (2012)

former group has −0.91. Apparently, countries with bottom policy scores receive more aid than countries with top policy scores do. Although recipient countries have improved their policies longitudinally, disproportionately more aid has been allocated to countries with the poorest policies cross-sectionally.

The question remains is, why do donor countries favor recipient countries with worse policies? During 1990–2013, amongst the 19 recipient countries rated as those with the bottom ten percent policy scores, nine of them are from the 13 countries with the bottom ten percent income—D.R. Congo, Zambia, Tanzania, Sierra Leone, Malawi, Ethiopia, Madagascar, Nigeria, and Syrian. Not surprisingly, most of the poorest

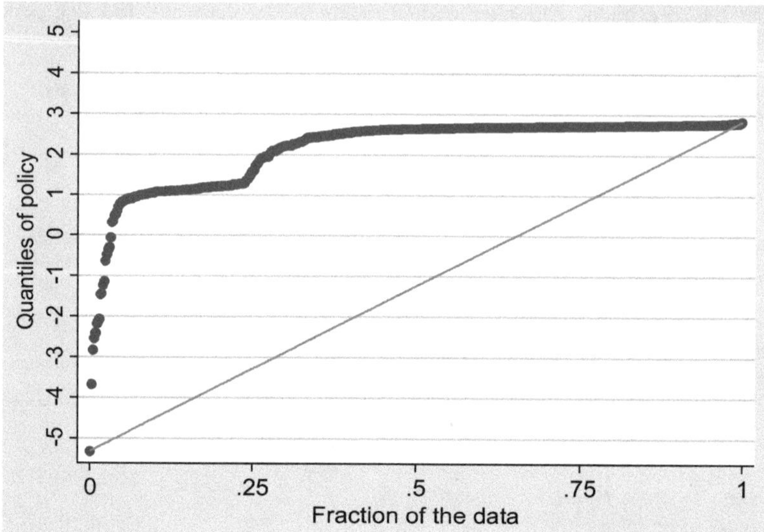

Fig. 2.2 Quantile plot of policy, BD specification, 1990–2013 full sample. (Source: Author's calculation based on data collected from World Bank (1978), Sachs and Warner (1995), Wacziarg and Welch (2008), and Clemens et al. (2012))

countries in the world are also those with the worst policies. Evidence suggests that the poorest countries are the neediest recipients for aid; countries with better policies are also wealthier. Better policy countries have higher growth rates regardless of foreign aid.

What if aid is allocated to countries with good policies, as BD would suggest? Would aid work then? Many studies addressing conditionality of aid—allocating aid conditionally on the commitment of policy reform has been largely ineffective. There is weak to no evidence supporting the positive role of policy in the aid-policy-growth relation. For example, Crawford (1997) discusses that the failure of aid conditionality-requiring political reform in recipient countries undermines both the credibility and effectiveness of aid. Dollar and Pritchett (1998) reveal that aid is "unlikely to bring about lasting reform" (p. 18), as it is difficult to monitor and force beyond the life of the aid program, let alone the incentives from the donors. Lu and Ram (2001) do not observe any impact of aid on growth, in the presence of good policies, once country fixed effects are controlled for. Brumm (2003), with improved econometric methodology, discovers negative effect of aid on economic growth even with sound policies; Dalgaard et al. (2004) conclude that not only the BD policy index, alternative policy measures, like the World Bank Country Policy and Institutional Assessment index (CPIA) introduced by Collier and Dollar (2001, 2002), also show very weak evidence supporting aid effectiveness on economic growth either.

Instead of policy, Hansen and Tarp (2001) identify that aid increases growth via the investment channel. Islam (2005) argues that political stability overrules economic policies and determines aid effectiveness; it is also policy that promotes growth with the assistance of more aid rather than aid increasing growth with a good policy environment. Rajan and Subramanian (2008) call for rethinking the current aid policies, as there is little robust evidence supporting that aid in any form contributes to growth, under any conditions. Doucouliagos and Paldam (2010) conducted a meta-study on the aid effectiveness literature but find no support for aid conditionality. Yusuf (2012) and Chatelain and Ralf (2014) contend that aid does not impact growth positively, with any type of policy.

In addition to the aid-policy-growth, Jia and Williamson (2019) add to the aid conditionality literature by replacing economic growth with four other well-being indicators, as suggested by the literature (Mosley et al. 2004; Watkins et al. 2005; Cogneau and Naudet 2007; Williamson 2008; Chong et al. 2009; Holtham and Hazelwood 2010; Guillaumont and Wagner 2014; Page and Shimeles 2015; Breitwieser and Wick 2016; Furukawa 2016; Gillanders 2016; Asongu and Nwachukwu 2017; Briggs 2017). These four alternative outcome measures are poverty, income inequality (GINI coefficient), unemployment rate, and Human Development Index (HDI). However, similar to economic growth, they are not affected by aid regardless of the quality of policy.

In fact, aid and policies are actually "substitutes", where a good policy environment may reduce the effectiveness of foreign aid (Dalgaard and Hansen 2001). Good policies stimulate growth, but they do necessarily relate to aid's effectiveness (Hudson and Mosley 2001); hence, policy does not necessarily play a role in the complex aid-growth relation.

Foreign Aid-Institutions-Growth

As Rodrik et al. (2004) simply put: institutions rule. Institutions, as defined by North (1991), are the "humanly devised constraints that structure political, economic and social interaction" that includes both formal rules (constitutions, laws, property rights) and informal constraints (customs, traditions) (North 1991, p. 97). Institutions "provide the incentive structure of an economy... and shapes the direction of economic change towards growth, stagnation, or decline" (North 1991, p. 97).

In the early institutional development literature, institutions are not completely separable from the term policy, and both are often used to explain cross-country income differences. For example, Olson (1996) points out that the differences in institutions and economic policies explain why some countries are rich or poor. Economic policy and institutions are considered cofactors to explain long run growth. For example, Dollar and Kraay (2003) find both institutions and trade policy are important determinants of growth in the very long run, with trade playing a larger role in the short run.

Developed along with the new institutional literature, the aid, institution, and growth relation or institutional conditionality of aid literature, also relates to the aid-policy-growth literature. In general, the aid-institutions-growth literature favors the positive role of selectivity based on institutional quality in a recipient country. For example, as one of the earliest research studies discussing the role of institutions in aid effectiveness, Boone (1994) confirms that institutional quality, together with a stable macroeconomic policy environment, determine the effectiveness of foreign aid—good policies and institutions promote economic growth and bad institutions are detrimental to growth. Boone (1996) further compares how aid works differently in countries with different types of political institutions and finds that aid targeted at liberal regimes might be more successful in poverty reduction.

Measured with Freedom House Index, Isham et al. (1997) find a positive relation between civil liberties and the economic performance of World Bank-financed government projects. In addition to civil liberties, Svensson (1999) adds to the aid-political institutions-growth literature that aid also promotes growth in countries with more political rights. In the same vein, foreign aid also impacts growth through the economic institutions channel. For example, aid is more effective in poverty reduction in countries with better economic institutions and policies (Collier and Dollar 1998). In their reply to arguments against the aid, policies, and growth debate, Burnside and Dollar (2004) expand their concept of good policy to include institutions, and conclude that the impact of foreign aid depends on sound institutions.

More recently, Kathavate and Mallik (2012) conclude that there exists a negative relation between aid volatility and economic growth, and this relation depends on institutional quality in a recipient country. Young and Sheehan (2014) find that economic institutions, not aid or political institutions, matter for growth. Wako (2018) confirms that the long-run negative growth effect of aid also exists through the political institutions channel.

Jia and Williamson (2019) test aid's impact on growth using an improved institutional quality measure, the economic freedom index (EFW) (Gwartney et al. 2016). As the most commonly cited measure for economic institutions, EFW covers a wide range of measures on protection of property rights, size of government, business regulations, stable money, and trade barriers. The results indicate that foreign aid decreases growth in recipient countries with poor (the bottom ten percent) institutional quality, and it does not increase growth in a country with good institutional qualities (the top ten percent). This result further adds to the literature that countries with good institutions do not need aid, and countries with poor institutions can be hurt by aid. Combined, this literature suggests that aid can be harmful at any level of policy and in economically unfree countries.

Conclusion

Does policy or institutions condition foreign aid's effect on economic growth? This answer is contingent on data availability, sample selection, and estimation techniques. As the debate between BD and ELR revealed, updating the sample could lead to the opposite conclusion, and sample driven results are not rare in the literature. Second, endogeneity and imperfect identification methodologies also attribute to disagreement in the aid literature. Poor countries with low economic growth rates attract more aid; hence, foreign aid should not be treated as purely exogenous.

The current literature relies on instrumental variables as the solution to identify reverse causality in the aid-growth relation; however, due to lack of valid and efficient instruments, it is difficult to capture and estimate the "small average effect on economic growth" (Roodman 2008, p. 2). In fact, instead of running from aid to growth, what dominates the aid-growth relation is a causal relationship from growth to aid with a negative sign. As GDP grows, the ratio of aid/GDP drops (Roodman 2007), even without assuming that donors decrease aid. What makes matter worse is that other explanatory variables other than aid could also be endogenous, which may magnify the estimation bias (Roodman 2008).

Assuming away the problems in data and methodology, why does aid in the presence of good policy tend to fail to promote the big economic growth development goal? The aid-policy-growth view argues that the reason aid has not been working is because it is not allocated to recipient countries with good policies. In practice, aid conditionality on policy relies on reform commitment from recipient countries. The good policy rule requires additional resources from donor countries to screen and evaluate the recipient countries, which does not align with the incentives of donor countries; hence, it is difficult to practice, if not impossible.

It seems that the necessary condition for a country to develop is "know how", not aid resources. Countries with good policies may develop despite foreign aid, and countries with poor policies do not know the way to use aid to grow. This idea is well known as the Foreign Aid Paradox or Bauer's Paradox. In fact, aid may negatively impact growth either under good policies (Lensink and White 2001) or at all levels of policies (Jia and Williamson 2019).

The development literature has found that the secret of economic development lies in institutional arrangements. Windfalls of aid change institutions, which also change entrepreneurs' incentives and behaviors in recipient countries. As an input, aid itself could not provide more 'productive' incentives, which are necessary for entrepreneurs to work toward economic growth (Baumol 1990; Easterly 2001, 2006; Moyo 2009; Coyne and Sobel 2010; Williamson 2010). However, aid may contribute to more incentives toward 'unproductive' entrepreneurial activities. This suggests that aid effectiveness may be hampered by the unintended consequences of deteriorating institutional qualities and changing incentives in recipient countries.

With or without foreign aid, sound institutions are the foundation of productive entrepreneurial activity and the resource of economic growth. Foreign aid is just like other policies; its effectiveness relies on the institutional foundation. Donor countries have practiced allocating aid through non-state channels like NGOs and multilateral organizations (Acht et al. 2015) to improve aid effectiveness. Given the relatively weak institutions in recipient countries, failure of aid seems to be often unavoidable.

Perhaps, what poor countries really need is not foreign aid, but "a decentralized economy that allows and rewards individuals to act on their entrepreneurial insights", as Hayek (1945) pointed out before the international community started allocating foreign aid.

Notes

1. The first person to have used the term 'poverty trap' is Rostow (1959) in his 'The Stages of Economic Growth'.
2. BD's policy index which has three components- trade openness, budget surplus, and inflation. The 1970–1993 period is provided by BD's original dataset; 1990–2013 policy index is calculated by Jia and Williamson (2019), following BD's methodology.

References

Acht, Martin, Toman Omar Mahmoud, and Rainer Thiele 2015. Corrupt Governments Do Not Receive More State-To-State Aid: Governance and The Delivery of Foreign Aid Through Non-State Actors. Journal of Development Economics, 114:20–33.

Alesina, Alberto, and Beatrice Weder 2002. Do Corrupt Governments Receive Less Foreign Aid?. American Economic Review, 92(4):1126–1137.

Ali, Abdiweli M., and Hodan S. Isse 2005. An Empirical Analysis of The Effect of Aid on Growth. International Advances in Economic Research, 11(1):1–11.

Alvi, Eskander, Debasri Mukherjee, and Elias Kedir Shukralla 2008. Aid, Policies, and Growth in Developing Countries: A New Look at the Empirics. Southern Economic Journal: 693–706.

Asongu, Simplice A., and Jacinta C. Nwachukwu 2017. Foreign Aid and Inclusive Development: Updated Evidence from Africa, 2005–2012. Social Science Quarterly, 98(1):282–298.

Baumol, William J. 1990. Entrepreneurship: Productive, Unproductive, and Destructive. Journal of Political Economy, 98(5, Part 1):893–921.

Becker, Gary S. 1962. Investment in Human Capital: A Theoretical Analysis. Journal of Political Economy, 70(5, Part 2):9–49.

Boone, Peter 1994. The Impact of Foreign Aid on Savings and Growth. London School of Economics and Political Science, Centre For Economic Performance.

Boone, Peter 1996. Politics and The Effectiveness of Foreign Aid. European Economic Review, 40(2):289–329.

Breitwieser, Anja, and Katharina Wick 2016. What We Miss by Missing Data: Aid Effectiveness Revisited. World Development, 78:554–571.

Briggs, Ryan C 2017. Does Foreign Aid Target the Poorest?. International Organization 71(1): 187–206.

Brumm, Harold J. 2003. Aid, Policies, and Growth: Bauer Was Right. Cato Journal, 23:167.

Burnside, Craig, and David Dollar 2000. Aid, Policies, and Growth. American Economic Review, 90(4): 847–868.

Burnside, Craig, and David Dollar 2004. Aid, Policies, and Growth: Reply. American Economic Review, 94(3):781–784.

Chatelain, Jean-Bernard, and Kirsten Ralf 2014. Spurious Regressions and Near-Multicollinearity, With an Application to Aid, Policies and Growth. Journal of Macroeconomics, 39: 85–96.

Chong, Alberto, Mark Gradstein, and Cecilia Calderon. 2009. Can Foreign Aid Reduce Income Inequality and Poverty? Public Choice 140 (1–2):59–84.

Clemens, Michael A., Steven Radelet, Rikhil R. Bhavnani, and Samuel Bazzi 2012. Counting Chickens When They Hatch: Timing and The Effects of Aid on Growth. The Economic Journal 122(561):590–617.

Cogneau, Denis, and Jean-David Naudet 2007. Who Deserves Aid? Equality of Opportunity, International Aid, and Poverty Reduction. World Development 35(1):104–120.

Collier, Paul, and David Dollar 1998. Aid Allocation and Poverty Reduction. Policy Research Working Paper, no. 2041, The World Bank.

Collier, Paul, and David Dollar 2001. Can the World Cut Poverty in Half? How Policy Reform and Effective Aid Can Meet International Development Goals. World Development, 29:1787–802.

Collier, Paul, and David Dollar 2002. Aid Allocation and Poverty Reduction. European Economic Review, 46(8):1475–1500.

Collier, Paul, and Jan Dehn 2001. Aid, Shocks, and Growth. World Bank Working Paper 2688.

Crawford, Gordon 1997. Foreign Aid and Political Conditionality: Issues of Effectiveness and Consistency. Democratization, 4(3):69–108.

Coyne, Christopher J., Russell S. Sobel, and John A. Dove 2010. The Non-Productive Entrepreneurial Process. The Review of Austrian Economics, 23(4):333–346.

Dalgaard, Carl-Johan, and Henrik Hansen 2001. On Aid, Growth and Good Policies. Journal of Development Studies, 37(6):17–41.

Dalgaard, Carl-Johan, Henrik Hansen, and Finn Tarp 2004. On the Empirics of Foreign Aid and Growth. The Economic Journal, 114(496):191–216.

Dayton-Johnson, Jeff, and John Hoddinott 2003. Aid, Policies, and Growth, Redux. Halifax: Department of Economics, Dalhousie University. Mimeo.

Dollar, David, and Aart Kraay 2003. Institutions, Trade, and Growth. Journal of Monetary Economics, 50(1):133–162.

Dollar, David, and Lant Pritchett 1998. Assessing Aid: What Works, What Doesn't, and Why. World Bank Publications.

Domar, Evsey 1946. Capital Expansion, Rate of Growth, and Employment. Econometrica, 14(2): 137–147.

Doucouliagos, Hristos, and Martin Paldam 2010. Conditional Aid Effectiveness: A Meta – Study. Journal of International Development 22(4):391–410.

Dreher, Axel, and Sarah Langlotz 2017. Aid and Growth. New Evidence Using an Excludable Instrument. Working Paper.

Easterly, William 2001. The Elusive Quest for Growth. Massachusetts: MIT

Easterly, William 2003. Can Foreign Aid Buy Growth? Journal of Economic Perspectives, 17(3): 23–48.

Easterly, William 2006. Reliving the 1950s: The Big Push, Poverty Traps, and Takeoffs in Economic Development. Journal of Economic Growth, 11(4):289–318.

Easterly, William, Ross Levine, and David Roodman 2004. Aid, Policies, and Growth: Comment. American Economic Review, 94(3):774–780.

Furukawa, Mitsuaki 2016. Aid Fragmentation and Effectiveness for Infant and Child Mortality and Primary School Completion. In the Fragmentation of Aid. London: Palgrave Macmillan:165–184.

Gillanders, Robert 2016. The Effects of Foreign Aid in Sub-Saharan Africa. The Economic and Social Review 47(3):339–360.

Grossman, Gene M., and Elhanan Helpman 1990. Trade, Innovation, and Growth. The American Economic Review, 80(2):86–91.

Guillaumont, Patrick, and Laurent Wagner 2014. Aid Effectiveness for Poverty Reduction: Lessons from Cross-country Analyses, with a Special Focus on Vulnerable Countries. Revue d'économie du développement 22 (HS01):217–261.

Guillaumont, Patrick, and Lisa Chauvet 2001. Aid and Performance: A Reassessment. Journal of Development Studies 37(6):66–92.

Gwartney, James, Robert Lawson, and Joshua. Hall 2016. Economic Freedom of the World Annual Report. The Fraser Institute, 2016.

Hansen, Henrik, and Finn Tarp 2001. Aid and Growth Regressions. Journal of development Economics 64(2):547–570.

Harrod, Roy F. 1939. An Essay in Dynamic Theory. The Economic Journal, 49 (193):14–33.

Hayek, Friedrich August 1945. The Use of Knowledge in Society. The American Economic Review, 35(4):519–530.

Holtham, Gerald, and Arthur Hazelwood 2010. Aid and Inequality in Kenya: British Development Assistance to Kenya. London and New York: Routledge.

Hudson, John, and Paul Mosley 2001. Aid Policies and Growth: In Search of The Holy Grail. Journal of International Development, 13(7):1023–1038.

Isham, Jonathan, Daniel Kaufmann, and Lant H. Pritchett 1997. Civil Liberties, Democracy, and the Performance of Government Projects. The World Bank Economic Review, 11(2):219–242.

Islam, Muhammed N 2005. Regime Changes, Economic Policies and The Effect of Aid on Growth. The Journal of Development Studies, 41(8):1467–1492.

Jia, Shaomeng, and Claudia R. Williamson 2019. Aid, Policies and Growth: Why So Much Confusion? Contemporary Economic Policy, forthcoming.

Juselius, Katarina, Niels Framroze Møller, and Finn Tarp 2014. The Long-Run Impact of Foreign Aid in 36 African Countries: Insights from Multivariate Time Series Analysis. Oxford Bulletin of Economics and Statistics, 76(2):153–184.

Kathavate, Jay, and Girijasankar Mallik 2012. The Impact of the Interaction Between Institutional Quality and Aid Volatility on Growth: Theory and Evidence. Economic Modelling, 29(3):716–724.

Kimura, Hidemi, Mori, Yuko, and Sawada Yasuyuki 2012. Aid Proliferation and Economic Growth: A Cross-Country Analysis. World Development, 40(1): 1–10.

Kohama, Hirohisa, Yasuyuki Sawada, and Hisaki Kono 2003. Aid, Policies and Growth Reconsidered. Center for Global Development.

Lensink, Robert, and Howard White 2001. Are There Negative Returns to Aid?. Journal of Development Studies, 37(6):42–65.

Lu, Shuang, and Rati Ram 2001. Foreign Aid, Government Policies, and Economic Growth: Further Evidence from Cross-Country Panel Data For 1970–1993. International Economics, 54(1):15–29.

Mincer, Jacob 1958. Investment in Human Capital and Personal Income Distribution. Journal of Political Economy, 66(4):281–302.

North, Douglass C. 1991. Institutions. Journal of Economic Perspectives, 5(1):97–112.

Malthus, Thomas R. 1789. An Essay on the Principle of Population. London: J. Johnson.

Miyamoto, Kaori, and Emilio Chiofalo 2015. Official Development Finance for Infrastructure: Support by Multilateral and Bilateral Development Partners. Paris: OECD Publishing, 25.

Mosley, Paul 1986. Aid-Effectiveness: The Micro-Macro Paradox. Institute of Development Studies Bulletin, 17(2): 22–27.

Mosley, Paul, John Hudson, and Arjan Verschoor 2004. Aid, Poverty Reduction and the 'New Conditionality'. The Economic Journal, 114 (496):F217-F243.

Moyo, Dambisa 2009. Dead Aid: Why Aid Is Not Working and How There Is a Better Way for Africa. Basingstoke: Macmillan Group.

OECD 2018. Development Aid at a Glance Statistics by Region 2018 Edition. Paris: OECD.

Olson, Mancur 1996. Distinguished Lecture on Economics in Government: Big Bills Left on The Sidewalk: Why Some Nations Are Rich, and Others Poor. Journal of Economic Perspectives, 10(2):3–24.

Page, John, and Abebe Shimeles 2015. Aid, Employment and Poverty Reduction in Africa. African Development Review, 27(S1):17–30.

Qian, Nancy 2015. Making Progress on Foreign Aid. Annual Review of Economics, 7(1):277–308.

Rajan, Raghuram, and Arvind Subramanian 2008. Aid and Growth: What Does the Cross-Country Evidence Really Show? The Review of Economics and Statistics, 90(4):643–665.

Ram, Rati 2003. Roles of Bilateral and Multilateral Aid in Economic Growth of Developing Countries. Kyklos, 56(1):95–110.

Ricardo, David. 1817. On the Principles of Political Economy and Taxation. London: John Murray.

Riddell, Abby, and Miguel Niño-Zarazúa. 2016. The Effectiveness of Foreign Aid to Education: What Can be Learned?. International Journal of Educational Development, 48:23–36.

Rodrik, Dani, Arvind Subramanian, and Francesco Trebbi 2004. Institutions Rule: The Primacy of Institutions Over Geography and Integration in Economic Development. Journal of Economic Growth, 9(2):131–165.

Romer, Paul M. 1990. Endogenous Technological Change. Journal of Political Economy, 98(5, Part 2): S71–S102.

Roodman, David 2007. Macro Aid Effectiveness Research: A Guide for The Perplexed. Center for Global Development Working Paper Number 134.

Roodman, David 2008. Through the Looking Glass, and What OLS Found There: On Growth, Foreign Aid, and Reverse Causality. Center for Global Development Working Paper Number 137.

Rostow, Walt Whitman 1959. The Stages of Economic Growth, Economic History Review, 13(1): 450–458.

Sachs, Jeffrey 2005. The End of Poverty: Economic Possibilities for Our Time. New York: Penguin Press.

Sachs, Jeffrey D., and Andrew Warner 1995. Economic Reform and the Process of Global Integration. Brookings Papers on Economic Activity 1:1–118.

Schultz, Theodore W. 1961. Investment in Human Capital. The American Economic Review, 51(1):1–17.

Skarbek, David B., and Peter T. Leeson 2009. What Can Aid Do. Cato J. 29:391.

Solow, Robert M. 1956. A Contribution to The Theory of Economic Growth. The Quarterly Journal of Economics, 70(1):65–94.

Svensson, Jakob 1999. Aid, Growth and Democracy. Economics & Politics, 11(3):275–297.

Svensson, Jakob 2000. Foreign Aid and Rent-Seeking. Journal of International Economics, 51(2): 437–461.

Tan, Kang Yong 2009. A Pooled Mean Group Analysis on Aid and Growth. Applied Economics Letters, 16(16):1597–1601.

United Nations 2015. 17 Sustainable Development Goals (SDGs) of the 2030 Agenda for Sustainable Development. New York: UN.

Verschoor, Arjan, and Adriaan Kalwij 2006. Aid, Social Policies and Pro-Poor Growth. Journal of International Development, 18(4):519–532.

Wacziarg, Romain, and Karen H. Welch 2008. Trade Liberalization and Growth: New Evidence. The World Bank Economic Review 22(2):187–231.

Wako, Hassen Abda 2018. Aid, Institutions and Economic Growth in Sub-Saharan Africa: Heterogeneous Donors and Heterogeneous Responses. Review of Development Economics 22(1):23–44.

Watkins, Kevin, Haishan Fu, Ricardo Fuentes, Arunabha Ghosh, Chiara Giamberardini, Claes Johansson, Christopher Kuonqui et al. 2005. Human Development Report 2005: International Cooperation at a Crossroads: Aid, Trade and Security in an Unequal World. New York: UNDP

Williamson, Claudia R. 2008. Foreign Aid and Human Development: The Impact of Foreign Aid to The Health Sector. Southern Economic Journal:188–207.

Williamson, Claudia 2010. Exploring the Failure of Foreign Aid: The Role of Incentives and Information. The Review of Austrian Economics, 23(1):17–33.

Williamson, John 1990. What Washington Means by Policy Reform. Latin American adjustment: How Much Has Happened, 1:90–120.

World Bank 1978. International Economics Dept. Development Data Group. World Development Indicators. World Bank.

Young, Andrew T., and Kathleen M. Sheehan 2014. Foreign Aid, Institutional Quality, and Growth. European Journal of Political Economy, 36:195–208.

Yusuf, Tashrifov. 2012. Foreign Financial Aid, Government Policies and Economic Growth: Does the Policy Setting in Developing Countries Matter?. Zagreb International Review of Economics & Business, 15(1): 1–22.

CHAPTER 3

Types of Foreign Aid

Christian Bjørnskov

Introduction

The likely consequences of foreign aid have led to heated discussions among economists since the 1950s (Rosenstein-Rodan 1957; Friedman 1958). Since Mosley et al. (1987), a long series of studies that have estimated the effectiveness of aid, either on growth, investments or a set of social outcomes, has found no robust effects (Werker et al. 2009; Licht 2010; Doucouliagos and Paldam 2011; Bjørnskov and Schröder 2013; Dreher et al. 2018). Small parts of the profession continue to argue either that aid in general works or that aid is always harmful (Hansen and Tarp 2000, 2001; Minoiu and Reddy 2010; Ovaska 2003; Djankov et al. 2008). However, systematic surveys document that the converging consensus in the literature is that aid overall has no significant growth effects (Rajan and Subramanian 2008; Doucouliagos and Paldam 2008, 2011; Nowak-Lehmann et al. 2012).

Most existing studies propose two main explanations for this result while this chapter follows an emerging literature in exploring a third option. First, some studies argue that there is an effect of aid, but that it is so small that econometric problems prevent clear identification (cf.

C. Bjørnskov (✉)
Aarhus University, Aarhus, Denmark
e-mail: chbj@econ.au.dk

N. Dutta, C. R. Williamson (eds.), *Lessons on Foreign Aid and Economic Development*, https://doi.org/10.1007/978-3-030-22121-8_3

Roodman 2008). A second strand of literature argues that foreign aid has positive direct effects but also comes with several negative indirect effects, yielding an average net development effect of zero. The side effects mentioned in this strand include Dutch Disease, which undermines competitiveness and the export and manufacturing sector (Arellano et al. 2009; Werker et al. 2009; Bjerg et al. 2011), in particular that aid inflows and larger projects may induce inflation and relative price changes that distort the economy (Tornell and Lane 1999; Torvik 2001; Acharya et al. 2006; Doces 2014; Rajan and Subramanian 2011). Aid may also allow governments to spend more resources on popular but unproductive purposes, and to ignore structural development problems for substantially longer than otherwise (Boone 1996; Moss et al. 2007). It may thereby undermine political incentives and institutional reforms that would be beneficial to long-run growth (Remmer 2004; Knack 2004; Djankov et al. 2008; Heckelman and Knack 2008; Bjørnskov and Schröder 2013). The problems of political incentives also relate to the issue of fungibility, which has the consequence that aid may contribute to activities well outside the interest of donors (Feyzioghlu et al. 1998; Collier and Hoeffler 2007; Werker et al. 2009).

However, recent studies have sketched a third argument: that foreign aid is given with such different purposes in mind that though precisely measured, the sheer diversity of disbursements makes identification of effects almost impossible (cf. Calderisi 2006; Dreher et al. 2008b; Wright and Winters 2010). Clemens et al. (2012) for example argue that 'early-impact' aid, which includes budget and balance of payments support and aid intended to support infrastructure and industrial development, affects growth within a time horizon detectable in standard regression design. Kilby and Dreher (2010) and Dreher et al. (2018) instead attempt to separate aid inflows depending on the motives of different donors, suggesting that aid given with political motives is less likely to contribute to development.[1] Rajan and Subramanian (2008) find no difference between bilateral and multilateral aid while Selaya and Thiele (2012) distinguish between program and project aid and show that the former, in particular when given as direct budget support, is likely to undermine governance. Other studies focus specifically on the effects of aid for education and health (Michaelowa and Weber 2007; Dreher et al. 2008b; Mishra and Newhouse 2009; Christensen et al. 2011).

The purpose of this chapter is to address the particular problem of aid diversity and to explore the dimensionality of foreign aid disbursements and the consequences of treating foreign aid as a multi-dimensional international transfer. The chapter addresses the particular potential problem stressed by Roodman (2007) that substantial multicollinearity can create the appearance of significance: if one estimates the effects of different elements of aid that are highly correlated, outlier observations in which the elements do not go together tend to gain undue influence and can create the appearance of significance. Conversely, if types of aid in general are disbursed together, studies of the effectiveness of specific types may not count all relevant disbursements and thus underestimate the effect.

To alleviate this problem, I use the AidData database, which is becoming a standard alternative to OECD/World Bank data in the aid literature (Nielson et al. 2010; Nielsen et al. 2011). Doing so allows me to separate aid into different types, based on 24 purpose codes in which AidData reports all development projects. This choice implies that aid effectiveness can be estimated without the heterogeneity problem inherent in most previous studies. The analysis shows that most foreign aid disbursements to developing countries between 1970 and 2005 can be split into three identifiable and separable groups, each with a joint overarching purpose, and a residual group consisting of aid for a number of fringe purposes. Separating the types of foreign aid thus allows for substantially more precise estimates of the consequences of aid. When trying to account for endogeneity problems, General Method of Moments (GMM) panel estimates suggest that most aid is without consequences. Yet, aid with the purpose of reconstruction exhibits a positive significant effect on growth, suggesting that aid is only effective under such specific circumstances.

The rest of the chapter is structured as follows. Section "Data and Estimation Strategy" describes the data and estimation strategies. Section "Separating Types of Foreign Aid" reports the results of estimating the dimensionality of foreign aid and outlines the structure of the separated data. Section "Types of Foreign Aid and Economic Growth" re-estimates two claims from the existing literature on aid effectiveness while section "Conclusions" concludes.

Data and Estimation Strategy

Main Data

The data on aid used in the following are all from the recent PLAID (Project Level Aid) database, as reported by AidData (Nielson et al. 2010), which offers a more inclusive account of global aid flows. Relative to the common database from the OECD's Development Assistance Committee (DAC), AidData offers nearly twice as large flows of aid when recorded as commitments and excluding concessional loans, not least by adding projects from NGOs and other additional sources not included in OECD statistics. All data are recorded in project form, categorized in 24 purpose codes listed in Table 3.1 and a 25th purpose code, 'Administrative costs of donors'. This feature of AidData allows the separation of different types of aid in a more comprehensive way than in previous studies. I elect to use data on actual disbursements instead of commitments, as some commit-

Table 3.1 Aid in purpose codes

Purpose code	*Mean*	*Standard deviation*	*Zero observations*
Agriculture, forestry and fishery	0.586	0.952	29
Banking and financial services	0.051	0.098	182
Business and other services	0.027	0.084	378
Communications	0.080	0.168	136
Development aid, food security assistance	0.168	0.416	155
Disaster prevention and preparedness	0.001	0.001	706
Education	0.276	0.608	29
Emergency response	0.110	0.421	100
Energy generation and supply	0.254	0.399	101
General budget support	0.489	1.103	205
General environmental protection	0.024	0.059	331
Government and civil society	0.196	0.493	81
Health	0.146	0.262	95
Industry, mining and construction	0.212	0.441	72
Other	0.570	1.032	30
Other commodity assistance	0.136	0.383	235
Other social infrastructure and services	0.083	0.188	116
Population policies	0.041	0.120	282
Reconstruction relief	0.039	0.151	450
Support to NGOs and government organizations	0.004	0.16	408
Trade and tourism	0.031	0.083	217
Transport and storage	0.594	0.878	31
Water supply and sanitation	0.209	0.301	64
Women	0.001	0.13	679

Note: All aid variables have 756 observations
Source: PLAID (Project Level Aid) database reported by AidData

ments are known not to be fulfilled. For similar reasons, I only include aid given to specific countries and thus exclude regional aid flows that cannot be assigned to one country.

Using AidData comes with a further benefit: compared to non-oil developing countries with full national accounts data in the Penn World Tables and aid flows recorded by the OECD, AidData allows adding 76 observations (10% of the sample), yielding a sample that is more balanced in terms of time, geography and level of development than previous datasets. This means more data from countries such as Congo (Brazzaville), Djibouti, Fiji and Vietnam, as well as substantially more data from small countries, including Dominica, Guyana, Kiribati, Micronesia and Sao Tomé and Principe. The use of a large sample size including more countries than previous studies alleviates the inherent problem in such literature that the inclusion of countries in datasets is not random (Hollyer et al. 2011; Bjerg et al. 2011). By allowing a large and more diverse dataset, using this source is a priori likely to yield more reliable results (cf. Easterly et al. 2004).

The size of aid flows in the 24 purpose codes varies considerably. Disaster prevention and preparedness, support to women and support to NGOs and civil society are the purposes for which donors give the smallest amounts of fund. The major posts are general budget support, agriculture, forestry and fishery, transport and storage and the general 'other' category; the average country within the sample period received 2.2% of GDP as foreign project aid in one of these four categories. Yet, while the smallest disbursement categories remain the same, the largest change over time, suggesting that even in a purely dynamic perspective, aid types can be separated.[2] Having total aid disbursements separated into purpose codes allows testing one additional potential source of effect heterogeneity. In the following, I also include the Herfindahl-Hirschmann index of aid in the 24 categories, which effectively measures the degree of concentration of aid to one purpose.[3] As Kimura, Mori and Sawada (2012) show that the bureaucratic and administrative difficulties increase with the number of donors to report to, a similar problem is likely to occur when aid is spread across more purposes, each of which necessitates its own reports (Moss et al. 2007).

While AidData represents an improvement over existing data sources, reporting nonetheless remains a potential problem. Holding total aid disbursements in AidData up against commitments of net official development assistance (ODA) data from the World Bank (2017), that is, comparing actual, documented flows with official promises including concessional loans, there is an average discrepancy of 4.8% of Gross National Income (GNI). In other words, a comparison suggests that AidData on average may underestimate aid inflows by up to one half, if the World Bank had accurately reported official aid disbursements. One should, however, be careful of interpreting the difference as pure under-reporting since the standard data from the World Bank and OECD not only report commitments instead of disbursements, but also includes concessional loans with a grant element of up to 25% and debt relief in the concept of net ODA. The average grant element of new loans extended to developing countries since 1980 has been approximately 38%, which is likely to substantially inflate OECD aid inflows (World Bank 2017). In addition, commitments have on average been 25% larger than disbursements since 1970 (OECD 2015). These two factors thus capture the bulk of the difference between the two sources.

These data first enter into a dimensionality analysis, which informs of how one can separate different types of aid in a statistically valid way. In the following, I also report and use the total aggregated aid inflows as well as aid separated according to the typology in Clemens et al. (2012) in a set of standard growth regressions.

Control Variables

In the following, all data are aggregated in the seven five-year periods 1970–1975, 1975–1980, 1980–1985, 1985–1990, 1990–1995, 1995–2000 and 2000–2005. Averaging aid and growth rates across five-year periods reduces the inevitable random noise in the data, implies that the estimates are more likely to reflect long-run consequences instead of activity effects within a business cycle, and avoids the spuriously co-integrated relations that often occur in annual data. All right-hand side variables are lagged, with the exception of growth rates that are captured in the five-year periods between 1975 and 2010. As such, I estimate the effects of aid disbursed in a given period on growth five years later. The data form an almost balanced panel with 110 non-oil developing countries and 753 observations with full data.

I employ two different sets of control variables: one adds a set of variables used by most studies of growth in developing countries while the other is restricted to the most basic factors. The problem, and the reason for using both, is that several variables that are standard in the growth literature could proxy for transmission mechanisms connecting foreign aid and growth (cf. Hodler and Knight 2012). Examples include the budget balance, added by Rajan and Subramanian (2008), which Remmer (2004) suggests is adversely affected by aid inflows; institutional quality, which a series of studies shows is negatively associated with aid (Knack 2004; Djankov et al. 2008); political instability that may be reduced by aid inflows to dictatorships (Licht 2010; Nielsen et al. 2011); and inflation and terms of trade, both of which are associated with the Dutch Disease phenomenon (Doucouliagos and Paldam 2008; Rajan and Subramanian 2011). The simple set of control variables thus only includes the initial logarithm to Purchasing Power Parity (PPP)-adjusted GDP per capita, openness to trade, and disasters (per million inhabitants); the former two variables are from the Penn World Tables, mark 7.1 (Heston et al. 2012) while the latter is the number of major natural disasters per one million inhabitants within each five-year period, which derives from EM-DAT (2012). In all specifications, I also add a full set of period fixed effects.

On the contrary, the variables in the full set include government expenditures as percent of GDP, the investment rate, both measured as the GDP share of total trade and population growth, all from the Penn World Tables. I also add life expectancy at birth, from World Bank (2017), the dichotomous democracy indicator developed by Cheibub et al. (2010), and the number of coups and confirmed coup attempts, taken from Marshall and Marshall (2010), both of which proxy for differences in institutional quality and political instability across countries. The controls thus capture convergence effects, and most other broadly important factors. In total, I estimate growth rates of country i in period $t-1$, GR_{ti}, with a vector of common control variables X_{t-1i} and a set of additional variables Z_{t-1i} that together make up the full specification in (3.1). A_{t-1i} is either total aid or vectors of types of aid following either Clemens et al. (2012) or the typology developed in the following; D_i is a full set of period dummies, and e_{t-1i} is a noise term.

$$GR_{ti} = a + bX_{t-1i} + cZ_{t-1i} + dA_{t-1i} + fD_i + ge_{t-1i} \tag{3.1}$$

I handle potential endogeneity problems by applying a set of GMM estimates including period fixed effects (Blundell and Bond 1998) as implemented in Stata by Roodman (2009). In these regressions, additional instruments include country voting patterns from the United Nations General Assembly and whether or not countries are enrolled in the Highly Indebted Poor Countries program (HIPC). The former set includes the shares of all votes within a period in which the country voted with the US or the Soviet Union / Russia and China, respectively (Voeten and Merdzanovic 2010). This choice is dictated by a series of studies showing that aid flows are affected by countries' voting patterns and influence in the Security Council (Dreher et al. 2008a, 2009; Kuziemko and Werker 2006). All data are summarized in Appendix Table 3.6.

Separating Types of Foreign Aid

While recent typologies may be informed by intuitive and theoretically well-founded arguments, all approaches nevertheless tend to be ad-hoc in a statistical sense (e.g. Rajan and Subramanian 2008; Kilby and Dreher 2010; Clemens et al. 2012). Although the theoretical arguments may be sound, estimates can suffer from severe bias if the resulting aid measures are either too highly correlated or differences occur due to problems associated with particular elements (Roodman 2007). Likewise, if ad-hoc typologies mix types of aid with actual effects and ineffective types, real consequences may go undetected, as invalid typologies bias estimates toward zero.

The main challenge is therefore how to separate different types of aid in a statistically valid way, that is, how to properly reduce the dimensionality of the data (cf. Morgenthau 1962). Some aid purposes are conceptually overlapping while others are not, but still pooled in the standard approach to aid regressions. For example, aid to agriculture, forestry and fisheries is similar in purpose to aid to industry and mining in that the overarching purpose is one of economic development. Similarly, general budget support, general environmental protection, health aid as well as most aid within the purpose code of 'government and civil society' share the feature that they are all given with the aim of enabling national governments to achieve specific public goals (Guillamont 2011). As such, aid given with different specific purposes may share an overarching purpose and thus tend to be packaged together by donors such that inflows of specific purposes within overarching types are correlated.

For the purpose of separating such overall types, I use principal factor analysis, a method that is occasionally used when separating types of what is apparently the same phenomenon. Munck and Verkuilen (2002) for example provide what has become a seminal illustration of the application of factor analytical tools to measurement problems by showing how a set of different democracy indices tend to fall into two separable types. The benefit of using this approach is that it provides a direct test of which of the 24 purpose codes in which the aid data are sorted typically go with which. In other words, principal factor analysis can reveal, based on the covariances between the 24 aid codes, which types of aid tend to be bundled with which other types, and which types are disbursed independently of other types.

Table 3.2 reports the results of a principal factor analysis, in which loadings can be interpreted as the degree to which different types are usually

Table 3.2 Principle components analysis: types of aid

Purpose code	*Factor 1*	*Factor 2*	*Factor 3*	*Factor 4*	*Factor 5*
Agriculture, forestry and fishery	0.61	0.34	−0.07	0.02	−0.35
Banking and financial services	0.15	0.20	−0.03	−0.07	0.00
Business and other services	−0.05	0.53	−0.10	0.07	0.22
Communications	0.58	0.12	−0.03	0.20	0.06
Development aid, food security assistance	0.70	0.02	0.14	−0.02	0.11
Disaster prevention and preparedness	0.00	0.01	0.08	−0.01	0.00
Education	0.34	0.43	−0.08	0.42	−0.09
Emergency response	0.06	0.16	0.64	0.00	0.04
Energy generation and supply	0.45	0.14	−0.01	−0.08	−0.01
General budget support	0.20	0.51	−0.04	−0.08	0.14
General environmental protection	−0.05	0.48	−0.08	0.06	0.32
Government and civil society	0.00	0.43	0.40	0.25	0.00
Health	0.32	0.65	0.16	0.12	0.13
Industry, mining and construction	0.52	0.09	−0.04	0.06	−0.02
Other	0.26	0.66	0.11	−0.09	−0.01
Other commodity assistance	0.70	−0.01	0.04	−0.04	0.12
Other social infrastructure and services	0.11	0.69	0.05	0.02	−0.22
Population policies	0.00	0.38	0.20	0.05	0.31
Reconstruction relief	0.07	0.12	0.59	0.00	−0.04
Support to NGOs and government organizations	0.09	0.31	0.10	0.55	0.05
Trade and tourism	0.21	0.10	0.01	0.04	0.03
Transport and storage	0.64	0.27	0.02	0.03	−0.17
Water supply and sanitation	0.50	0.31	−0.07	−0.06	0.05
Women	0.09	0.08	−0.04	−0.06	−0.03
Eigenvalue	4.846	1.859	1.013	0.571	0.526
Proportion explained	0.582	0.223	0.122	0.069	0.063

Note: Components are rotated with Oblimin
Source: PLAID (Project Level Aid) database reported by AidData

disbursed together.[4] Yet, as factor scores cannot be interpreted directly, I use the pattern revealed by this analysis to sort actual disbursement data into interpretable categories. Table 3.3 reports the weighting scheme derived from factor analysis that I use to calculate how much of each type of foreign aid a country receives in each period.[5]

Table 3.3 Separating types of aid, factor weight

Purpose code	*Factor 1*	*Factor 2*	*Factor 3*	*Residual*	*Early impact*	*Residual*
Agriculture, forestry and fishery	0.64	0.36			1	
Banking and financial services				1	1	
Business and other services		1			1	
Communications	1				1	
Development aid, food security assistance	1					1
Disaster prevention and preparedness				1		1
Education	0.44	0.56				1
Emergency response			1			1
Energy generation and supply	1				1	
General budget support		1			1	
General environmental protection		1				1
Government and civil society		0.52	0.48			1
Health	0.33	0.67				1
Industry, mining and construction	1				1	
Other		1				1
Other commodity assistance	1					1
Other social infrastructure and services		1				1
Population policies		0.55		0.45		1
Reconstruction relief			1			1
Support to NGOs and government organizations				1		1
Trade and tourism				1		1
Transport and storage	1				1	
Water supply and sanitation	0.62	0.38				1
Women				1		1

Note: The purpose codes in italics are collapsed in a residual category since they load unto none of the factors extracted. The two right-hand columns report the way purpose codes are aggregated according to the typology in Clemens et al. (2012)

Source: PLAID (Project Level Aid) database reported by AidData

Table 3.2 reports a solution with five interpretable components of which only three have eigenvalues above one. In other words, only the first three components capture more variation than one of the underlying 24 types; the remaining components thus entail less information than any single purpose code. A scree plot also shows a clear elbow at a solution with three components—the fourth component explains only a very small share of the variation—and the first three factors capture 92% of the variation in the aid data. As such, the additional factors are likely to be of relatively little importance and very far from robustly identified. In the following, I therefore provide analyses with a solution of three types; I aggregate aid flows in all remaining purpose codes that do not fit within these three types into a residual component. Table 3.3 provides the particular weights used to score the aid variables.

This typology, in which all aid flows are divided into four types and which I refer to as the 3 + 1 typology in the following, appears to be both statistically robust and intuitively valid.[6] Above its robustness, the particular benefit of the typology is that the different purpose codes are split into an intuitively valid and easily interpretable pattern.

The first type (i.e. the first dimension identified by the analysis) includes two thirds of aid with the purpose of building capacity in agriculture, all aid for forestry and fishery, communications and food security, almost half of education aid, all energy infrastructure aid, a third of all aid for health projects, all industry, mining and construction aid, all other commodity assistance, transport and storage aid and about two thirds of aid for water supply. These types of aid can all be considered first-generation aid with an overall purpose of funding directly productive economic investments or infrastructure investments thought to be complementary to industrial development. I therefore term this type 'economic aid', although it might also be thought of as very traditional development assistance along the paradigm outlined by the two-gap model and take-off models (Calderisi 2006; Easterly 2002).

The second overall aid type consists of about a third of projects in the 'agriculture, forestry and fishery' purpose code, all aid for business and other services, the other half of education aid, aid for general budget support and environmental purposes, half of the support for government and civil society, two thirds of health aid, the 'other' category of aid flows, social infrastructure aid, half of the projects in the 'population policy' purpose code and roughly a third of investments in water fall within this category. As all these investments can be construed under the heading of 'social aid', that is, aid with the purpose of non-pecuniary social development through government policy, that is the term and interpretation of this type.

The third type clearly focuses on reconstruction after some type of emergency or preparations for future emergencies and emergency management, as it includes all financing of emergency responses, half of all aid to government and civil society and all reconstruction relief. Reconstruction aid is thus very easy to place as an entirely separate type of foreign aid. Finally, the remaining purpose codes—aid to the banking and financial sector, disaster prevention (i.e. not traditional emergencies), the other half of aid for population policy, support for NGOs and civil society, trade and tourism and aid to women fall outside of the typology. These types of aid that on average form 2.4% of total aid disbursements are therefore pooled into a residual category.

A potential problem solved in the present context is that Clemens et al. (2012)—which provide an alternative aid typology—use OECD-DAC data and do not report disbursement data on types of aid, only commitments. Despite this difference, the way Clemens et al. (2012) separate types maps easily onto the AidData purpose codes. Their early-impact aid category consists of aid for infrastructure, including transportation, communications, energy, banking, agriculture and industry, and also includes budget support. It is therefore easy to form two measures of aid, following this typology, which I compare to the 3 + 1 typology of the present chapter. I define early-impact aid as reported in Table 3.3 as the aggregate of agriculture, banking, business, communications, energy, budget support, industry and mining and transport aid; the remaining purpose codes form the Clemens et al. residual category.

One way of validating these solutions, apart from yielding a readily interpretable pattern and passing a standard test, is to trace the development over time of the typology. Figure 3.1 therefore provides an illustration of the share of total aid to an average country that fell into one of four types during the period between 1970 and 2005. The figure rather clearly demonstrates that the purpose and intentions of foreign aid have changed over time similar to those traced by Easterly (2009), reflecting changes in international aid 'paradigms' (Hodler and Dreher 2013).

The most dramatic change documented by the figure is the decline of aid for purely economic purposes, that is, aid with the intention of creating 'old-fashioned' economic development, and thus the death of 'big push' mentality. From the mid-1980s, economic aid declined from an average of

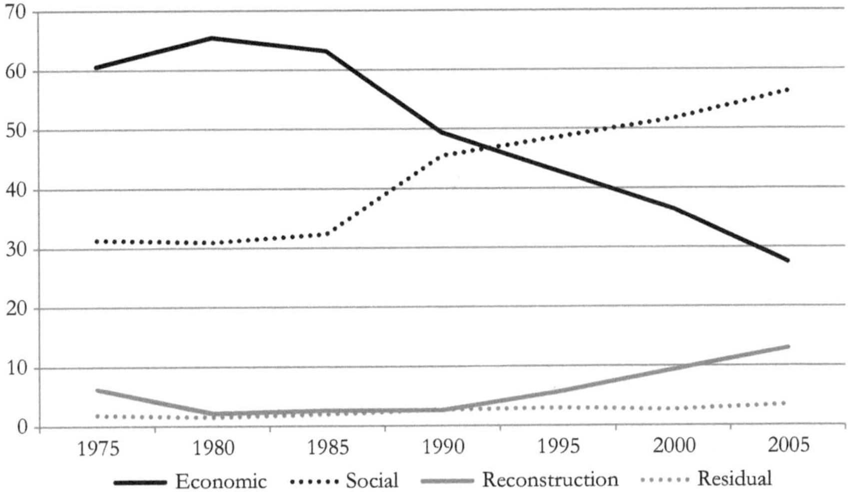

Fig. 3.1 Shares of aid in types, 1975–2005. (Source: PLAID (Project Level Aid) database reported by AidData)

3% of GDP to about 1% in the early 2000s. At the same time, aid with social purposes was stable before the 1981–1982 debt crises, but has increased steadily since. In other words, economic aid constituted more than 60% of all aid in the 1970s, but less than 30% by the mid-2000s. Conversely, social aid has increased from about 30% to more than half of all aid, and reconstruction aid now takes up approximately 15% of total aid. Most of the decline in economic aid since 1990 is thus a reflection of aid flows shifting toward social purposes and reconstruction. The residual category, which includes business support, NGOs, trade and tourism, women as well as a small share of total aid disbursed as disaster aid has decreased since 1990. There is therefore evidence of a refocusing of foreign aid since the early 1980s and the series of development failures that became obvious with the debt crises in Latin America. This shift of focus is moreover consistent with the changing official priorities of the international community (Easterly 2002, 2009). However, whether this has led to a concentration of aid efforts or contributed to distributing aid disbursements thinly across more purposes is indicated by Fig. 3.2.

Figure 3.2 clearly depicts that foreign aid has become less concentrated over the years, at least until the mid-1990s, as more issues came on the aid

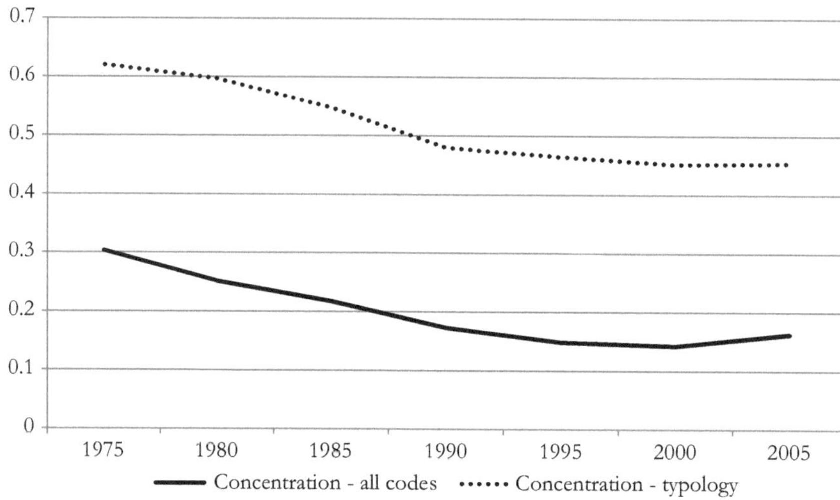

Fig. 3.2 Concentration of aid: raw data and types. (Source: PLAID (Project Level Aid) database reported by AidData)

agenda and intentions broadened (Easterly 2009). Prima facie, the development of aid in all 24 purpose codes suggests that aid efforts have become more diverse. When separating aid into types, the evidence of diversification remains similar with a typology of four components; evidently, the reduction of dimensionality does not alter the broad pattern. In other words, the figure rather clearly shows that regardless of whether aid is separated according to specific project descriptions or statistically separable types, foreign aid is now distributed across more purposes and intentions than in previous decades.

However, it remains an open question whether one can separate the *consequences* of aid. In previous studies as in the following, the problem of fungibility may imply that one cannot separate effects of foreign aid, even though one can separate types of aid by disbursement or purpose. If a type of aid is perfectly or sufficiently fungible, aid for any purpose within that type may effectively finance projects or expenditures of any other type and intention. As such, consequences of types of foreign aid are logically only separable to the degree that they are not fungible across types. The concentration or diversification of aid may nevertheless include information on the likely severity of fungibility and Dutch Disease. In particular, price hikes leading to Dutch Disease are arguably more likely when aid is concentrated in specific sectors or purposes because such projects are more likely to demand the same type of resources and labor. Relatively more concentrated aid is therefore more likely to cause Dutch Disease stemming from bottlenecks in particular markets while appreciation of the nominal exchange rate occurs regardless of the use of aid inflows. Likewise, one would expect reconstruction aid mainly to affect countries hit by disasters, although the largest probably have consequences beyond the ability of aid. Effects of particular types may also rest on institutional quality or countries' own political and economic ability to solve problems (cf. Chauvet 2002).

In the following, I estimate the effectiveness of a vector of types of aid as separated according to this typology. To take care of the potential conditionality of effects, I add interactions with the Herfindahl-Hirschmann index of aid concentration, political instability and disasters.

Types of Foreign Aid and Economic Growth

The litmus test of the value of separating types of aid is whether separation affects the measurement of consequences of foreign aid. If previous studies have failed to pick up substantial effects because total aid flows provide a too noisy measure, using a statistically valid typology should reduce the noise and reveal a clean estimate of the 'true' effect of aid. If, on the other hand, aid skeptics are correct and the average return to aid is counterweighed by side effects, the theoretical effects may still be ambiguous although estimates on conditional effects may be more precise.

In order to ensure that the approach in this chapter can be compared to the standard of using a simple sum of all aid disbursements, I first report estimates with the simple aggregate measure of aid, secondly with aid divided according to the Clemens et al. (2012) typology, and finally in the 3 + 1 typology of this paper; throughout, growth is the dependent variable. Odd-numbered columns report the simple specification while even-numbered columns include the full specification. Table 3.4 provides the estimates, based on an assumption that aid flows have approximately similar effects across countries.

First, while there is significant first-order autocorrelation, GMM estimates appear unbiased as the Arellano-Bond test of second-order autocorrelation is never significant (Arellano and Bond 1991).[7] Furthermore, in separate tests, the standard lagged first differences of vari-

Table 3.4 Growth effects, total aid versus typologies, GMM

	Total aid		*Clemens et al.*		*3 + 1 types*	
	1	*2*	*3*	*4*	*5*	*6*
Disasters	−0.019	0.030	−0.029	0.007	−0.022	0.018
	(0.031)	(0.024)	(0.032)	(0.024)	(0.028)	(0.022)
Openness	0.054***	0.025**	0.048***	0.025**	0.041***	0.021*
	(0.020)	(0.013)	(0.018)	(0.012)	(0.015)	(0.011)
Lagged growth	0.050	0.036	0.045	0.040	0.047	0.039
	(0.068)	(0.064)	(0.068)	(0.061)	(0.075)	(0.057)
Log initial GDP per capita	−0.406	−2.244***	−0.191	−2.245***	0.173	−1.967***
	(0.578)	(0.512)	(0.525)	(0.511)	(0.603)	(0.537)
Investment rate		0.064*		0.065*		0.071**
		(0.035)		(0.036)		(0.036)
Government expenditures		−0.049		−0.041		−0.056**
		(0.031)		(0.029)		(0.028)
Life expectancy		0.186***		0.169***		0.186***
		(0.071)		(0.059)		(0.059)
Democracy (Cheibub)		−0.054		0.479		0.412
		(0.593)		(0.698)		(0.681)
Coups		−0.607***		−0.631***		−0.588**
		(0.224)		(0.246)		(0.232)
Total aid disbursement	0.025	−0.000				
	(0.065)	(0.063)				
Early impact aid (Clemens)			−0.092	−0.149		
			(0.117)	(0.106)		
Residual aid (Clemens)			0.170	0.166		
			(0.144)	(0.126)		

(*continued*)

Table 3.4 (continued)

	Total aid		*Clemens et al.*		*3 + 1 types*	
	1	*2*	*3*	*4*	*5*	*6*
Economic aid					0.031	−0.086
					(0.137)	(0.109)
Social aid					0.019	0.092
					(0.115)	(0.112)
Reconstruction aid					1.059*	1.133**
					(0.629)	(0.462)
Residual aid					−1.157	−1.359
					(1.447)	(1.345)
Country fixed effects	Yes	Yes	Yes	Yes	Yes	Yes
Period fixed effects	Yes	Yes	Yes	Yes	Yes	Yes
Observations	620	620	621	620	620	620
Countries	109	109	109	109	109	109
Wald Chi sq.	57.26	113.91	51.80	140.35	76.89	153.36
1st order corr.	−3.04***	−3.07***	−3.05***	−3.16***	−3.11***	−3.27***
2nd order corr.	−0.18	−0.12	−0.16	−0.13	−0.06	0.03
Hansen test, $p<$	0.923	1.000	0.997	1.000	1.000	1.000

Note: *** (**) [*] denote significance at $p < 0.01$ ($p < 0.05$) [$p < 0.10$]

Source: PLAID (Project Level Aid) database reported by AidData, World Bank and Penn World Tables

ables (the default option for instruments) perform quite well as instrumental variables (as suggested by the significant first-order autocorrelation). The GMM estimates are thus not likely to be biased by over- or under-identification.

The results pertaining to control variables are in general comparable to standard results, with initial GDP and political instability negatively associated with growth and openness, investment rates and health positively so, and government expenditures only significant in column 6. With respect to the aid variables, taking the typology seriously nonetheless makes a substantial difference. Neither the standard total aid variable, nor those based on the typology in Clemens et al. (2012) turn out significant. Using the 3 + 1 aid variables based on the factor analysis, neither economic and social aid nor the residual category significantly affects growth, but the estimate of reconstruction aid is positive, large and significant at conventional levels.[8] As these findings are robust to a set of additional tests (not shown), including changes to instruments and excluding observations with no or very small aid inflows, a final question to ask is whether they generalize to most situations or if they are conditional.[9]

However, these estimates are based on an assumption that the effects are homogenous across conditions. Since Svensson (1999) and Burnside and Dollar (2000), a long list of studies has explored whether aid has effects conditional on specific factors being present. Table 3.5 provides estimates that take three such conditionalities into account: political instability, natural disasters and aid concentration.

First, political instability is likely to be associated with a number of factors suggested as conditioning aid effects, such as good policies, institutional quality, social conflict and debt burdens (cf. Doucouliagos and Paldam 2010). Second, Chauvet (2002) finds that aid is mainly effective in countries hit by political or natural disasters. One would also strongly suspect that if reconstruction aid actually has a significant effect on growth as in Table 3.4, this effect would only be likely to appear when countries are hit by natural disasters or conflict of a relatively manageable size. Finally, the nature of the specific data in this chapter allows a direct test of whether or not aid diversification across many purposes, and thus many projects and recipient government institutions, is associated with transaction costs of a size that undermine aid effectiveness. On the other hand, while aid diversification might increase such costs, an opposite theoretical possibility exists that aid concentration causes stronger adverse price responses to increased aid inflows. In Table 3.5, I therefore repeat the

Table 3.5 Conditional aid effects, GMM

	Total aid			*3 + 1 types*		
Interacting variable	*Coups*	*Disasters*	*Concentration*	*Coups*	*Disasters*	*Concentration*
Total aid disbursement	0.022 (0.064)	0.069 (0.071)	0.188 (0.258)			
Economic aid				0.073 (0.173)	0.127 (0.124)	−0.556 (0.785)
Social aid				0.038 (0.132)	−0.039 (0.120)	1.006 (0.722)
Reconstruction aid				−0.957 (0.847)	1.890*** (0.624)	−7.667 (6.332)
Residual aid				−0.051 (1.422)	−2.092 (1.510)	0.3689 (5.261)
Coups	−0.778*** (0.246)			−0.562*** (0.201)		
Disasters		−0.031 (0.029)			−0.014 (0.022)	
Aid concentration, typology			2.231 (2.336)			1.689 (2.667)
Total aid interaction	0.002 (0.039)	0.069 (0.071)	−0.381 (0.485)			
Economic aid interaction				0.025 (0.070)	−0.007 (0.007)	0.823 (1.157)
Social aid interaction				−0.218 (0.179)	0.005 (0.011)	−1.905 (1.282)
Reconstruction aid interaction				2.318** (0.933)	−0.196* (0.101)	20.587 (15.663)

(*continued*)

Table 3.5 (continued)

	Total aid			*3 + 1 types*		
Interacting variable	*Coups*	*Disasters*	*Concentration*	*Coups*	*Disasters*	*Concentration*
Residual aid interaction				−0.379	0.130	−2.587
				(1.389)	(0.096)	(13.193)
Country fixed effects	Yes	Yes	Yes	Yes	Yes	Yes
Period fixed effects	Yes	Yes	Yes	Yes	Yes	Yes
Observations	620	620	620	620	620	620
Countries	109	109	109	109	109	109
Wald Chi sq.	80.21	52.41	62.51	97.66	104.28	87.85
1st order corr.	−3.18***	−3.04***	−3.05***	−3.56***	−3.26***	−3.32***
2nd order corr.	0.10	−0.27	−0.15	0.34	−0.05	0.16
Hansen test, $p<$	1.000	0.999	1.000	1.000	1.000	1.000

Note: *** (**) [*] denote significance at $p < 0.01$ ($p < 0.05$) [$p < 0.10$]

Source: PLAID (Project Level Aid) database reported by AidData, World Bank and Penn World Tables

regressions of Table 3.4, but add an interaction between aid inflows in the 3 + 1 typology and each of these variables. Although all control variables are included, I only report the aid results.

The estimates in the table suggest that the overall measure of aid, reported in columns 1–3, remains insignificant regardless of the interacting factor. However, two of three interacting factors in columns 4–6 yield significant heterogeneous effects of reconstruction aid; no other type of aid exhibits any conditional effects.

First, interacting aid types with coups and evaluating conditional aid impacts on their conditional standard errors (cf. Brambor et al. 2006) suggests that reconstruction aid is insignificant when countries are politically stable. Yet, if countries are likely to experience at least one coup or coup attempt, reconstruction aid becomes significant and positive. Second, interacting reconstruction aid with the number of disasters per million people suggests that aid is only effective in contributing to growth when disasters are of medium size.[10]

While reconstruction aid *on average* provides positive growth input, it remains uncertain whether it is effective after major disasters. Similarly, reconstruction aid is not likely to (and logically should not) affect growth when no disaster has struck, that is, when there is nothing to reconstruct. Overall, though, the results suggest that the majority of disbursements of foreign aid in general are inconsequential for the growth of poor countries. The results nevertheless indicate different effects of different statistically separable types of foreign aid, since GMM estimates of the effects of reconstruction aid appear significant and positive.

Conclusions

The discussion of whether foreign aid is an effective tool with which to further development remains one of the most heated in the social sciences. A minority of economists continues to claim that aid is effective; another minority finds that aid is directly harmful, while most independent economists find no evidence of any growth effect (cf. Doucouliagos and Paldam 2011). Different solutions to the inherent endogeneity problem have tended to reproduce the zero result, which underlines Mosley's micro-macro paradox: that projects financed by foreign aid are often successful but total aid disbursements seem to make no difference at the macro level. How to resolve this problem has generated an entire literature of its own, including a number of different theoretical perspectives.

Part of the discussion in recent years has revolved around which types of aid are likely to be effective, and by extension, how one could restructure and reallocate aid in order to get significant results. Clemens et al. (2012) for example argue that budget and balance of payments support and aid for infrastructure and industrial development are likely to lead to measurably faster growth. Guillamont (2011), on the other hand, argues that aid ought to be given as a supplement to social expenditures.

The present paper has followed the line of logic of this strand of the aid literature by first employing factor analysis to generate a statistically valid way of separating types of aid. Based on data on actual disbursements of foreign aid from AidData, reported in 24 purpose codes, this analysis suggests that aid can be separated into three distinct categories covering about 92% of all disbursements. These categories can be subsumed as aid for economic purposes, aid for social purposes, reconstruction aid as well as a small residual category that aggregates the last 8% of total aid flows. Counting aid in these four categories and estimating growth regressions for a large set of 110 non-oil developing countries in the seven five-year periods between 1975 and 2010 suggests that different types of aid may have different effects.

The positive finding in the chapter is that inflows of reconstruction aid are significantly positively associated with subsequent economic growth. However, reconstruction aid is obviously given as a response to actual or latent events that would also slow down growth. When estimating effects of four types of foreign aid with GMM, thereby alleviating the perennial endogeneity bias, reconstruction aid still turns out positively associated with growth, while aid given for any other purpose remains insignificant. Further estimates suggest that this effect may be stronger in politically instable countries.

On the one hand, the positive estimate of reconstruction aid is positive news that some aid may have the intended consequences. On the other hand, reconstruction aid has in recent years only made up about 15% of total aid flows, suggesting that the majority of aid is entirely inconsequential. This particular result provides more insights into why a priori peaceful and politically stable countries such as Tanzania or Zambia, that have received comparatively large inflows of both economic and social aid, have nevertheless developed slowly since the early 1970s.

In other words, although reconstruction aid has become somewhat more prevalent in recent decades, implying that overall aid flows are less harmful than before, most of the change of focus and intentions of foreign aid appears to have been negligible. The findings in this chapter indicate that most aid, on average, simply remains without the intended consequences although being reallocated to other types and intentions. Separating aid into different identifiable types suggest that the average contribution to long-run growth of aid with long-run development purposes has at best been zero.

Appendix

Table 3.6 Descriptive statistics

Variable	*Mean*	*Standard deviation*	*Observations*
Economic aid	2.121	2.591	756
Social aid	1.859	2.541	756
Reconstruction aid	0.243	0.635	756
Residual aid (3 + 1 types)	0.106	0.152	756
Total aid (AidData)	4.329	4.847	756
Early impact aid (Clemens)	2.292	2.775	756
Residual aid (Clemens)	2.036	2.581	756
Aid concentration, all purpose codes	0.199	0.155	756
Aid concentration, 3 + 1 types	0.515	0.124	756
Net official development assistance (WDI)	9.097	10.602	680
Government expenditures, % of GDP	13.888	10.629	756
Growth rate	1.323	4.493	754
Initial GDP per capita	3184	3113	756
Investment rate, % of GDP	23.698	12.106	756
Life expectancy	58.188	10.125	746
Openness (trade volume, % of GDP)	72.891	38.669	756
Democracy (Cheibub)	0.379	0.485	736
Disasters (per million)	3.497	7.661	756
Arable land, % of total	11.571	12.148	748
Coups	0.412	0.891	755
Voting with the US	0.184	0.095	713
Voting with Russia	0.617	0.169	713

Source: PLAID (Project Level Aid) database reported by AidData, World Bank and Penn World Tables

Notes

1. Dreher et al. (2018) provide suggestive evidence that foreign aid disbursed to countries for purely political reasons tend to consist of or fund projects that are poorly designed and implemented, or simply designed to benefit political insiders. As such, a larger share of aid given for political purposes means a smaller impact as many politically motivated projects are not really designed to have a development impact.
2. In addition, the dataset enables researchers to assess donors' administrative costs from delivering foreign aid. Administrative costs have almost entirely been reported after 2000, but the available evidence shows that only 0.32% of total reported aid in the total AidData database consists of administrative costs. Only 14 country-year observations on administrative costs are above 2% of total aid to the country in a given year, and only two of those are not small island states.
3. The Herfindahl-Hirschmann index is the sum of all squared shares of total aid flows for each of the 24 (or 4) categories. If all aid is disbursed in a single category, the index will be 1 while smaller scores indicate that the aid distribution is less concentrated.
4. I use the Oblimin rotation procedure with a gamma of 0.5; results are almost identical with a gamma of 0. The alternative orthogonal rotation technique Varimax, which is standard in most studies, yields comparable results.
5. While procedures exist that can rescale factor components back to the original scale of the variables entering the analysis, these procedures all rest on first performing factor analysis based on the covariance matrix. They are therefore not practically applicable in the present situation, as analyses based on the covariance matrix are highly sensitive to differences in variance of the raw variables. As the averages, and thus the variances, of the 24 aid variables vary widely, such procedures merely identify factors based on the absolute levels and thus rely on very little relevant information.
6. An earlier working paper version of this paper provides a full discussion of the robustness of the aid typology to, for example, using different rotation techniques, only using observations receiving more than 1% of GDP as foreign aid, that is, avoiding spurious correlations due to a large number of zero-observations, and basing the analysis on aid per capita instead of aid as a percent of GDP.
7. Roodman (2009) notes that the Hansen test may be particularly weak in situations with multiple instruments and may in some cases approach non-credible values close to one. This is indeed presently the case, which may question the findings even if the standard moment restrictions are satisfied. In such cases, Roodman recommends performing robustness tests by

reducing the set of instruments. When doing so, all main results in the following remain unchanged and Hansen tests remain far from significant. In particular, the estimate of reconstruction aid proves very stable.

8. In simpler fixed effects estimates in a working paper version, the residual category in the Clemens et al. (2012) typology is significantly negative. The social aid type is also significantly negatively associated with growth when endogeneity issues are ignored.
9. The additional tests of instrument strength consist of either excluding one of the additional instruments—UN voting shares with the US and Russia and a HIPC dummy, and adding voting shares with China and a dummy for membership in the UN Security Council.
10. Further tests (not shown) nevertheless provide additional information. When measuring the absolute number of disasters, instead of disasters per inhabitant, reconstruction aid only becomes significantly positive when countries are hit by more than one disaster per year. Measuring disasters relative to initial GDP suggests similar conclusions.

References

Acharya, Arnab, Ana Teresa Fuzzo de Lima and Mick Moore. 2006. Proliferation and Fragmentation: Transaction Costs and the Value of Aid. Journal of Development Studies, 42 (1): 1–21.

Arellano, Cristina, Aleš Bulíř, Timothy Lane and Leslie Lipschitz. 2009. The Dynamic Implications of Foreign Aid and its Variability. Journal of Development Economics, 88 (1): 87–102.

Arellano, Manuel and Stephen Bond. 1991. Some Tests of Specification for Panel Data: Monte Carlo Evidence and an Application to Employment Equations. Review of Economic Studies, 58 (2): 277–297.

Bjerg, Christina, Christian Bjørnskov, and Anne Holm. 2011. Growth, Debt Burdens and Alleviating Effects of Foreign Aid in Least Developed Countries. European Journal of Political Economy, 27(1): 143–153.

Bjørnskov, Christian, and Philipp J.H. Schröder. 2013. Are Debt Repayment Incentives Undermined by Foreign Aid? Journal of Comparative Economics, 41(4): 1073–1091.

Boone, Peter. 1996. Politics and the Effectiveness of Foreign Aid. European Economic Review, 40(2): 289–329.

Blundell, Richard, and Stephen Bond. 1998. Initial Conditions and Moment Restrictions in Dynamic Panel Data Models. Journal of Econometrics, 87 (1): 11–143.

Brambor, Thomas, William Clark and Matt Golder. 2006. Understanding Interaction Models: Improving Empirical Analyses. Political Analysis, 14 (1): 63–82.

Burnside, Craig, and David Dollar. 2000. Aid, Policies, and Growth. American Economic Review, 90 (4): 847–868.
Calderisi, Robert. 2006. The Trouble with Africa: Why Foreign Aid isn't Working. New Haven: Yale University Press.
Chauvet, Lisa. 2002. Socio-Political Instability and the Allocation of International Aid by Donors. European Journal of Political Economy, 19 (1): 33–59.
Cheibub, José Antonio, Jennifer Gandhi and James Raymond Vreeland. 2010. Democracy and Dictatorship Revisited. Public Choice, 143 (1-2): 67–101.
Christensen, Zachary, Dustin Homer and Daniel L. Nielson. 2011. Dodging Adverse Selection: How Donor Type and Governance Condition Aid's Effects on School Enrollment. World Development, 39 (11): 2044–2053.
Clemens, Michael A., Steven Radelet, Rikhil R. Bhavnani and Samuel Bazzi. 2012. Counting Chickens When They Hatch: The Short-Term Effect of Aid on Growth. The Economic Journal, 122 (561): 590–617.
Collier, Paul, and Anke Hoeffler. 2007. Unintended Consequences: Does Aid Promote Arms Races? Oxford Bulletin of Economics and Statistics, 69 (1): 1–27.
Djankov, Simeon, José G. Montalvo, and Marta Reynal-Querol. 2008. The Curse of Aid. Journal of Economic Growth, 13 (3): 169–194.
Doces, John A. 2014. Saving Sudan, Starving Uganda: Aid, Growth, and Externalities in Africa. Journal of African Development, 16 (1): 61–81.
Doucouliagos, Hristos, and Martin Paldam. 2008. Aid Effectiveness on Growth: A Meta Study. European Journal of Political Economy, 24 (1): 1–24.
Doucouliagos, Hristos, and Martin Paldam. 2010. Conditional Aid Effectiveness: A Meta-Study. Journal of International Development, 22 (4): 391–410.
Doucouliagos, Hristos, and Martin Paldam. 2011. The Ineffectiveness of Development Aid on Growth: An Update. *European Journal of Political Economy, 27 (2):* 399–404.
Dreher, Axel, Peter Nunnenkamp, and Rainer Thiele. 2008a. Does US Aid buy UN General Assembly Votes? A Disaggregated Analysis. Public Choice, 136 (1–2): 139–164.
Dreher, Axel, Peter Nunnenkamp, and Rainer Thiele. 2008b. Does Aid for Education Educate Children? Evidence from Panel Data. World Bank Economic Review, 22 (2): 291–x.
Dreher, Axel, Jan-Egbert Sturm, and James R. Vreeland. 2009. Development Aid and International Politics: Does Membership on the UN Security Council Influence World Bank Decisions? Journal of Development Economics, 88 (1): 1–18.
Dreher, Axel, Vera Eichenauer, and Kai Gehring. 2018. Geopolitics, Aid and Growth: The Impact of UN Security Council Membership on the Effectiveness of Aid. World Bank Economic Review, 32 (2): 268–286
Easterly, William. 2002. The cartel of good intentions: the problem of bureaucracy in foreign aid. Journal of Policy Reform, 5 (4): 223–250.

Easterly, William. 2009. Can the West Save Africa? Journal of Economic Literature, 47 (2): 373–344.

Easterly, William, Ross Levine, and David Roodman. 2004. New Data, New Doubts: A Comment on Burnside and Dollar's 'Aid, Policies, and Growth (2000)'. American Economic Review, 94 (3): 774–780.

EM-DAT. 2012. EM-DAT: The International Disaster Database. Center for the Epidemiology of Disasters, Catholic University of Louvain. Available at http://www.emdat.be/ (accessed January 2012).

Feyzioghlu, Tarhan, Vinaya Swaroop and Min Zhu. 1998. A Panel Data Analysis of the Fungibility of Foreign Aid. World Bank Economic Review, 12 (1): 29–58.

Friedman, Milton. 1958. Foreign Economic Aid: Means and Objectives. Yale Review, 47: 500–516.

Guillamont, Patrick. 2011. Aid Effectiveness for Poverty Reduction: Macroeconomic Overview and Emerging Issues. HAL working paper halshs-00554285. Auvergne: Université d'Auvergne.

Hansen, Henrik, and Finn Tarp. 2000. Aid Effectiveness Disputed. Journal of International Development, 12 (3): 375–98.

Hansen, Henrik, and Finn Tarp. 2001. Aid and Growth Regressions. Journal of Development Economics, 64 (2): 547–570.

Heckelman, Jac, and Stephen Knack. 2008. Foreign Aid and Market-Liberalizing Reform. Economica, 75 (299): 524–548.

Heston, Alan, Robert Summers, and Betina Aten. 2012. Penn World Tables Version 7.1. Philadelphia: Center for International Comparisons, University of Pennsylvania.

Hodler, Roland, and Axel Dreher. 2013. Development (Paradigm) Failures. Journal of Development Economics, 101: 63–74.

Hodler, Roland and David S. Knight. 2012. Ethnic Fractionalization and Aid Effectiveness. Journal of African Economies, 21 (1): 65–93.

Hollyer, James R., B. Peter Rosendorff, and James R. Vreeland. 2011. Democracy and Transparency. Journal of Politics, 73 (4): 1191–1205.

Kilby, Christopher, and Axel Dreher. 2010. The Impact of Aid on Growth Revisited: Do Donor Motives Matter? Economics Letters, 107 (3): 338–340.

Kimura, Hidemi, Yuko Mori and Yasuyuki Sawada. 2012. Aid Proliferation and Economic Growth: A Cross-Country Analysis. World Development, 40 (1): 1–10.

Knack, Stephen. 2004. Does Foreign Aid Promote Democracy? International Studies Quarterly, 48 (1): 251–266.

Kuziemko, Ilyana, and Eric D. Werker. 2006. How Much is a Seat on the Security Council Worth? Foreign Aid and Bribery at the United Nations. Journal of Political Economy, 114 (5): 905–930.

Licht, Amanda A. 2010. Coming Into Money: The Impact of Foreign Aid on Leader Survival. Journal of Conflict Resolution, 54 (1): 58–87.

Marshall, Monty G., and Donna R. Marshall. 2010. Coup d'Etat Events, 1946–2008. Codebook and data. Available at http://www.systemicpeace.org/inscr/inscr.htm (accessed May 2014).
Michaelowa, Katharina, and Anke Weber. 2007. Aid Effectiveness in the Education Sector: A Dynamic Panel Analysis. In *Theory and Practice of Foreign Aid*, edited by Sajal Lahiri. Amsterdam: Elsevier, pp. 357–385.
Minoiu, Camelia, and Sanjay Reddy. 2010. Development Aid and Economic Growth: A Positive Long-Run Relation. Quarterly Review of Economics and Finance, 50 (1): 27–39.
Mishra, Prachi, and David L. Newhouse. 2009. Does Health Aid Matter? Journal of Health Economics, 28 (4): 855–872.
Morgenthau, Hans. 1962. A Political Theory of Foreign Aid. American Political Science Review, 56 (2): 301–309.
Mosley, Paul, John Hudson, and Sara Horrell. 1987. Aid, the Public Sector and the Market in Less Developed Countries. The Economic Journal, 97 (387): 616–641.
Moss, Todd, Gunilla Pettersson, and Nicolas van de Walle. 2007. An Aid-Institutions Paradox? A Review Essay on Aid Dependency and State Building in Sub-Saharan Africa. In *Reinventing Foreign Aid*, edited by William Easterly. Cambridge, MA: MIT Press.
Munck, Gerardo L. and Jay Verkuilen. 2002. Conceptualizing and Measuring Democracy: Evaluating Alternative Ideas. Comparative Political Studies 35 (1): 5–34.
Nielsen, Richard A., Michael G. Findley, Zachary S. Davis, Tara Candland and Daniel L. Nielson. 2011. Foreign Aid Shocks as a Cause of Violent Armed Conflict. American Journal of Political Science, 55 (2): 219–232.
Nielson, Daniel L., Ryan M. Powers, Michael J. Tierney, Michael G. Findley, Darren G. Hawkins, Robert L. Hicks, Bradley C. Parks, J. Timmons Roberts and Sven E. Wilson. 2010. AidData: Tracking Development Finance. Presented at the PLAID Data Vetting Workshop, Washington DC; available at http://www.aiddata.org/research/releases (accessed May 2011).
Nowak-Lehmann, Felicitas, Axel Dreher, Dierk Herzer, Stefan Klasen and Immaculada Martínez-Zarzoso. 2012. Does Foreign Aid Really Raise per Capita Income? A Time Series Perspective. Canadian Journal of Economics, 45 (1): 288–313.
OECD. 2015. International Development Statistics. Paris: OECD.
Ovaska, Tomi. 2003. The Failure of Foreign Aid. Cato Journal, 23 (2): 175–188.
Rajan, Raghuram G. and Arvind Subramanian. 2008. Aid and Growth: What Does the Cross-Country Evidence Really Show? Review of Economics and Statistics, 90 (4): 643–665.
Rajan, Raghuram G. and Arvind Subramanian. 2011. Aid, Dutch Disease, and Manufacturing Growth. Journal of Development Economics, 94 (1): 106–118.

Remmer, Karen. 2004. Does Foreign Aid Promote the Expansion of Government? American Journal of Political Science, 48 (1): 77–92.

Roodman, David M. 2007. The Anarchy of Numbers: Aid, Development, and Cross-Country Empirics. World Bank Economic Review, 21 (2): 255–277.

Roodman, David M. 2008. Through the Looking Glass, and What OLS Found There: On Growth, Foreign Aid, and Reverse Causality. Center for Global Development Working Paper 137.

Roodman, David M. 2009. How to do Xtabond2: An Introduction to Difference and System GMM in Stata. Stata Journal, 9 (1): 86–136.

Rosenstein-Rodan, Paul N., 1957. Notes on the Theory of the 'Big Push'. Cambridge, MA: Center for International Studies, MIT.

Selaya, Pablo, and Rainer Thiele. 2012. The Impact of Aid on Bureaucratic Quality: Does the Mode of Delivery Matter? Journal of International Development, 24: 379–386.

Svensson, Jakob. 1999. Aid, Growth and Democracy. Economics and Politics, 11 (3): 275–297.

Tornell, Aaron, and Philip R. Lane. 1999. The Voracity Effect. American Economic Review, 89 (1): 22–46.

Torvik, Ragnar. 2001. Learning by Doing and the Dutch Disease. European Economic Review, 45 (2): 285–306.

Voeten, Erik, and Adis Merdzanovic. 2010. United Nations General Assembly Voting Data. Available at: http://hdl.handle.net/1902.1/12379 (accessed June 2014).

Werker, Eric D., Faisal Z. Ahmed and Charles Cohen. 2009. How Is Foreign Aid Spent? Evidence from a Natural Experiment. American Economic Journal: Macroeconomics, 1 (2): 225–244.

World Bank. 2017. World Development Indicators. Washington DC: the World Bank.

Wright, Joseph and Matthew Winters. 2010. The Politics of Effective Foreign Aid. Annual Review of Political Science, 13: 61–80.

CHAPTER 4

An Effectiveness, Efficiency, and Equity Approach to Examining Subnational Health Aid

Carrie B. Dolan

Introduction

The ratification of the Sustainable Development Goals (SDGs) in all 193 UN member nations in 2015 represents the opportunity for a transformative, worldwide policy agenda (United Nations General Assembly 2015). The SDGs reflect a "no one left behind" policy agenda that recognizes the inequalities that persist and that progress has become uneven (United Nations General Assembly 2015). The majority of the 17 goals call for economic and social development and environmental protection; SDG 3 calls for ensuring healthy lives and promoting well-being, which is necessary for the success of the other goals.

Achieving SDG 3 requires a multifaceted development approach to ensure the effectiveness, efficiency, and equity of policy solutions. This requires answering questions such as, is it possible to reach the world's most vulnerable and marginalized populations? Moreover, what do these groups really want or need from development efforts? The answer to these

C. B. Dolan (✉)
William and Mary, Williamsburg, VA, USA
e-mail: cbdolan@wm.edu

N. Dutta, C. R. Williamson (eds.), *Lessons on Foreign Aid and Economic Development*, https://doi.org/10.1007/978-3-030-22121-8_4

questions will, in turn, require the rethinking of policies developed to reach only aggregate outcomes and the ability to formulate and implement policies at varying levels of national and local government.

There is a need for substantial investments in health and well-being (Schmidt-Traub and Shah 2015; Stenberg et al. 2017). Since the adoption of the Millennium Development Goals (MDGs) in 2008 as a blueprint for development efforts, substantial although varied advances in public health have been achieved through investments in the use of vaccines, medicines, and diagnostic tests (Ruducha et al. 2017; Kuruvilla et al. 2014; United Nations Department of Public Information 2009; Andrus et al. 2008; Dye 2018). However, more efforts are needed to continue to improve population level health. SDG 3 outlines a number of measures aimed to reduce maternal and infant mortality, end epidemics of communicable disease, provide access to reproductive healthcare and universal health coverage, and reduce harm associated with drug abuse, tobacco pollution, and traffic, and mitigate non-communicable diseases. This call for increased focus on health comes at a time when funding for health aid is stagnant. While there was a period of rapid growth from 2000 to 2010, it was essentially flat between 2015 and 2016 (IHME 2016). In particular, Low and Middle Income Countries (LMICs) are facing a substantial health financing gap. Stenberg et al. have estimated that an additional US$ 371 billion will be needed each year up until 2030 to reach the health-related Sustainable Development Goals (SDGs) in LMICs (Stenberg et al. 2017). Therefore, it is critical to know how well we are targeting health aid resources at the populations they aim to benefit. For multilateral and bilateral organizations as well as private foundations to address the allocation of this limited funding, attention must be paid to policies at multiple levels to ensure sustainable scale-up. Reaching the health targets outlined in SDG 3, in 67 low and middle-income countries that account for 95% of the total population of low and middle-income countries (Stenberg et al. 2017) requires addressing two major issues. The first is the ethical decision that determines distribution—how much and to whom. The second addresses the practical dimensions of when and where (Brown et al. 2014).

To address the questions policymakers face, this chapter presents an argument for using disaggregated (micro-level) information to bridge the policy gap and provide actionable information to develop evidence-based health aid policies. Given that aid may be channeled to varying levels of government and that the determinants of population health and the infrastructure to improve health varies within countries, efficacious aid policies require disaggregated data. Measuring the allocation of resources at a disaggregated level makes it possible to identify gaps in program placement and fund interventions in the places and for the populations that need them the most. This chapter approaches the rethinking of traditional notions of health aid allocation in two ways: first, by providing a broader perspective grounded in theory and research for assessing the performance of health aid in achieving effectiveness, efficiency, and equity (Aday et al. 2004). Second, by discussing the challenges that have constrained the research on health aid, and subsequently the innovations researchers are using to address these challenges. Although based in the decades of extensive literature on foreign aid, this chapter focuses on relatively recent established findings related to health aid from a subnational perspective.

Why We Should Use Evidence and Which Evidence to Use

Global health programs have saved millions of lives (Levine 2007). The use of empirical evidence to develop interventions has been crucial to the success of programs such as those aimed at polio elimination in Latin America and the Caribbean, the control of river blindness in sub-Saharan Africa, and eradicating smallpox worldwide (Levine 2007). By contrast, understanding the relationship between the money used to fund these interventions and health outcomes has been challenging. The question of whether or not international aid can improve health remains one of the fundamental challenges for understanding the impact of global development interventions. Substantial reductions in child mortality have occurred worldwide during the past 35 years (Wang et al. 2016). Despite these gains, in 2015, 23 countries reported under-5 mortality rates three times higher than the proposed SDG target for 2030, and it is not clear whether the aid the development community has offered to save them will lower this number (Coyne and Williamson 2014; Wang et al. 2016).

It is absolutely vital to determine whether health aid works, given limited public health resources and the need to use them wisely (Yamey and Volmink 2014). Understanding how to make health aid work is also vital to the success of the SDGs. This chapter will seek an answer to the question as to which evidence should be used and how to determine what makes health aid work, first, in the existing literature. Until recently, researchers examined health aid from a macro perspective: they employed cross-country regression methods in an effort to determine the nationwide impact of health aid on aggregated outcomes such as growth or national measures of poverty. These studies suggest that health aid has had little effect on infant mortality, life expectancy, death rates, child health, and immunizations (Williamson 2008; Wilson 2011; Bavinger et al. 2017). In the last 10 years, researchers began taking a micro-level approach to look at subnational outcomes. These studies have found some evidence that selected public health intervention programs such as building hospitals, providing vaccines, and bed nets have been successful (BenYishay and Kranker 2015; Marty et al. 2017).

A few studies of health aid have found meaningful changes in targeted health outcomes, making recent work by Bendavid et al. (2012) and Ng et al. (2011) on HIV outcomes and Akachi and Atun (2011) on malaria notable. Using a controlled pre/post study design, Bendavid et al. (2012) found that the first four years of the President's Emergency Plan for AIDS Relief (PEPFAR) on HIV-related outcomes decreased HIV-related deaths in sub-Saharan African countries. Ng et al. (2011) conducted an observational study in India to examine the number of HIV infections averted with a donor-funded AIDS treatment initiative, concluding that the AIDS mortality rate fell from 6.4 per 1000 person-years in the pre-antiretroviral therapy (ART) period, to 2.7 after implementation of ART. They also found a limited but nonetheless significant decrease in the number of new HIV infections attributable to the ART intervention.

Akachi and Atun (2011) quantified the relationship between malaria investments and malaria-attributed mortality using longitudinal data from 24 sub-Saharan African countries. They estimated that the increase in coverage of insecticide-treated nets (ITNs) and indoor residual spraying saved the lives of 237,971 children under five. Studies examining the percent of households that owned at least one ITN found that efforts to fund and expand programs were successful (Akachi and Atun 2011; Chizema-Kawesha et al. 2010; Steketee et al. 2008; Flaxman et al. 2010; Noor et al. 2007). However, these studies were all conducted at the country level using country-level data, or had a narrow focus and only included a small number of facilities or subnational districts.

New evidence suggests that cross-country differences explain approximately 20% of the variation in project outcomes and within-country variation explains 80% of the variation in project outcomes (Denizer et al. 2013). Despite the US $30 billion-a-year global investment in health, very few studies examine how health funding translates to health outcomes at the subnational level, a key issue if global health actors are to use sound research evidence to shape policy. BenYishay and Kranker (2015) estimated the reduction in all-cause child mortality after countrywide measles vaccination campaigns across countries and subnational regions. The research showed that the campaigns raised the probability of children's survival to 60 months by approximately 2.4 percentage points for treated cohorts. Marty et al. (2017) examined the subnational allocation of health aid, determining that health aid contributed to reduced malaria prevalence and improved self-reported healthcare quality. They found that health aid had the most notable impacts on its intended target if it was allocated toward improving health infrastructure and infectious disease.

If nations are to reach SDG 3, the development community must allocate aid according to scientific evidence. Barriers to the integration of this evidence into health policy include lack of timeliness and relevance of the research, competing influences, and a perceived knowledge gap between researchers and the policy community (Yamey and Volmink 2014). To address these barriers, it is necessary to create a common foundation in which to view health aid research. The effectiveness, efficiency, and equity perspectives provide a useful set of criteria for linking health aid to health outcomes.

Effectiveness, Efficiency, and Equity

Given that it is impossible for health aid to address all problems within all countries, the framework of effectiveness, efficiency, and equity can provide a policy mechanism for deciding which criteria to focus on and at which point in time. Health aid policies can be evaluated through the lens of effectiveness to determine if they result in significant improvements in population level health. An equity perspective can determine if a health aid policy makes the best use of limited resources subject to a budget constraint. Finally, an equity focus can determine if resources are distributed across groups fairly (Aday et al. 2004). The following discussion highlights the application of the effectiveness, efficiency, and equity criteria to recent research.

Effectiveness

What allocation approach contributes most to the health of the population? There are conflicting claims about what it means for health aid to contribute to the health of the population. What constitutes aid improvement could vary due to political and economic incentives as well as recipient need or donor interests (Alesina and Dollar 2000; Mishra et al. 2012). In the context of health, the effective aid objective typically considers population level improvement such as improved health-related quality, reduction in mortality rates, increased life expectancy, and decreased disease prevalence (Aday et al. 2004). One tangible example of health aid supporting a population level approach is the reduction of the guinea worm in Asia and sub-Saharan Africa. This multi-partner eradication effort reduced the prevalence of guinea worm by 99% in 20 endemic African and Asian countries (Levine 2007). Another is an immunization campaign the Pan American Health Organization led in Latin America and the Caribbean, eliminating polio as a public health problem in the Western Hemisphere (Levine 2007).

Whereas in the past research has focused at the country level, the emergence of georeferenced information on both aid and outcomes has permitted the examination of aid effectiveness in smaller geographic units such as districts or regions. This emerging literature has highlighted the contribution of targeted programs such as PEPFAR in Tanzania and Rwanda and measles catch-up campaigns (Bendavid et al. 2012; BenYishay and Kranker 2015). Researchers have begun to use subnational data to examine health aid effectiveness beyond targeted programs. Malawi has been studied most often because georeferenced data for individual and health facility outcomes, as well as aid indictors, exists. For example, Marty et al. (2017) find that aid contributed to the reduction of malaria prevalence and improving self-reported quality of care, while De and Becker (2015) find an association between aid and reduced prevalence and severity of diarrhea. Wayland (2017) compared the spatial distribution of aid projects in the water, sanitation, and hygiene sector, finding that under certain circumstances, households located near these projects experienced lower rates of water-related illness. Two studies that go beyond targeted data in examining subnational units are focused in other countries: Odokonyero et al. (2015) found that health aid significantly reduced disease burden and severity in Uganda; Kotsadam et al. (2017) demonstrated that aid in Nigeria was associated with decreased infant mortality.

Taken together, the emerging literature on health aid effectiveness examined at a subnational level provides far stronger evidence of benefit than cross-country studies (Williamson 2008; Wilson 2011; Bavinger et al. 2017). However, the fact that research examining subnational areas has generally focused on targeted interventions represents a substantial limitation. Also, those studies that go beyond targeted interventions focus on a single country. This research gives little information as to whether aid can improve the population level health of an entire region. Until georeferenced data for individual and health facility outcomes becomes available for a greater number of countries, examining aid effectiveness at the subnational level will continue to be limited.

Efficiency

How do donors decide to allocate health aid compared to the other things they can do with the same resources? Health aid is inherently limited as it is impossible to address all health problems in developing countries at the same time. Therefore, it is important to understand the costs and consequences associated with aid allocation. However, since we are not interested in the efficiency of ineffective aid, successful economic evaluation assumes some baseline indication of effectiveness (Drummond et al. 2015). It is also necessary to accurately measure and value the most relevant costs and consequences for each alternative allocation.

Some aid programs seek to reward countries with good policies by allocating aid to more efficient and less corrupt regimes (Alesina and Dollar 2000). Others allocate aid based on cost-effectiveness of available interventions, prioritizing the highest impact interventions among the most affected populations (Glassman et al. 2013). Research indicates that the value for money agenda encouraged programs such as ITNs and malaria treatment, which have high value for money and have been proven to provide health gains (Jamison et al. 2013). A more recent analysis reviewed the cost-effectiveness of interventions targeting HIV, malaria, tuberculosis, non-communicable diseases, and maternal, newborn, and child health. This work found that diseases with more cost-effective interventions tend to attract funding (Bendavid et al. 2015).

Equity

Does health aid promote an equal distribution for health improvement? Making progress toward the SDG 3 is not only contingent on generating sufficient resources, but also equitable allocation across regions and districts (Ensor et al. 2012). Equity implies maximizing the fairness of distribution and minimizing disparities across groups. Significant disparities exist between racial, ethnic, age, and socioeconomic groups. These disparities have an impact beyond the groups facing the disparities, as they limit improvement in health for the broader population and impose unnecessary costs (Kaiser Family Foundation 2012). The World Health Organization's Commission on Social Determinants of Health consequently recommended more even distribution of resources within and among countries to ensure fair financing (WHO 2008).

Policymakers often assume that aid has an egalitarian effect despite the fact few formal efforts have investigated whether it does (Chong et al. 2009). Exceptions have generally used a subnational perspective. Marty et al.'s (2017) finding that areas of Malawi that were poor, urban, or had existing health infrastructure were more likely to receive healthcare services suggests that need does not entirely drive the allocation of aid. Further, Briggs's (2017) study of subnational allocation across 17 diverse African countries found no association between poverty and the likelihood that a region will receive aid. Skirbekk et al. (2017) found an inequitable distribution of health aid by age in that people younger than 60 received 90% of assistance, in spite of the greater vulnerability and need of older people.

Up to this point, this chapter has focused on the synthesis and integration of recent health aid literature into the theoretical criteria of effectiveness, efficiency, and equity. Taken together this literature implies that these criteria can compete with each other and therefore policymakers may need to focus on one of these areas at a time. This chapter has also focused on literature that uses a subnational approach, because the determinants of population health and the infrastructure to improve health vary within countries. Achieving SDG 3 will require targeted aid policies that improve health outcomes.

As the introduction to a special issue of the *Review of International Organizations* recently outlined, three major challenges constrain research designed to understand the relationship between health aid and health outcomes (Nielson et al. 2017). First, the data on aid is of poor quality and coverage, representing a fundamental lack of accountability of the official aid system or any kind of independent monitoring (Easterly and Williamson 2011; Nielson et al. 2017). Second, data on development finance are generally aggregated broadly across sectors, geographies, distribution channels, and implementation partners (Nielson et al. 2017). Third, the methods are limited due to the lack of random assignment of aid, making causal identification more difficult (Nielson et al. 2017). The next few sections explore the limitations of data coverage and quality, aggregation, and research methods in more detail and focus on the innovations of the most recent generation of health aid effectiveness, efficiency, and equity studies.

Data Coverage and Quality at a Subnational Level

Coverage

Health aid and health outcomes often have an unclear relationship, because of a lack of the data rigorous scientific investigation would require (Nielson et al. 2017). The organizations that gather health aid data include the Organization for Economic Co-operation and Development, the Development Assistance Committee, AidData, the Institute for Health Metrics and Evaluation (IHME) Development Assistance for Health database, and donor specific tracking mechanisms from the Global Fund to Fight AIDS, Tuberculosis, and Malaria, the GAVI Alliance, the Bill and Melinda Gates Foundation, the World Bank, USAID, and regional development banks (Grépin et al. 2011). Each of these data sets was developed for a different purpose, for a different audience, and using a different approach (Grépin et al. 2011). Therefore, consolidating this information into an analysis data set is not always possible. Uncertainties in the evidence related to data coverage and quality has made it particularly challenging for researchers of health aid to make a significant contribution to the existing evidence. The drive for evidence-based policy making assumes that the necessary data exist for the entire region of study, but it often does not. For example, the many donors contributing to malaria control efforts in the Democratic Republic of Congo, including the Global Fund, the World Bank, the Department for International Development, the President's Malaria Initiative, UNICEF, the Korea International Cooperation Agency, the Sweden International Development Agency, the Canadian International Development Agency and the World Health Organization, all collect disparate data on the timing, location, purpose, and amount of malaria aid distribution (President's Malaria Initiative 2015). The absence of this type of information is widely regarded as one of the fundamental problems with measuring aid effectiveness (Easterly and Williamson 2011).

A more accurate description of the state of aid requires much better data (Easterly and Williamson 2011). However, existing literature reveals that researchers do not agree as to the data they need or the most important health aid research questions. Questions can be excessively broad and unsuited to data constraints. Two different approaches to developing research questions have been adopted for addressing these coverage challenges. The first is a "top-down" approach that relies on data source from a donor such as the World Bank. The other is "bottom-up," which relies on recipient-sourced data, typically supplied by an aid information management system housed within an aid recipient country that draws data from multiple donor organizations (AidData 2017). Either way data coverage will vary based on quality and availability of project documentation. However, typically, top-down data has a wider geographic coverage and bottom-up data has wider donor coverage (AidData 2017). The construction of these datasets mean that specific research questions call for different methodological approaches.

Quality

In addition to coverage, health aid researchers must also consider data quality issues that are specific to micro-level analysis. For example, one of the most important questions for policymakers who focus on malaria interventions is the impact of malaria treatment services on population-level transmission of malaria and on the consequent prevalence of malaria in young children. As the data necessary to estimate this policy relationship becomes available, researchers must confront practical obstacles to the consistent estimation of this impact parameter. These include missing data and locational error, both of which will bias the estimated impact of the policy variable (malaria treatment) on the health outcome variable (malaria prevalence). A growing literature aims to integrate information on the geographic data needed to improve the accuracy of modeling efforts (Worboys 1998; Aerts et al. 2003; Ogryczak and Śliwiński 2009). Researchers have proposed several solutions to this problem, from the efficient estimation of probability density to sensitivity models (Lilburne and Tarantola 2009). Recently, geoSIMEX has been introduced, which expands on these methods by integrating an extrapolation step into traditional Monte Carlo approaches to avoid bias due to imprecision. The approach mitigates a key limitation of simulation alone—namely, a failure to account for imprecision during the estimation of standard errors and parameter estimates during each iteration of a simulation (Runfola et al. 2017). geoSIMEX outperforms model averaging approaches in its ability to capture the true coefficient at all levels of spatial imprecision (Runfola et al. 2017).

Data Aggregation

Existing research on health aid has largely relied on transformed country-level data, because systematic collection of subnational data was unavailable (Easterly and Williamson 2011). These studies have contributed greatly to our knowledge of aid effectiveness and inspired the design of many follow-on or new aid programs. But the use of aggregate data to make important decisions regarding individual- or project-level programs is vulnerable to the ecological fallacy. The grouping of individuals creates aggregation bias and the fact that it ignores the possibility that grouping the data distributes confounding factors in a way that is biased creates specification bias (Morganstern 1982; King 2013). Analyzing project-level data, grouped to country levels, can lead to incorrect inference and, therefore, incorrect policy conclusions (Robinson 1950). For example, some aggregate level studies suggest that health aid is an ineffective policy tool (Wilson 2011; Williamson 2008), while others find that health aid significantly reduces infant mortality and increases life expectancy (Bendavid and Bhattacharya 2014; Mishra and Newhouse 2009). Such conflicting evidence suggests that analyzing the association between aid and outcomes requires alternative approaches. In the past 10 years, aid research has begun to disaggregate development projects by sector as well as by geographic location (Clemens et al. 2012; Hicks et al. 2010; Marty et al. 2017; Bendavid et al. 2012). Within the health sector, this subnational perspective allows researchers to examine variation in health outcomes within targeted regions and sectors.

Research Methods

A growing trend in international development aid research is to use experiments for causal identification. However, in addition to limitations associated with quality and coverage, random assignment of health aid is often impractical or unethical. Without a randomized or natural experiment, it is difficult to make causal claims in terms of the impact of health aid on health outcomes. Some studies employ Geospatial Impact Evaluations (GIEs), approximating randomized controlled trials (RCTs) through the use of subnationally georeferenced intervention, outcome, and covariate data as well as quasi-experimental methods of inference. GIEs are significantly cheaper and faster than RCTs as a rule, but more rigorous than performance evaluations. Thus, they make impact evaluation of a larger number of development programs possible than RCTs would permit. One study used a GIE to present evidence that aid used to fund a nationwide malaria bed net campaign had substantially different impacts on all-cause child mortality in the Democratic Republic of Congo (Dolan et al. 2019). However, GIEs are not appropriate for all development interventions (BenYishay et al. 2017). They require spatially explicit intervention data that vary in both timing and geography, obtainable measurements of outcomes, and covariates at the same spatial and temporal scale. Conducting a GIE requires intervention, outcome, and covariate data that can be computationally joined at a common spatial unit of collaboration. Researchers also must have the econometric tools to address the challenges of spatial uncertainty, spatial spillovers, and spatially heterogeneous effects (BenYishay et al. 2017).

Conclusion

Evidence indicates that investments in health are critical for better health outcomes, but the majority of existing research has relied on aggregate (i.e., country-level) information (Boone 1996; Kosack and Tobin 2006; Gomanee et al. 2005). Although these studies have added to our understanding of the use of aid, and have been influential in the overall design of health programs, using aggregate information to make essential decisions regarding individual- or project-level programs may impede outcomes. Careful planning and evaluation using subnational data will be necessary to sustain the current improvements in health, as well as extend health improvements to reach the SDGs (IHME 2016). This chapter has discussed the emerging literature within the context of effectiveness, efficiency, and equity which provides policymakers a set of criteria to examine emerging micro-level health aid allocation. It also discusses some of the limitations of examining health aid at a subnational level with a focus on three areas where the most recent generation of health aid research has innovated: in the data set used for analysis, in the unbundling of aid by sector and region, and in the analytical methods.

As the review of the extant literature suggests, more research is warranted to investigate the association between the allocation of health aid and health outcomes. It is increasingly important to understand the aid allocation patterns of countries like China that are becoming large players in the global development space but who may be less bound to compacts that aim to curb regional favoritism in aid allocation than countries with a longer history of involvement in aid. Thanks to the growing availability of recent aid and outcome data disaggregated at the subnational level, it is now possible to add new evidence to this decades-long debate. This chapter's examination of subnational health aid, within the context of effectiveness, efficiency, and equity, makes four broad recommendations for future research on subnational aid flows, as listed below.

First and foremost, policymakers, donors, and researchers should collectively place greater emphasis on tracking aid placement (Dieleman and Hanlon 2014). The limitations of current data require researchers to rely on complicated estimation methods that are poor substitutes for precise information. Data that is more accurately measured, collected, and tracked allows for more exact measurements (Dieleman and Hanlon 2014) and makes possible broader examinations of aid that use more donors and countries while still maintaining granularity and disaggregation at a fine level. Existing research is circumscribed not by the complexity of questions, but rather by the kinds of data available, and the level of detail at which the data can be successfully analyzed.

Second, in addition to increased efforts toward better data on aid placement, the development community should emphasize tracking health outcomes. One of the most important tasks health policymakers face is testing causal effects of policies on health outcomes. A lack of outcome data frustrates these efforts. The development literature should create, validate, and disseminate measurement tools that can reliably detect health outcomes. Jean et al. (2016) provided an example, using satellite imagery and machine learning to provide better measurements of poverty.

Third, data on current subnational aid flows is a valuable resource for researchers wishing to examine aid at greater levels of disaggregation. Yet understanding the limitations of these data is a challenge, hampering uptake within the research community. Users of the data should consider collectively detailing the limitations of subnational aid flows and the methodological challenges of measuring aid at this level in academic as well as policy-relevant outlets (e.g., peer-reviewed journals and policy briefs). Finally, as more scholars integrate geospatial data from multiple sources to examine health outcomes, researchers must confront practical obstacles stemming from where and how measurements are obtained. Past literature has shown that uncertainty regarding the locations where measurements are taken can produce biased estimates in empirical analyses (Perez-Heydrich et al. 2013; Warren et al. 2016). In current practice, researchers attempt to overcome these obstacles by using approaches that range from ad hoc to the highly methodologically sophisticated (Runfola and Napier 2016; Runfola et al. 2017; Warren et al. 2016; Perez-Heydrich et al. 2013). Additional research should provide data producers with a rigorous framework to assist their choices when using spatially referenced data sets, especially when data is displaced to preserve confidentiality.

References

Aday, Lu Ann, Charles E. Begley, David R. Lairson, and Rajesh Balkrishnan. 2004. Evaluating the Healthcare System: Effectiveness, Efficiency, and Equity. Third Edition. Chicago: Health Administration Press.

Aerts, Jeroen, Michael F. Goodchild, and Gerard Heuvelink. 2003. Accounting for Spatial Uncertainty in Optimization with Spatial Decision Support Systems. Transactions in GIS, 7(2): 211–230.

AidData Research Evaluation Unit. 2017. Geocoding Methodology (Version 2.0).

Akachi, Yoko, and Rifat Atun. 2011. Effect of Investment in Malaria Control on Child Mortality in Sub-Saharan Africa in 2002–2008. PLoS One, 6(6): e21309.

Alesina, Alberto, and David Dollar. 2000. Who Gives Foreign Aid to Whom and Why? Journal of Economic Growth, 5(1): 33–63.

Andrus, Jon Kim, Alan Arthur Crouch, John Fitzsimmons, Andrea Vicari, and Gina Tambini. 2008. Immunization and the Millennium Development Goals: Progress and Challenges in Latin America and the Caribbean. Health Affairs, 27(2): 487–493.

Bavinger, J. Clay, Paul Wise, and Eran Bendavid. 2017. The Relationship between Burden of Childhood Disease and Foreign Aid for Child Health. BMC Health Services Research, 17(1): 655.

Bendavid, E., A. Duong, C. Sagan, and G. Raikes. 2015. Health Aid is Allocated Efficiently, but Not Optimally: Insights from A Review of Cost-Effectiveness Studies. Health Affairs (Project Hope), 34(7): 1188–1195.

Bendavid, Eran, and Jay Bhattacharya. 2014. The Relationship of Health Aid to Population Health Improvements. JAMA Internal Medicine, 174(6): 881–887.

Bendavid, Eran, Charles B. Holmes, Jay Bhattacharya, and Grant Miller. 2012. HIV Development Assistance and Adult Mortality in Africa. JAMA, 307(19): 2060–2067.

BenYishay, A., D. Runfola, R. Trichler, C. Dolan, S. Goodman, B. Parks, J. Tanner, S. Heuser, G. Batra, and A. Anand. 2017. A Premier on Geospatial Impact Evaluation Methods, Tools, and Applications. AidData Working Paper No. 44, Williamsburg, VA: AidData.

BenYishay, Ariel, and Keith Kranker. 2015. All-Cause Mortality Reductions from Measles Catchup Campaigns in Africa. Journal of Human Resources, 50(2): 516–547.

Boone, Peter. 1996. Politics and the Effectiveness of Foreign Aid. European Economic Review, 40(2): 289–329.

Briggs, Ryan C. 2017. Does Foreign Aid Target the Poorest? International Organization, 71(1): 187–206.

Brown, Garrett W., Gavin Yamey, and Sarah Wamala. 2014. The Handbook of Global Health Policy. Annapolis, MD: John Wiley & Sons.

Chizema-Kawesha, Elizabeth, John M. Miller, Richard W. Steketee, Victor M. Mukonka, Chilandu Mukuka, Abdirahman D. Mohamed, Simon K. Miti, and Carlos C. Campbell. 2010. Scaling Up Malaria Control in Zambia: Progress and Impact 2005–2008. The American Journal of Tropical Medicine and Hygiene, 83(3): 480–488.

Chong, Alberto, Mark Gradstein, and Cecilia Calderon. 2009. Can Foreign Aid Reduce Income Inequality and Poverty? Public Choice, 140(1): 59–84.

Clemens, Michael A., Steven Radelet, Rikhil R. Bhavnani, and Samuel Bazzi. 2012. Counting Chickens when they Hatch: Timing and the Effects of Aid on Growth. The Economic Journal, 122(561): 590–617.

Coyne, Christopher J., and Claudia R. Williamson. 2014. Can International Aid Improve Health? The Handbook of Global Health Policy, edited by Garrett W. Brown, Gavin Yamey, and Sarah Wamala. City: Publisher. 375–392.

De, Rajlakshmi, and Charles Becker. 2015. The Foreign Aid Effectiveness Debate: Evidence from Malawi. AidData Working Paper No. 6, Williamsburg, VA: AidData.

Denizer, Cevdet, Daniel Kaufmann, and Aart Kraay. 2013. Good Countries Or Good Projects? Macro and Micro Correlates of World Bank Project Performance. Journal of Development Economics, 105:288–302.

Dieleman, Joseph L., and Michael Hanlon. 2014. Measuring the Displacement and Replacement of Government Health Expenditure. Health Economics, 23(2): 129–140.

Dolan, Carrie B., Ariel BenYishay, Karen A. Grépin, Jeffery C. Tanner, April D. Kimmel, David C. Wheeler, and Gordon C. McCord. 2019. The impact of an insecticide treated bednet campaign on all-cause child mortality: A geospatial impact evaluation from the Democratic Republic of Congo. PloS one 14(2): e0212890.

Drummond, Michael F., Mark J. Sculpher, Karl Claxton, Greg L. Stoddart, and George W. Torrance. 2015. Methods for the Economic Evaluation of Health Care Programmes. Oxford, UK: Oxford University Press.

Dye, Christopher. 2018. Expanded Health Systems for Sustainable Development. Science, 359(6382): 1337–1339.

Easterly, William, and Claudia R. Williamson. 2011. Rhetoric Versus Reality: The Best and Worst of Aid Agency Practices. World Development, 39(11): 1930–1949.

Ensor, Tim, Hafidz Firdaus, David Dunlop, Alex Manu, Ali Ghufron Mukti, Diah ayu Puspandari, Franz von Roenne, Stephanus Indradjaya, Untung Suseno, and Patrick Vaughan. 2012. Budgeting Based on Need: A Model to Determine Sub-National Allocation of Resources for Health Services in Indonesia. Cost Effectiveness and Resource Allocation, 10(1): 11.

Flaxman, Abraham D., Nancy Fullman, Mac W. Otten Jr, Manoj Menon, Richard E. Cibulskis, Marie Ng, Christopher J.L. Murray, and Stephen S. Lim. 2010. Rapid Scaling Up of Insecticide-Treated Bed Net Coverage in Africa and its Relationship with Development Assistance for Health: A Systematic Synthesis of Supply, Distribution, and Household Survey Data. PLoS Medicine, 7(8): e1000328.

Glassman, A., Victoria Fan, Mead Over, Rachel Silverman, Kate McQueston, and Denizhan Duran. 2013. More Health for the Money: A Practical Agenda for the Global Fund and its Partners. A Report of the Center for Global Development Working Group on Value for Money in Global Health. Consultation Draft.

Gomanee, Karuna, Oliver Morrissey, Paul Mosley, and Arjan Verschoor. 2005. Aid, Government Expenditure, and Aggregate Welfare. World Development, 33(3): 355–370.

Grépin, Karen A., Katherine Leach-Kemon, Matthew Schneider, and Devi Sridhar. 2011. How to do (Or Not to do)… Tracking Data on Development Assistance for Health. Health Policy and Planning, 27(6): 527–534.

Hicks, Robert L., Bradley C. Parks, J. Timmons Roberts, and Michael J. Tierney. 2010. Greening Aid?: Understanding the Environmental Impact of Development Assistance. Oxford, UK: Oxford University Press.

Institute for Health Metrics and Evaluation. 2016. Financing Global Health 2015: Development Assistance Steady on the Path to New Global Goals. Seattle, WA: IHME.

Jamison, Dean T., Lawrence H. Summers, George Alleyne, Kenneth J. Arrow, Seth Berkley, Agnes Binagwaho, Flavia Bustreo, et al. 2013. Global Health 2035: A World Converging within a Generation. The Lancet, 382(9908): 1898–1955.

Jean, Neal, Marshall Burke, Michael Xie, W. Matthew Davis, David B. Lobell, and Stefano Ermon. 2016. Combining Satellite Imagery and Machine Learning to Predict Poverty. Science, 353(6301): 790–794.

Kaiser Family Foundation. 2012. Focus on Health Care Disparities. Menlo Park, CA: Kaiser Family Foundation.

King, Gary. 2013. A Solution to the Ecological Inference Problem: Reconstructing Individual Behavior from Aggregate Data. Princeton, NJ: Princeton University Press.

Kosack, Stephen, and Jennifer Tobin. 2006. Funding Self-Sustaining Development: The Role of Aid, FDI and Government in Economic Success. International Organization, 60(01): 205–243.

Kotsadam, Andreas, Gudrun Østby, Siri Aas Rustad, Andreas Forø Tollefsen, and Henrik Urdal. 2017. Development Aid and Infant Mortality. AidData Working Paper No.39, Williamsburg, VA: AidData.

Kuruvilla, Shyama, Julian Schweitzer, David Bishai, Sadia Chowdhury, Daniele Caramani, Laura Frost, Rafael Cortez, Bernadette Daelmans, Andres de Francisco, and Taghreed Adam. 2014. Success Factors for Reducing Maternal and Child Mortality. Bulletin of the World Health Organization, 92: 533–544.

Levine, Ruth. 2007. Case Studies in Global Health: Millions Saved. Sudbury, MA: Jones & Bartlett.

Lilburne, Linda, and Stefano Tarantola. 2009. Sensitivity Analysis of Spatial Models. International Journal of Geographical Information Science, 23(2): 151–168.

Marty, Robert, Carrie B. Dolan, Matthias Leu, and Daniel Runfola. 2017. Taking the Health Aid Debate to the Subnational Level: The Impact and Allocation of Foreign Health Aid in Malawi. BMJ Global Health, 2(1): e000129.

Mishra, Prachi, and David Newhouse. 2009. Does Health Aid Matter? Journal of Health Economics, 28(4): 855–872.

Mishra, Tapas, Bazoumana Ouattara, and Mamata Parhi. 2012. International Development Aid Allocation Determinants. Economics Bulletin, 32(2): 1385–1403.

Morganstern, H. 1982. Uses of Ecologic Analysis in Epidemiologic Research. American Journal of Public Health, (72):1336–1344.

Nielson, Daniel L., Bradley Parks, and Michael J. Tierney. 2017. International organizations and development finance: Introduction to the special issue: 157–169.

Ng, Marie, Emmanuela Gakidou, Alison Levin-Rector, Ajay Khera, Christopher JL Murray, and Lalit Dandona. 2011. Assessment of population-level effect of Avahan, an HIV-prevention initiative in India. The Lancet 378(9803): 1643–1652.

Noor, Abdisalan M., Abdinasir A. Amin, Willis S. Akhwale, and Robert W. Snow. 2007. Increasing Coverage and Decreasing Inequity in Insecticide-Treated Bed Net use among Rural Kenyan Children. PLoS Medicine, 4(8): e255.

Odokonyero, Tonny, Alex Ijjo, Robert Marty, Tony Muhumuza, and Godfrey Owot Moses. 2015. Sub-National Perspectives on Aid Effectiveness: Impact of Aid on Health Outcomes in Uganda. AidData Working Paper No. 18, Williamsburg, VA: AidData.

Ogryczak, Włodzimierz, and Tomasz Śliwiński. 2009. On Efficient WOWA Optimization for Decision Support Under Risk. International Journal of Approximate Reasoning, 50(6): 915–928.

Perez-Heydrich, Carolina, Joshua Warren, Clara Burgert, and Michael Emch. 2013. Guidelines on the use of DHS GPS Data. Calverton, MD: Demographic Health Survey.

President's Malaria Initiative. 2015. Democratic Republic of Congo: Malaria Operational Plan FY2015.

Robinson, William. 1950. Ecological Correlations and the Behavior of Individuals. American Sociological Review, 15(June): 351–357.

Ruducha, Jenny, Carlyn Mann, Neha S. Singh, Tsegaye D. Gemebo, Negussie S. Tessema, Angela Baschieri, Ingrid Friberg, Taddese A. Zerfu, Mohammed Yassin, and Giovanny A. Franca. 2017. How Ethiopia Achieved Millennium Development Goal 4 through Multisectoral Interventions: A Countdown to 2015 Case Study. The Lancet Global Health, 5(11): e1151.

Runfola, Daniel, Robert Marty, Seth Goodman, Michael Lefew, and Ariel BenYishay. 2017. geoSIMEX: A Generalized Approach to Modeling Spatial Imprecision. AidData Working Paper No.38, Williamsburg, VA: AidData.

Runfola, Daniel Miller, and Ashley Napier. 2016. Migration, Climate, and International Aid: Examining Evidence of Satellite, Aid, and Micro-Census Data. Migration and Development, 5(2): 275–292.

Schmidt-Traub, Guido, and A. Shah. 2015. Investment Needs to Achieve the Sustainable Development Goals. Paris and New York: Sustainable Development Solutions Network.

Skirbekk, V., T. Ottersen, H. Hamavid, N. Sadat, and J.L. Dieleman. 2017. Vast Majority of Development Assistance for Health Funds Target those Below Age Sixty. Health Affairs (Project Hope), 36(5): 926–930.

Steketee, Richard W., Naawa Sipilanyambe, John Chimumbwa, James J. Banda, Abdirahman Mohamed, John Miller, Suprotik Basu, Simon K. Miti, and Carlos C. Campbell. 2008. National Malaria Control and Scaling up for Impact: The Zambia Experience through 2006. The American Journal of Tropical Medicine and Hygiene, 79(1): 45–52.

Stenberg, Karin, Odd Hanssen, Tessa Tan-Torres Edejer, Melanie Bertram, Callum Brindley, Andreia Meshreky, James E. Rosen, John Stover, Paul Verboom, and Rachel Sanders. 2017. Financing Transformative Health Systems Towards Achievement of the Health Sustainable Development Goals: A Model for Projected Resource Needs in 67 Low-Income and Middle-Income Countries. The Lancet Global Health, 5(9): e887.

United Nations General Assembly. 2015. Transforming our World: The 2030 Agenda for Sustainable Development. New York: United Nations.

United Nations Department of Public Information. 2009. Millennium Development Goals Report 2009 (Includes the 2009 Progress Chart). New York: United Nations.

Wang, Haidong, Zulfiqar A. Bhutta, Matthew M. Coates, Megan Coggeshall, Lalit Dandona, Khassoum Diallo, Elisabeth Barboza Franca et al. 2016. Global, regional, national, and selected subnational levels of stillbirths, neonatal, infant, and under-5 mortality, 1980–2015: a systematic analysis for the Global Burden of Disease Study 2015. The Lancet 388, no. 10053: 1725–1774.

Warren, Joshua L., Carolina Perez-Heydrich, Clara R. Burgert, and Michael E. Emch. 2016. Influence of Demographic and Health Survey Point Displacements on Distance-Based Analyses. Spatial Demography, 4(2): 155–173.

Wayland, Joshua. 2017. Constraints on Foreign Aid Effectiveness in the Water, Sanitation, and Hygiene (WaSH) Sector. Journal of Water, Sanitation, and Hygiene for Development, 8(1): 44–52.

Williamson, Claudia R. 2008. Foreign Aid and Human Development: The Impact of Foreign Aid to the Health Sector. Southern Economic Journal, 75(1): 188–207.

Wilson, Sven E. 2011. Chasing Success: Health Sector Aid and Mortality. World Development, 39(11): 2032–2043.

Worboys, Michael. 1998. Imprecision in Finite Resolution Spatial Data. GeoInformatica, 2(3): 257–279.

World Health Organization Commission on Social Determinants of Health and World Health Organization. 2008. Closing the Gap in a Generation: Health Equity through Action on the Social Determinants of Health: Commission on Social Determinants of Health Final Report. Geneva, Switzerland: World Health Organization.

Yamey, Gavin, and Jimmy Volmink. 2014. An Argument for Evidence-based Policy-making in Global Health. The Handbook of Global Health Policy, edited by Garrett W. Brown, Gavin Yamey, and Sarah Wamala. Annapolis, MD: John Wiley & Sons. 133–155.

SECTION II

The Political Economy of Donor Behavior

CHAPTER 5

Evaluating Aid Agencies: Challenges, Comparisons, and Causes of Best Aid Practices

Liya Palagashvili

Introduction

Why has foreign aid fallen short in achieving its development goals?[1] One such answer lies in the aid effectiveness movement. Aid effectiveness refers to improving the *quality* (rather than *quantity*) of aid flows and following a set of "best practices" that can make foreign aid more effective in poverty reduction. These best practices range from encouraging aid agencies or donors to be more transparent about their aid practices, to giving aid only to democratic and poor countries, to donors specializing in geographic regions or sectors, and other practices aimed to develop more effective aid disbursements.

Scholars, the development community, and policymakers believe that aid can better achieve its intended results if donors commit to following the aid effectiveness principles.[2] This idea has led to several formal international agreements to engage in better aid disbursement practices. It is important to note that while the formal agreements contain best aid

L. Palagashvili (✉)
State University of New York, Purchase, Purchase, NY, USA
e-mail: Liya.palagashvili@purchase.edu

N. Dutta, C. R. Williamson (eds.), *Lessons on Foreign Aid and Economic Development*, https://doi.org/10.1007/978-3-030-22121-8_5

practices for both donors and recipient countries, much of the literature (and accordingly this chapter) focuses on evaluating and ranking the donors rather than the recipient countries. These international aid effectiveness agreements are made by both bilateral and multilateral donors. Bilateral donor refers to the country itself as the aid donor (i.e. the USA, France, New Zealand), while multilateral donor refers to international institutions, such as the IMF, World Bank, or Global Fund.

The official launch of the aid effectiveness movement began with the "First High Level Forum on Aid Effectiveness" in 2003 in Rome, organized by the Organization for Economic Cooperation and Development (OECD). In that same year, the OECD's Development Assistance Committee created a subsidiary body called the "Working Party for Aid Effectiveness," whose mission was to improve the "effectiveness of aid for greater impact on development and poverty reduction" (OECD 2008a, pg. 115). The Development Assistance Committee (DAC) is a group of high-income donor countries (such as the USA and members of the European Union) that discuss issues surrounding aid, coordinate efforts to collect and publish statistics on aid flows, and create common objectives, resolutions, and guidelines on aid-giving—as such, it was in their initiative to formally launch the aid effectiveness movement.

At this first forum, the participants created the Rome Declaration of 2003, where donors along with the aid recipient countries, made public commitments to coordinate donor aid efforts, to share information, and to reduce the duplication of aid projects. Donors also made commitments that aid should be delivered in accordance with recipient country's priorities—including their national goals, budgets, project planning cycles, and public expenditure and financial management systems.

In 2005, the members of the development community met again to create a more comprehensive plan on aid effectiveness, which they called the Paris Declaration on Aid Effectiveness. Donor bilateral and multilateral institutions, alongside recipient countries, committed to a more thorough set of aid effectiveness principles. The Paris Declaration became a landmark agreement because it created an implementation plan, set with clear indicators, measurement criterion, and targets set for specific years for both donors and recipients.

Three years later, members of the development community met again in Accra, Ghana, to check the progress and make a similar set of commitments on aid effectiveness—with donors pledging once again to better coordinate their actions and both donors and recipients agreeing to be more accountable. They signed the Accra Agenda for Action (AAA) on September 4, 2008.

Despite these efforts to unite and create commitments and pledges, the implementation of these agreements has been difficult. Both bilateral and multilateral agencies were found to be ineffective in meeting their own commitments. In an OECD monitoring report, "Aid Effectiveness: 2005–2010: Progress in Implementing the Paris Declaration," it concluded that the "results were sobering" and only one of the 13 targets established for 2010 was met, albeit by a narrow margin (OECD 2011, pg. 15). The findings called for more dialogue, cooperation, and action to better meet the aid effectiveness goals.

The Fourth High Level Forum on Aid Effectiveness was held in Busan, Korea in 2011. After addressing the challenges on why donors were unable to keep their commitments, they again reaffirmed their pledges. During this forum, the Global Partnership for Effective Development Cooperation was created and signed by 161 countries and 56 organizations—with the goal of tracking the progress and implementation of the Busan commitments. In the latest 2016 report monitoring the Busan agreements, the Global Partnership found that while some progress has been made, the goals and commitments have yet to be achieved (OECD/UNDP 2016).

Why have donors failed to achieve their own commitments and implement changes to best aid practices? Are there differences in the types of donors that perform better or worse? This chapter will summarize the findings in the literature on donor performance and rankings, as well as examine patterns, highlight major findings, and investigate what factors influence donors' decisions to engage in best aid practices.

The Components of Aid Effectiveness

The components of effective aid are formed in two main ways: (1) through the development community and the commitments that donors and recipients make in the agreements, and (2) by development researchers and scholars. While there is overlap on what constitutes as best aid practices, there is also a lot of variation depending on the specific international agreements, or on the different types of research and methodologies. As a result, there is not one set of agreed-upon best aid practices, but a good starting point often comes from the Paris Declaration of 2005. The principles are as follows:

1. ***Ownership:*** *Partner countries exercise effective leadership over their development policies and strategies and co-ordinate development actions*
2. ***Alignment:*** *Donors base their overall support on partner countries' national development strategies, institutions, and procedures*
3. ***Harmonization:*** *Donors' actions are more harmonized, transparent and collectively effective*
4. ***Managing for results:*** *Managing resources and improving decision-making for results*
5. ***Mutual accountability:*** *Donors and partners are accountable for development results*

Both donors and recipients commit to best aid practices, but for the purposes of this chapter and following the academic literature on donor best practices, I focus mainly on the donor-side commitments.

The **ownership** commitment is mostly for the developing countries to better exercise leadership in poverty reduction, improving their institutions, and tackling corruption. Donors are merely encouraged to "respect partner country leadership" (OECD 2008b, pg. 3). As such, the ownership commitment is not commonly utilized when assessing donor performance and rankings for best aid practices.

Alignment refers to donors respecting recipient country priorities, utilizing the recipient country's local institutions, and human resources, untying aid, and disbursing aid in a predictable fashion, among other commitments. Some of the measurements used to assess donor performance on this principle are percentage of donors using the recipient country's public financial management system and percent using the procurement systems, percent of aid disbursements disbursed according to agreed schedules, and percent of bilateral aid that is untied.

For **harmonization**, the general idea is that donor countries coordinate with each other, simplify procedures, and share information to avoid duplication. This includes donors engaging in joint field mission projects and country work analytics and implementing common arrangements for funding, disbursements, monitoring, evaluating, and reporting. In other words, harmonization is a commitment to share missions and coordinate with other donors to reduce duplication, burden, and costs (especially transaction costs) on recipient countries.

For **results,** the main indicator for assessment is on the recipient country side to provide transparent and measurable assessment frameworks to measure progress and evaluate results. Donors agreed to work with recipient country's results-orientated reporting and framework systems.

Lastly, **mutual accountability** refers to a commitment to transparency such that donors and recipients can hold each other accountable to implementing these agreements on aid effectiveness. On the donor side, they commit to providing "timely, transparent, and comprehensive information on aid flows."

These principles in the Paris Declaration form the backbone of effective aid. While some researchers have followed these principles closely when evaluating donor performance, others select their own methods for evaluation on academic grounds. There is not one single, agreed-upon methodology nor is there agreement on the specific components to address aid effectiveness—scholars and the development community pursue a variety of methodologies and differ on how closely to follow the Paris Declaration components of effective aid. As a result, the outcomes of each study and the discussions on aid effectiveness and the performance of donors can cause confusion because each set of donor performance measures uses its own unique components of what constitutes as effective aid or best aid practices. In other words, there is no common "best aid practices" index, and that makes it difficult to evaluate whether donors are in fact improving over time.

Stemming from aspects of the harmonization principle, the development community and scholars began to focus on the component of **specialization** (sometimes discussed as fragmentation or proliferation of aid). Aid fragmentation/proliferation or a lack of specialization is identified as one of the main challenges for effective aid.[3] Too many donors in one country or sector leads to a duplication of efforts and high bureaucratic costs in recipient countries as well as increasing transactions costs in donor countries.[4] Too many donors and too many projects also weaken the capacity of recipient governments to manage aid and their relations with donors, and can also reduce economic growth (Djankov et al. 2009; Kimura et al. 2012). Some of the main indicators for specialization are geographic concentration, sector concentration, or average size of aid projects.

Furthermore, another best practice component highlighted by development researchers is called **aid selectivity,** which measures whether donors give aid to mostly poor and mostly democratic countries. This component is included because aid is believed to be more effective at reducing poverty if it is selectively allocated to the poorest countries and to countries with the more democratic institutions (and less corrupt governments). Burnside and Dollar (2000) and several other studies also provided empirical support for this. One main challenge with aid selectivity is that the poorest countries are more likely to be undemocratic and corrupt, so donors must create a balance between supporting the poorest and those with better governance.

With the discussion of accountability in the Paris Declaration, the development community began to focus broadly on the concept of **transparency**, and it has yielded several methodologies for how to measure transparency of aid and whether donors are becoming more transparent over time. Transparency is arguably the most critical component to aid effectiveness because it enables outside monitoring. If aid is not transparent, agencies are not accountable for ineffective use or misappropriation of aid. Droop et al. (2008) explains that we cannot evaluate agencies if we cannot monitor where the money goes, and if we cannot evaluate aid agencies, then there is an absence of accountability on the part of the donors.

Lastly, while not in the Paris Declaration, **overhead costs** are frequently included as a best practice measure. Overhead costs are sometimes used as a component for a broader principle, but their purpose is to examine an agency's costs relative to aid disbursements. Exceptionally high overhead costs are signs of inefficiency because it implies that a large proportion of the agency's budget is going more toward supporting the organization rather than delivering aid to intended recipients—thus, an indicator of inefficient aid practices.

It is important to note that these best practices are organized differently for different studies measuring donor performance and aid effectiveness, and not all studies include the same best practices. For example, in one major study, Birdsall et al. (2010) create four pillars of aid effectiveness: maximizing efficiency, fostering institutions, reducing burden, and transparency. In their study, overhead costs are an indicator for "maximizing efficiency," as is selectivity and specialization. But in Easterly and Pfutze (2008), Easterly and Williamson (2011), and Palagashvili and Williamson (2018), overhead costs, selectivity, and specialization are their own separate best aid practice indices. In Knack et al. (2011), overhead costs are not included at all, but selectivity and specialization are separate indices. Furthermore, even when the components are the same across studies, the underlying indicators for a component are different. In Birdsall et al. (2010), whether members are part of the International Aid

Transparency Initiative is an indicator for the transparency pillar, but it does not count for Easterly and Pfutze (2008), Easterly and Williamson (2011), and Palagashvili and Williamson (2018).

Donor Performance and Rankings

How well have donors performed to meet best aid practices? The OECD began monitoring and measuring whether donors would meet the 2010 targets set in Paris Declaration and Accra Agenda for Action. In the OECD 2011 report of the results, they conclude: "For the most part, the findings are clear: while many donors and partner country governments have made significant progress towards the targets that they set themselves for 2010, few of them have been met" (OECD 2011, pg. 17). In fact, only 1 of the 13 targets was met—which was donors coordinating efforts to support the recipient countries' capacity development objectives. In some areas, donor performance made no progress at all or progress declined, which was the case for aid fragmentation. The reports also noted that donor efforts and progress significantly "vary across countries and donor organizations" (pg. 17).

In the most recent 2016 Global Partnership monitoring report, the donor performance results are mixed—with important progress on some components, little progress on others, and slight declines on a few. Alignment and transparency are moving in the right direction, but "further progress also needs to be made in promoting the use of the countries' public financial management and procurement system" (OECD/UNDP 2016, pg. 25). The report also finds that untying aid is "leveling off" as little progress has been made since 2010 (pg. 32). For aid predictability, donors also agreed to distribute funds in a timely and predictable fashion, but the progress on that has slightly declined since 2010, with the target still out of reach (pg. 33).

In addition to the monitoring schemes organized by the OECD and its partners on aid effectiveness, there have been a plethora of academic and scholarly research attempts to measure and rank how well the donors are doing as a group, and also to analyze the variation in best practices by donors.

Birdsall et al. (2010) rank aid quality across 31 bilateral and multilateral donors based on four pillars of maximizing efficiency, fostering institutions, reducing burden, and transparency. Overall, donors have not been successful in meeting best aid practices, but there are large differences among individual donors and components. As a group, multilateral agencies outperform bilateral agencies in three out of the four indicators (transparency is where bilaterals are better than multilaterals). The International Development Association (IDA, part of the World Bank Group) and Ireland are the only two donors that score in the top ten across all four components, and Greece, Switzerland, and the USA are among the bottom rankings for all four indicators.

In another major study, Knack et al. (2011) create a comprehensive index closely following the main commitments that donors have made at the Paris Declaration. They construct an overall rank grouped into four dimensions of selectivity, alignment, harmonization, and specialization. They include 38 bilateral and multilateral donors and find that the top donors are the Asian Development Bank, the World Bank, and the IMF. The worst performing donors are Turkey and Greece. The USA and the United Nations earned considerably low scores as well.

Easterly and Pfutze (2008) evaluate 39 bilateral and multilateral donors and construct indices of transparency, overhead costs, specialization, selectivity, ineffective aid channels (includes tied aid). They find that development banks tend to rank among the best, bilateral agencies second, and UN agencies among the worst. Following the same methodology and evaluating 44 donors, Easterly and Williamson (2011) find that agencies are not improving overtime: only modest improvements in transparency and ineffective channels, and there is no evidence of improvement in the other channels. They also find that as a group, multilateral agencies are the best performers, and UN agencies among the worst. In the most recent analysis of evaluating donor performance along the same methodology set up by Easterly and Pfutze (2008), Palagashvili and Williamson (2018) find that between 2004–2012, multilateral and UN agencies improved their best aid practices (especially in transparency and specialization), while bilateral donors have declined (particularly in specialization). Overall, multilateral agencies are the best performers.

In addition to constructing overall performance-based measures, other scholars are using specific components of aid effectiveness to study how donors measure in those areas. Nunnenkamp et al. (2013) test whether donors have specialized and coordinated activities since Paris Declaration and find that there is no statistically significant impact on donor specialization—hence concluding that donors did not keep their promises to "specialize" and "coordinate." Bürcky (2011) finds that aid fragmentation and aid proliferation has *increased* since the Paris Declaration.

Ghosh and Kharas (2011) rank donors on transparency by constructing an index that looks at the accessibility and completeness of aid information, whether donors publish to the International Aid Transparency Initiative (IATI), and the share of aid that go to recipients with good monitoring and evaluation frameworks. They find that being a member of IATI is a powerful signal of a donor being transparent across most other dimensions. Among the best are the IDA, Australia, Ireland, and European Commission (EC) Korea, IDB Special Fund, and Greece are the least transparent. Publish What You Fund (PWYF) maintains a comprehensive yearly transparency index that assesses agencies based on the information that they provide on their organization and specific project activities, and their commitment to transparency. In the latest 2018 report, they find overall progress in transparency. Among their best performers are the Asian Development Bank and UNDP, while the worst performers are China, United Arab Emirates, and Japan (PWYF 2018, pg. 6–7).

Dollar and Levin (2006) rank donors based solely on the aid selectivity component: they create sub-indices of poverty selectivity (whether donors allocate aid based on recipient poverty levels) and policy selectivity (whether donors allocate aid based on recipient country's good institutions/policies). They assess 31 bilateral and multilateral donors, and find that, in general, multilateral aid is more policy and poverty focused than bilateral aid. They also find that between 1984 and 2002 donors increased in policy and poverty selectivity. Jimmy Adedokun and O. Folawewo (2017) find similar results when studying aid between 1980 and 2012 in Sub-Saharan Africa: there has been significant improvement in aid effectiveness due to better aid selectivity practices. This is also in line with Winters and Martinez (2015) who find that donors in general have become more selective from 2004–2010.

These have been some of the main findings in the aid effectiveness and donor performance rankings research. Table 5.1 presents a summary of the studies, and includes other studies that assess donor performance, containing the criterion of evaluation, the type of donors assessed, and the main results.

While there are differences in methodologies and components of aid effectiveness, there are important patterns that emerge across various studies on donor performance. First, donors as a whole tend to be increasing in the transparency component, though "full transparency" has yet to be achieved. Bilateral donors also tend to do better than multilateral and UN donors on the transparency measures. Second, aid fragmentation and

Table 5.1 Summary of aid agency rankings & findings

Source	*Criterion*	*Donors*	*Major findings*
Palagashvili and Williamson (2018): "Are Aid Agencies Changing their Practices?"	Transparency, overhead costs, specialization, selectivity, and ineffective channels	40 bilateral and multilateral donors	Multilateral and UN agencies are improving (especially in transparency and specialization), bilateral donors have declined (especially in specialization). Overall, multilateral agencies are the best performers.
Easterly and Williamson (2011): "Rhetoric vs. Reality: The Best and Worst of Aid Agency Practices"	Transparency, overhead costs, specialization, selectivity, and ineffective channels	44 bilateral and multilateral donors	Agencies not improving overtime: Only modest improvements in transparency and ineffective channels; no evidence of improvement in the other channels. Multilateral donors are the best performers, and UN agencies are among the worst.
Easterly and Pfutze (2008): "Where Does the Money Go?"	Transparency, overhead costs, specialization, selectivity, and ineffective channels	39 bilateral and multilateral donors	Development banks tend to rank second among the best, bilateral agencies, and UN agencies are among the worst. Among bilateral agencies, New Zealand, Spain, and Greece are the worst performers, and UK, Norway, and Sweden the best.
Knack et al. (2011). "Aid Quality and Donor Rankings"	Selectivity, alignment, harmonization, and specialization	38 bilateral and multilateral donors	Asian Development Bank, the World Bank, and the IMF are among the best performers. The worst performing donors are Turkey, Greece, and the USA. United Nations also earned considerably low scores.

(*continued*)

Table 5.1 (continued)

Source	*Criterion*	*Donors*	*Major findings*
Birdsall et al. Center for Global Development (2010): "Quality of Official Development Assistance Assessment"	Maximizing efficiency, fostering institutions, reducing burden, and transparency	31 bilateral and multilateral donors (UN agencies counted as one multilateral group)	As a group, multilateral agencies outperform bilateral agencies in 3 out of the 4 indicators (transparency is where bilateral agencies outcompete); Greece, Switzerland, and the USA are among the bottom rankings for all 4 indicators.
Roodman (2012); Center for Development. "Index on Donor Performance"	Tied aid, selectivity, proliferation/ fragmentation, along with quantity of aid given and fiscal policies for private charity aid	21 bilateral donors	Sweden, Norway, Denmark, and the Netherlands score the highest; The USA and Japan are at the bottom.
OECD: "2011 survey on monitoring the Paris declaration"	Ownership, alignment, harmonization, managing for results, mutual accountability	33 donors	1 of 13 targets established for 2010 has been met (donors coordinating efforts to support country's capacity development objectives).
UK DFID: "Multilateral Development Review 2016"	Match with UK development objectives, organizational strength	38 multilateral donors	DFID's multilateral partners align closely with UK's development and humanitarian goals and organizational capacity is improving. Some agencies need urgent reform. World Bank, Global Fund, GAVI are among the best. UNESCO received the worst score.

(*continued*)

Table 5.1 (continued)

Source	*Criterion*	*Donors*	*Major findings*
Ghosh and Kharas (2011): "The Money Trail: Ranking Donor Transparency in Foreign Aid"	Transparency	31 bilateral and multilateral donors	Being a member of IATI is a powerful signal of donor being transparent across most other dimensions. IDA, Australia, Ireland, and EC are most transparent; Korea, IDB Special Fund, and Greece are least transparent. No strong systemic difference between bilateral and multilateral agencies on transparency.
Nunnenkamp et al. (2013); "Donor Coordination and Specialization: Did the Paris Declaration Make a Difference?"	Specialization, coordination	19 bilateral DAC donors plus two multilateral: EU institutions & IDA	Aid fragmentation persisted after Paris Declaration, and coordination among donors has weakened
Dollar and Levin (2006) "The Increasing Selectivity of Foreign Aid"	Selectivity	41 bilateral and multilateral donors	Between 1984 and 2002, donors increased in policy and poverty selectivity. In general, multilateral aid is more policy & poverty focused than bilateral. Among the best performers are IDA, IMF's ESAF, Denmark, the UK, Norway, Ireland, and Netherlands. The USA and France are not particularly selective.
OECD/UNDP 2016: "Making Development Co-operation More Effective: 2016 Progress Report"	Focus on results, country ownership, inclusive partnerships for development, transparency and mutual accountability	Bilateral and multilateral donors	Results are mixed—in some areas there are improvements, in others there are slight declines or no improvements. The report concludes that "important progress" had been made, but goals have yet to be achieved.

(*continued*)

Table 5.1 (continued)

Source	*Criterion*	*Donors*	*Major findings*
Publish What You Fund "Aid Transparency Index 2018"	Transparency	45 bilateral and multilateral donors	Progress overall in transparency. Among the best performers are the Asian Development Bank and UNDP, while the worst performers are China, United Arab Emirates, and Japan.

Source: Stated in the table

Table 5.2 Performance of bilateral and multilateral across components

	Bilateral	*Multilateral*
Easterly and Pfutze (2008)	Transparency, overhead	Specialization, selectivity, ineffective channels
Easterly and Williamson (2011)	Overhead	Transparency, specialization, selectivity, ineffective channels
Palagashvili and Williamson (2018)	Transparency, overhead	Specialization, selectivity, ineffective channels
Birdsall et al. (2017)	Transparency	Maximizing efficiency, fostering institutions, reducing burden
Knack et al. (2011)		Selectivity, alignment, harmonization, specialization
Dollar and Levin (2006)		Selectivity

Source: Stated in the table

a lack of specialization remain as one the biggest weaknesses across all studies. Third, UN agencies are highlighted in many of the studies as being among the worst performers, and on an individual level, the USA and Greece come up in the bottom of several aid effectiveness components across studies.

Moreover, one of the most important patterns is that multilateral donors consistently outperform bilateral donors. There is even a similarity across which type of components. Table 5.2 provides a summary across the studies that evaluate both bilateral and multilateral donors on which components multilateral and bilateral donors tend to do better.

As shown across studies, bilateral donors tend to do better on transparency, partly because the DAC membership requires the bilateral donors to report aid flows and to engage in other transparency-related commitments. In some studies, bilateral donors also do better in overhead costs.[5] This may be because multilateral and UN agencies undertake more program-based aid work and they are involved in activities beyond dispersing funds, thus increasing their overhead expenses. Also, it is important to note that bilateral agencies disperse part of their aid through multilateral agencies, so bilateral donors can be seen as "outsourcing" part of their expenses.

Multilateral donors tend to outperform in all other areas, especially in specialization and selectivity. Because the Birdsall et al. (2010) study creates broader categories, the common aid components are hidden as indicators—but within their Maximizing Efficiency pillar, multilateral donors also outperform bilateral donors on specialization and fragmentation. The fact that bilateral donors tend to be the most fragmented lends support to the hypothesis that bilateral donors respond to political lobbying to "plant their flags" across countries and different projects to increase visibility (Kilby 2011). And on selectivity, multilateral donors adhere more to a poverty agenda as part of their missions, whereas bilateral donors may allocate aid based on geopolitical or political economy reasons. The next section will dive more into these determinants and incentives of best aid practices.

The Determinants of Best Aid Practices

Why are donors unable to meet the principles of aid effectiveness, and what determines whether donors engage in best aid practices? Why do multilateral donors tend to outperform bilateral donors? These questions are a natural extension of the growing literature on evaluating aid effectiveness, and scholars have begun to inquire into the variables that determine donors implementing these effective strategies.

One reason why donors may not be meeting aid effectiveness best practices is because aid is given for intentions other than to relieve poverty and spur development. Maizels and Nissanke (1984) find that bilateral aid agencies give aid based on political/security reasons, investment incentives, and trade interests, while multilateral aid agencies are more likely to give aid based on poverty level of the recipient country.

Alesina and Dollar (2000) also find that the colonial past of the country and political alliances are the major determinants of foreign aid allocation. They do identify a small number of donors who allocate aid based on "correct" reasons (income levels, less corruption in the country), but for the most part, the aid allocation flows are determined by strategic, political reasons. These strategic reasons include such things as voting in the UN, as Kuziemko and Werker (2006) show that donors will give foreign aid in order to "buy" votes from the UN Security Council rotating members on important international issues such as declaring war and engaging in economic sanctions. Similarly, Dreher et al. (2009) argue that temporary membership on the UN Security Council determines the number of World Bank projects a country receives.

Using a natural experiment of the Eastern European transitions, Frot et al. (2014) find that commercial and strategic concerns determined aid flows and allocation during the first half of the post-communist transitions in the late twentieth century—an important phase for foreign policy interests. Fleck and Kilby (2010) also find that the War on Terror significantly reduced US aid flows for need-based recipients. These studies show that the reasons donors give foreign aid may have less to do with development intentions for the recipient country and have more to do with geopolitical or "self-interest" reasons of the donor countries. This plays an important role in the incentives that donors have to engage in some of the best practices and provides an explanation for why the rhetoric in terms of committing to best aid practices diverges from the reality of the practices they actually employ.

This line of research may also help explain why multilateral donors tend to do better than bilateral donors on the selectivity component of aid effectiveness—bilateral donors have a stronger incentive to allocate aid based on geopolitical, historical, or political economy reasons (thus potentially ignoring need or governance). But multilateral agencies do not face the same political economy incentives and may adhere to need as a guide for aid disbursements.

Furthermore, Knack (2013) points to a rational response by donors to adhere to the "use of the recipient country's system" component of the alignment principle in the Paris Declaration: donors will choose to use the recipient country system if the recipient countries are less corrupt, if the donors have a greater share of aid in the recipient countries, and if there is greater public support in the donor countries for aid-giving. In another paper, Knack and Smets (2013) seek to test whether there are potential trade-offs or complementarities between two components of the Paris Declaration: untying aid and reducing fragmentation. They find that donors with a large share of the aid market have a stronger incentive to maximize the development impact of aid, and hence will engage in less aid tying. Thus, one "determinant" of reducing aid tying is gaining a greater share of the aid market in a particular country.

A further problem with aid fragmentation is that it may be a rational response by donors: more donors in one country means less donor accountability creating a free-rider problem and strategic donor competition. Rahman and Sawada (2012) empirically test the free-riding problem with donor proliferation and conclude that there needs to be a fundamental change in aid-giving incentives in order to lower aid proliferation. And similarly, Kilby (2011) finds that donors may fragment their aid because of the strong presence of bureaucratic competition in donor countries as they attempt to "plant their flags" in as many countries as possible in order to increase their budgets for the following year. In other words, these studies show that donors face incentives to fragment aid, and it will continue unless there are changes to incentivize donors to act otherwise.[6]

Although improvement in aid fragmentation has leveled-off or declined, transparency of aid has increased. What incentives did donors secure in improving transparency? For one, the DAC bilateral donors are already required to meet a baseline of transparent aid as part of their membership. Furthermore, Honig and Weaver (2018) found that the International Aid Transparency initiative was successful in influencing more transparent aid across donors via social pressure and "community dynamics" incentives. Interestingly they note that because these incentives to improve transparency operate on social pressure, they will not influence donors who overtly reject the goals and are not part of the community in which the social pressure operatives may function (i.e. China and the UAE).

This line of research that seeks to understand donor incentives is fundamental to the overall discussion of aid effectiveness since it helps to provide an understanding of why aid agencies may not choose to engage in the best aid practices.

Conclusion

Moving forward, research on aid effectiveness should continue to uncover patterns and determinants of best aid practices in order to better understand the incentives and conditions that donors face to meet effective aid principles. In doing so, it should also address some of the current limitations and challenges in the aid effectiveness research. First, there are data limitation problems. While transparency of aid is increasing, there is still a lot more that donors can do to provide more information, which is fundamental to deepen the research on aid effectiveness. Studies that evaluate donor transparency should continue highlighting the most and least transparent donors, as a way to at least put pressure on donors to improve transparency.

Second, Clist (2014) pointed out the donor rankings research has potential measurement and sensitivity problems. He illustrates how making some marginal alterations to the measurements and cutoffs in the donor rankings indices can vastly alter the position of individual donor rankings—thus making these studies sensitive to marginal changes.[7] BenYishey and Wiebe (2009) also challenge the ranking assessments. They reproduce Easterly and Pfutze's rankings and show how the US Millennium Challenge Corporation (MCC) moves up in the rankings after a few adjustments.[8] These challenges raise the importance of focusing on the larger patterns that emerge rather than individual donor rankings. For example, a pattern emerging from the rankings research shows that multilateral agencies tend to do better than bilateral agencies, and this finding is robust across several studies.

Third, and following this similar line of thought, there are also patterns on best aid practices when evaluating non-DAC bilateral donors, which include countries such as China, Russia, United Arab Emirates, and now many Eastern European countries such as Bulgaria, Estonia, and Romania. Despite the emergence of non-DAC aid in the development context, there has not been enough research on it. In one of the few papers, Dreher et al. (2011) provide an analysis of whether there are differences in aid allocation between DAC and non-DAC donors. They find that on average, the emerging donors do not discriminate with regard to the recipient country as much as DAC donors on certain margins—for example, the poverty level of recipient countries. However, in general, there are several aspects in which non-DAC and DAC donors behave similarly, such as their disregard for corruption in recipient countries. Furthermore, Dreher and Fuchs (2012) find that Chinese aid allocation is determined by political considerations but that it is not significantly different when compared to some DAC donors, who also allocate aid for political reasons. Palagashvili and Williamson (2018) also find that DAC and non-DAC donors both rank poorly on best aid practices, but there are differences across the components: DAC donors tend to be more transparent, while non-DAC are better in terms of specialization and providing aid through more effective channels. Despite these efforts to understand DAC versus non-DAC aid, more research is needed, which means that there need to be improvements in the transparency of non-DAC aid.

Overall, the aid effectiveness research demonstrates that there is potential for better quality aid to help with poverty reduction, but that donors face great difficulty in committing and sticking to these practices. There is a lot of variation among individual donors—but some individual donors are consistently better or worse across many studies. Beyond individual donor performances, there are patterns that emerge alongside the type of donor and type of best practice components that seem to improve. Multilateral donors tend to outperform bilateral donors, and the transparency component seems to be improving (and to a lesser extent also selectivity), while harmonization, fragmentation, and lack of specialization either decline or do not show much improvement. This leads to important questions on donor motivations and incentives to engage in best aid practices. Some of the literature indicates that bilateral donors are motivated to give aid based on geopolitical or political economy reasons, lending support to why bilateral donors often perform worse than multilateral agencies.

Other studies also indicate how aspects such as aid fragmentation are rational responses by donors, given the incentives they face. This line of research is particularly important moving forward. If the goal is to have donors engage in better aid practices, then we should continue to uncover what incentives donors have to engage in those best aid practices. Once there is a better understanding of the determinants of best aid practices and donor incentives, it may help the development community to rethink commitments and/or restructure incentives for donors to better meet those best aid practices.

Notes

1. For empirical studies supporting the ineffectiveness of foreign aid in achieving development, see Boone (1996), Svensson (1999, 2000), Easterly (2001, 2006), Knack (2001), Bräutigam and Knack (2004), Easterly et al. (2004), Djankov et al. (2008), Heckelman and Knack (2008), Williamson (2008), Moyo (2009), Shleifer (2009), Skarbek and Leeson (2009), and Young and Sheehan (2014).

2. For example, Minasyan et al. (2017) find that only recipient countries with increased aid flows of "high quality" benefited in terms of increasing GDP per capita. Djankov et al. (2009) find that a lack of aid specialization leads to more corruption in recipient countries and reduces economic growth. Kimura et al. (2012) also find that aid proliferation has a negative effect on the economic growth of recipient countries, especially in Africa.
3. See, Accra Agenda for Action (2008, pg. 17), World Bank (1998, pg. 25), Commission for Africa (2005, pgs. 62, 320), IMF and World Bank (2005, pg. 171, 2006, pg. 62, 2010, pg. 131), Easterly (2007), Frot and Santiso (2009), Kimura et al. (2012).
4. Anderson (2012) finds that bilateral donors could reduce transaction costs by $2.5 billion per year if they specialized more.
5. Though in Birdsall et al. (2010), bilateral donors are worse than multilateral donors in administrative costs (which falls in the broader Maximizing Efficiency pillar).
6. See also, Acharya et al. (2006), Kharas (2009), Anderson (2012), Annen and Moers (2012), Barthel et al. (2014), Fuchs et al. (2015).
7. However, most of the deviations that Clist points to are not dramatic changes—the donor rankings do change, but they stay relatively within the same vicinity. For example, Clist calls Sweden a "large" fall when altering Easterly and Williamson's measurements, but Sweden falls from 8th to the 12th rank.
8. MCC's ODA commitments rather than disbursements are used. However, they only alter MCC's data from disbursements to commitments and analyze the other agencies with disbursements. If all of the donors' changes were made to commitments, it is not clear whether the MCC would have jumped in the rankings.

References

Acharya, Arnab, Ana Teresa Fuzzo de Lima, and Mick Moore. 2006. "Proliferation and Fragmentation: Transactions Costs and the Value of Aid." Journal of Development Studies, 42(1): 1–21.

Adedokun, Adeniyi J., and Abiyodun O. Folawewo. 2017. "Aid Selectivity Practice and Aid Effectiveness in Sub-Saharan Africa." Journal of Economic and Social Development, 4(2): 23–39.

Alesina, Alberto, and David Dollar. 2000. "Who Gives Foreign Aid to Whom and Why?" Journal of Economic Growth, 5(1): 33–63.

Anderson, E. 2012. "Aid fragmentation and donor transactions costs." Economic Letters, 117: 799–802.

Annen, K., and L. Moers. 2012. "Donor competition for aid impact, and aid fragmentation." International Monetary Fund, Working Paper No. 12/204.

Barthel, F., E. Neumayer, and P. Nunnenkamp, and P. Selaya. 2014. "Competition for export markets and the allocation of foreign aid: The role of spatial dependence among donor countries." World Development, 64: 350–365.
BenYishey, A., and F.S. Wiebe. 2009. "Can Aid Agencies Follow Best Practices? An Assessment of the Millennium Challenge Corporation's Aid Practices Based on Easterly & Pfutze (2008)." Millennium Challenge Corporation Working Paper.
Birdsall, N., Kharas, H., Mahgoub, A., & Perakis, R. (2010). A Quality of Development Assistance Index. Center for Global Development and the Wolfensohn Center for Development at the Brookings Institution.
Birdsall, Nancy, Homi Kharas, and Rita Perakis. 2017. "Measuring the Quality of Aid: QuODA Second Edition." In The Imperative of Development: The Wolfensohn Center at Brookings, edited by Kharas, Homi, Geoffrey Gertz, and Johannes F. Linn, 83–91. Washington, D.C.: Brookings Institution Press.
Boone, P. 1996. "Politics and the effectiveness of foreign aid." European Economic Review, 40: 289–329.
Bräutigam, D., and S. Knack. 2004. "Foreign Aid, Institutions and Governance in Sub- Saharan Africa." Economic Development and Cultural Change, 52: 255–86.
Bürcky, Urs. 2011. "Trends in In-Country Aid Fragmentation and Donor Proliferation: An Analysis of Changes in Aid Allocation Patterns between 2005 and 2009." OECD Publishing.
Burnside, Craig, and David Dollar. 2000. "Aid, Policies, and Growth." The American Economic Review, 90(4): 847–868.
Clist, Paul. 2014. "Do Performance Measures of Donors' Aid Allocation Underperform?" The World Economy, 38(5).
Djankov, S., J.G. Montalvo, and M. Reynal-Querol. 2008. "The curse of aid." Journal of Economic Growth, 13(3): 169–194.
Djankov, S., J.G. Montalvo, and M. Reynal-Querol. 2009. "Aid with multiple personalities." Journal of Comparative Economics, 37: 217–229.
Dollar, David, and Victoria Levin. 2006. "The Increasing Selectivity of Foreign Aid, 1984–2003." World Development, 34(12): 2034–2046.
Dreher, Axel, and Andreas Fuchs. 2012. "Rogue Aid? The Determinants of China's Aid Allocation." Courant Research Centre 'Poverty, Equity and Growth' Discussion Paper No. 93.
Dreher, Axel, Peter Nunnenkamp, and Rainer Thiele. 2011. "Are 'New' Donors Different? Comparing the Allocation of Bilateral Aid Between nonDAC and DAC Countries." World Development, 39(11): 1950–1968.
Dreher, Axel, Jan-Egbert Sturn, and James R. Vreeland. 2009. "Development Aid and International Politics: Does membership on the UN Security Council influence World Bank decisions?" Journal of Development Economics, 88(1): 1–18.

Droop, J., P. Isenman, and B. Mlalazi, 2008. "Paris declaration on aid effectiveness: Study of existing mechanisms to promote mutual accountability (MA) between donors and partner countries at the international level." Oxford Policy Management, Oxford, UK.

Easterly, W. 2001. "The elusive quest for growth: Economists' adventures and misadventures in the tropics." MIT Press, Cambridge, MA.

Easterly, W. 2006. "The white man's burden: Why the west's efforts to aid the rest have done so much ill and so little good." Penguin Press, New York, NY.

Easterly, W. 2007. "Inequality does cause underdevelopment: Insights from a new instrument." Journal of Development Economics, 84(2): 755–776.

Easterly, W., R. Levine, and D. Roodman. 2004. "New data, new Doubts: A comment on Burnside and Dollar's 'Aid, Policies, and Growth'." American Economic Review, 94: 774–780.

Easterly, William, and Tobias Pfutze. 2008. "Where Does the Money Go? Best and Worst Practices in Foreign Aid." Journal of Economic Perspectives, 22(2): 29–52.

Easterly, William, and Claudia R. Williamson. 2011. "Rhetoric vs. Reality: The Best and Worst of Aid Agencies Practices." World Development, 39(11): 1930–1949.

Fleck Robert K., and Christopher Kilby. 2010. "Changing aid regimes? U.S. foreign aid from the Cold War to the War on Terror." Journal of Development Economics, 91(2): 185–197.

Frot, Emmanuel, Anders Olofsgård, and Maria P. Berlin. 2014. "Aid Effectiveness in Times of Political Change: Lessons from Post-Communist Transition." World Development, 56: 127–138.

Frot, E., and J. Santiso. 2009. "Development aid and portfolio funds: Trends, volatility and fragmentation." OECD Development Centre, Working Paper No. 275.

Fuchs, A., P. Nunnenkamp, and H. Öhler. 2015. "Why donors of foreign aid do not coordinate: The role of competition for export markets and political support." The World Economy, 38: 255–285.

Ghosh, Anirban, and Homi Kharas. 2011. "The Money Trail: Ranking Donor Transparency in Foreign Aid." World Development, 39(11): 1918–1929.

Heckelman, J., and S. Knack. 2008. "Foreign aid and market-liberalizing reform." Economica, 75: 542–548.

Honig, Dan, and Catherine Weaver. 2018. "A Race to the Top?: The Aid Transparency Index and the Social Power of Global Performance Indicators." Conditional Acceptance, International Organization.

IMF & World Bank. 2005. "Global Monitoring Report 2005: Millennium Development Goals: From Consensus to Momentum." World Bank, Washington, DC.

IMF & World Bank. 2006. "Global Monitoring Report 2006: Strengthening Mutual Accountability—Aid, Trade, and Governance." World Bank, Washington, DC.

IMF & World Bank. 2010. "Global Monitoring Report 2010: The MDGs after the Crisis." World Bank, Washington, DC.
Kharas, H. 2009. "Development Assistance in the 21st Century." Contribution to the VIII Salamanca Forum, The Fight Against Hunger and Poverty.
Kilby, Christopher. 2011. "What Determines the Size of Aid Projects." World Development, 39(11): 1981–1994.
Kimura, H., Y. Mori, and Y. Sawada. 2012. "Aid proliferation and economic growth: A cross-country analysis." World Development, 40(1): 1–10.
Knack, S. 2001. "Aid Dependence and the Quality of Governance: Cross-Country Empirical Tests." Southern Economic Journal, 68(2): 310–329.
Knack, Stephen. 2013. "Aid and donor trust in recipient country systems." Journal of Development Economics, 101: 316–329.
Knack, Stephen, F. Halsey Rogers, and Nicholas Eubank. 2011. "Aid Quality and Donor Rankings." World Development, 39(11): 1907–1917.
Knack, Stephen, and Lodewijk Smets. 2013. "Aid Tying and Donor Fragmentation." World Development, 44: 63–76.
Kuziemko, Ilyana, and Eric Werker. 2006. "How Much is a Seat on the Security Council Worth? Foreign Aid and Bribery at the United Nations." Journal of Political Economy, 114(5): 905–930.
Maizels Alfred, and Machiko K. Nissanke. 1984. "Motivations for aid to developing countries." World Development, 12(9): 879–900.
Minasyan, Anna, et al. "Does Aid Effectiveness Depend on the Quality of Donors?" World Development, vol. 100, 01 Dec. 2017, pp. 16–30.
Moyo, D. 2009. "Dead Aid: Why Aid is Not Working and How There is a Better Way for Africa." Farrar, Straus and Giroux, New York, NY.
Nunnenkamp, Peter, Hannes Öhler, and Rainer Thiele. 2013. "Donor Coordination and Specialization: Did the Paris Declaration Make a Difference?" Review of World Economics, 149(3): 537–563.
OECD. 2008a. "The DAC at Work." Development Co-operation Report 2007, Vol 1(9).
OECD. 2008b. "The Paris Declaration on Aid Effectiveness and the Accra Agenda for Action."
OECD. 2011. "Busan Partnership for Effective Development Co-operation." OECD, Busan.
OECD/UNDP. 2016. "Making Development Co-operation More Effective: 2016 Progress Report." OECD Publishing, Paris.
Palagashvili, Liya, and Claudia R. Williamson. 2018: "Are Emerging Donors Engaging in Poor Foreign Aid Practices? A Comparison of Traditional versus Non-Traditional Aid Agencies." Working Paper.
Publish What You Fund (2018). Aid Transparency Index 2018. London, Publish What You Fund. Available here: http://www.publishwhatyoufund.org/reports/2018-Aid-Transparency-Index.pdf

Rahman, Aminur, and Yasuyuki Sawada. 2012. "Can donor coordination solve the aid proliferation problem?" Economic Letters, 116: 609–612.

Roodman, David. 2012. "An Index of Donor Performance." Center for Global Development, Working Paper Number 67, October 2012 Edition.

Shleifer, A. 2009. "Peter Bauer and the failure of foreign aid." Cato Journal, 29: 379–90.

Skarbek, D., and P.T. Leeson. 2009. "What can aid do?" Cato Journal, 29: 391–97.

Svensson, J. 1999. "Aid and growth: Does democracy matter?" Economics & Politics, 11: 275–297.

Svensson, J. 2000. "Foreign Aid and rent-seeking." Journal of International Economics, 51: 437–461.

Williamson, C.R. 2008. "Foreign aid and human development: The impact of foreign aid to the health sector." Southern Economic Journal, 75(1): 188–207.

Winters, M., and G. Martinez. 2015. "The role of governance in determining foreign aid flow composition." World Development, 66: 516–531.

World Bank. 1998. "Assessing Aid." World Bank, Washington, DC.

Young, A., and K. Sheehan. 2014. "Foreign Aid, Institutional Quality, and Growth." European Journal of Political Economy, 36: 195–208.

CHAPTER 6

What Influences World Bank Project Evaluations?

Christopher Kilby and Katharina Michaelowa

Introduction

In July of 2011, the World Bank's Independent Evaluation Group (IEG) made its evaluation ratings—the IEG World Bank Project Performance Ratings database—public as part of the World Bank's new "Access to Information" policy (World Bank 2012a).[1] The database includes information on more than 8500 completed projects and programs with funds administered by the World Bank. Although there has been some previous academic work using these data, difficulty obtaining official permission limited access by World Bank outsiders so that, until recently, the bulk of earlier research has been done by insiders.[2]

Evaluating project performance is to a degree subjective and there is evidence of systematic bias in some World Bank assessments at project appraisal (Pohl and Mihaljek 1992) as well as changes over time in the

C. Kilby (✉)
Villanova University, Villanova, PA, USA

K. Michaelowa
University of Zurich, Zurich, Switzerland
e-mail: katja.michaelowa@pw.uzh.ch

N. Dutta, C. R. Williamson (eds.), *Lessons on Foreign Aid and Economic Development*, https://doi.org/10.1007/978-3-030-22121-8_6

evaluation system (Grasso et al. 2003). In addition, there is a large empirical literature outlining the impact of geopolitics on World Bank lending. Hence it is natural to ask if there is a similar impact on ratings.[3]

Evaluation bias or process changes are of particular concern to researchers if these are correlated with key explanatory variables. A few researchers have devised clever ways to check for evaluation bias related to their particular question (Dreher et al. 2013) but it is an issue that anyone using these data must address to draw meaningful conclusions.

For many World Bank projects, the database contains more than one set of ratings. First, Implementation Completion Reports (ICRs) are written for virtually all projects under the responsibility of Team Task Leaders, that is, staff supervising project implementation in its final stages. Second, IEG selects about a quarter of these projects for additional review and prepares a Project Performance Assessment Report (PPAR). This chapter explores IEG's role in evaluation, examining both the PPAR selection process and how PPAR ratings differ from ICR ratings. In addition to considering the effect of project and country characteristics, we examine the role of internal institutional forces and external geopolitical factors. In doing so we have three objectives: (1) improving the understanding of the World Bank's evaluation procedures; (2) identifying evaluation biases; and (3) guiding future research.

The next section provides an overview of World Bank project evaluation. The third section analyses PPAR selection in a hazard model framework. The fourth section explores the determinants of PPAR ratings. The final section concludes.

World Bank Project Evaluation

Evaluation is the final step in the World Bank's project cycle and involves two branches of the World Bank, Operations and the Independent Evaluation Group. Figure 6.1 provides the World Bank organizational chart to illustrate where Operations and IEG fit into the overall structure. Evaluation at the World Bank serves two functions. First, it allows lessons learned to shape country assistance strategies and the identification, preparation, and implementation of new projects. Second, it promotes accountability, holding staff accountable to management and, especially, holding management accountable to stakeholders. World Bank President Robert McNamara formalized ex post project evaluation at the World Bank (initially referred to as an audit) with the creation of the Operations Evaluation

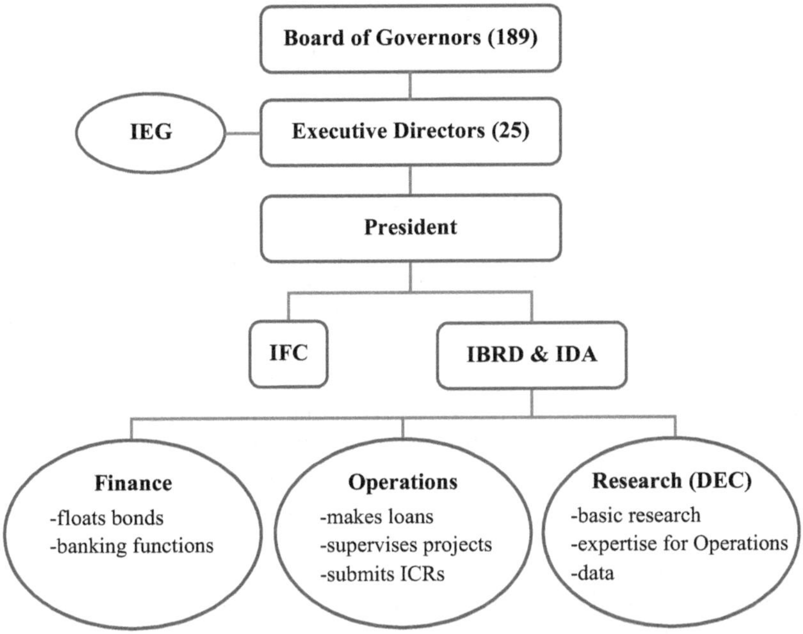

Fig. 6.1 World Bank organizational chart (IBRD, IDA, IFC). (Source: IEG database, World Bank)

Unit in 1970. This unit was elevated to a separate division in 1971 and then to a department—the Operations Evaluation Department (OED)—in 1973. To ensure the independence of the evaluation department, in 1975 OED top management was promoted to Director General, Operations Evaluation (DGO), appointed by and reporting directly to the World Bank Executive Directors (EDs) rather than the President. Operations staff and management, as well as borrowing governments, can comment on but not edit draft reports (IEG 2015a, vi). In November of 2005, OED merged with the much smaller evaluation units for World Bank's International Finance Corporation and Multilateral Investment Guarantee Association and was reincarnated as IEG (IEG 2015b).[4]

As part of this move toward systematic evaluation, starting in 1973 the World Bank has required a Project Completion Report (PCR)—since 1995 more accurately called an ICR—for all World Bank-funded projects; this report now includes project ratings.

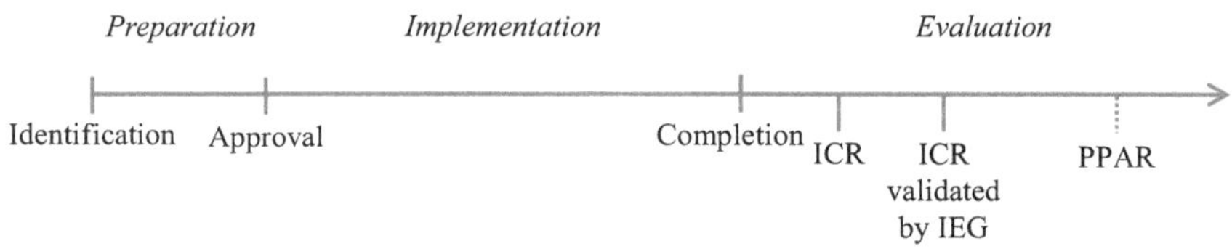

Fig. 6.2 Project timeline. (Adapted from Geli et al. (2014) (not to Scale)

One key function of IEG is to prepare additional ex post evaluations (PPARs). PPARs start with a desk review of the ICR and project files and typically include field research in the borrowing country. Figure 6.2 illustrates this evaluation process within the overall project timeline. IEG initially attempted to reassess all ICRs (essentially achieved by 1981 (IEG 2015b, 2)) but selective ex post evaluation was introduced in 1983 and the percent of projects with PPARs was gradually reduced over time to 25% in 1997 (Grasso et al. 2003, 178).[5] PPAR performance ratings can differ from ICR ratings and do 16% of the time in our data.[6]

The availability of ratings in the IEG database merits some discussion. Up through the end of 1996, ICR ratings appear in the database as PCRs. Phased in starting in early 1995, IEG policy shifted to include a "validation" step—termed Evaluation Memorandum (EVM) and later Evaluation Summary (ES)—before these ratings enter the database (Denizer et al. 2013). If IEG conducts a PPAR, it includes the associated rating in the database. For simplicity, we refer to this as a PPAR rating though the IEG database uses the code PAR based on an older name for these reports (Project Assessment Report).[7] In early years, the database reports only PPARs, systematically replacing previous PCR ratings. Starting in FY 1983, some projects report an initial PCR rating as well as a PPAR and from 1995 onward virtually all projects report an initial PCR/EVM/ES rating.[8] Figure 6.3 shows the type of the first ratings reported in the database (in % of total first ratings).

IEG acknowledges that selection of projects for PPARs is nonrandom (Grasso et al. 2003). PPAR selection reportedly depends on several factors, including particularly good or bad outcomes, sectors subject to an IEG sector-wide review, and geography (discussed in detail below).[9] IEG staff typically complete PPARs one to five years after the project closes (i.e., the close of disbursement of the IBRD loan or IDA credit).

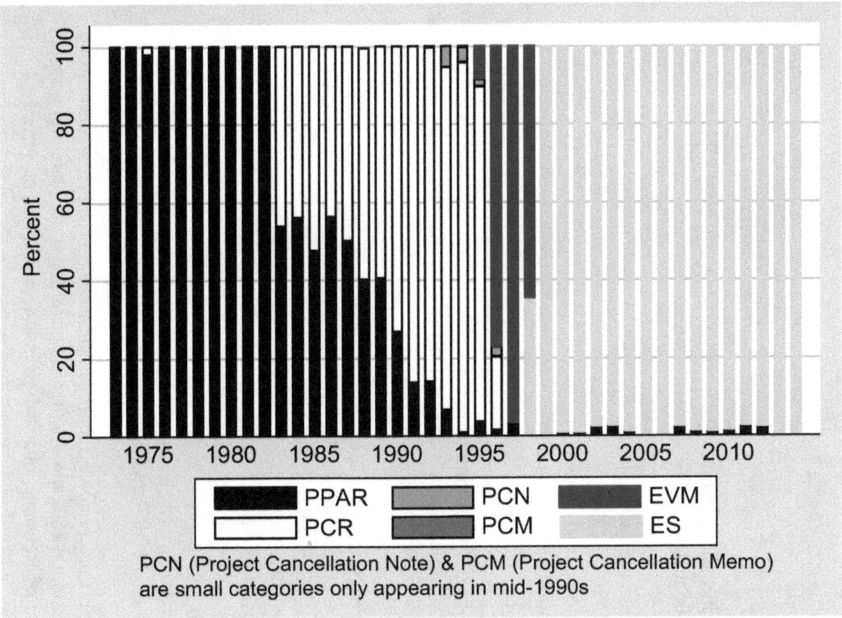

Fig. 6.3 First evaluation type by evaluation fiscal year. (Source: IEG database, World Bank)

Ratings have expanded over time from a single 0/1 outcome rating into numerous multi-category ratings. Most research and policy discussion continues to focus on the original outcome rating reduced to a binary variable. Studies examining ratings in both raw and binary forms (Denizer et al. 2013; Dreher et al. 2013) generally do not find compelling reasons to use the more fine-grained version except Sud and Olmstead-Rumsey (2012), who argue that rating system changes facilitated illusory improvements in performance. The outcome rating ostensibly measures project outcomes relative to objectives stated in the project appraisal and loan documents though there is evidence that an economic rate of return cut-off of 10% (i.e., an absolute standard) is used to distinguish between "Satisfactory" and "Not Satisfactory" where such figures are available (Kilby 2000; Grasso et al. 2003, 11).[10]

IEG ratings cover a number of topics in addition to the overall project performance ("outcome") rating. Table 6.1 provides details on these ratings.

Table 6.1 IEG evaluation ratings

Rating	*Coverage*[a]	*Scale*[b]	*Description*
Overall performance			
Outcome	1972–1992 1993 1994–	Binary 4 point 6 point[c]	"extent to which the operation's major relevant objectives were achieved, or are expected to be achieved, efficiently" (IEG 2015b, 14)
Sustainability	1989–2000 2000.5–2008	3 point 5 point	"At the time of the evaluation, the resilience to risk of future net benefits flows." (IEG 2015b, 29)
Risk to development outcome (gradually replaced Sustainability)	2006.5–	4 point	"risk, at the time of evaluation, that development outcomes (or expected outcomes) will not be maintained (or realized)" (IEG 2015b, 16)
Institutional development impact	1989–1999 1999.5–2007	3 point 4 point	"extent to which a project improves the ability of a country or region to make more efficient, equitable and sustainable use of its human, financial, and natural resources" (IEG 2015b, 27)
World Bank performance			
Quality at entry	1994–2006 2006.5–	4 point 6 point	"extent to which the Bank identified, facilitated preparation of, and appraised the operation such that it was most likely to achieve planned development outcomes and was consistent with the Bank's fiduciary role" (IEG 2015b, 17)
Quality of supervision	1991–1992 1993–2006 2006.5–	Binary 4 point 6 point	"extent to which the Bank proactively identified and resolved threats to the achievement of relevant development outcomes and the Bank's fiduciary role" (IEG 2015b, 18)
Overall bank performance	1997–2006 2006.5–	4 point 6 point	"The quality at entry and quality of supervision ratings should be combined into a rating of overall Bank Performance." (IEG 2015b, 19)
Borrower performance			
Borrower preparation	1993–2003	4 point	"government/implementing agency performance on the preparation of this project. Consider specifically whether the government/implementing agency took account of economic, financial, technical, policy, and resource considerations, and ensured participation of major stakeholders in preparing the project" (IEG 2015b, 30)

Government compliance	1993–2006	4 point	Renamed Government Performance
Government performance	2006.5–	6 point	"extent to which the borrower … government … ensured quality of preparation and implementation, and complied with covenants and agreements, towards the achievement of development outcomes" (IEG 2015b, 21)
Implementing agency performance	1993–2006 2006.5–	4 point 6 point	"extent to which the borrower…implementing agency or agencies…ensured quality of preparation and implementation, and complied with covenants and agreements, towards the achievement of development outcomes" (IEG 2015b, 21)
Overall borrower performance	1997–2006 2006.5–	4 point 6 point	"The ratings for government performance and implementing agency or agencies' performance should be combined into a rating of Borrower Performance, per guidance below." (IEG 2015b, 22)
Evaluation process			
Quality of ICR	1983–1989 1990–1996 1997–	Binary 4 point 3 point	IEG evaluator assessment of PCR/ICR quality. Prior to 1997, very few projects have ratings (2% prior to 1990, 14% 1990–1996). After 1996, 80% of projects rated. See IEG (2015b, 24).
Quality of M&E	2006.5–	4 point	"based on an assessment of three main elements: (i) M&E design; (ii) M&E implementation; and (iii) use of M&E data…The evaluator is asked to discuss separately each of the three elements of M&E quality and to arrive at an overall quality of M&E rating on a 4-point scale." (IEG 2015b, 25)

[a]Reflects effective dates in rating data rather than official dates of policy changes. See IEG (2015b) for official dates. A suffix of 0.5 indicates change on or after July 1 (start of fiscal year); otherwise, calendar years

[b]Ratings also include "NOT AVAILABLE," "NOT APPLICABLE," "NOT RATED," and "NON-EVALUABLE" as well as missing values

[c]Database includes two "MARGINALLY SATISFACTORY" and three "MARGINALLY UNSATISFACTORY" ratings. These are not officially recognized designations (IEG 2015b). See Sud and Olmstead-Rumsey (2012) and IEG (2015b) for detailed discussions on the evolution of ratings and its implications for aggregate reporting

Source: IEG, World Bank

PPAR Selection

As noted above, selection for performance review depends on a number of factors and is not simply random. Since IEG periodically reviews a long sequence of projects, a project might be selected for a PPAR years after completion; the longest interval in the database between ICR and PPAR is 18 years.[11] Of the 158 countries and territories with projects included in the database, 14 have not yet had a project with a completed PPAR.[12] In principle, a project always has some positive PPAR selection probability, no matter when it was completed. For this reason, a hazard model that treats unselected projects as not-yet-selected is appropriate.[13] We start with a baseline model that includes the variables suggested by IEG (such as ICR rating), IEG's assessment of the quality of the ICR, and some basic project characteristics such as project size, geographical region, project type and so on. We include additional variables reflecting institutional peculiarities and bureaucratic preferences that may be relevant. The latter includes the attractiveness of the borrowing country (proxied by tourist arrivals) and a dummy for the ICR being completed in the month of June to capture the spike in the number of ICRs at the end of the financial year. We expect that given the high number of ICRs completed simultaneously in June IEG would select a smaller share for reevaluation. We also include recipient-country characteristics to account for the general economic and political context. The data section below provides more detail.

The baseline model excludes all variables reflecting geopolitical importance and the interests of powerful shareholder countries. We consider these variables separately thereafter, as they are of special interest given the strong evidence of the role these factors play in other areas of World Bank activity.

We start with cumulative hazard rate function graphs presenting simple bivariate relationships. Figure 6.4, Panel A plots separate cumulative probabilities of a PPAR for projects with IDA funding (including "blend projects" with both IDA and IBRD funding) and projects with IBRD funding only. There is very little difference. Panel B presents the graph for investment projects and program loans, illustrating the much higher frequency of PPARs for the latter group. Panel C confirms that PPARs are more likely for projects initially rated "Satisfactory" ("Moderately Satisfactory" or better in detailed ratings) than for those initially rated as "Unsatisfactory" ("Moderately Unsatisfactory" or worse in detailed ratings). Panel D reveals that projects where the ICR was rated as low quality by IEG in its

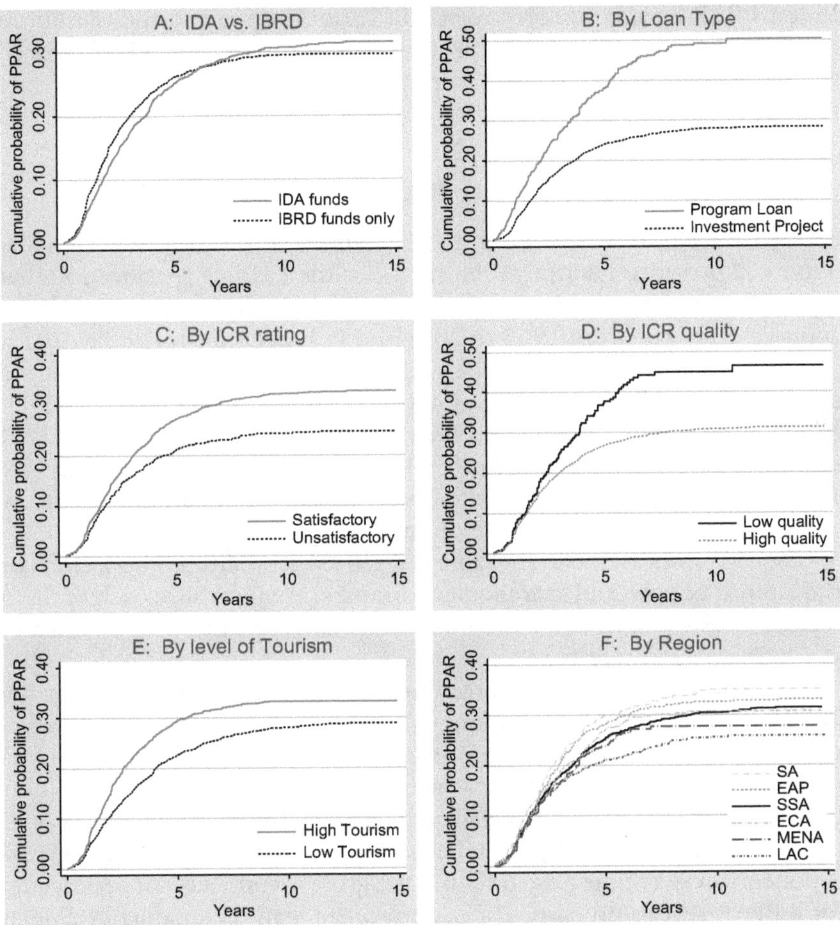

Fig. 6.4 Cumulative hazard rate functions for selected variables. Notes: Nelson-Aalen estimates. (Source: IEG database, World Bank)

initial validation step (6% of the sample) are much more likely to be subject to additional review. Panel E highlights variation in PPAR hazard rates by the number of tourist arrivals per year in the project country. The odds that IEG staff will complete a PPAR—typically including travel to the country—rise faster for projects in countries that are popular with tourists (which may, of course, proxy a variety of things such as better connectivity or safety). Finally, Panel F illustrates differences between regions, with the lowest PPAR hazard rate for projects in Latin America and the Caribbean (LAC) and the highest rate for projects in South Asia (SA). Of course, all the above patterns could reflect compositional differences or confounding factors so we now turn to estimation results.

Data Description

Along with Fig. 6.4, Table 6.2 and Figs. 6.5 and 6.6 describe the data. Table 6.2 presents descriptive statistics. For the baseline specification that excludes geopolitical variables, the sample includes 5155 projects. Project approval dates run from 1963 to 2011 and ICR dates from 1983 to 2012.

To allow for the possibility of an ICR followed by a PPAR, we limit the sample to cases where the PPAR is not the first recorded evaluation rating. As mentioned above, before FY1983 the IEG database only reports PPAR ratings. Only by FY1994, virtually all projects report an ICR rating. We further limit the baseline sample to observations with inflation rates below 1000% to avoid undue influence of outliers on our results.

The last seven variables in Table 6.2 reflect geopolitical importance or the interest of powerful shareholder countries. We introduce each of them separately as candidates for the potential political and institutional biases in which we are interested.

Figure 6.5 shows the (censored) time between ICR and PPAR for the 1590 projects for which both ratings are available.[14] This ranges from a few days to almost 13 years (median 2 years). Figure 6.6 provides similar information for the 3784 projects for which IEG has yet to conduct a PPAR (as of September 30, 2013). Time since ICR ranges from less than 1 year to over 30 years (median 12 years). The risk of a PPAR rises and then tails off exponentially over time (Fig. 6.5), but the group of projects not yet selected for a PPAR reveals no particular pattern other than the gradual decline in the PPAR selection rate between 1983 and 1997 (Fig. 6.6).

The previous section suggests the initial ICR rating is an important factor. In this context, we focus primarily on a dichotomous version of the overall ICR rating of project performance, *Outcome* (*ICR*), which indicates a 73% satisfactory rate in this sample. However, we also consider a 6-point scale introduced in 1995 (Table 6.3, Column 4).

In addition to the ICR rating, a number of other institutional/bureaucratic variables may play a role in PPAR selection. We include the *IDA* dummy even though Fig. 6.4 shows only small differences between IDA- and IBRD-funded projects as well as *ICR quality*, which Fig. 6.4 suggests impacts PPAR selection. We also include the amount the borrower owes

Table 6.2 Descriptive statistics for hazard rate estimation

Variable	*N*	*Mean*	*SD*	*Min*	*Max*	*Description*
Outcome (ICR)	5155	0.73	0.44	0	1	=1 if project rated "Satisfactory"
IDA	5155	0.54	0.50	0	1	=1 if project included IDA funding
ICR quality	5155	0.94	0.24	0	1	=1 if ICR quality rated "Satisfactory"[a]
log World Bank debt	5155	0.68	1.51	−4.75	3.53	log of debt to IBRD/IDA in billions of 2005 USD[b,c]
log Project size	5155	4.00	1.21	−0.63	8.00	log of loan amount in 2005 USD (millions)
log # WB projects	5155	1.40	0.77	0	3.04	log of # ICRs completed same fiscal year (by country)
June ICR	5155	0.18	0.38	0	1	=1 if ICR published in June (end of FY)
Tourism	5155	13.98	1.81	9.53	17.51	log of Tourist Arrivals (country average)
Years in office	5155	7.30	7.67	1	45	Executive years in office[b]
Freedom House	5155	3.93	1.50	1	7	Average of political rights and civil liberties (7 is best)[b,c]
log Population	5155	17.10	1.87	11.48	21.02	log of population
log GDP PC	5155	7.00	1.04	4.78	9.31	log of GDP per capita in 2000 USD[b,c]
GDP growth	5155	4.61	3.43	−17.49	28.65	GDP growth rate[b,c]
Inflation	5155	0.16	0.44	−0.13	8.07	Inflation rate[b,c]
Program Loan	5155	0.14	0.35	0	1	=1 if Program Loan
SIL	5155	0.54	0.50	0	1	=1 if Specific Investment Loan
East Asia-Pacific	5155	0.16	0.36	0	1	=1 if East Asia-Pacific region

(*continued*)

Table 6.2 (continued)

Variable	*N*	*Mean*	*SD*	*Min*	*Max*	*Description*
Europe and Central Asia	5155	0.13	0.33	0	1	=1 if Europe and Central Asia region
Latin America and Caribbean	5155	0.20	0.40	0	1	=1 if Latin America and Caribbean region
Middle East and North Africa	5155	0.09	0.28	0	1	=1 if Middle East and North Africa region
South Asia	5155	0.13	0.33	0	1	=1 if South Asia region
Sub-Saharan Africa	5155	0.31	0.46	0	1	=1 if Sub-Saharan Africa region
log US Aid	4845	4.07	1.50	0	8.58	log of (US bilateral aid + 1) in 2005 USD (millions)[b,c]
log G7 Aid	4845	6.17	1.32	0.98	8.93	log of (G7 bilateral aid + 1) in 2005 USD (millions)[b,c]
US military aid	5140	0.41	0.49	0	1	=1 if US military aid>2 million (2012 USD)[b]
US UN voting	5154	0.42	0.17	0.00	0.85	UN voting alignment with US on important votes[b]
G7 UN voting	5154	0.63	0.15	0.26	0.95	UN voting alignment with G7 on important votes[b]
UNSC@ICR	5155	0.09	0.28	0	1	=1 if nonpermanent UNSC member[b]
WBEB@ICR	5155	0.33	0.47	0	1	=1 if Executive Board member in last 3 years[b]

[a]Missing values imputed using Sustainability, Supervision, Institutional Development Impact, and Risk to Development Outcome ratings
[b]At time of most recent ICR
[c]Three-year moving average (*t*-2 to *t*)

Source: See Table 6.8

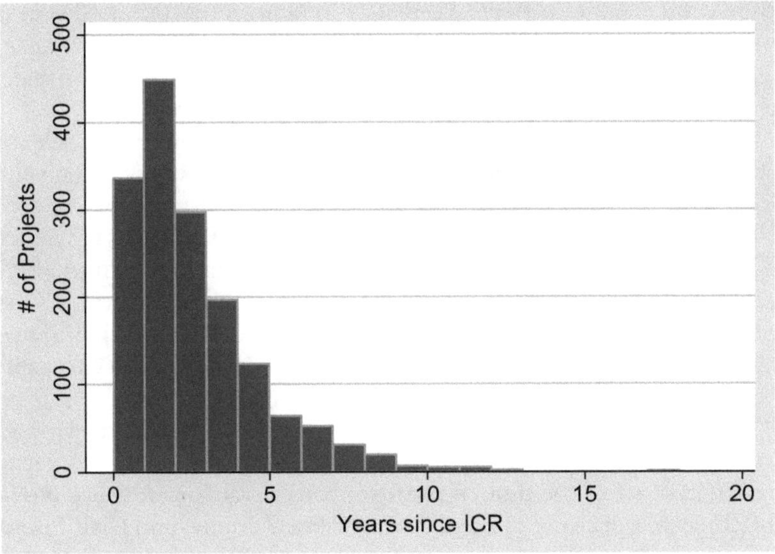

Fig. 6.5 Time between ICR and PPAR. (Source: IEG database, World Bank)

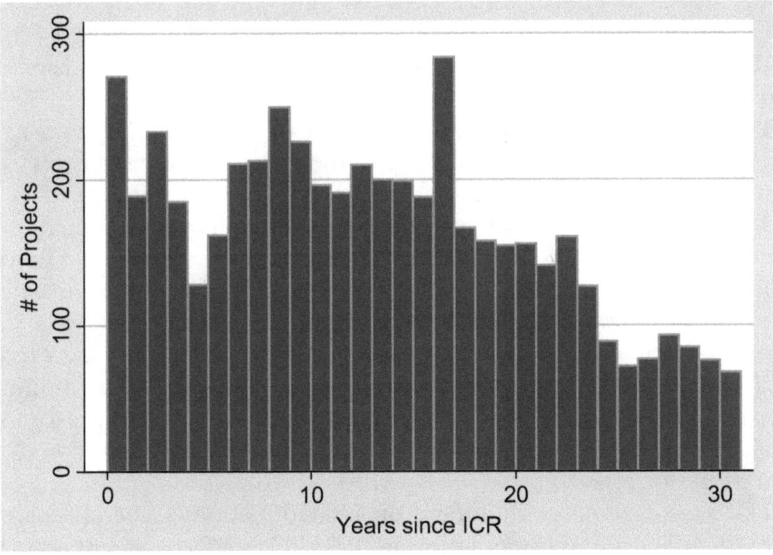

Fig. 6.6 Time since ICR for projects without a PPAR (as of September 30, 2013). (Source: IEG database, World Bank)

to the World Bank (*log World Bank debt* in billions of 2005 USD) in case the World Bank treats major borrowers differently and *log Project size* (in millions of 2005 USD) in case larger projects are more likely to be selected due to their greater relevance for both bank and borrower.

Three other bureaucratic factors may play a role in PPAR selection. First, we include (log) number of ICRs in the same country in a given fiscal year to allow for IEG's cost-saving practice of "cluster audits." Second, we include a June ICR dummy to account for end of fiscal year effects; 18% of ICR ratings appear in the IEG database in June. Third, PPARs typically include a trip ("mission") to the borrowing country. IEG staff have input into PPAR selection so we also include the variable *Tourism*, the log of the annual number of tourist arrivals in the country to capture the desirability of the country as a travel destination.[15]

The next set of variables captures characteristics of the borrowing government and country. *Years in office* is the number of years the executive has been in office at the time of the first project evaluation. *Freedom House* is the three-year moving average of the Political Rights and Civil Liberties indicators; higher values indicate more democratic.

We measure country size with *log Population* and level of development with *log GDP PC*, the log of a three-year moving average of GDP per capita measured in year 2000 USD. We also include *GDP growth*, the three-year moving average of GDP growth and *Inflation* based on the GDP deflator (again, three-year moving average), excluding hyperinflation cases (*Inflation* > 1000%) as mentioned above.

The baseline variables include a final set of dummies: *Program Loan*, *SIL* (Specific Investment Loans—one of the major project loan types), and regional dummies (Sub-Saharan Africa as the omitted category).

The geopolitical variables in Table 6.2 cover aid flows, alignment measures, and membership on powerful committees. We measure aid flows as either *log US Aid* or *log G7 Aid* (bilateral total official gross disbursements in millions of 2005 USD) to capture US and broader G7 interests.[16] *US Military Aid* is a dummy variable, equal to one if US military aid exceeds 2 million 2005 USD, the case in 40% of observations. We use a dummy because military aid has both a skewed distribution (which argues for logs) and many zeros (which argues against logs). Results are insensitive to the military aid threshold.

UN voting measures alignment on United Nations General Assembly votes identified as important in the annual US State Department report to Congress. For any two countries, we code matching votes as 1, opposite votes as 0, and cases where one party abstained/was absent but the other party voted as 0.5. We average these values across all relevant votes in a given year, then include the resulting alignment variable in our specifications with a one-year lag since UN votes fall late in the calendar year. For the G7, the alignment measure is an average of the alignments with each of the seven countries.

The final two variables reflect membership in important committees. *UNSC@ICR*=1 if the country holds a nonpermanent United Nations Security Council (UNSC) seat in the year of the ICR evaluation. *WBEB@ICR = 1* if the country held a seat on the World Bank's Executive Board in the ICR year or either of the two previous years.[17] With a 25-member board, many countries belong to groups that share an ED seat; their representative comes from one of the countries in the group. As Kaja and Werker (2010), Morrison (2013), and Kilby (2013b) demonstrate, this can be a powerful position that improves access to World Bank resources for the ED's home country. Any of these characteristics might play a role in the selection of projects for performance assessment by IEG.

Hazard Model Estimation

Table 6.3 reports hazard ratios from a parametric survival time model using a proportional hazard specification and the Weibull distribution (Columns 1 and 3–5) as well as odds ratios from a logit selection model for comparison (Column 2).[18] Reported z-statistics reflect country-clustered standard errors. Results are similar using an accelerated failure-time model, alternative distributions, or a Cox proportional hazard model.[19] All specifications include unreported ICR fiscal year dummies.

Column 1 is the baseline model using the full sample. Mirroring Fig. 6.4, the risk of a PPAR is significantly higher for projects with a positive ICR outcome rating (hazard ratio greater than one). More specifically, the increase is 48% for projects with satisfactory ICR ratings, ceteris paribus. This could reflect a desire to learn lessons from successful projects, to correct overly optimistic ICR ratings, or to incentivize staff to report accurate ICR ratings. Further in-line with Fig. 6.4, the source of funds (IBRD versus IDA) does not influence IEG's decision to conduct a performance assessment.[20] Conversely, *ICR quality* is a strong predictor—ceteris paribus, the risk of a PPAR decreases by 50% for projects with high-quality ICRs, presumably because IEG feels the learning phase of the project cycle is short-circuited by a low-quality ICR.

The hazard ratio for *log World Bank debt* is marginally greater than one, becoming insignificant in the slightly smaller samples of Columns (4) and

Table 6.3 Baseline hazard rate for PPAR

	(1)	*(2)*	*(3)*	*(4)*	*(5)*
Outcome (ICR)	1.476***	1.609***	0.933		1.592***
	(4.33)	(4.62)	(−0.89)		(4.42)
Unsatisfactory				2.405**	
				(2.35)	
Moderately Unsatisfactory				2.955***	
				(2.85)	
Moderately Satisfactory				3.659***	
				(3.40)	
Satisfactory				3.936***	
				(3.77)	
Highly Satisfactory				4.638***	
				(4.13)	
IDA	1.080	1.132	0.788**	1.193	1.197
	(0.76)	(1.02)	(−2.30)	(1.52)	(1.54)
ICR quality	0.497***	0.464***	1.070	0.551***	0.559***
	(−7.82)	(−6.42)	(0.62)	(−5.76)	(−5.64)
log World Bank debt	1.134*	1.157*	1.038	1.111	1.107
	(1.72)	(1.77)	(0.56)	(1.33)	(1.29)
log Project size	1.140***	1.178***	1.029	1.156***	1.149***
	(3.03)	(3.28)	(0.81)	(3.00)	(2.89)
log of # WB projects	1.137**	1.157*	1.051	1.141*	1.148*
	(2.01)	(1.81)	(0.88)	(1.78)	(1.84)
June ICR	0.854**	0.822**	0.929	0.828**	0.828**
	(−2.07)	(−2.05)	(−0.83)	(−2.03)	(−2.04)
Tourism	1.161***	1.176**	1.124**	1.171***	1.171***
	(2.77)	(2.55)	(2.05)	(2.70)	(2.67)
Years in office	1.011**	1.014**	0.998	1.011*	1.011*
	(2.01)	(1.99)	(−0.53)	(1.82)	(1.85)
Freedom House	1.137***	1.161***	0.988	1.119***	1.125***
	(3.81)	(3.66)	(−0.35)	(2.72)	(2.84)
log Population	0.874*	0.859*	0.899	0.851**	0.855*
	(−1.84)	(−1.82)	(−1.44)	(−2.00)	(−1.93)
log GDP PC	0.709***	0.660***	1.025	0.698***	0.699***
	(−3.71)	(−3.58)	(0.28)	(−3.52)	(−3.48)
GDP growth	1.017	1.019	1.021*	1.009	1.011
	(1.36)	(1.34)	(1.91)	(0.64)	(0.84)
Inflation	0.997	0.989	1.024	1.168	1.127
	(−0.04)	(−0.12)	(0.69)	(0.93)	(0.63)
Program Loan	2.035***	2.006***	0.987	1.686***	1.710***
	(6.14)	(4.68)	(−0.12)	(4.20)	(4.33)
× *Inflation*	1.464***	2.364**	1.214**	1.299	1.358

(*continued*)

Table 6.3 (continued)

	(1)	*(2)*	*(3)*	*(4)*	*(5)*
	(3.19)	(2.11)	(2.08)	(1.45)	(1.54)
SIL	1.171**	1.177*	1.094	1.053	1.053
	(2.18)	(1.90)	(1.47)	(0.57)	(0.57)
East Asia-Pacific	0.888	0.909	0.716**	0.892	0.899
	(−0.97)	(−0.66)	(−2.47)	(−0.83)	(−0.77)
Europe and Central Asia	1.747***	1.950***	0.877	1.601**	1.609**
	(3.13)	(3.09)	(−0.95)	(2.43)	(2.47)
Latin America and Caribbean	1.019	1.088	0.864	1.136	1.142
	(0.12)	(0.43)	(−1.00)	(0.71)	(0.74)
Middle East and North Africa	1.097	1.216	0.761**	1.043	1.039
	(0.50)	(0.92)	(−2.03)	(0.22)	(0.20)
South Asia	0.731	0.729	1.156	0.895	0.880
	(−1.46)	(−1.34)	(0.95)	(−0.47)	(−0.52)
Observations	5155	5047	1371	4282	4282

z-statistics in parentheses based on country-clustered standard errors. All specifications include unreported evaluation year dummies. Hazard models use a Weibull regression; all coefficients reported as hazard or odds ratios. *p < 0.1, **p < 0.05, ***p < 0.01

(1) Hazard model with dichotomous ICR Outcome rating, full sample

(2) Logit PAR selection model (probability of being selected for PPAR by September 30, 2013); some observations drop due to lack of variation by year

(3) Hazard model with dichotomous ICR Outcome rating, uncensored sample

(4) Hazard model with dummy variables reflecting 6-point ICR Outcome rating; omitted category is "Unsatisfactory." Sample starts in 1995 with the introduction of 6-point scale

(5) Hazard model with dichotomous ICR Outcome rating, =1 if rating is "Moderately Satisfactory" or above. Sample constrained to match (4)

Source: See Table 6.8

(5). Thus, there is only weak evidence that World Bank exposure in a country influences the decision to conduct a PPAR. As anticipated, larger projects have a significantly higher PPAR risk. Consistent with IEG's practice of clustering PPARs by country to control costs, the hazard ratio for *log # WB projects* is significantly greater than one.

The end-of-fiscal-year ICR spike does reduce PPAR selection risk ("safety in numbers"). The hazard ratio for *June ICR* is significantly below one. The estimated hazard ratio for *June ICR* indicates a 15% decrease in the PPAR hazard rate for projects with June ICRs relative to ICRs completed in other months, ceteris paribus. Thus, the June ICR effect is about one-third that of a satisfactory *Outcome* (*ICR*) rating or low-quality ICR, but still substantial. One explanation is that IEG flags projects for PPARs when it receives the ICRs from Operations but is reluctant to commit to too many PPARs in a given month. Alternatively, projects with June ICRs might be different in some dimension not captured by our covariates.

Our last institutional variable, *Tourism*, is also significant at the 1% level with a hazard ratio greater than one. Ceteris paribus, countries that attract tourists also attract PPARs—and the IEG staff and consultants who travel on mission to conduct these PPARs.

We turn now to borrower variables. The hazard ratios for *Years in office* and for *Freedom House* are significantly greater than one, indicating a higher PPAR selection risk for more established and more democratic governments.[21] Why do we see this? This is not simply an effect driven by China with its large number of projects. One interpretation is that more experienced, more democratic governments complete their part in PPARs faster. These characteristics might impact how quickly PPARs are released, not whether a PPAR is undertaken. If so, the delay between ICR and PPAR—when a PPAR is observed—should depend on these characteristics but the odds of a PPAR being undertaken should not. Because of the censoring issue that motives the hazard model, only a rough test of this conjecture is possible. We return to this when discussing Columns 2 and 3.

Projects in more populous countries have a lower PPAR hazard rate, ceteris paribus. Level of development (measured by *log GDP PC*) is a significant factor, with a lower PPAR risk in more advanced countries. *GDP growth* is not a significant factor. For inflation, we differentiate between investment projects and program loans (where macroeconomic performance is a core focus). The estimated equation includes *Inflation*, *Program Loan*, and their interaction. Table 6.3 shows inflation is significant only in for program loans; high inflation is associated with higher PPAR selection risk in the full sample (Columns 1–3). As expected, PPAR risk is higher for program loans.

Finally, the hazard ratio is significantly higher for SILs compared to other types of investment loans in the full sample. A SIL increases the risk of a PPAR by 17%, an effect similar in size as the June ICR. We considered other categorical project characteristics (financial instrument type, sector) but only one proved relevant. To streamline presentation, we omit all these factors other than *SIL*.

Considering regional differences, we find that PPAR selection risk is higher for projects in *Europe and Central Asia* relative to Sub-Saharan Africa, ceteris paribus. This underscores the importance of controlling for compositional effects since the unconditional hazard rate for *South Asia* (Fig. 6.4) was highest.

As discussed above, it is possible to roughly test of what drives hazard rate results—which projects are (eventually) selected or the length of the delay between ICR and PPAR for selected projects. The first step—selection estimation—suffers from right censoring and must be interpreted in this context (as the probability of being selected for a PPAR by September 30, 2013) but may still be informative. To this end, Column 2 presents odds ratios from a logit model of whether or not there is a PPAR by September 30, 2013, while Column 3 presents results from a hazard model estimated with only uncensored data (cases with a PPAR—see also Table 6.5 below). Column 2 should mirror effects in Column 1 that operate through selection while Column 3 should mirror those due to delayed (or accelerated) release of a PPAR. Comparing the three columns, the high odds ratio for *Outcome* (*ICR*) in Column 2 coupled with the low (though insignificant) hazard ratio in Column 3 suggests ICR ratings influence PPAR selection—making PPARs more likely—but not the length of time to complete a PPAR for selected projects. The low hazard ratio on the *IDA* dummy in Column 3 suggests IDA project PPARs take longer. *ICR quality* is significant only for the first two columns, suggesting it matters for selection only. The marginally significant effect of World Bank debt also appears driven by selection, a pattern seen again for project size, number of World Bank projects, and June ICRs. *Tourism*, however, enters with odds/hazard ratios significantly greater than one in all three columns; projects in tourist locations are both more likely to be selected and, if selected, more likely to have their PPAR completed quickly.

With respect to higher PPAR risk for projects under more experienced, more democratic governments, the estimates do not support the "delay" story suggested above. If effects were due to recipient government delays, the uncensored hazard model (Column 3) should drive *Years in office* and *Freedom House* results while these variables should be insignificant in the selection logit (Column 2). However, we find the opposite: neither is statistically significant in the uncensored hazard model; both are strongly statistically significant in the logit model. Apparently, the World Bank prefers to conduct PPARs with more democratic, more established governments. Such PPARs might be more agreeable to all partners because they expect better results. Alternatively, IEG might expect a smoother process and increased learning for both the World Bank and the recipient-country government in stable, democratic environments.[22]

The last two columns examine the role of detailed ICR outcome ratings. Does the ICR outcome rating enter PPAR selection in monotonically (with the hazard rate declining consistently as ratings decline)? Alternatively, one might imagine that IEG specifically targets projects: (1) with the most inflated ICR ratings ("Highly Satisfactory"); (2) that were exceptionally effective to learn from success ("Highly Satisfactory"); and (3) that were exceptionally awful to learn from failure ("Highly

Unsatisfactory"). Column 4 reports results for projects with post-1994 ICRs that include a 6-point rating. Each rating category is a separate dummy (omitted category: "Highly Unsatisfactory").

Results support the first two conjectures: ICR outcome ratings enter PPAR selection monotonically. The remaining column demonstrates that changes in other coefficient estimates are due to the reduced sample.

Thus far we examine only two of ten project ratings. Controlling for ICR outcome and ICR quality, other ratings do not have a significant impact. One exception is Borrower Compliance; middling ratings enter with positive and significance coefficient estimates as compared to the lowest category. Perhaps IEG expects the difficulty of the cooperation to extend to evaluation, so that PPARs are less fruitful. Estimated coefficients are not significantly different for program loans compared to investment projects. Other results remain substantially unchanged.

Table 6.4 explores whether the interests of powerful World Bank shareholders play a role in PPAR selection. The table summarizes results from hazard ratio estimations that add individual political economy variables to Column 1 of Table 6.3. Sample sizes differ due to data availability.

Table 6.4 Hazard ratios for PPAR: political economy variables

	(1)	*(2)*	*(3)*	*(4)*	*(5)*	*(6)*	*(7)*
log US Aid	1.075**						
	(2.13)						
log G7 Aid		1.181**					
		(2.31)					
US military aid			0.998				
			(−0.02)				
US UN voting				1.139			
				(0.36)			
G7 UN voting					0.927		
					(−0.19)		
UNSC@ICR						0.999	
						(−0.01)	
WBEB@ICR							0.976
							(−0.21)
Observations	4845	4845	5140	5154	5154	5155	5155

z-statistics in parentheses based on country-clustered standard errors. All specifications include baseline variables from Table 6.3, Column 1. Number of observations vary due to data availability. Estimates from hazard function with Weibull distribution reported as hazard ratios. *p < 0.1, **p < 0.05, ***p < 0.01

Source: See Table 6.8

For *log US Aid*, the estimated hazard ratio is statistically significant but greater than one. The hazard ratio for the G7 is also greater than one. These results indicate a higher—not lower—PPAR risk for countries that receive more US/G7 aid, that is, if there is specific interest of major World Bank shareholders in these countries, this does not imply that their governments are protected from further evaluations. Rather G7 donors may desire PPARs to learn more for their own aid programs. Alternatively, more bilateral aid may signal greater need or more collaborative recipient governments—with results matching those regarding Borrower Compliance, rather than pressure by powerful World Bank members. We explore this result further by including instead bilateral aid from the so-called like-minded donors (Denmark, the Netherlands, Norway, Sweden). Model donors whose aid allocations more closely mirror need and effectiveness, these small countries have very limited ability to pressure the World Bank to serve narrow geopolitical objectives (though they may influence best practices). Thus, like-minded donor aid should proxy for elements of need and effectiveness not captured by variables already included. The hazard ratio for like-minded donor aid is again greater than one with similar size and significance. If we also include US aid, we cannot reject that the effects are the same (though neither is estimated precisely). It appears our other controls do not sufficiently capture need/effectiveness so that bilateral aid (whether like-minded, US, or G7) proxies for need/effectiveness rather than measuring geopolitical influence in a meaningful fashion. Alternatively, IEG's PPARs might be more useful in countries that also receive aid from many bilateral donors due to learning synergies or due to generally more successful cooperation.

The other geopolitical variables—US military aid, UN voting, UNSC nonpermanent membership, and World Bank Executive Board membership—have no impact on the PPAR hazard rate; all the hazard ratios are very close to one. Thus, Table 6.4 provides little evidence that political economy factors play a role in PPAR risk. Yet a more nuanced picture emerges below.

Do Rating Revisions Delay PPARs?

One factor that could delay a PPAR's release is a rating change between the ICR and the PPAR. Such cases may be more complex, perhaps requiring more deliberation within IEG, feedback from Operations or the borrowing government. Delay could also be a result of external pressure.[23] This issue can only be examined for cases with PPARs.

Using binary ratings, we define *Downgrade* as a "Satisfactory" ICR followed by an "Unsatisfactory" PPAR and *Upgrade* as an "Unsatisfactory" ICR followed by a "Satisfactory" PPAR. "Satisfactory" ICR ratings outnumber "Unsatisfactory" ICR ratings in the overall estimation sample (73% vs. 27%); for the PPAR sample, this pattern is stronger. The result is far more downgrades (157) than upgrades (45) in our sample. However comparing the incidence of downgrades and upgrades, the imbalance disappears: P(*Downgrade*|ICR="Satisfactory")=14.6% and P(*Upgrade*|ICR="Unsatisfactory")=15.4%.

Regarding whether rating changes are associated with longer delays between ICR and PPAR, Fig. 6.7 provides separate *PPAR lag* distributions by rating change (no change, *Downgrade*, *Upgrade*). This shows the time between ICR and PPAR is substantially longer when there is a rating change than when there is not; the mean difference is about one year. The pattern looks similar for both downgrades and upgrades.

Table 6.5 presents hazard model results for the 1371 projects with PPARs (uncensored cases) to explore the role of rating changes. Column 1 repeats the Table 6.3, Column 3 specification for comparison. Column

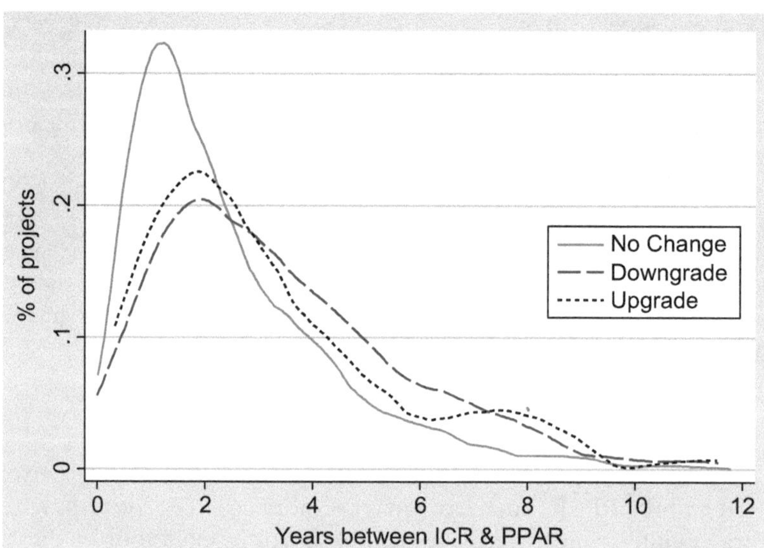

Fig. 6.7 *PPAR lag* by outcome rating change. (Source: IEG database, World Bank)

Table 6.5 Role of rating changes: PPAR hazard ratios for projects with completed PPARs

	(1)	*(2)*	*(3)*	*(4)*
Outcome (ICR)	0.933	0.945	0.950	0.957
	(−0.89)	(−0.69)	(−0.61)	(−0.52)
Downgrade		0.705***	0.792**	0.766**
		(−3.81)	(−2.08)	(−2.42)
Upgrade		0.749	0.640*	0.653*
		(−1.54)	(−1.86)	(−1.83)
WBEB@ICR			0.887	0.860*
			(−1.45)	(−1.88)
× *Downgrade*			0.702**	0.719*
			(−2.13)	(−1.95)
× *Upgrade*			1.760**	1.678**
			(2.02)	(1.97)
UNSC@ICR				1.041
				(0.27)
UNSC@PPAR				0.659***
				(−3.51)
IDA	0.788**	0.793**	0.790**	0.760***
	(−2.30)	(−2.16)	(−2.13)	(−2.59)
ICR quality	1.070	1.032	1.030	1.030
	(0.62)	(0.30)	(0.30)	(0.31)
log World Bank debt	1.038	1.029	1.025	1.039
	(0.56)	(0.43)	(0.40)	(0.62)
log Project size	1.029	1.033	1.033	1.038
	(0.81)	(0.90)	(0.87)	(1.02)
log # WB projects	1.051	1.046	1.040	1.038
	(0.88)	(0.80)	(0.74)	(0.68)
June ICR	0.929	0.902	0.901	0.907
	(−0.83)	(−1.11)	(−1.14)	(−1.12)
Tourism	1.124**	1.134**	1.145**	1.124**
	(2.05)	(2.26)	(2.54)	(2.19)
Years in office	0.998	0.997	0.996	0.998
	(−0.53)	(−0.75)	(−0.94)	(−0.47)
Freedom House	0.988	0.984	0.991	0.984
	(−0.35)	(−0.48)	(−0.26)	(−0.49)
log Population	0.899	0.891	0.907	0.917
	(−1.44)	(−1.59)	(−1.38)	(−1.25)
log GDP PC	1.025	1.019	1.018	1.044
	(0.28)	(0.21)	(0.21)	(0.50)
GDP growth	1.021*	1.017	1.018	1.022**
	(1.91)	(1.57)	(1.57)	(1.98)

(*continued*)

Table 6.5 (continued)

	(1)	*(2)*	*(3)*	*(4)*
Inflation	1.024	1.031	1.031	1.055
	(0.69)	(0.85)	(0.88)	(1.42)
Program Loan	0.987	0.983	0.991	1.016
	(−0.12)	(−0.17)	(−0.09)	(0.14)
× *Inflation*	1.214**	1.181*	1.173*	1.153
	(2.08)	(1.80)	(1.71)	(1.48)
SIL	1.094	1.083	1.073	1.085
	(1.47)	(1.23)	(1.08)	(1.20)
East Asia-Pacific	0.716**	0.721**	0.733**	0.685***
	(−2.47)	(−2.34)	(−2.27)	(−2.92)
Europe and Central Asia	0.877	0.866	0.828	0.781*
	(−0.95)	(−1.05)	(−1.32)	(−1.80)
Latin America and Caribbean	0.864	0.869	0.889	0.885
	(−1.00)	(−0.96)	(−0.81)	(−0.88)
Middle East and North Africa	0.761**	0.771*	0.758**	0.691***
	(−2.03)	(−1.91)	(−2.04)	(−2.89)
South Asia	1.156	1.206	1.229	1.191
	(0.95)	(1.32)	(1.55)	(1.32)
Observations	1371	1371	1371	1371

z-statistics in parentheses based on country-clustered standard errors. All specifications include unreported evaluation year (ICR) dummies. Weibull regression with coefficients reported for log relative-hazard form. *$p < 0.1$, **$p < 0.05$, ***$p < 0.01$

Source: See Table 6.8

2 adds *Downgrade* and *Upgrade* (compared against no rating change). Both have hazard ratios less than one and of similar magnitude, but only *Downgrade* is statistically significant, perhaps due to the scarcity of upgrades. Other hazard ratio estimates are essentially unaffected.

Column 3 introduces *WBEB*, the dummy variable indicating World Bank Executive Board membership. Of the geopolitical variables considered thus far, only *WBEB* enters the specification with a statistically significant hazard ratio in this sample (though only at the 10% level). Column 3 interacts Board membership with the *Downgrade* and *Upgrade* dummies. The *WBEB*×*Downgrade* hazard ratio is significantly less than one while the *WBEB*×*Upgrade* hazard ratio is significantly greater than one. For the uninteracted terms, the hazard ratio for *Downgrade* continues to be significantly less than one and that for *Upgrade* is marginally significantly less than one; *WBEB* is not significant. These results imply: (1) PPARs that downgrade ratings experience delays which are longer when the borrowing country occupies an important position in World Bank governance;

(2) PPARs that upgrade ratings are also delayed except when the borrowing country occupies an important position in the World Bank, in which case the PPAR is instead accelerated; and (3) when PPAR findings are unremarkable (no rating change), the borrowing country's importance within the World Bank does not impact the release of these findings. This pattern suggests both a bureaucratic procedure (e.g., another layer of review) when PPARs change ratings but also a response to power within the institution, delaying bad news and expediting good news when countries hold an institutionally important position.

Column 4 introduces dummy variables for nonpermanent UNSC membership, at the time of the ICR and at the time of the PPAR. As in Table 6.4, *UNSC@ICR* is statistically insignificance. In contrast, *UNSC@PPAR* is statistically significant, with a hazard ratio less than one. For countries that are nonpermanent UNSC members at the time of the PPAR, the time between the ICR and PPAR is significantly longer.[24]

PPAR Outcome Ratings

Understanding the selection of projects for PPARs explored above is important for understanding differences between ICR and PPAR ratings. We now turn to examining what factors influence IEG's evaluation process and how resulting PPAR ratings differ from ICR ratings. Does IEG's design and reporting structure provide sufficient protection from outside pressure—or do bureaucratic and geopolitical forces influence IEG ratings?

A few simple graphs for variables that were significant in the hazard model are illuminating. Figure 6.8 explores the bivariate relationship between rating changes and nonpermanent UNSC membership at the time of the PPAR. For each project with a PPAR, we subtract the detailed ICR rating from the PPAR rating; negative values indicate a downgrade, positive values, an upgrade. Then for each year with available data, we calculate the average of this difference for projects in countries that are nonpermanent UNSC members that year and for others. We plot each resulting point, UNSC values on the Y-axis and non-UNSC on the X-axis. Each point is plotted as a circle proportional to the number of underlying projects. No relationship between UNSC membership and ratings implies symmetry about the 45-degree line.

This is not the case. Figure 6.8 has two interesting features. First, FY2002 (July 1, 2001–June 30, 2002) is a clear outlier. Given the 9/11 attacks, this is perhaps unsurprising, though why this would be linked to rating downgrades for UNSC members' projects is unclear. Second, rather than clustering symmetrically about the 45-degree line, the bulk of the

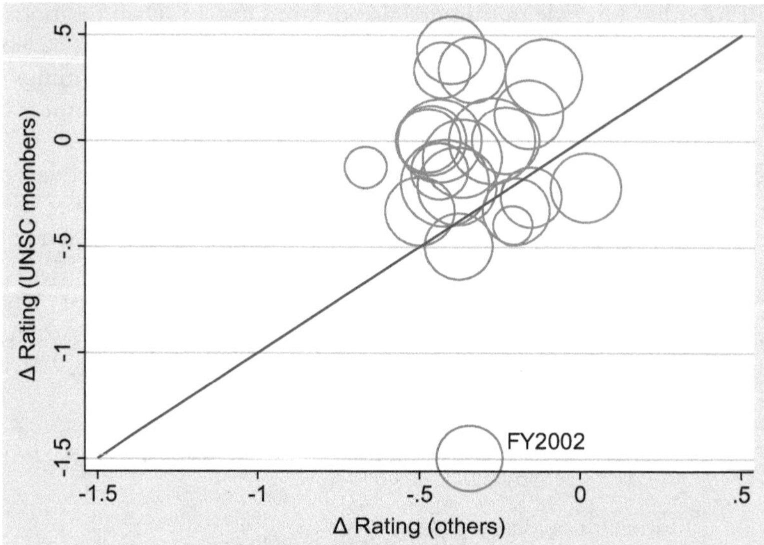

Fig. 6.8 Rating change and nonpermanent UNSC membership by evaluation fiscal year. (Source: IEG database, World Bank)

data lie above the line. This indicates that projects of countries that are nonpermanent UNSC members at the time of the PPAR rating are less likely to be downgraded/more likely to be upgraded by IEG than are projects of other borrowers. This pattern is even more pronounced if we exclude FY2002.

Figure 6.9 repeats the exercise for World Bank Executive Board membership. Now data points fall symmetrically about the 45-degree line. These graphs suggest that external geopolitical importance might influence IEG ratings but internal bureaucratic power, while slowing reports of bad news as seen earlier, does not skew results.

We explore the determinants of PPAR ratings more systematically by estimating the PPAR rating equation:

$$PPAR_{ij} = \beta_0 + \beta_1 ICR_{ij} + \beta_2{}' \boldsymbol{X}_{ij} + \beta_3{}' \boldsymbol{Z}_{ij} + \varepsilon_{ij} \quad (6.1)$$

where ICR_{ij} is the ICR rating for project i in country j, $\boldsymbol{X}_{ij}$ is a matrix including project and country characteristics measured at the relevant time for project i, and $\boldsymbol{Z}_{ij}$ is a matrix that includes bureaucratic or geopolitical

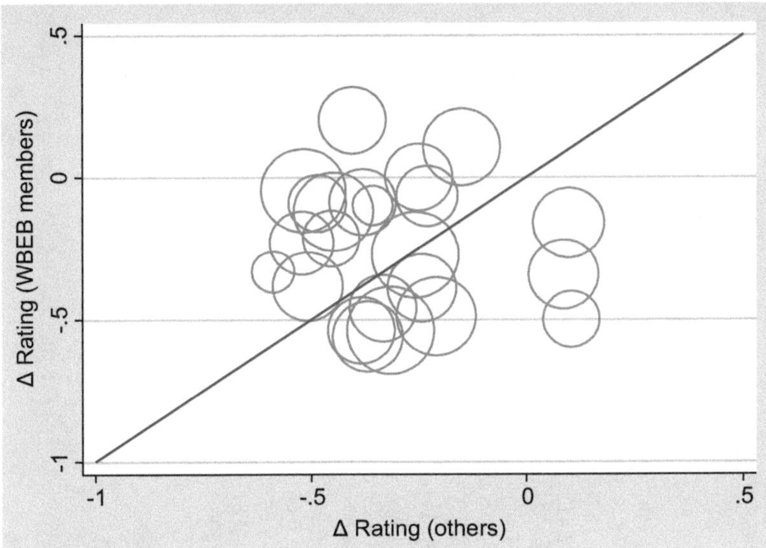

Fig. 6.9 Rating change and World Bank Executive Board membership by evaluation fiscal year. (Source: IEG database, World Bank)

factors describing country *j* at the relevant time for project *i*. We estimate this in three ways. Using binary PPAR and ICR ratings, we estimate Eq. (6.1) via probit and via OLS. Using the detailed 6-point PPAR and ICR ratings available from 1994 on, we again estimate Eq. (6.1) via OLS but replace ICR_{ij} with dummy variables *ICR*2 to *ICR*6 for the individual rating values where *ICR*1 ("Highly Unsatisfactory") is the excluded category.[25]

Table 6.6 presents estimation results and marginal effects for nonpermanent UNSC membership. Columns 1–4 use a parsimonious specification with the ICR rating and nonpermanent UNSC membership at project approval, at ICR and at PPAR. Column 1 reports probit estimation results; Column 2 presents marginal effects. Column 3 reports OLS results. Column 4 repeats this but using the 6-point PPAR rating as the dependent variable and the set of ICR dummies as independent variables. The last four columns repeat this for our "full specification" (country fixed effects, approval year dummies, PPAR year dummies, project characteristics, time-varying country characteristics). We include the full specification to check for omitted variable bias but the vast majority of the additional variables prove insignificant and we do not report these coefficients in the table. Based on Fig. 6.8, we exclude PPARs completed in FY2002.[26]

Table 6.6 PPAR ratings and nonpermanent UNSC membership

	(1)	*(2)*	*(3)*	*(4)*	*(5)*	*(6)*	*(7)*	*(8)*
ICR	2.051***	0.695***	0.692***		2.428***	0.774***	0.676***	
	(23.83)	(34.25)	(33.92)		(17.75)	(28.68)	(29.33)	
ICR2 (Unsatisfactory)				0.465				0.805***
				(1.01)				(2.75)
ICR3 (Moderately Unsatisfactory)				1.138**				1.352***
				(2.41)				(4.45)
ICR4 (Moderately Satisfactory)				2.032***				2.305***
				(4.44)				(7.97)
ICR5 (Satisfactory)				2.574***				2.869***
				(5.71)				(10.73)
ICR6 (Highly Satisfactory)				3.534***				3.686***
				(7.82)				(12.00)
UNSC@PPAR	0.356***	0.110***	0.0751***	0.220***	0.360**	0.101**	0.0638**	0.241***
	(2.65)	(2.96)	(2.89)	(3.60)	(2.08)	(2.41)	(2.35)	(3.16)
UNSC@ICR	−0.0284	−0.00993	−0.00676	−0.0637	0.0550	0.0174	−0.000553	−0.0782
	(−0.17)	(−0.17)	(−0.18)	(−0.66)	(0.30)	(0.30)	(−0.02)	(−1.16)
UNSC@approval	0.0412	0.0141	0.00896	−0.0438	0.131	0.0403	0.0262	−0.0364
	(0.37)	(0.37)	(0.34)	(−0.81)	(0.79)	(0.82)	(0.87)	(−0.59)
Observations	1500	1500	1500	1500	1219	1219	1329	1329

z/*t*-statistics in parentheses based on country-clustered standard errors
Probit on binary PPAR rating: (1) Basic specification, (5) Full specification
Marginal effects for probit: (2) Basic specification, (6) Full specification
OLS on binary PPAR rating: (3) Basic specification, (7) Full specification
OLS on 6-point PPAR rating: (4) Basic specification, (8) Full specification
Marginal effects for ICR rating calculated with other variables set at sample mean. Marginal effects for each UNSC variable calculated with other UNSC variables at zero and all other variables at sample mean
$*p < 0.1$, $**p < 0.05$, $***p < 0.01$

Source: See Table 6.8

A consistent pattern emerges. ICR ratings are strongly predictive of PPAR ratings; a satisfactory ICR rating increases the chances of a satisfactory PPAR rating by 68–77 percentage points, ceteris paribus. If a country holds a nonpermanent seat on the UNSC at the time of the PPAR rating, the chances of a satisfactory rating increase by 6.4–11 percentage points. In contrast, earlier membership (at approval or ICR) does not directly influence PPAR ratings. Dreher et al. (2013) and Kilby (2015) find evidence of a negative effect of nonpermanent UNSC membership at approval in certain settings; however, the included ICR rating captures such effects. We expect a negative coefficient on *UNSC@ICR* if PPAR ratings correct for a bias in ICR ratings; point estimates are negative in five of six specifications but never significant.

Table 6.7 explores these findings. We define World Bank debt dummies for the bottom 25% (*Low Debt*), middle 50% (*Medium Debt*), and top 25% (*High Debt*) and then interact these with *UNSC@PPAR* to determine if a subset of cases drives the results. This is the case. The estimated coefficient on *UNSC@PPAR* is small (even negative) and statistically insignificant for *Low Debt* countries. For *High Debt*, the estimate for *UNSC@PPAR* is consistently significant and almost always larger than in Table 6.6 *Medium Debt* falls in between—positive coefficient estimates but with varying statistical significance across specifications. Looking at *High Debt*, the probit, for example, indicates the probability of a satisfactory PPAR rating is 13–15 percentage points higher for countries owing a lot to the World Bank when they serve as nonpermanent UNSC members at the time of the PPAR rating as compared to cases where they do not serve on the UNSC, ceteris paribus and evaluated at the mean. We also explored other measures that the literature suggests might condition the effects of geopolitics in international financial institutions (Stone 2008; Dreher et al. 2013) including the ratio of short-term debt to total debt and the debt service ratio. None of the categories (low, medium, high) associated with these other variables identify the cases driving UNSC results.

World Bank debt, however, is closing linked to country size. The correlation between population and World Bank debt in our sample is 0.9. Reproducing Table 6.7 but interacting ICR@PPAR with indicator variables for low, medium, and high population levels instead of debt volume leads to essentially the same results. Thus, we cannot separately identify whether UNSC membership matters for countries that are large borrowers or large countries that are borrowers.

In a series of unreported estimations, we repeat the Table 6.6 exercise with other geopolitical variables from Table 6.4. We do not find robust

Table 6.7 Interaction of UNSC membership and World Bank debt

	(1)	*(2)*	*(3)*	*(4)*	*(5)*	*(6)*	*(7)*	*(8)*
ICR	2.066***	0.698***	0.695***		2.431***	0.775***	0.672***	
	(24.15)	(34.93)	(35.00)		(17.28)	(27.68)	(29.15)	
ICR2 (Unsatisfactory)				0.466				0.775***
				(1.00)				(2.80)
ICR3 (Moderately Unsatisfactory)				1.168**				1.334***
				(2.41)				(4.58)
ICR4 (Moderately Satisfactory)				2.047***				2.283***
				(4.37)				(8.33)
ICR5 (Satisfactory)				2.576***				2.835***
				(5.60)				(11.27)
ICR6 (Highly Satisfactory)				3.528***				3.654***
				(7.65)				(12.50)
UNSC@PPAR × *Low Debt*	0.159	0.0540	0.0373	−0.00347	−0.105	−0.0415	−0.00263	−0.0365
	(0.46)	(0.48)	(0.47)	(−0.03)	(−0.22)	(−0.22)	(−0.04)	(−0.19)
UNSC@PPAR × *Medium Debt*	0.342*	0.108*	0.0730*	0.269***	0.214	0.0572	0.0524	0.281**
	(1.70)	(1.89)	(1.86)	(2.81)	(0.90)	(0.97)	(1.37)	(2.50)
UNSC@PPAR × *High Debt*	0.481***	0.135***	0.0901***	0.214**	0.747***	0.150***	0.118***	0.296**
	(3.89)	(3.69)	(3.43)	(2.31)	(4.11)	(2.61)	(3.62)	(2.49)
Low Debt	−0.0204	−0.0162	−0.00518	−0.0855	−0.635*	0.0240	−0.138**	−0.108
	(−0.18)	(−0.28)	(−0.19)	(−1.07)	(−1.91)	(0.41)	(−2.16)	(−0.73)
High Debt	0.0869	0.00886	0.0207	0.0890	0.0235	0.0303	0.0308	0.121
	(0.64)	(0.23)	(0.66)	(1.13)	(0.07)	(0.59)	(0.40)	(0.57)

UNSC@ICR	−0.0463	−0.00716	−0.0111	−0.0782	0.0776	−0.223*	0.00126	−0.0675
	(−0.28)	(−0.18)	(−0.29)	(−0.86)	(0.40)	(−1.80)	(0.04)	(−0.97)
UNSC@approval	0.0257	0.0294	0.00534	−0.0811	0.0986	0.00655	0.0238	−0.0419
	(0.23)	(0.65)	(0.21)	(−1.50)	(0.58)	(0.07)	(0.78)	(−0.66)
Observations	1451	1451	1451	1451	1219	1219	1329	1329

z/t-statistics in parentheses based on country-clustered standard errors. $*p < 0.1$, $**p < 0.05$, $***p < 0.01$
Probit on binary PPAR rating: (1) Basic specification, (5) Full specification
Marginal effects for probit: (2) Basic specification, (6) Full specification
OLS on binary PPAR rating: (3) Basic specification, (7) Full specification
OLS on 6-point PPAR rating: (4) Basic specification, (8) Full specification
Marginal effects for ICR rating calculated with other variables set at sample mean. Marginal effects for each UNSC variable calculated with other UNSC/debt variables at zero and all other variables at sample mean

Source: See Table 6.8

effects on PPAR ratings, whether based on values at approval, ICR or PPAR. Furthermore, interactions with low, medium, and high levels of World Bank debt or the short-term debt to total debt ratio (parallel to Table 6.7) do not identify any categories with robust effects.

Finally, we explore whether selection impacts our results. We estimate a Heckman model where the PPAR selection equation is a probit (following Table 6.3, Column 2) and the PPAR outcome equation is either the linear probability model (Table 6.6, Column 3 or 7) or the 6-point rating (Column 4 or 8). This set-up lends itself well to a Heckman model since there are a number of theoretically valid exclusion restrictions (ICR quality, # World Bank projects finishing in same year, June ICR). Whether or not we can reject the independence of the error terms in the two equations depends on which variables we include. However, in all cases the estimated coefficient for *UNSC@PPAR* remains positive and statistically significant with little variation in magnitude. Thus, selection effects, if any, do not materially influence our findings.

Conclusion

This chapter investigates two functions of the World Bank's Independent Evaluation Group. We first examine how IEG selects projects for a Project Performance Assessment Report, a comprehensive review carried out for about a quarter of World Bank-funded projects. We then turn to how PPAR ratings done by IEG staff differ from initial ratings by Operations staff in their Implementation Completion Report.

IEG makes clear that PPAR selection is nonrandom. IEG focuses on projects with positive initial ratings—the higher the rating, the more likely a review. Poorly done ICRs also increase the odds of a PPAR. PPAR selection favors large projects and projects from less developed countries. Program loans, especially in high inflation environments, are more likely to be subject to a PPAR. Furthermore, there is a surge of Implementation Completion Reports filed at the end of the World Bank's fiscal year; these June ICRs are individually less likely to be selected for a PPAR as IEG attempts to allocate scarce resources in a balanced way over the year. When multiple projects in a single country are completed in the same year, these projects are more likely to be selected for a PPAR as IEG staff undertake "cluster audits" to economize on travel expenses and time. All these patterns are in-line with IEG's mission.

However, some elements of PPAR selection may not be in-line with the mission. IEG is more likely to review projects in countries with easier working conditions such as well-established, democratic governments. IEG is more likely to conduct a PPAR—including a country visit by IEG staff/consultants—and conduct it sooner rather than later if the country is a popular tourist destination. Institutional power appears to impact the PPAR release date. PPARs that result in rating changes on average take an additional year to be released. If the borrowing country is on the World Bank Executive Board and the rating change is a downgrade, the release of this bad news is delayed twice as long. Conversely, if the country is on the Board and rating change is an upgrade, IEG releases the PPAR more quickly than if there had been no rating change. PPAR releases also take longer for nonpermanent UNSC members.

We find some, albeit limited, evidence linking IEG ratings to geopolitics. Controlling for the previous ICR rating, the PPAR rating is more likely to be positive if the borrowing country happens to hold a nonpermanent UN Security Council seat at the time the PPAR rating is released. This result is driven primarily by higher ratings for countries that both occupy a nonpermanent UNSC seat and are important World Bank customers (i.e., large World Bank borrowers). Such countries are also populous; due to the correlation between population and borrowing, we cannot separately identify the two effects. These results are robust. For other geopolitical variables from the aid literature, we find no robust relationship. On the one hand, this is remarkable given the strong association between World Bank lending activities and geopolitics in the literature and may indicate that attempts to maintain the evaluation function as an institutionally independent unit have been relatively successful. On the other hand, of the geopolitical variables we consider, only UNSC membership has substantial variation over the one-to-three-year period between ICR and PPAR. That is, UNSC membership is the only geopolitical variable well suited to our application.

This chapter does not explain why these patterns exist. Some PPAR selection patterns may reflect a bureaucratic tendency toward a more pleasant work environment and may have little consequence in terms of the effectiveness of the organization. Delaying the release of "bad news" (rating downgrades) for institutionally important Board members is perhaps more troubling (because it suggests IEG is not entirely independent) but there is no evidence of other Board member privileges. EDs may be able to delay or expedite a PPAR but we do not find convincing evidence that they prevent PPARs or impact ratings. Furthermore, we cannot explain why borrowing governments want to delay or expedite a PPAR release and can only speculate that PPAR ratings might influence elections or access to additional aid resources.

For the link between UNSC nonpermanent membership and higher PPAR ratings, the channel of influence may be US/G7 pressure or an expectation thereof. Tangible benefits from higher project ratings might be political or financial but exactly what they are remains an open question for future research.

The implications of these results in terms of possible institutional reforms at the World Bank are in the eye of the beholder. Given the insignificance of a number of geopolitical factors tested, one might conclude that the World Bank's evaluation function is well positioned to carry out independent assessments. Conversely, evidence of delayed negative reports for institutionally important countries and inflated project performance ratings for UNSC members suggests the need for additional measures to safeguard the independence of the Independent Evaluation Group.

For researchers who intend to use World Bank project ratings as proxies for project quality, our results suggest including nonpermanent UNSC membership and certain bureaucratic factors as control variables to avoid omitted variable bias. Researchers should also look more broadly at the patterns we uncover and consider how issues of timing and type of rating could impact their identification strategy. If researchers control for such potential biases, World Bank project ratings can provide a valuable and meaningful way to measure project quality in many applications.

Appendix

Table 6.8 Data sources

Beck et al. (2001):	*Years in office*
Freedom House (2012):	*Freedom House*
IEG (2014):	*Outcome (ICR); ICR quality; log # WB projects; June ICR*
Kaja and Werker (2010):	*WBEB@ICR*
OECD (2015):	*log US Aid; log G7 Aid*
Strezhnev and Voeten (2012); U.S. State Department (1984–2013):	*US UN voting; G7 UN voting*
United Nations (2014):	*UNSC@ICR*
USAID (2014):	*US military aid*
World Bank (2012b):	*IDA; Program Loan; SIL;* Regional dummies
Azevedo (2011); World Bank (2014):	*log World Bank debt; log Project size; Tourism; log Population; log GDP PC; GDP growth; Inflation*

Table 6.9 Acronym list

DAC	Development Assistance Committee (also called Development Co-operation Directorate) of the Organization for Economic Cooperation and Development (OECD)
DGO	Director General, Operations
EAP	East Asia and Pacific
ECA	Europe and Central Asia
ED	Executive Director
ES	Evaluation Summary
EVM	Evaluation Memorandum
FY	Fiscal Year (July 1–June 30)
G7	Group of 7 (Canada, France, Germany, Italy, Japan, United Kingdom, United States)
GDP	Gross Domestic Product
IBRD	International Bank for Reconstruction and Development
ICR	Implementation Completion Report or Implementation Completion and Results Report
IDA	International Development Association
IEG	Independent Evaluation Group
LAC	Latin America and the Caribbean
MENA	Middle East and North Africa
OED	Operations Evaluation Department
PAR	Project Assessment Report
PCM	Project Cancellation Memorandum
PCN	Project Cancellation Note
PCR	Project Completion Report
PPAR	Project Performance Audit Report
SA	South Asia
SIL	Specific Investment Loan
SSA	Sub-Saharan Africa
UN	United Nations
UNSC	United Nations Security Council
USD	US Dollar
WBEB	World Bank Executive Board

Notes

1. In response NGO and donor pressure, the World Bank has gradually increased the amount of information it makes public. The "Access to Information" policy adopted in 2010 under World Bank President Robert Zoellick marked a major step forward, providing access to new information on projects and putting in place procedures to request information and to appeal when requests are initially denied.

2. Outsider papers: Buntaine and Parks (2013), Dreher et al. (2013), Girod and Tobin (2016), Kilby (2015), Malik and Stone (2018), Michaelowa and Borrmann (2006), Sud and Olmstead-Rumsey (2012), and Winters (2014). Insider papers: Blum (2014), Bulman et al. (2017), Chauvet et al. (2010), Chauvet et al. (2017), Cruz and Keefer (2013), Deininger et al. (1998), Denizer et al. (2013), Dollar and Levin (2005), Dollar and Svensson (2000), Geli et al. (2014), Guillaumont and Laajaj (2006), Isham and Kaufmann (1999), Isham et al. (1997), Kaufmann and Wang (1995), Limodio (2011), Malesa and Silarszky (2005), Moll et al. (2015), Pohl and Mihaljek (1992), Ralston (2014) and Smets et al. (2013).
3. The influence of geopolitics has been demonstrated at every stage of the project cycle (preparation: Kilby (2013b); approval (number of loans): Dreher et al. (2009), Kaja and Werker (2010); disbursement (speed): Kilby (2013a); disbursement (enforcement of conditionality): Kilby (2009); disbursement (electioneering): Kersting and Kilby (2016)) *except* at the evaluation stage. Most of the literature focuses on US informal influence over the World Bank, which is headquartered just two blocks from the White House and depends on the US for funding and leadership.
4. For a detailed history of OED, see Grasso et al. (2003). In the text below we use IEG to refer to the evaluation department even before 2005.
5. This reduction was driven by an expanding World Bank project portfolio but also increasing demands on IEG to generate other products at the country and sector levels (Grasso et al. 2003). More than 70% of IEG's budget was devoted to PPARs in 1976 (Grasso et al. 2003, 169); the figure was less than 10% of IEG's USD 34 million budget in 2011 when the time devoted to a PPAR averaged six staff weeks (IEG 2011, 38). PPAR coverage differs across activities, depending on "novelty" and importance. For example, IEG kept PPAR coverage of structural adjustment programs at 100% in the 1980s while it reduced coverage of investment projects.
6. Calculated from 1590 IBRD/IDA-funded projects with overall outcome ratings measured as "Satisfactory" or "Unsatisfactory." For our estimation sample, it is 17.6%.
7. PPAR is the report (also called a Project Performance Audit Report or just Project Audit Report in early IEG documents); PAR is the database name for its associated ratings.
8. In a few cases, a second PPAR rating is available. To allow such variation, we take the project's last PCR/EVM/ES entry as its ICR rating and the project's first PPAR entry as its PPAR rating.
9. Despite some selection based on ICR ratings, the overall share of projects initially rated satisfactory does not vary much between those projects that get reevaluated and others: ICR ratings average 72% satisfactory for projects with no subsequent PPAR versus 78% for projects with a subsequent

PPAR. Starting in the mid-1980s, IEG began "group audits" for sequences of projects in the same sector in a given country and "cluster audits" of similar projects in several neighboring countries (Grasso et al. 2003, 48–49). Selection of projects for a PPAR is ultimately the decision of IEG division chiefs but with input from staff (Grasso et al. 2003, 49).

10. This pattern is apparent in IEG (2010); Appendix B reports that only 12% of projects with an economic rate of return above 10% were rating "moderately unsatisfactory" or lower. Denizer et al. (2013) argue that World Bank procedures promote applying relatively uniform standards to goal setting and evaluation.
11. The Vocational Training and Technological Development Project in Uruguay was approved in 1978 and completed in 1986. Its PCR (equivalent to an ICR) was issued in 1988 and the project was included with two subsequent Uruguayan education projects in a 2006 PPAR. The longest interval in our estimation sample is 12.75 years.
12. Countries with ICRs (# ICRs in parentheses) but no PPARs as of 9/30/2013 are: Angola (15), Cape Verde (22), Sao Tome and Principe (13), Tonga (5), the Bahamas (5), Grenada (9), St. Kitts and Nevis (5), St. Vincent and the Grenadines (6), Turkmenistan (3), West Bank and Gaza (40), Kosovo (20), Namibia (2), Montenegro (5), South Sudan (1).
13. The hazard model explores how the time until PPAR depends on institutional, country, and project characteristics. This is a form of a duration model that allows for censoring. Specifically, the model treats cases without a PPAR as not yet having a PPAR, since in principle a project could be audited at any point in the future. Estimation results are reported in terms of a hazard ratio relative to the baseline so that a ratio greater than one indicates a higher likelihood ("greater risk") of a PPAR/shorter time until a PPAR; a ratio less than one indicates a lower likelihood of a PPAR/longer time until a PPAR. Hazard ratios have the advantage of not depending on values of the other variables (just as slope terms in a linear model do not depend on where you evaluate them).
14. The hazard model sample includes all years with available data whereas the PPAR rating sample below excludes FY2002 (which proves to be an outlier in that setting perhaps due to the 9/11 attacks). Hazard model results are largely unchanged if we also exclude FY2002 here.
15. Tourism data are sparse so we average across available years for each country, resulting in a purely cross-sectional variable. The specification also includes log population so that the tourism coefficient would be the same if we measured tourist arrivals per capita.
16. We add one before taking logs; we disregard the few negative values reported by the OECD since this is defined as a gross measure.
17. Results are similar if we use current year membership only. However, the three-year period has a few advantages. It allows for the delay between the

decision to carry out a PPAR and the release of the PPAR. It also simplifies treatment of cases where the country held the WBEB seat for only part of the calendar year (since WBEB membership follows the World Bank's fiscal year).

18. The Weibull distribution is a generalization of the exponential distribution and is commonly used in hazard models because it is more flexible than the exponential and results in constant hazard ratios. We select logit (which estimates the probability of a PPAR by the end date) rather than probit because logit odds ratios can easily be compared to hazard ratios.
19. Results comparable for Gompertz, loglogistic, and lognormal distributions. A likelihood ratio test rejects the shape assumption of the exponential model in favor of Weibull though results are again similar. Estimates are similar with gamma distribution but standard errors are larger and a few variables (notably *June ICR*) fail to reach statistical significance.
20. However, if we omit GDP per capita in this multivariate model, the *IDA* hazard ratio becomes significantly greater than one. The two variables are strongly correlated as only low-income countries qualify for IDA's concessional credits. (This may also explain why, in the specifications of Table 6.5 below, *IDA* is significant while *log GDP PC* is not).
21. The impact of a single year is trivial but years in office range from 1 to 45 so there is a sizeable effect some cases. Because years in office might be related to conflict, we explored the impact of a conflict dummy derived from PRIO data. The magnitude of the *Years in office* hazard rate is unchanged and so is not driven by omitted information about conflict.
22. Again, controlling for conflict does not change results.
23. IEG states: "Each PPAR is subject to internal IEG peer review, Panel review, and management approval. Once cleared internally, the PPAR is commented on by the responsible Bank department. The PPAR is also sent to the borrower for review. IEG incorporates both Bank and borrower comments as appropriate, and the borrowers' comments are attached to the document that is sent to the Bank's Board of Executive Directors. After an assessment report has been sent to the Board, it is disclosed to the public." (IEG 2015a, vi)
24. We do not interact *UNSC* with *Downgrade* or *Upgrade* because, in combination, these are rare events, for example, only seven cases where a UNSC member has a downgrade. Looking at UNSC membership, timing is critical (since nonpermanent membership lasts only two years) whereas it is less critical when considering other geopolitical variables (bilateral aid, UN voting alignment, etc.) that vary less over time. This explains why results differ between *UNSC@ICR* and *UNSC@PPAR* while results for the other geopolitical variables do not depend on whether measured at the time of the ICR or the PPAR.

25. We do not present ordered probit results because of the challenges involved in presenting useful marginal effects in this setting. However, the sign and significance of estimated coefficients for the ordered probit latent variable model match the linear model.
26. Project characteristics include an IDA dummy and a Program Loan dummy. Country characteristics include GDP per capita, GDP growth rate, inflation, openness, the ratio of short-term debt to total debt, the average number of years of schooling, the combined Freedom House rating, and government years in office, all at approval. Sample size falls from 1500 observations (on 120 countries) in the parsimonious specifications to 1329 observations (on 93 countries) in the full specification. This is less than the 1371 observations in Table 6.5 because we exclude FY2002 PPARs. The full specification probit sample is slightly smaller still, at 1219 observations (on 69 countries) due to lack of variation in PPAR ratings (all Satisfactory or all Unsatisfactory) in some countries.

References

Azevedo, João Pedro. 2011. wbopendata: Stata module to access World Bank databases, Statistical Software Components S457234, Boston College Department of Economics. http://ideas.repec.org/c/boc/bocode/s457234.html

Beck, Thorsten, George Clarke, Alberto Groff, Philip Keefer, and Patrick Walsh. 2001. New tools in comparative political economy: The Database of Political Institutions. World Bank Economic Review 15:165–176.

Blum, Jürgen René. 2014. What factors predict how public sector projects perform? A review of the World Bank's public sector management portfolio. World Bank Policy Research Working Paper 6798.

Bulman, David, Walter Kolkma, and Aart Kraay. 2017. Good countries or good projects? Comparing macro and micro correlates of World Bank and Asian Development Bank project performance. Review of International Organizations 12(3):335–363.

Buntaine, Mark, and Bradley C. Parks. 2013. When do environmentally-focused assistance projects achieve their objectives? Evidence from World Bank post-project evaluations. Global Environmental Politics 13(2):67–90.

Chauvet, Lisa, Paul Collier, and Marguerite Duponchel. 2010. What explains aid project success in post-conflict situations? World Bank Policy Research Working Paper 5418.

Chauvet, Lisa, Paul Collier, and Andreas Fuster. 2017. Supervision and Project Performance: A Principal-Agent Approach.⟨hal-01516966⟩.

Cruz, Cesi, and Philip Keefer. 2013. The organization of programmatic parties and the politics of bureaucratic reform. World Bank Policy Research Working Paper 6686.

Deininger, Klaus, Lyn Squire, and Swati Basu. 1998. Does economic analysis improve the quality of foreign assistance? World Bank Economic Review 12(3):385–418.
Denizer, Cevdet, Daniel Kaufmann, and Aart Kraay. 2013. Good countries or good projects? Macro and micro correlates of World Bank project performance. Journal of Development Economics 105:288–302.
Dollar, David, and Victoria Levin. 2005. Sowing and reaping: Institutional quality and project outcomes in developing countries. World Bank Policy Research Working Paper # 3524.
Dollar, David, and Jakob Svensson. 2000. What explains the success or failure of structural adjustment programmes? The Economic Journal 110(466):894–917.
Dreher, Axel, Jan-Egbert Sturm, and James Vreeland. 2009. Development aid and international politics: Does membership on the UN Security Council influence World Bank decisions? Journal of Development Economics 88: 1–18.
Dreher, Axel, Stephan Klasen, James Raymond Vreeland, and Eric Werker. 2013. The costs of favoritism: Is politically-driven aid less effective? Economic Development and Cultural Change 62(1):157–191.
Freedom House. 2012. Freedom in the World.
Geli, Patricia, Aart Kraay, and Hoveida Nobakht. 2014. Predicting World Bank project outcome ratings. World Bank Policy Research Working Paper 7001.
Girod, Desha M., and Jennifer Tobin. 2016. Take the money and run: The determinants of compliance with aid agreements. International Organization 70(1) 209–239.
Grasso, Patrick G., Sulaiman S. Wasty, Rachel V. Weaving (Eds). 2003. World Bank Operations Evaluation Department: The First 30 Years. Washington, DC: The World Bank.
Guillaumont, Patrick, and Rachid Laajaj. 2006. When instability increases the effectiveness of aid projects. World Bank Policy Research Working Paper # 4034.
IEG (World Bank Independent Evaluation Group). 2010. Cost-Benefit Analysis in World Bank Projects. Washington, DC: The World Bank.
IEG (World Bank Independent Evaluation Group). 2011. IEG Work Program and Budget (FY12) and Indicative Plan (FY13–14). Washington, DC: The World Bank.
IEG (World Bank Independent Evaluation Group). 2014. Independent Evaluation Group - World Bank Project Performance Ratings. http://ieg.worldbankgroup.org/ratings
IEG (World Bank Independent Evaluation Group). 2015a. Project Performance Assessment Report. Brazil: First Programmatical Reform Loan for Environmental Sustainability. Report No.: 92270-BR.
IEG (World Bank Independent Evaluation Group). 2015b. World Bank Project Performance Ratings - Codebook. https://ieg.worldbankgroup.org/Data/reports/ieg-wb-project-performance-ratings-codebook_092015.pdf

Isham, Jonathan, Daniel Kaufmann, and Lant Pritchett. 1997. Civil liberties, democracy, and the performance of government projects. World Bank Economic Review 11(2):219–242.

Isham, Jonathan, and Daniel Kaufmann. 1999. The forgotten rationale for policy reform: The productivity of investment projects. Quarterly Journal of Economics 114(1):149–184.

Kaufmann, Daniel, and Yan Wang. 1995. Macroeconomic policies and project performance in the social sectors: A model of human capital production and evidence from LDCs. World Development 23(5)751–765.

Kaja, Ashwin, and Eric Werker. 2010. Corporate governance at the World Bank and the dilemma of global governance. World Bank Economic Review 24(2):171–198.

Kersting, Erasmus, and Christopher Kilby. 2016. With a little help from my friends: Global electioneering and World Bank lending. Journal of Development Economics 121:153–165.

Kilby, Christopher. 2000. Supervision and performance: The case of World Bank projects. Journal of Development Economics 62(1):233–259.

Kilby, Christopher. 2009. The political economy of conditionality: an empirical analysis of World Bank loan disbursements. Journal of Development Economics 89(1):51–61.

Kilby, Christopher. 2013a. An empirical assessment of informal influence in the World Bank. Economic Development and Cultural Change 61(2):431–464.

Kilby, Christopher. 2013b. The political economy of project preparation: An empirical analysis of World Bank projects. Journal of Development Economics 105:211–225.

Kilby, Christopher. 2015. Assessing the impact of World Bank preparation on project outcomes. Journal of Development Economics 115:111–123.

Limodio, Nicola. 2011. The success of infrastructure projects in low income countries and the role of selectivity. World Bank Policy Research Working Paper # 5694.

Malesa, Thaddeus, and Peter Silarszky. 2005. Does World Bank effort matter for success of adjustment operations? In Stefan Koeberle, Harold Bedoya, Peter Silarsky, and Gero Verheyen (Eds.), Conditionality Revisited: Concepts, Experiences, and Lessons. (Washington: The World Bank). Chapter 13, pages 127–141.

Malik, Rabia, and Randall W. Stone. 2018. Corporate influence in World Bank lending. Journal of Politics 80(1):103–1118.

Michaelowa, Katharina, and Axel Borrmann. 2006. Evaluation bias and incentive structures in bi- and multilateral aid agencies. Review of Development Economics 10(2):313–329.

Moll, Peter, Patricia Geli, and Pablo Saavedra. 2015. Correlates of success in World Bank development policy lending. World Bank Policy Research Working Paper 7181.

Morrison, Kevin M. 2013. Membership no longer has its privileges: The declining informal influence of board members on IDA lending. Review of International Organizations 8(2):291–312.

OECD (Organization for Economic Cooperation and Development). 2015. Geographical distribution of financial flows: Flows to developing countries. OECD International Development Statistics (database). https://doi.org/10.1787/data-00566-en.

Pohl, Gerhard, and Dubravko Mihaljek. 1992. Project evaluation and uncertainty in practice: A statistical analysis of rate-of-return divergences of 1,015 World Bank projects. The World Bank Economic Review 6(2):255–277.

Ralston, Laura. 2014. Success in difficult environments: A portfolio analysis of fragile and conflict-affected states. World Bank Policy Research Working Paper 7098.

Smets, Lodewijk, Stephen Knack, and Nadia Molenaers. 2013. Political ideology, quality at entry and the success of economic reform programs. Review of International Organizations 8(4):447–476.

Stone, Randall. 2008. The scope of IMF conditionality. International Organization 62:589–620.

Strezhnev, Anton, and Erik Voeten. 2012. United Nations General Assembly Voting Data, https://dataverse.harvard.edu/dataset.xhtml?persistentId=hdl:1902.1/12379.

Sud, Inder, and Jane Olmstead-Rumsey. 2012. Development outcomes of World Bank projects: Real or illusory improvements. George Washington University Institute for Global and International Studies Working Paper #1.

United Nations. 2014. Countries Elected Members of the Security Council. http://www.un.org/en/sc/members/elected.asp Accessed 9/15/2014.

USAID (United States Agency for International Development). 2014. U.S. overseas loans and grants: Obligations and loan authorizations, July 1, 1945–September 30, 2012 (Greenbook). https://explorer.usaid.gov/reports-greenbook.html Accessed 3/20/2014.

U.S. State Department. 1984–2013. Voting Practices in the United Nations. GPO, Washington.

Winters, Matthew S. 2014. Targeting, accountability and capture in development projects. International Studies Quarterly 58(2):393–404.

World Bank. 2012a. Access to Information. Annual Report FY 2011. Moving Forward Transparency and Accountability. (Washington: The World Bank).

World Bank. 2012b. Projects database. http://go.worldbank.org/KPMUDAVVT0 Accessed 11/30/2012.

World Bank. 2014. World Development Indicators. http://databank.worldbank.org/data/reports.aspx?source=world-development-indicators Accessed 10/14/2014.

CHAPTER 7

Aid Allocation and Outcomes: What Role Do Political Motives Play?

Nabamita Dutta and Claudia R. Williamson

Introduction

An extensive literature has emerged in both economics and political science that investigates political motivations behind aid allocation to recipient nations. A separate but related strand of literature talks about the impact of such aid allocation resulting out of political motivations on different development outcomes including economic growth. While this chapter briefly touches on the impact of aid on economic growth, it mainly focuses on donor motivations behind aid allocation. It summarizes the nuances of political and sometimes economic incentives of donors while making aid allocation decisions and describes the literature that has emerged in this regard over the decades. Finally, the chapter briefly touches on the statistical challenges faced by these studies due to endogeneity and other biases.

N. Dutta (✉)
University of Wisconsin-La Crosse, La Crosse, WI, USA
e-mail: ndutta@uwlax.edu

C. R. Williamson
Mississippi State University, Mississippi, MS, USA
e-mail: claudia.williamson@msstate.edu

N. Dutta, C. R. Williamson (eds.), *Lessons on Foreign Aid and Economic Development*, https://doi.org/10.1007/978-3-030-22121-8_7

Literature over the decades has started emphasizing that donors may not be actively pursuing effective development strategies. Rather, role of bilateral foreign aid can include goals like provide stability to the recipient government (Yuichi Kono and Montinola 2009), counter-terrorism (Bapat 2011; Boutton and Carter 2014), access to resources (Kapfer et al. 2007), and democratization (Wright 2009; Bermeo 2011). In fact, political, economic, and strategic interests of donors can far outweigh the development objectives in the context of aid allocation (Neumayer 2003a, b; Svensson 2000).

In both economics and political science literature, the significance of politics and leaders in molding development policies for their countries has moved to prominence (see e.g. Jones and Olken 2005, 2009; McGillivray and Smith 2004; Dreher and Jensen 2013; Potrafke 2009 among others). Yet, studies on foreign aid assumed for a long time motives of donors to be unitary and did not account for differences of ideologies of governments, political incentives, and how political leadership can shape allocation of aid. As Tingley (2010) stresses, aid can be a variable source of revenue for recipient nations and out of several factors, the above stated reasons can affect aid flow variability.

One of the earliest papers to study donor motives for aid allocation is Dudley and Montmarquette (1976). Using the OECD commitment data from 1970, they find the per capita income of recipient nations as one of the primary reasons for giving aid. Other important reason includes population though the impact is more ambiguous.

Dudley and Montmarquette's (1976) model was extended by Trumbull and Wall (1994). In their paper, donors could assign different weights to aid impact for recipient nations. The weights can vary by recipients and can capture, among other factors, the historical, strategic, and geographical differences among recipient nations as perceived by the donors.

Studies emerged after the earlier papers stressing how aid flow to nations can vary based on donor preferences and incentives. By correlating separately by year donor effort with various measures of government policy, Noël and Thérien (1995) find no significant link between partisan orientation and foreign aid effect. In the following decades and more so in the recent ones, a vast number of studies have explored donor motives for aid allocation and have found factors like political motivations, political favoritism, and donors' ideology to be playing crucial roles in such allocations. Government ideology can be an important explanation in this context (Dreher et al. 2013; Fuchs et al. 2012; Tingley 2010; Meernik et al. 1998; Imbeau 1988). In the following sections, we summarize the literature based on the different factors and briefly summarize the findings.

Political Motivations and Aid Allocation

Aid allocation by official donors of the OECD's Development Assistance Committee (DAC) has been investigated by several studies. Many such studies conclude that aid may not be motivated just by altruism but instead by the self-interest of donors. For example, in this context, Alesina and Dollar (2000: 33) find "considerable evidence that the direction of foreign aid is dictated as much by political and strategic considerations, as by the economic needs and policy performance of the recipients". As Ruttan (1996) points out in this context, every US administration considered foreign aid to be important in achieving foreign policy goals since the late 1940s. Promotion of overall US policy objectives can be the primary purpose of US economic assistance (Zimmermann 1993).

As an indicator of political aid motivations, Alesina and Dollar rely on UN voting patterns. When recipients vote in line with the donor country in the UN General Assembly, they receive more aid. As stated by Morgenthau (1962: 302), "the transfer of money and services from one government to another performs here the function of a price paid for political services rendered or to be rendered".

Likewise, Dreher, Nunnenkamp, and Thiele (2008) ask: does US aid buy UN general assembly votes? Using 143 countries over the period 1973–2002, the paper empirically analyzes the influence of US aid on voting patterns in the UN General Assembly. They used disaggregated aid data to account for the fact that various forms of aid may differ in their ability to induce political support by recipients. The authors obtain strong evidence that US aid buys voting compliance in the Assembly. More specifically, their results suggest that general budget support and grants are the major aid categories by which recipients have been induced to vote in line with the United States. When replicating the analysis for other G7 donors, no comparable patterns emerge.

In a similar context, Höffler and Outram (2011) show that recipient nations receive more aid when voting in line with the donor country in the UN General Assembly. Employing fixed effect estimates, they find, inter alia, that Germany's aid allocation responds positively to recipient countries' voting in line with the United States. Yet, they find that voting in line with Germany itself has no significant effects on German aid.

An important study in this regard is by Dreher, Sturm, and Vreeland (2009a) who investigate whether World Bank lending is used by the institution's major shareholders for just helping countries in situations of dire need or if international politics also play a role. They explain that major shareholders control over 40 percent of the votes and they have veto power in important decision-making. Constituting a near majority, they need the support of only a handful of allies to guarantee control of the Bank's loans and grants to developing countries.

Why would stakeholders want to influence UNSC voting instead of simply providing direct aid packages? Dreher, Strum, and Vreeland (2009a) identify three types of benefits from indirect aid packages: (1) political coverage: delegating "dirty work" to international organizations allows government to escape nationalist resentment; (2) leverage: this is an additional benefit because leverage is explicitly built into the arrangement through conditionality; and (3) decreased costs since major stakeholders pay a fraction of the cost. The relative efficiency therefore depends on the perceived costs of achieving consensus among the major stakeholders and the reduced costs of not using one's own funds.

The results of the paper contribute to the growing literature that documents how foreign policy of powerful nations incorporates International Financial Institutions as a tool to influence such policy. Projects by such an institution, the World Bank, can be given to developing countries with political importance rather than catering to the main goal of advancing development goals of poor nations. The authors state that one was of establishing political importance is serving a term of UN Security Council (UNSC), a deal that can be negotiated with the help of the powerful nations (mainly the United States but also Japan, France, Germany, and the United Kingdom) who happen to be the major shareholders.

Recent research has come up with more sophisticated measures of political and strategic interest. Studies indicate that membership in the UNSC has a strong relation with receiving foreign aid. Dreher et al. (2009a) provide evidence that elected UNSC members are more likely to participate in International Monetary Fund (IMF) programs. Additionally, as pointed out by Dreher et al. (2009b), Kuziemko and Werker (2006), Lim and Vreeland (2013), UNSC members receive more aid from the United States, the World Bank, the Asian Development Bank, and the United Nations Development Program.

Aid can be donated for commercial motives too like trade-related interests. Studies like Berthélemy and Tichit (2004) find evidence of a strong impact of bilateral trade intensity on the allocation of aid. They state that such interests vary between donors. Papers have ranked elasticity of aid with respect to bilateral trade intensity. In this context, Berthélemy (2006) find Germany to be “moderately egoistic”. The altruistic nature of donors for giving aid is revealed when it comes donating aid to countries with sound institutions and economic policies (Dollar and Levin 2006; Claessens et al. 2009). Contrasting evidence have been found by Nunnenkamp and Ohler (2011) who show that German exports to recipient countries were negatively associated with German aid in recent years (2005–2007). But as Dreher, Nunnenkamp, and Schmaljohann (2015c) state that whether these changes are persistent is subject to debate.

Political Favoritism and Allocation of World Bank and IMF Projects

In their paper, “Development Aid and International Politics: Does Membership on the UN Security Council Influence World Bank Decisions?” Dreher, Strum, and Vreeland (2009a) argue that World Bank loans are not used exclusively for development but used for political purpose. They test the hypothesis: whether temporary members of the UN Security Council receive favorable treatment from the World Bank. Using a data for 157 countries over the period 1970–2004, they find a robust positive relation between temporary UN Security Council membership and the number of World Bank projects a country receives (even after controlling for all relevant factors). The authors claim that this shows that World Bank loans have not been exclusively used to promote development but it has been used as a political tool, where project funding is made available to countries regardless of economic policy or economic need.

In the same vein, Dreher, Strum, and Vreeland (2009b) in the paper, “Global Horse Trading: IMF Loans for Votes in the United Nations Security Council,” test whether temporary members of the United Nations Security Council receive favorable treatment from IMF. Using 197 countries from 1951 to 2004, they find a positive relation between temporary Security Council membership and IMF funds. They also find evidence that Security Council membership reduces the number of conditions included in the IMF programs. The IMF loans seem to be a mechanism by which the major shareholders of the Fund can win favor with voting members of the Security Council.

Dreher went further to show how the IMF and World Bank influence voting in the UN General Assembly. Using a panel of 188 countries over the 1970–2008 period, Dreher and Strum (2012) empirically test the influence of the IMF and the World Bank on voting patterns in the UN General Assembly. They find evidence that countries receiving adjustment projects and larger non-concessional loans from the World Bank vote more frequently in line with the average G7 country. The same is true for countries obtaining non-concessional IMF programs. Regarding voting coincidence with the United States, World Bank non-concessional loans have a significant impact, while the IMF loans do not.

These papers clearly show how politics and self-interest of stakeholders in the IMF and World Bank drive allocation of project funding. Dreher, Strum, and Vreeland (2015a) provide additional evidence of this in the paper, "Political and IMF Conditionality". The authors investigate the claim that bailouts by IMF are famous for their conditionality: in return for continued installments of desperately needed loans, governments must comply with austere policy changes. The authors show that politically important countries, measured by UNSC membership, face weaker and fewer conditions. Security Council members receive about 30 percent fewer conditions. This clearly suggests that the major shareholders of the IMF trade softer conditionality in return for political influence over the Security Council.

Dreher and Gassebner (2012) further examine the consequence of World Bank and IMF lending by investigating if these programs induce government crises, and if true, under which circumstances. Analyzing 90 developing countries over the period 1970–2002, they find that World Bank projects and IMF programs affect the likelihood of major government crises. That is, the IMF and World Bank programs significantly increase crisis probability. One other interesting finding by the article is that recipient governments face an increasing risk to enter a crisis when they remain under an arrangement (with World Bank or IMF) once the economy performs better.

Dreher, Klasen, Vreeland, and Werker (2013) elaborate in detail as to why political favoritism might hamper the influence of foreign aid and specifically affect the performance of World Bank projects. Cold War is a good example of politically motivated aid and how nations wanted to help allies to be successful economically. Economic development of East Asian Tigers was boosted by receiving politically motivated aid assistance. Critics can further argue that bureaucrats might aim to implement effective programs irrespective of the political motivations of donors. Examples, in this context, come from economic aid to Pakistan for increased political support for anti-Taliban operations. An US aid official said, “We had to choose a method of funding that was most likely to produce results efficiently and effectively” (Perlez 2009). Additionally, as Dreher, Klasen, Vreeland, and Werker (2013) note political bias in aid allocation may not reduce effectiveness as there may be a plethora of worthwhile possible projects with similar potential effectiveness.

Dreher Klasen, Vreeland, and Werker (2013) use a comprehensive data set of nearly 6000 World Bank project evaluations (approved after 1975 and evaluated by 2008) to test the hypothesis that political motivations hurt aid effectiveness. Specifically, they investigate whether World Bank project performance suffers when the projects are awarded to countries that experience fleeting increases in their political power resulting from membership on the UN Security Council or the World Bank Board of Executive Directors. They find little evidence that project performance suffers, on average. They do find evidence, however, that projects awarded to UNSC members facing economic vulnerability or mismanagement perform worse than other projects.

Yet, politically motivated aid might fail to deliver development outcomes. Lower quality projects to favored countries compared to competing projects from other countries might gain approval when aid is politically motivated. Thus, politics can change the order of the queue that ranks projects based on marginal returns and, thus, development outcomes can suffer.

Politically motivated aid is prone to face less intense supervision by the World Bank or the recipient country to achieve success on development outcomes. This is especially true if intense supervision results in reduced or delayed resource transfers. Important policy reforms that promote project success can also be delayed due to granting of a project. Kilby (2009) finds that the credibility of conditionality is undermined in the case of aid when there is favoritism in project allocation and, thus, aid is rendered less effective.

Dreher, Klasen, Vreeland, and Werker (2013) go on to suggest that while there are multiple reasons to believe that development outcomes can suffer when aid is politically motivated, it is not true in absolute terms that countries receiving such aid follow unsound or inefficient economic policy. Government and World Bank can sometimes agree on policies. Vreeland (2003) suggests that some government can even invite policy conditionality. In other situations, governments may not follow policy recommendations by the World Bank and rather choose a set of policies that result in better outcomes.

Yet, World Bank conditionally may also fail in the face of political connections even when they are important. As Stone (2008) shows, politically important countries employ their leverage on the IMF conditionality when they are economically vulnerable. Under such situations, politically important country can also avoid following policies that are painful in the short run irrespective of that this may be damaging for the development outcome of the country.

Dreher, Sturm, and Vreeland (2013) have also concluded with similar findings. They mention that in exchange for the IMF loans at continuous installments, governments of recipient countries need to adhere to the conditionality imposed on them in terms of policy adoption. Yet, politically important countries can bargain and possibly face weaker stringency. Using temporary membership on the UN Security council as the measure of political importance, Dreher, Sturm, and Vreeland (2013) show that member countries receive about 30 percent fewer conditions.

Aid Allocation: Role of Leadership and Ideology

Based on multiple studies, it is now widely believed that individual leaders can make a difference with respect to a country's policies. Research on this topic is more upcoming and not as extensive as the other strands of studies that explore political motivations behind aid allocation in general. The role of political ideology has been investigated while investigating the role of individual leaders in aid allocation. The link between foreign aid and political left is well established. Studies like Thérien and Noël (2000) and Milner and Tingley (2010) have shown that left-wing politicians are more supportive of foreign aid than right-wing politicians. To summarize from the paper by Noël and Thérien (2008), "Motivated by an ethics that looked upon the inequitable sharing of wealth as a barrier to human dignity, progressives considered that the values of solidarity and democracy upheld in the developed world had to be projected on a world scale … [T]he welfare state had to be extended across borders in order to bring about a 'welfare world'" (Noël and Thérien 2008, p. 132). Redistribution of income and wealth via government intervention to reduce inequality is at the crux of beliefs for socialists. On the other hand, government intervention is not preferred by conservatives who believe in market's power to restore the economy back to normal in the face of any disruptions. Thus, conservations have less faith aid giving as a means to reduce poverty and income inequality.

Donor countries are often sharply divided in their preferences over policy options toward developing countries. Populace who self-identify themselves as being more on the left ideologically support more economic aid to developing countries (Paxton and Knack 2012; Chong and Gradstein 2008). Similar ideological divide among university students of Germany have been found by Potrafke and Ursprung (2013). Voting behavior can also be a sharp predictor in this context. The probability of members of US Congress located on the political left voting in favor of foreign aid is higher than those on the political right (Milner and Tingley 2011; Milner and Tingley 2010). Members on the political right are more likely to support substitution of trade for aid (Fleck and Kilby 2006).

But basing aid allocation based on political ideologies can become overtly simplistic. Many times conservative governments can have altruistic motives in aid giving since Christian roots can call for international solidarity (Thérien and Noël 2000). Further, to promote business interests such as export promotion, conservative governments can be in favor of aid giving (Round and Odedokun 2004).

The empirical findings in the literature, as far as the impact of political ideology on overall size of foreign aid budgets is concerned, is mixed. Along with Thérien and Noël (2000), Chong and Gradstein (2008) also find that left-leaning governments grant more aid. Brech and Potrafke (2014) conform to these findings for bilateral aid but not for other kinds of aid. Some studies found no significant effect of partisanship on aid allocation (Lundsgaarde et al. 2010). Many studies, on the contrary, found that the size of aid donation by right-wing governments is stronger than left-wing governments (Bertoli et al. 2007; Goldstein and Moss 2005; Round and Odedokun 2004).

Dreher, Minasyan, and Nunnenkamp (2015b) test the hypothesis that political proximity between donor and recipient governments, measured by left-right political ideology, affects aid effectiveness. Political similarity could promote favoritism, but political misalignment could make aid less effective. Overall, aid tends to be less effective when political ideology differs between the donor and the recipient.

Dreher, Nunnenkamp, and Schmaljohann (2015c) focus on the distribution of a given aid budget across recipient countries rather than the overall size of aid. The authors stress the importance of leaders in shaping the policies of their country. They argue leadership change can affect economic policy and outcomes, democratization, and conflict. Using bilateral allocation of German aid to 138 countries over the 1973–2010 period, the authors examine the importance of geostrategic and commercial motives in conjunction with indicators of political ideology and partisanship. The authors find that geostrategic and commercial motives matter. In addition, the results suggest that geostrategic and commercial interest matter at least as much under Socialist leadership, but the amount of aid commitments is reduced under Socialist leadership.

The only other study adopting a similar approach to this one is Fleck and Kilby's (2006) study on US aid over the 1960–1997 period. Fleck and Kilby rate the US presidents and congresses on a liberal-conservative scale. Conservative governments give greater weight to commercial interests. But the impact of shifts toward Republican presidents and more conservative congresses on geostrategic aid motivations (proxied by UN voting affinity) proves to be weak and ambiguous.

Political Motivations, Aid, and Economic Growth

The literature documenting and exploring the political determinants of foreign aid also emphasize the failure of development aid in significantly affecting economic growth (Hodler and Dreher 2013; Doucouliagos and Paldam 2009; Rajan and Subramanian 2008; Easterly et al. 2004; Boone 1996). As Dreher, Klasen, Vreeland, and Werker (2013) point out, the political implications associated with aid allocation can very well be the reason for aid ineffectiveness in the context of economic growth.

One of the pioneering studies in this context by Alesina and Dollar (2000) stresses that political allocation of aid "provides evidence as to why it is not more effective at promoting growth and poverty reduction". Dreher (2006) examines whether the IMF programs and conditionality influence economic growth in recipient countries. Using 98 countries from 1970 to 2000, after controlling for endogeneity, he reports that the IMF programs reduce growth rates. Evidence indicates that complying with the IMF conditionality mitigates the negative effect. Although the overall impact remains negative, the IMF loans have no robust statistically significant impact on economic growth.

The main challenge faced by all empirical studies on aid that have shown contemporaneous effect of aid on growth is endogeneity of aid flows. Multiple studies have exploited the idea that donors might give aid for geopolitical reasons that are inessential to a country's economic performance (Alesina and Dollar 2000; Easterly 2003, 2005; Rajan and Subramanian 2008). These variables capture the "friends of the donors" variables. These instruments can be UN voting patterns, whether the recipient country is a member of or a signatory to a strategic alliance, whether it has been a colony of the donor, and whether the donor and the recipient share a common language.

In terms of identification strategies, temporary UNSC membership is exogenous to variables that might be directly related to foreign aid (Bueno de Mesquita and Smith 2010; Dreher et al. 2016). Countries enter the UNSC for two years and are precluded from immediate re-election. This makes the membership variable truly exogenous in nature. Thus, it has a direct advantage over other geostrategic variables in terms of being exogenous. Dreher, Eichenauer, and Gehring (2016) utilize short-term UNSC membership as a quasi-random experiment to help determine the effectiveness of aid. They find that economic growth is significantly reduced when aid is committed during a county's membership on the UNSC. This suggests that political favoritism reduces the effectiveness of aid. In addition, this finding raises concern over using political interest variables as instruments for overall aid.

While political motives behind aid allocation has been cited as a significant reason of aid ineffectiveness with respect to development outcomes like growth, studies have also pointed out the lack of statistical precision like a clear identification strategy to be the reason for the mixed findings (Dreher et al. 2016).

Additional studies point out the downside of using geostrategic variables as instruments for total aid. Many times these instruments are prone to capture aid flows motivated by donors' geostrategic considerations and thus, they may not be donated to recipient countries for developmental purposes but rather to build and sustain political allegiances (Fleck and Kilby 2006). Other studies have commented that certain geostrategic variables may fail the exogeneity and exclusion restrictions. As stressed by Headey (2005, 2007) expectations of aid flows from certain members of geostrategic alliances may be correlated with membership in such groups. Variables capturing colonial heritage as determined by initial levels of technological advancement may also lead to a direct causal effect on growth (Price 2003; Grier 1999; Bertochhi and Canova 1996; Bagchi 1982).

References

Alesina, A., and D. Dollar. 2000. Who gives foreign aid to whom and why? Journal of Economic Growth, 5(1): 33–63.

Bagchi, A.K. 1982. The political economy of underdevelopment. Cambridge University Press.

Bapat, N.A. 2011. Transnational terrorism, US military aid, and the incentive to misrepresent. Journal of Peace Research, 48(3), 303–318.

Bermeo, S.B. 2011. Foreign aid and regime change: a role for donor intent. World Development, 39(11), 2021–2031.

Berthélemy, J.C. 2006. Bilateral donors' interest vs. recipients' development motives in aid allocation: do all donors behave the same? Review of Development Economics, 10(2): 179–194.

Berthélemy, J.-C., and A. Tichit. 2004. Bilateral donors' aid allocation decisions: a three-dimensional panel analysis. International Review of Economics and Finance. 13: 253–274.

Bertochhi, G., and F. Canova. 1996. Did colonialization matter for growth? An empirical exploration into the historical causes of Africa's underdevelopment, CEPR Working Paper No. 1444 (Washington: Center for Economic Policy and Research).

Bertoli, S., G.A. Cornia, and F. Manaresi. 2007. Aid performance and its determinants. A comparison of Italy with the OECD norm. Banca Nazionale del Lavoro Quarterly Review, 60(242): 271.

Boone, P. 1996. Politics and the effectiveness of foreign aid, European Economic Review, 40(2): 289–329.

Boutton, A., and D.B. Carter. 2014. Fair-weather allies? Terrorism and the allocation of US foreign aid. Journal of Conflict Resolution, 58(7), 1144–1173.

Brech, V., and N. Potrafke. 2014. Donor ideology and types of foreign aid, Journal of Comparative Economics, 42: 61–75.

Bueno de Mesquita, B., and A. Smith. 2010. The pernicious consequences of UN Security Council membership. Journal of Conflict Resolution 54, 5: 667–686.

Chong, A., and M. Gradstein. 2008. What determines foreign aid? The donors' perspective, Journal of Development Economics, 87: 1–13.

Claessens, S., D. Cassimon and B. Van Campenhout. 2009. Evidence on changes in aid allocation criteria. World Bank Economic Review, 23: 185–208.

Dollar, D. and V. Levin. 2006. The increasing selectivity of foreign aid. 1984–2003. World Development, 34: 2034–2046.

Doucouliagos, H., and M. Paldam. 2009. The Aid Effectiveness Literature: The Sad Results of 40 Years of Research. Journal of Economic Surveys, 23 (3): 433–61.

Dreher, A. 2006. IMF and Economic Growth: The Effects of Programs, Loans, and Compliance with Conditionality. World Development, 34(5): 769–788.

Dreher, A., P. Nunnenkamp, and R. Thiele. 2008. Does US aid buy UN general assembly votes? A disaggregated analysis. Public Choice (136): 139–164.

Dreher, A., J. Strum, and V.R. James. 2009b. Global horse trading: IMF loans for votes in the United Nations Security Council, European Economic Review (53): 742–757.

Dreher, A., and M. Gassebner. 2012. Do IMF and World Bank Programs Induce Government Crises? An Empirical Analysis. International Organization, 66(2): 329–358.

Dreher, A., and J. Strum. 2012. Do the IMF AND World Bank influence voting in the UN General Assembly. Public Choice (151): 363–397.

Dreher, A., J.-E. Sturm, and J.R. Vreeland. 2015a. Politics and IMF Conditionality, Journal of Conflict Resolution, 59(1):120–148.

Dreher, A., A. Minasyan, and P. Nunnenkamp. 2015b. Government ideology in donor and recipient countries: Does ideological proximity matter for the effectiveness of aid?. European Economic Review, 79: 80–92.

Dreher, A., P. Nunnenkamp, and M. Schmaljohann. 2015c. The Allocation of German Aid: Self-interest and Government Ideology. Economics & Politics, 27(1): 160–184.

Dreher, A., S. Klasen, J.R. Vreeland, and E. Werker. 2013. The Costs of Favoritism: Is Politically Driven Aid Less Effective? Economic Development and Cultural Change, 62 (1): 157–191.

Dreher, A., and N.M. Jensen. 2013. Country or leader? Political change and UN General Assembly voting, European Journal of Political Economy, 29: 183–196.

Dreher, A., J.-E. Sturm, and J.R. Vreeland. 2009a. Development Aid and International Politics: Does Membership on the UN Security Council Influence World Bank Decisions? Journal of Development Economics, 88(1): 1–18.

Dreher, A., V.Z. Eichenauer, and K. Gehring 2016. Geopolitics, aid, and growth: the impact of UN Security Council membership on the effectiveness of aid. The World Bank Economic Review, 32 (2): 268–286.

Dudley, L., and C. Montmarquette. 1976. A model of the supply of bilateral foreign aid. The American Economic Review, 66(1): 132–142.

Easterly, W. 2003. Can foreign aid buy growth? Journal of Economic Perspectives, 17(3): 23–48.

Easterly, W. 2005. What did structural adjustment adjust? The association of policies and growth with repeated IMF and World Bank adjustment loans, Journal of Development Economics, 76(1): 1–22.

Easterly, W., R. Levine, and D. Roodman. 2004. New Data, New Doubts: A Comment on Burnside and Dollar's 'Aid, Policies, and Growth' (2000), American Economic Review, 94(3): 774–80.

Fleck, R.K., and C. Kilby. 2006. How do political changes influence US bilateral aid allocations? Evidence from panel data, Review of Development Economics, 10: 210–223.

Fuchs, Andreas, A. Dreher, and P. Nunnenkamp. 2012. Determinants of Donor Generosity: A Survey of the Aid Budget Literature. Courant Research Centre Poverty, Equity and Growth – Discussion Papers 121. Göttingen.

Goldstein, M.P., and T.J. Moss. 2005. Compassionate conservatives or conservative compassionates? US political parties and bilateral foreign assistance to Africa, Journal of Development Studies, 41: 1288–1302.

Grier, R.M. 1999. Colonial legacies and economic growth. Public choice, 98(3–4): 317–335.

Headey, D.D. 2007. Geopolitics and the effect of foreign aid on economic growth: 1970–2001, Journal of International Development, 20(2): 161–180.

Headey, D.D. 2005. "Foreign aid and foreign policy: how donors undermine the effectiveness of overseas development assistance," CEPA Working Paper No. 5, (Queensland: Centre for Efficiency and Productivity Analysis, School of Economics, University of Queensland).

Hodler, R., and A. Dreher. 2013. Development (Paradigm) Failures, Journal of Development Economics, 101:63–74.

Imbeau, L.M. 1988. Aid and ideology. European Journal of Political Research, 16(1): 3–28.

Jones, B.F., and B.A. Olken. 2005. Do leaders matter? National leadership and growth since World War II, Quarterly Journal of Economics, 120: 835–864.

Jones, B.F., and B.A. Olken. 2009. "Hit or miss? The effect of assassinations on institutions and war, American Economic Journal: Macroeconomics, 1, 55–87.

Kapfer, S., R. Nielsen, and D. Nielson. 2007. If you build it, will they come? Foreign aid's effects on foreign direct investment. In MPSA National Conference (Vol. 14).

Kilby, C. 2009. The Political Economy of Conditionality: An Empirical Analysis of World Bank Loan Disbursements, Journal of Development Economics, 89 (1), 51–61.

Kuziemko, I., and E. Werker. 2006. How much is a seat on the Security Council worth? Foreign aid and bribery at the United Nations, Journal of Political Economy, 114: 905–930.

Höffler, A., and V. Outram. 2011. Need, merit, or self-interest: what determines the allocation of aid?, Review of Development Economics, 15, 237–250.

Lim, D., and J.R. Vreeland. 2013. Regional organizations and international politics: Japanese influence over the Asian Development Bank and the UN Security Council, World Politics, 65: 34–72.

Lundsgaarde, E., C. Breunig, and A. Prakash. 2010. Trade versus aid: donor generosity in an era of globalization, Policy Sciences, 40, 157–179.

McGillivray, F., and A. Smith. 2004. The impact of leadership turnover on trading relations between states, International Organization, 58: 567–600.

Meernik, J., E.L. Krueger, and S.C. Poe. 1998. Testing models of US foreign policy: Foreign aid during and after the Cold War. The journal of Politics, 60(1): 63–85.

Milner, H.V., and D.H. Tingley. 2010. The political economy of US foreign aid: American legislators and the domestic politics of aid. Economics and Politics, 22: 200–232.

Milner, Helen V., and Dustin H. Tingley. 2011. Who supports global economic engagement? The sources of preferences in American economic policy. International Organization 65 (1), 37–68.

Morgenthau, H. 1962. A political theory of foreign aid. American Political Science Review, 56: 301–309.

Neumayer, E. 2003a. What factors determine the allocation of aid by Arab countries and multilateral agencies?. Journal of Development Studies, 39(4), 134–147.

Neumayer, E. 2003b. Do human rights matter in bilateral aid allocation? A quantitative analysis of 21 donor countries. Social Science Quarterly, 84(3), 650–666.

Noël, Alain, and Jean-Phillipe Thérien. 1995, From Domestic to International Justice: The Welfare State and Foreign Aid, International Organization 49, 3: 523–553.

Noël, Alain, and Jean-Philippe Thérien. 2008. Left and Right in Global Politics. Cambridge University Press, Cambridge.

Nunnenkamp, P. and H. Ohler. 2011. Aid allocation through various official and private channels: need, merit and self-interest as motives of German donors. World Development, 39: 308–323.

Paxton, P., and S. Knack. 2012. Individual and country-level factors affecting support for foreign aid. International Political Science Review, 33(2), 171–192.

Perlez, J., 2009. US push to expand in Pakistan meets resistance. New York Times, October 6, 2009.

Potrafke, N. 2009. Does government ideology influence political alignment with the US? An empirical analysis of voting in the UN General Assembly. Review of International Organizations, 4: 245–268.

Potrafke, Niklas, and Heinrich W. Ursprung. 2013. Development aid as expressive giving. Paper presented at the European Public Choice Society Meeting 2013, Zurich.

Price, G.N. 2003. Economic Growth in a Cross-section of Nonindustrial Countries: Does Colonial Heritage Matter for Africa?. Review of Development Economics, 7(3): 478–495.

Rajan, R., and A. Subramanian. 2008. "Aid and growth: What does the cross-country evidence really show?, Review of Economics and Statistics, 90(4): 643–665.

Round, J.I., and M. Odedokun. 2004. Aid effort and its determinants, International Review of Economics and Finance, 13: 293–309.

Ruttan, V.W. 1996. United States Development Assistance Policy: The Domestic Politics of Foreign Economic Aid. The Johns Hopkins University Press, Baltimore.

Stone, R.W. 2008. The scope of IMF conditionality. International Organization, 62(4): 589–620.

Svensson, J. 2000. When is foreign aid policy credible? Aid dependence and conditionality. Journal of development economics, 61(1), 61–84.

Thérien, J.-P., and A. Noël. 2000. "Political parties and foreign aid",. *American Political Science Review*, 94: 151–162.

Tingley, Dustin. 2010. Donors and Domestic Politics: Political Influences on Foreign Aid Effort, Quarterly Review of Economics and Finance, 50, 2: 40–49.

Trumbull, W.N., and H.J. Wall. 1994. Estimating aid-allocation criteria with panel data. The Economic Journal, 104(425): 876–882.

Vreeland, J.R. 2003. The IMF and Economic Development. Cambridge, MA: Cambridge University Press.

Wright, J. 2009. How foreign aid can foster democratization in authoritarian regimes. American journal of political science, 53(3), 552–571.

Yuichi Kono, D., and G.R. Montinola. 2009. Does foreign aid support autocrats, democrats, or both?. The Journal of Politics, 71(2), 704–718.

Zimmermann, R. 1993. Dollars, Diplomacy and Dependency – Dilemmas of US Economic Aid. Lynne Reinner Publishers, Colorado.

SECTION III

Foreign Aid's Effect on Institutional Quality

CHAPTER 8

Foreign Aid and Recipient State Capacity

Andrew T. Young and Estefania Lujan Padilla

Introduction

An important stylized fact of economic development is the fact that rich economies are characterized by relatively high rates of taxation and markets that are well functioning under the rule of law (Johnson and Koyama 2017). This has led many scholars to argue that investments in *state capacity* are a necessary condition for development (e.g., Besley and Persson 2009, 2010, 2011; Acemoglu et al. 2011, 2015, 2016; Gennaioli and Voth 2015). According to this view, a state's capacity to suppress internal conflict, promote the rule of law, and provide common-interest public goods is fundamental to the creation of wealth over time. Doing so requires both *fiscal capacity* to tax its citizenry and the *legal capacity* to use the revenues in the ways listed above rather than for predation and/or arbitrary redistribution. Such state capacity must consist of a combination of infrastructure and institutions that simultaneously empowers and constrains a government.

Much of the state capacity literature has been motivated by the state-building experiences of early-modern Europe (e.g., Tilly 1990; Ertman 1997; Stasavage 2011; Strayer 2016 [1970]). However, the subsequent

A. T. Young (✉) • E. L. Padilla
Texas Tech University, Lubbock, TX, USA
e-mail: a.t.young@ttu.edu; estefania.lujan-padilla@ttu.edu

N. Dutta, C. R. Williamson (eds.), *Lessons on Foreign Aid and Economic Development*, https://doi.org/10.1007/978-3-030-22121-8_8

exceptionalism of the West in achieving sustainable economic development has led other researchers to emphasize the importance of building state capacity for developing economies. (To wit: if investing in state capacity made the West rich, then it behooves the developing world to do the same.) This has especially been the case regarding fiscal capacity, that is, the capacity for a state to extract revenue from its citizenry (e.g., Bräutigam 2002; Bräutigam et al. 2008; Bird 2008; Bird and Jantscher 1992; Gupta and Tareq 2008; Di John 2006, 2011; Addison et al. 2018). As Bräutigam (2002, p. 10) succinctly notes: "Before a state can protect its citizens, before it can provide justice or administer a bureaucracy, it needs to raise money."

The era of the Millennium Development Goals has been one of increased attention to state capacity on the part of the development community. This is evidenced by, inter alia, the 2002 Monterrey Consensus on Financing and Development, the founding of the African Tax Administration Forum in 2009, the 2010 communication on "Tax and Development" issued by the European Commission, and the 2015 Addis Abada Action Agenda.[1] Addison et al. (2018, p. 162) summarize as such: "The Millennium Development Goals (MDGs) and now the Sustainable Development Goals (SDGs) [established in 2015] have placed fiscal policy, including domestic resource mobilization, at the center of national and international development efforts."

Attached to the MDGs was a push to have donor nations increase their official development assistance (ODA) to at least 0.7 percent of their GDP. An important question is then: does foreign aid help or hinder developing countries in building fiscal capacity? Straightforwardly, proponents of increased foreign aid hope that it provides recipient governments with resources to invest into such capacity (e.g., administrative capital and technologies).[2] However, there are reasons that aid may have perverse effects on the capacity of a recipient government to extract revenues from its citizenry. Recipient governments may perceive aid as a close substitute for domestic revenues, decreasing their incentives to build fiscal capacity (Kaldor 1963). The citizens of recipient countries, in turn, may identify the provision of public goods with aid donors rather than their governments, making them prone to shirk on (evade) their taxes (Bräutigam 2002; Bräutigam and Knack 2004).

Here we provide some evidence on the relationship between aid flows and recipient fiscal capacity during the MDG era. For a sample of up to 73 ODA recipients, we explore this relationship for both the total tax share of

GDP (the most commonly used measure of fiscal capacity) and the direct tax share of total taxes. States with high fiscal capacity collect a disproportionate share of their revenues in the form of direct taxes (Besley and Persson 2009). Even within the sample of aid recipients analyzed in this paper, there is a positive relationship between income per capita and the direct tax share (Fig. 8.1). Doing so requires relatively complex administrative structures and direct taxes are often a means toward broadening the tax base to be more inclusive of economic elites. We also provide evidence on aid's relationship with legal capacity using a measure of legal system and property rights quality. With greater legal capacity, a government will limit its use of fiscal capacity to providing common-interest public goods (rather than predation and arbitrary redistribution). In both cases, the evidence is very preliminary and causal inferences are perilous. Those caveats given, we hope to contribute to an understanding of whether foreign aid was associated with progress toward the MDG-era goals for fiscal capacity.

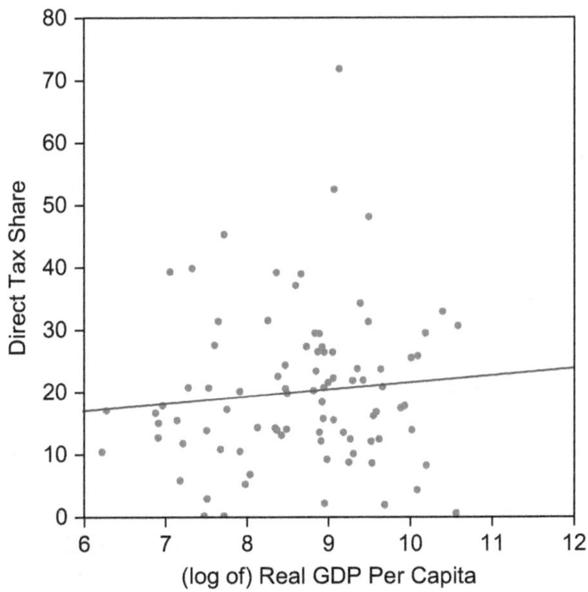

Fig. 8.1 Share of direct taxes in GDP versus (log of) real GDP per capita. Notes: Based on 89 aid recipient countries; direct taxes are those on income, profits, and capital gains. (Source: World Development Indicators)

Previous Literature

The empirical literature on the foreign aid–fiscal capacity relationship is relatively small. Of the small number of extant studies, nearly half focus on sub-Saharan African countries exclusively and none of them are focused on the MDG era. Furthermore, none of them emphasize the direct tax share of total tax revenues; this despite the fact that developing countries rely more on indirect taxes (e.g., excise taxes, sales taxes, and tariffs) than their developed counterparts and "there is, in principle, considerably scope for a broader personal income tax base across the developing world, which in turn makes it possible to introduce more progressivity into the income tax system" (Addison et al. 2018, p. 165). Progressivity is important in this context given the emphasis on how the economic elites of many developing countries are "largely outside the fiscal net" (Bräutigam 2002, p. 11).[3]

Among studies focused on sub-Saharan African exclusively is Leuthold (1991) who examines eight African countries over the 1973–1981 period and finds that aid is not a significant correlate with tax GDP shares. A later study by Ghura (1998) expands the scope to 39 African countries for a slightly later period (1985–1996) and reports a significant and negative correlation between the two variables. Also, Bräutigam and Knack (2004) examine 24 African nations over a similar period (1982–1999) and also report a significant, negative correlation. However, Bhushan and Samy (2012) explore a longer period (1972–2008) for a sub-Saharan sample as well as other regional samples of developing countries and they generally find no significant correlations between aid and fiscal capacity.

In addition to Bhushan and Samy (2012), there are a handful of studies covering a broader set of countries. Remmer (2004) considers 120 middle and lower income nations from 1970 to 1999 and reports that aid reduces tax GDP shares. However, Teera and Hudson consider a similar sample size (116 countries) and period (1975–1998) and find no significant correlation between aid and fiscal capacity. Finally, Gupta et al. (2003) assemble a large sample of 107 developing countries and find that the estimated aid-fiscal capacity relationship differs depending on whether one considers the grant (negative) or loan (positive) component of ODA.

Understanding if and how aid affects state capacity is important because state capacity is one channel through which aid may affect overall economic development. There is already a large literature on the relationship between aid and overall development. Influential papers by Burnside and

Dollar (2000, 2004) report that a positive effect of aid can only be identified for countries that already had good policy environments. Subsequent studies by Collier and Dehn (2001), Collier and Dollar (2002, 2004), and Collier and Hoeffler (2004) echo this claim. However, Easterly (2003) and Easterly et al. (2000) challenge these findings, reporting such results are very sensitive to changes in the countries included and time period covered. A recent paper by Jia and Williamson (2016) find that the Burnside and Dollar result is not robust to even updated data for the same countries and time period. In general, numerous studies during the 2000s and 2010s have reported different results (e.g., Hansen and Tarp 2000, 2001; Dalgaard et al. 2004; Karras 2006; Barro and Lee 2005; Rajan and Subramanian 2008; Young et al. 2014).[4] While it would be inaccurate to say that a consensus has emerged, a fair reading of the literature suggests that there is not much to warrant confidence in aid's effectiveness toward positive development outcomes.

Regarding the relationship between aid and legal capacity, there is a literature on the effect of aid on recipient institutional quality within which some contributions lend insights. Heckelman and Knack (2008) and Powell and Ryan (2006) find that aid hinders market-oriented reforms. However, in a later paper Heckelman and Knack (2009) conclude that aid has no significant effect on economic institutions. Alternatively, Young and Sheehan (2014) consider the legal system and property rights measure used in this chapter and report that aid flows have a negative and significant association with changes in that measure for recipient countries.[5]

Data

We wish to focus on the MDG era, which is 2000–2015. Data availability—in particular for GDP per capita and the legal capacity measure—limit us to analyzing the 2000–2014 period. The sources for the data will be the World Bank's World Development Indicators (WDIs), the Penn World Table 9.0 (PWT; Feenstra et al. 2015), the Fraser Institute's Economic Freedom of the World (EFW) Project (Gwartney et al. 2017), and the Polity IV Project (Marshall et al. 2016). The estimations that are reported in section "Results" are all cross-sectional where the 2000–2014 growth/change in a state capacity variable is regressed on initial state capacity levels and average ODA as a share of GDP.

A cross-sectional (rather than panel) analysis of averages is appropriate in this context for two reasons. First, while the underlying data are annual, any effect that aid has on state capacity is unlikely to be (at least in large part) contemporaneous at that frequency. Second, for the countries included in our estimations, most do not have continuous 2000–2014 observations for the state capacity variables. (Considering tax revenue GDP share, for example, only about 60 percent of the possible observations have values; many countries also have gaps between values with observations.) This makes panels of shorter averages (e.g., three 5-year averages) very unbalanced. Our approach, then, is to exploit the overall (15-year) averages to explore whether countries that generally received more aid experienced more or less growth in state capacity.

Our first measure of fiscal capacity is a country's tax revenue as a share of its GDP. These data are drawn from the WDIs. Also drawn from the WDIs is data on a country's share of direct tax revenue in its total tax revenue. *Direct taxes* in this measure are taxes on income, profits, and capital gains. Data on both measures are sparse for many countries during the MDG period. Values for 2000 are often not available and taking growth rates over the entire 2000–2014 period is in most cases not possible. To keep the number of country observations reasonably high, we construct "initial" levels at the average of available 2000–2002 values. (If none of the three years is available, the country is not included in the estimations.) We then use average annual growth rates, for the available data within the 2000–2014 period, as dependent variable measures of changes in fiscal capacity.

As a measure of legal capacity, we follow Young and Sheehan (2014) and draw on the legal system and property rights area of the EFW index. Each country is evaluated based on the extent of judicial independence and the impartiality of its courts; also the extent to which property rights are protected by law and their exchange is not restricted by government. Each country is scored on a scale of 0–10 with 10 indicating the highest quality of legal system and the most secure property rights.[6] For initial values, we again use the average of available 2000–2002 values. We use 2000–2014 average annual changes as a dependent variable.

The control variable of interest is average ODA as a share of a county's GDP over the 2000–2014 period. ODA is the most common measure of foreign aid and includes, in principle, all grants and concessional loans that are intended to promote economic development and welfare in the recipient country. Net official development assistance and official aid data are from the WDIs while GDP data are from the PWT.

A number of additional controls are introduced into some estimations. These include per capita real GDP and an index of human capital from the PWT (2000 values); also a country's polity democracy score and the overall EFW index.[7] I also consider oil rents as a share of a country's GDP and, separately, positive and negative terms of trade shocks. These variables are drawn from the WDIs. Terms of trade shocks are average values of, separately, positive and negative growth rates of the terms of trade during 2000–2014. Terms of trade are the national accounts exports price index divided by the imports price index. Oil rent shares are 2000–2014 averages. While causal inferences regarding ODA remain perilous, we want to see if any correlations between aid and changes in state capacity are robust to including some basic additional right-hand-side variables.

All variables are summarized, sources are reported, and summary statistics provided in Table 8.1. Also, correlations between the state capacity variables are reported in Table 8.2. All of the measures are positively correlated with one another. The two fiscal capacity measures have the highest of the correlations (0.460). The lowest correlation is between the legal system and property rights measure and the direct taxes share of total taxes (0.095).

Results

Baseline estimations are reported in Table 8.3. They are based on regressing the 2000–2014 average annual growth rate or change in a state capacity variable on its initial level and average ODA over the 2000–2014 period. These estimations are based on the largest number of observations available given the state capacity and ODA variables: between 72 and 85 countries.

ODA is negatively (though not statistically significantly) associated with growth in the tax shares of GDP and legal system and property rights scores. The ODA coefficient point estimates are very small in those cases. Alternatively, ODA is positively and significantly (5 percent level) associated with direct tax shares. Based on the point estimate, however, the effect is modest. A one standard deviation increase in ODA (11.10) is associated with between a 0.01 and 0.02 increase in the average annual growth rate of the direct tax share. That is only about one-third of the standard deviation associated with that variable (0.05).

Table 8.1 Summary of variables included in regression analyses

Variable	*Description*	*Source*	*Mean*	*Std. Dev.*
(a) Tax revenue as share of GDP	Tax revenue as share of GDP (%) (2000–2002 avg.)	WDI	15.06	7.90
(b) Direct taxes as share of total taxes	Taxes on income, profits, and capital gains as a share of total taxes (%) (2000–2002 avg.)	WDI	20.31	12.49
(c) Legal system and property rights	EFW area 2: legal structure and property rights (2000–2002 avg.)	Fraser Inst.	4.76	1.57
Average growth (a)	Average of available annual growth rates, 2000–2014	WDI	0.01	0.05
Average growth (b)	Average of available annual growth rates, 2000–2014	WDI	0.01	0.05
Average change (c)	Average of available annual changes, 2000–2014	Fraser Inst.	−0.01	0.08
ODA	Net official development assistance and official aid as share of GDP (%) (2000–2014 avg.)	WDI/ PWT	4.89	11.10
Real GDP per capita	2000 real GDP per capita (2011 US$)	PWT	$8894	$11,749
Economic freedom	2000–2002 avg. of the economic freedom of the world index	Fraser Inst.	6.32	0.94
Democracy	2000–2002 avg. of the polity IV democracy score	Polity	4.93	3.54
Human capital	2000 human capital index, based on years of schooling and returns to education	PWT	2.16	0.62
Pos. terms of trade shocks	Average value of positive terms of trade growth rates, 2000–2014	WDI	0.05	0.01
Neg. terms of trade shocks	Average value of negative terms of trade growth gates, 2000–2014	WDI	−0.04	0.02
Oil rent GDP share	Oil rents as a share of GDP (%), 2000–2014	WDI	5.13	10.42

Notes: "WDI" = World Development Indicators; "Fraser Inst." = Fraser Institute (see Gwartney et al. 2017); "PWT" = Penn World Table 9.0 (see Feenstra et al. 2015); "Polity" = Polity IV Project (see Marshall et al. 2016)

Table 8.4 reports analogous results when several additional controls are included. These are the (log) of real GDP per capita, the human capital index, and the initial polity democracy and overall economic freedom (EFW) scores. (This is done at the sacrifice of a number of country observations; the samples are now between 59 and 78 countries.) The results

Table 8.2 Correlation matrix for state capacity measures

	Tax revenue as share of GDP	*Direct taxes as share of total taxes*	*Legal system and property rights*
Tax revenue as share of GDP	1.0000		
Direct taxes as share of total taxes	0.4603	1.0000	
Legal system and property rights	0.3305	0.0953	1.000

Notes: All variables are "initial" values, that is, the average of available values from 2000 to 2002

Source: See Table 8.1

Table 8.3 Regressions of state capacity growth on foreign aid and initial state capacity

	(1) Average growth	*(2) Average growth*	*(3) Average change*
	Tax revenue as share of GDP	*Direct taxes as share of total taxes*	*Legal system and property rights*
ODA	−0.0003	0.0013**	−0.0004
	(0.0004)	(0.0005)	(0.0005)
Initial state capacity	−0.0019***	0.0005	−0.021***
	(0.0006)	(0.0004)	(0.0041)
R^2	0.1479	0.0849	0.2420
Observations	73	72	85

Notes: *, **, and *** denote statistical significance the 10, 5, and 1 percent levels, respectively. Standard errors are reported in parentheses. Constants are included in all regressions though not reported

Source: See Table 8.1

are essentially unchanged. Aid has a negative but not significant association with both the tax share of GDP and the legal system and property rights measure. Aid again enters positively and significantly (1 percent level) into the direct taxes share regression. The size of the point estimate is comparable to the one reported in Table 8.3 so, again, the estimated effect is a modest one.

Finally, we introduce a second set of control variables (positive and negative terms of trade shocks; oil rent GDP share) and report the results in Table 8.5. (Countries included in each estimation are between 61 and 62.) The point estimates look very similar to those from the

Table 8.4 Regressions of state capacity growth on foreign aid, initial state capacity, and controls for income, institutions, and human capital

	(1) *Average growth*	*(2)* *Average growth*	*(3)* *Average change*
	Tax revenue as share of GDP	*Direct taxes as share of total taxes*	*Legal system and property rights*
ODA	−0.0008	0.0016***	−0.0002
	(0.0005)	(0.0005)	(0.0007)
Initial state capacity	−0.0020***	0.0000	−0.0176**
	(0.0007)	(0.0004)	(0.0076)
Log(real GDP per capita)	−0.0070	−0.0157**	−0.0057
	(0.0079)	(0.0081)	(0.0109)
Economic freedom	−0.0201**	0.0141*	0.0080
	(0.0076)	(0.0078)	(0.0098)
Democracy	0.0011	0.0038*	−0.0009
	(0.0018)	(0.0019)	(0.0024)
Human capital	0.0043	−0.0212*	−0.0002
	(0.0121)	(0.0124)	(0.0180)
R^2	0.3475	0.3004	0.2018
Observations	59	58	78

Notes: *, **, and *** denote statistical significance the 10, 5, and 1 percent levels, respectively. Standard errors are reported in parentheses. Constants are included in all regressions though not reported

Source: See Table 8.1

previous tables. The only change is that now aid is no longer statistically significant for the growth rate of the share of direct taxes in total tax revenues.

Summarizing what we see in the data, the MDG era does not appear to be one where foreign aid flows were clearly associated with increases in either fiscal or legal capacity, as captured by the measures employed here. Considering tax shares of GDP and a measure of legal system and property rights quality, aid flows correlate negatively but not significantly. The only positive and significant relationship that appears is between aid and the direct tax share of total tax revenues, yet that relationship is not robust to changes in a small number of additional controls. (The size of the estimated effect is also small.) At the end of the day, these preliminary findings suggest that the aid-state capacity relationship remains somewhere between murky and modest.

Table 8.5 Regressions of state capacity growth on foreign aid, initial state capacity, and controls for terms of trade shocks and oil rents

	(1) *Average growth*	*(2)* *Average growth*	*(3)* *Average change*
	Tax revenue as share of GDP	*Direct taxes as share of total taxes*	*Legal system and property rights*
ODA	−0.0005	0.0012	−0.0005
	(0.0009)	(0.0011)	(0.0021)
Initial state capacity	−0.0020***	−0.0002	−0.0186***
	(0.0006)	(0.0005)	(0.0044)
Pos. terms of trade	0.0389	0.4339	0.2608
shocks	(0.4778)	(0.5100)	(0.5206)
Neg. terms of trade	−0.5269	0.2467	0.4630
shocks	(0.423)	(0.4450)	(0.4901)
Oil rent GDP share	0.0000	−0.0005	0.0002
	(0.0009)	(0.0010)	(0.0024)
R^2	0.1919	0.0848	0.2085
Observations	62	61	81

Notes: *, **, and *** denote statistical significance the 10, 5, and 1 percent levels, respectively. Standard errors are reported in parentheses. Constants are included in all regressions though not reported

Source: See Table 8.1

Discussion

How do countries build state capacity? Regarding the early-modern European experience, Charles Tilly (1990) argued that investments in state capacity were in response to the need to conduct warfare. Tilly's argument remains influential today. Regardless of whether or not Tilly's interpretation of European history accurate, most would agree that encouraging warfare is not a solution for developing economies that lack sufficient state capacity today.

Assuming that a peaceful approach is preferable, how can the governments of developing economies be encouraged to invest in the infrastructure necessary to raise sufficient revenues to provide the rule of law and other common-interest public goods? How can they develop the capacity to not only raise those sufficient revenues, but also to do so in a broad-based way that includes the economic elites of their countries? And importantly, how can they be encouraged to invest in additional infrastructure that makes sure that they revenues are not used for predation and arbitrary redistribution?

This latter question is something left unaddressed by the Tilly hypothesis. As Johnson and Koyama (2017, p. 3) note: "Economies governed by *strong, cohesive, and constrained* states are better able to overcome vested interests and avoid disastrous economic policies, while societies ruled by weak states are prone to rent-seeking, corruption and civil war" [emphases added]. Governments possessing the capacity to suppress conflict, enforce rule of law, and provide public goods may not necessarily have infrastructure that provides them with the information and incentives to do so (Salter and Young 2018).[8]

Foreign aid is one potential tool to encourage and provide the means to developing economy governments to build both fiscal and legal capacity. Indeed, during the Millennium Development Goal era (2000–2015) the development community has emphasized both the increase in foreign aid flows and investments in state capacity. Yet the literature the empirical relationship between aid flows and economic development generally has not been particularly optimistic in its findings. Furthermore, the empirical literature on aid-state capacity links is very small and there is little consensus regarding the findings.

And while one hopes that foreign aid does encourage and make possible developing country investments in state capacity, there are good reasons to believe that the effects will be perverse. Recipient governments may treat aid as a substitute for domestic revenues and see little reason to invest in the capacity to extract revenues domestically. Furthermore, their citizens may come to believe that they rely on donors rather than their governments for public goods, leading them to see little harm in evading their taxes. For reasons such as these, the relationship between aid and changes in recipient state capacity must be seriously explored.

Given the emphasis on building state capacity during the MDG era, we have tried above to begin such and exploration of the aid-state capacity relationship during that time period. We have considered the most basic of fiscal capacity measures—the tax share of a country's GDP—along with a measure of direct taxes as a share of total tax revenues. Along with these measures of fiscal capacity, we have also considered a measure of legal system and property rights quality. We have related growth rates or changes in these measures during the MDG era to ODA flows.

The resulting evidence is very preliminary and we make no strong claims of causation. However, prima facie, there does not appear to be much in the data to suggest that aid promotes increases in recipient state capacity. At best, there is some evidence that aid flows are associated with modest increases in the direct tax share of total tax revenue; but that result is not robust to controlling for terms of trade shocks and oil rents. At worst, the point estimates indicate that aid flows are associated with decreases in both the total tax share of GDP and the measure of legal system and property rights quality. Thus, it is not at all clear that recipient governments are using aid to build the infrastructure and institutions necessary to extract revenues and then use them in productive and protective, rather than predatory, ways.

This paper represents only a first look at the aid-state capacity relationship during the MGD era. Exploring this relationship further is worthy of future research. The development community's emphasis on building state capacity has carried over into the Sustainable Development Goals (SDGs; established in 2015) era. That emphasis makes sense only to the extent that we understand the links between development community policies and (i) developing country state capacity, (ii) the uses toward which that state capacity is put, and (iii) the effects of the use of state capacity on economic development. At any of these links, well-intentioned policies may stall toward their ultimate goals or, worse, have unintended consequences that are perverse.

Notes

1. United Nations (2002), https://www.ataftax.org/en/ (last accessed August 3, 2018), European Commission (2010), and United Nations (2015). For example, the European Commission communication states: "Supporting developing countries in mobilising domestic revenues and in fighting tax evasion is key in efforts to eradicate poverty as measured by the millennium development goals."
2. For example, Crivelli and Gupta (2016); also see the discussion in the World Bank's 2017 *World Development Report: Governance and the Law* (pp. 26–28).
3. Bräutigam (2002, p. 11) notes: "If economic elites are largely outside of the fiscal net, as they are in many developing countries, taxation may not stimulate effective demands for power sharing from authoritarian rules." She notes that a link between taxation of elites and the development of representative government is fundamental to the well-known theory of North and Thomas (1973) and North and Weingast (1989) of the 1688 Glorious Revolution in England and how it set the stage for the Industrial Revolution.
4. See Williamson (2010) for a discussion of the incentive and information problems that may lead to foreign aid failing to achieve its goals.

5. Young and Sheehan also address the aid-income growth relationship, finding that after institutional quality is controlled for, aid flows are not significantly related to economic growth. There work implies that aid only has a direct (significant and negative) effect on institutional quality, which in turn leads it to indirectly harm recipient development. Though not focusing on the legal system and property rights area specifically, Dutta and Williamson (2016) temper Young and Sheehan's finding somewhat by reporting evidence that aid can increase economic freedom in recipients that have high-quality political institutions. (As Dutta and Williamson note, however, most developing countries are not characterized by high-quality political institutions).
6. The underlying data are from the PRS Group's *International Country Risk Guide*, the World Economic Forum's *Global Competitiveness Report*, and the World Bank's *Doing Business Survey*. Se Gwartney et al. (2017, pp. 265–267) for details.
7. Numerous studies have documented a positive relationship between the EFW index and economic outcomes that include income levels, income growth rates, life expectancy, and reports of subjective well-being (Hall and Lawson 2014). Polity scores the level of democracy in a country, emphasizing the level of political competition and executive constraint. The scale is from 0 to 10, with 10 representing a fully institutionalized democracy. The PWT human capital index is constructed as a function of average years of schooling (Barro and Lee 2013) and the rate of return to that schooling (Psacharopoulos 1994).
8. Recent work by Bologna Pavlik and Young (2017, 2018) highlights how medieval and early-modern European experiences with representative assemblies left cultural legacies that facilitate high levels of state capacity and institutional quality generally today.

References

Acemoglu, Daron, Davide Ticchi, and Andrea Vindigni. 2011. Emergence and Persistence of Inefficient States. Journal of the European Economic Association 9(2): 177–208.

Acemoglu, Daron, Camilo Garcia-Jimeno, and James A. Robinson. 2015. State Capacity and Economic Development: A Network Approach. American Economic Review 105(8): 2364–2409.

Acemoglu, Daron, Jacob Moscona, and James A. Robinson. 2016. State Capacity and American Technology: Evidence from the 19th Century. American Economic Review 106(5): 61–67.

Addison, Tony, Miguel Niño-Zarazúa, and Jukka Pirttilä. 2018. Fiscal Policy, State Building and Economic Development. Journal of International Development 30(2): 161–172.

Barro, Robert, and Jong-Wha Lee. 2005. IMF programs: Who is chosen and What are the Effects? Journal of Monetary Economics 52(7): 1245–1269.

Barro, Robert, and Jong-Wha Lee. 2013. A New Data Set of Educational Attainment in the World, 1950–2010. Journal of Development Economics 104(September): 184–198.

Besley, Tim, and Torsten Persson. 2009. The origins of state capacity: property rights, taxation, and politics. American Economic Review 99(4): 1218–1244.

Besley, Tim, and Torsten Persson. 2010. State Capacity, Conflict, and Development. Econometrica 78(1): 1–34.

Besley, Tim, and Torsten Persson. 2011. Pillars of Prosperity: The Political Economics of Development Clusters. New Haven: Princeton University Press.

Bird, Richard M. 2008. Tax Challenges Facing Developing Countries. Background Paper for DFID Project 'Taxation for Effective Governance and Shared Growth'. London, Department for International Development.

Bird, Richard M., and Mika Casanegra de Jantscher, eds. 1992. Improving Tax Administration in Developing Countries. Washington, DC: International Monetary Fund.

Bologna Pavlik, Jamie, and Andrew T. Young. 2017. The Legacy of Representation in Medieval Europe for Incomes and Institutions Today. SSRN Working Paper. https://papers.ssrn.com/sol3/papers.cfm?abstract_id=3032584

Bologna Pavlik, Jamie, and Andrew T. Young. 2018. Medieval European Traditions in Representation and State Capacity Today. Working Paper.

Bräutigam, Deborah. 2002. Building Leviathan: Revenue, State Capacity and Governance. IDS Bulletin 33(3), 10–20.

Bräutigam, Deborah, Odd-Helge Fjeldstad, and Mick Moore, eds. 2008. Taxation and State-Building in Developing Countries: Capacity and Consent. Cambridge: Cambridge University Press.

Bräutigam, Deborah, and Stephen Knack. 2004. Foreign Aid, Institutions, and Governance in Sub-Saharan Africa. Economic Development and Cultural Change 52(2): 255–286.

Burnside, Craig, and David Dollar. 2000. Aid, Policies, and Growth. American Economic Review 90(4), 847–868.

Burnside, Craig, and David Dollar. 2004. Aid, Policies, and Growth: Revisiting the Evidence. World Bank Policy Research Paper O-2834.

Bhushan, Aniket, and Yiagadeesen Samy. 2012. Aid and Taxation: Is Sub-Saharan Africa Different? Research Report, The North South Institute. www.nsi-ins.ca/wp-content/uploads/2013/02/2012-Aid-and-Taxation.pdf

Collier, Paul, and Jan Dehn. 2001. Aid, Shocks, and Growth. SSRN Working Paper. http://ssrn.com/abstract=632756

Collier, Paul, and David Dollar. 2002. Aid Allocations and Poverty Reductions. European Economic Review 46(8): 1475–1500.

Collier, Paul, and David Dollar. 2004. Development Effectiveness: What have we Learnt? Economic Journal 114(496): F244–F271.

Collier, Paul, and Anke Hoeffler. 2004. Aid Policies and Growth in Post-Conflict Societies. European Economic Review 48(5), 1125–1145.

Crivelli, Ernesto, and Sanjeev Gupta. 2016. Does Conditionality in IMF-Supported Programs Promote Revenue Reform? International Tax and Public Finance 23(3): 550–579.

Dalgaard, Carl-Johna, Henrik Hansen, and Finn Tarp. 2004. On the Empirics of Foreign Aid and Growth. Economic Journal 114(496): F191–F216.

Di John, Jonathan. 2006. The political economy of taxation and tax reform in developing countries. WIDER Research Paper No. 2006/74. https://www.wider.unu.edu/publication/political-economy-taxation-and-tax-reform-developing-countries

Di John, Jonathan. 2011. Taxation, developmental state capacity and poverty reduction. International Journal of Social Welfare 20(3): 270–279.

Dutta, Nabamita, and Claudia R. Williamson. 2016. Aiding Economic Freedom: Exploring the Role of Political Institutions. European Journal of Political Economy 45(S): 24–38.

Easterly, William. 2003. Can Foreign Aid Buy Growth? Journal of Economic Perspectives 17(3): 23–48.

Easterly, William, Ross Levine, and David Roodman. 2000. New Data, New Doubts: A Comment on Burnside and Dollar's 'Aid, Policies, and Growth' (2000). American Economic Review 94(3): 774–780.

Ertman, Thomas. 1997. Birth of the Leviathan. New York: Cambridge University Press.

European Commission. 2010. Tax and Development: Promoting Good Governance in Taxation as Part of Development Cooperation. MEMO/10/146 (April 21, 2010). Brussels. www.europa.eu/rapid/press-release_MEMO-10-146_en.pdf

Feenstra, Robert C., Robert Inklaar, and Marcel P. Timmer. 2015. The Next Generation of the Penn World Table. American Economic Review 105(10): 3150–3182.

Gennaioli, Nicola, and Hans-Joachim Voth. 2015. State Capacity and Military Conflict. Review of Economic Studies 82(4): 1409–1448.

Ghura, Dhaneshwar. 1998. Tax Revenue in Sub-Saharan Africa: Effects of Economic Policies and Corruption. IMF Working Paper 98/135. Washington, DC: International Monetary Fund.

Gupta, Sanjeev, and Shamsuddin Tareq. 2008. Mobilizing Revenue. Finance and Development 45(3): 44–47.

Gupta, Sanjeev, Benedict Clements, Alexander Pivovarsky, Erwin H. Tiongson. 2003. Foreign aid and revenue response: does the composition of aid matter? Applied Economic Letters 11(1): 209–212.

Gwartney, James, Robert A. Lawson, and Joshua C. Hall. 2017. Economic Freedom of the World: 2016 Annual Report. Fraser Institute, Vancouver.

Hall, Joshua C., and Robert A. Lawson. 2014. Economic Freedom of the World: An Accounting of the Literature. Contemporary Economic Policy 32(1): 1–19.

Hansen, Henrik, and Finn Tarp. 2000. Aid Effectiveness Disputed. Journal of International Development 12(3): 375–398.
Hansen, Henrik, and Finn Tarp. 2001. Aid and Growth Regressions. Journal of Development Economics 64(2), 547–570.
Heckelman, Jac. C., Stephen Knack. 2008. Foreign aid and market-liberalizing reform. Economica 75(299): 524–548.
Heckelman, Jac. C., Stephen Knack. 2009. Aid economic freedom and growth. Contemporary Economic Policy 27(1): 46–53.
Jia, Shaomeng, and Claudia R. Williamson. 2016. Aid, Policies and Growth: Revisiting with New Data. SSRN Working Paper. https://papers.ssrn.com/sol3/papers.cfm?abstract_id=2841926
Johnson, Noel D., and Mark Koyama. 2017. States and Economic Growth: Capacity and Constraints. European Journal of Political Economy 64(C): 1–20.
Kaldor, Nicholas. 1963. Will underdeveloped countries learn to tax? Foreign Affairs 41(January): 410–419.
Karras, Georgios. 2006. Foreign aid and long-run economic growth: empirical evidence for a panel of developing countries. Journal of International Development 18(1): 15–28.
Leuthold, Jane H. 1991. Tax Shares in Developing Countries: A Panel Study. Journal of Development Economics 35(1): 173–185.
Marshall, Monty G., Ted Robert Gurr, and Keith Jaggers. 2016. Polity IV Project: Political Regime Characteristics and Transitions, 1800–2015. Center for Systemic Peace.
North, Douglass C., and Robert P. Thomas. 1973. The Rise of the Western World: A New Economic History. New York: Cambridge University Press.
North, Douglass C., and Barry R. Weingast. 1989. Constitutions and Commitment: The Evolutions of Institutions Governing Public Choice in Seventeenth Century England. Journal of Economic History 49(4): 803–832.
Powell, Benjamin, Matthew Ryan. 2006. Does development aid lead to economic freedom? Journal of Private Enterprise 22(1): 1–21.
Psacharopoulos, George. 1994. Returns to Investment in Education: A Global Update. World Development 22 (9): 1325–1343.
Rajan, Raghuram G., and Arvind Subramanian. 2008. Aid and Growth: What does the Cross-Country Evidence Really Show? Review of Economics and Statistics 90(4): 643–655.
Remmer, Karen L. 2004. Does Foreign Aid Promote the Expansion of Government? American Journal of Political Science 48(1): 77–92.
Salter, Alexander W., and Andrew T. Young. 2018. Polycentric Sovereignty: The Medieval Constitution, Governance Quality, and the Wealth of Nations. Social Science Quarterly (forthcoming).
Stasavage, David. 2011. States of Credit: Size, Power, and the Development of European Polities. Princeton: Princeton University Press.

Strayer, Joseph R. 2016 [1970]. The Medieval Origins of the Modern State. Princeton: Princeton University Press.

Tilly, Charles. 1990. Coercion, Capital, and European States, AD 990–1990. Oxford: Blackwell.

United Nations. 2002. Monterrey Consensus on Financing for Development. New York: United Nations. http://www.un.org/esa/ffd/monterrey/MonterreyConsensus.pdf

United Nations. 2015. Addis Ababa Action Agenda of the Third International Conference on Financing for Development. New York: United Nations. http://www.un.org/esa/ffd/wp-content/uploads/2015/08/AAAA_Outcome.pdf

Williamson, Claudia R. 2010. Exploring the Failure of Foreign Aid: The Role of Incentives and Information. Review of Austrian Economics 23(1): 17–33.

World Bank. 2017. World Development Report: Governance and the Law. Washington, DC: World Bank.

Young, Andrew T., and K.M. Sheehan. 2014. Foreign Aid, Institutional Quality, and Growth. European Journal of Political Economy 36(C): 195–208.

CHAPTER 9

Foreign Aid and Repression

Faisal Z. Ahmed

Introduction

In official statements, US foreign aid is declared to promote political liberalization in recipient countries. For instance, the US Department of State proclaims: "The protection of fundamental human rights was a foundation stone in the United States over 200 years ago. Since then, a central goal of U.S. foreign aid has been the promotion of human rights, as embodied in the Universal Declaration of Human Rights."[1] This democracy-enhancing objective is shared by many other bilateral donors, such as Canada, Germany, Japan, and the United Kingdom. These pronouncements are guided by the view that democratic governance facilitates economic development. Yet for many recipient governments, aid inflows may offer an opportunity to politically repress their populations; thus, undermining a key feature of democracy.

This seems to be one of the tragic political ramifications associated with the world's largest bilateral aid donor: the United States. Using an instrumental variables research design, this chapter argues and presents evidence that US aid *causes* a reduction in the quality of political rights in recipient

F. Z. Ahmed (✉)
Princeton University, Princeton, NJ, USA
e-mail: fzahmed@princeton.edu

N. Dutta, C. R. Williamson (eds.), *Lessons on Foreign Aid and Economic Development*, https://doi.org/10.1007/978-3-030-22121-8_9

countries.[2] US aid does so in large part by reducing a government's tax effort which weakens its incentive to be politically accountable to its population. This finding runs counter to the stated intentions of the US government—and other donors—to foster political liberalization abroad via foreign aid.

How Foreign Aid Can Affect Political Rights

Foreign Aid and Political Liberalization

Existing scholarship identifies several channels through which aid can foster political liberalization.[3] For instance, building on modernization theories of democracy, Finkel et al. (2007, 410) argue that aid can "indirectly" transform the structural conditions that serve as prerequisites for regime transition (e.g., level of economic development, such as per capita GDP) and/or "directly" by empowering agents (individuals, political institutions, and social organizations) that struggle for regime change in the domestic arena. Reform-minded governments can also leverage aid to accelerate political liberalization. As Wright (2009) shows dictators with large distributional coalitions and who have a good chance of winning fair elections tend to respond to aid by democratizing.

The "context" (e.g., geopolitical considerations) in which aid is disbursed can also matter. For example, Dunning (2004) examines the importance of donor "intent" during and after the Cold War. No longer concerned with the potential defection to the Soviet Union, Western donors are less willing to prop up authoritarian governments with aid. Building on this argument, Bermeo (2011) provides evidence that aid from democratic donors (e.g., the United States, the United Kingdom) in the post-Cold War era is associated with improvements in democracy in recipient countries.

Foreign Aid and Repression

While aid has the potential to foster political liberalization, aid can also empower governments to restrict political freedom. Existing scholarship identifies at least two broad channels through which aid can foster political repression: by affecting the relationship between taxation and government accountability; and by curbing rent seeking.

The first channel stems from models of government insularity, which views the evolution of the state as the result of bargaining between revenue-maximizing leaders and their citizens (Tilly 1992). In these models, the political bargains governments make hinge on the distribution of this income in exchange for staying in power, as opposed to relinquishing some influence over policy choice in exchange for taxes. Foreign aid has been situated within such models. For example, Moore (1998) argues that as the share of government income from unearned income (e.g., foreign aid) increases, state/society relations are less likely to be "characterized by accountability, responsiveness, and democracy" (85). Thus, governments that do not collect taxes from their citizens because they are being financed by unearned income do not need to be as responsive to the needs of their populations (as would be the case with direct taxation) and may pursue policies that repress their populations.

A second, and not necessarily mutually exclusive, channel posits that aid can hurt political rights by exacerbating group conflict over unearned income. Basically, unearned government income increases the "size of the pie", and if there are multiple groups dividing the pie, rent seeking can contribute to increased fighting over it. As applied to autocracies where groups are less likely to attain their share of the pie through non-violent means, an exogenous financial windfall is likely to raise internal domestic discontent and incidences of political violence. In response, an incumbent regime is likely to employ additional repressive tactics to quell this domestic unrest (Besley and Persson 2011).

Empirical Challenges

Given these divergent predictions, scholars have turned to the data to reconcile the effect of aid on political rights (see Ahmed 2016 for a literature review). Of course, untangling the causal impact of aid on "politics" is problematic as aid disbursements are often correlated with a recipient's political conditions. On the one hand, aid may reward countries committed to political liberalization, such as US aid to shore up nascent Eastern Europe democracies after the end of the Cold War. On the other hand, aid may help stabilize autocratic allies (e.g., Egypt) and thus undermine political liberalization. To overcome this challenge, the subsequent sections leverage an instrumental variables strategy to evaluate the causal effect of the foreign aid from the world's largest bilateral aid donor—the United States—on political liberalization in over 150 recipient countries.

Evaluating the Causal Impact of US Aid

The Importance of US Aid

This chapter examines the effect of US foreign aid on political liberalization, as the United States is the world's largest bilateral aid donor. Since 1960, the United States has allocated over $700 billion in bilateral economic assistance. This figure excludes US military aid, US aid disbursements to multilateral organization (e.g., World Bank, regional development banks), and food aid. Figure 9.1 captures the temporal variation in total US bilateral economic aid (left scale) and as a share of total DAC (right scale) aid since 1960. US economic aid averaged nearly $17 billion per annum in the 1960s, during a period when robust domestic economic growth coupled with relatively intense Cold War tensions increased. As super-power rivalry eased during the period of détente and the US experienced a recession in the 1970s, US economic assistance fell to around $10 billion per annum (and maintained that annual average throughout the 1980s and 1990s). In the 2000s, primarily in response to the events of 9/11, US economic aid increased substantially. Since 2001, US economic

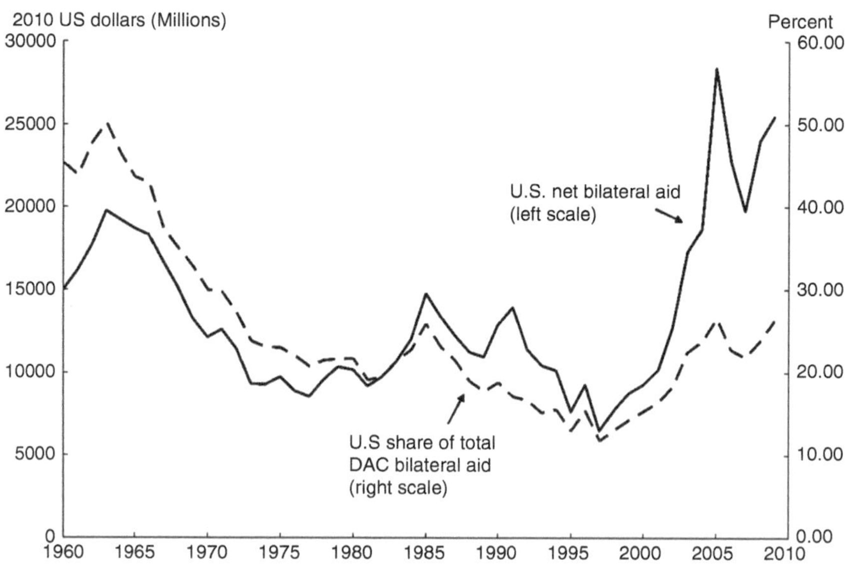

Fig. 9.1 US bilateral economic aid, 1960–2009. (Source: OECD DAC)

aid has averaged over $21 billion per year. Some of the largest recipients of US aid in the past 15 years have been Afghanistan, Iraq, Israel, and Egypt.

The US share of total DAC aid has also varied over time, ranging from a high of 50% in 1963 to a low of 12% in 1997. Since 1960, aggregate US aid has amounted to 28.5% of total DAC bilateral assistance, which exceeds the share of all other bilateral aid donors. Moreover, compared to the other four largest bilateral donors (France, Germany, Japan, and the United Kingdom), US aid also tends to be more volatile (annually). From an econometric standpoint this greater variability is advantageous because it will generate more precise estimates of the effect of US aid on political rights.

Political Economy of US Economic Aid

While recipient characteristics (e.g., "need", "merit") are important factors in shaping their annual receipts of foreign assistance, a significant component of the United States' foreign aid budget is determined through a political process. The majority of US aid is contained in the international affairs budget and is allocated through the State, Foreign Operations, and Related Agencies appropriations bill in the US Congress. The Legislative Branch plays a critical role in US foreign assistance, possessing the power both to authorize policy and to appropriate funds. In response to the President's budget submission (by February 2 every year), the House and Senate Budget committees are the first to act, setting funding ceilings for various parts of the budget and guiding the work of both authorizing and appropriations committees. Each year, 11–12 appropriations bills, including the State, Foreign Operations, and Related Agencies bill, make their way through a long deliberative process in both the House and the Senate. The appropriations committees, in coordination with the authorizing committees, determine and allocate federal spending each year, including foreign aid. Frequently, the resulting appropriations bills and accompanying reports include numerous detailed directives on how funds should be spent by country and account (Lancaster 2000).

This legislative process frequently reflects the political and partisan interests of Congressional representatives. For instance, members with a more right-leaning political ideology (e.g., Republicans) tend to oppose economic aid than members from more left-leaning districts (Fleck and Kilby 2006; Milner and Tingley 2010).[4] The existence of these partisan differences over aid allocation suggests that the legislative composition of Congress influences aid disbursements. In particular, existing theories and empirical evidence suggest that a more fragmented legislature contributes to higher government spending, including foreign aid appropriations (Roubini and Sachs 1989; Alesina and Tabellini 1990). The theoretical explanations stem from the well-established proposition that higher levels of aggregate political conflict (e.g., stemming from greater ideological/partisan differences in legislatures) will result in equilibrium fiscal outcomes that favor greater spending, since politicians will exhibit a greater proclivity in providing voters with program benefits. Moreover, greater heterogeneity in partisan preferences over fiscal policy is likely to require legislative logrolling, thus contributing to higher overall spending to accommodate different spending initiatives and to better ensure the bill's passage in Congress. A number of studies confirm this legislative fragmentation-spending relationship, both cross-nationally (Roubini and Sachs 1989; Alesina and Tabellini 1990) and, in particular for presidential systems, such as the United States (Alesina and Rosenthal 1995).

With respect to US bilateral aid disbursements, such a relationship is apparent in the legislative fragmentation of the US House of Representatives. Figure 9.2 depicts a robust positive correlation between average US bilateral aid disbursements and a measure of legislative fragmentation based on the difference in number of Democrats and Republicans in the US House of Representatives. Specifically, fragmentation ($FRAG_t$) in year t is defined as $\left(1-\frac{|DEMOCRAT_t - REPUBLICAN_t|}{435}\right)\times 100$, where a higher value corresponds to greater fragmentation. Using the *absolute* difference in the number of House Democrats and Republicans avoids explicitly incorporating measures of partisanship or ideology (e.g., DW-NOMINATE), which are potentially endogenous with actual preferences for foreign aid (e.g., Fleck and Kilby 2006).

Exploiting the legislative fragmentation from the US House of Representatives (rather than from the Senate) is advantageous for a number of reasons. First, all 435 members of the House are subject to reelection every two years as opposed to only one-third of the 100 senators. Empirically, this means the House $FRAG_t$ exhibits greater temporal variation than the Senate $FRAG_t$ and generates a statistically stronger and more precise instrumental variable for US aid. Second, and most importantly,

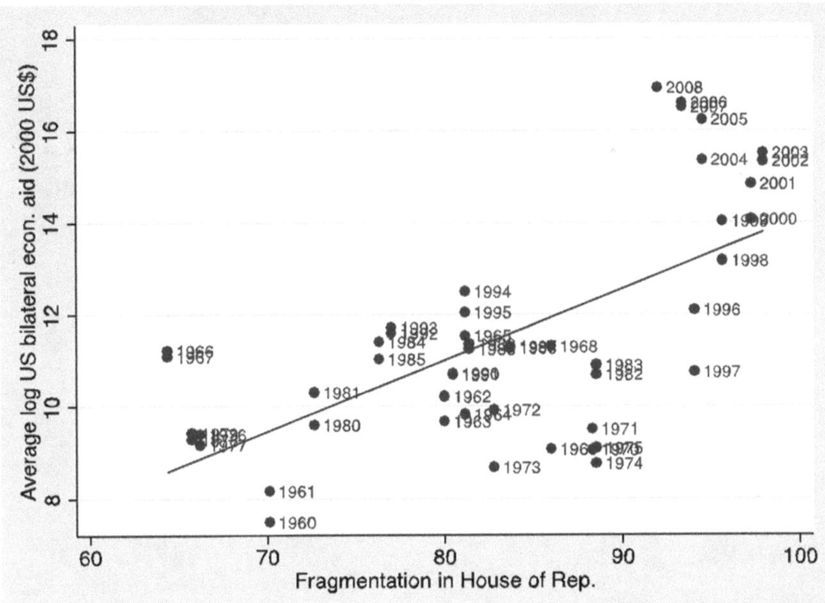

Fig. 9.2 Fragmentation in the US House of Representatives and average US bilateral aid disbursements. (Source: OECD DAC and United States Congress)

FRAG$_t$ is a plausibly exogenous source of temporal variation in US aid disbursements that is uncorrelated with political (and economic) conditions *within* aid recipients. Changes in the composition of the US House of Representatives occur bi-annually as a consequence of elections that are largely determined by local and national political and economic conditions, including (but not limited to) federal spending in Congressional districts, Presidential coattails, midterm elections, and retrospective economic voting. To the best of my knowledge, political conditions in poor developing countries have not been identified as a determinant for electoral outcomes in the US House of Representatives.

Heterogeneity in US Aid Recipients

The sensitivity of any particular country's receipts of aid to *FRAG$_t$* will be affected by that country's probability of actually receiving US aid in any given year. As Fig. 9.3 demonstrates, the US government tends to dole

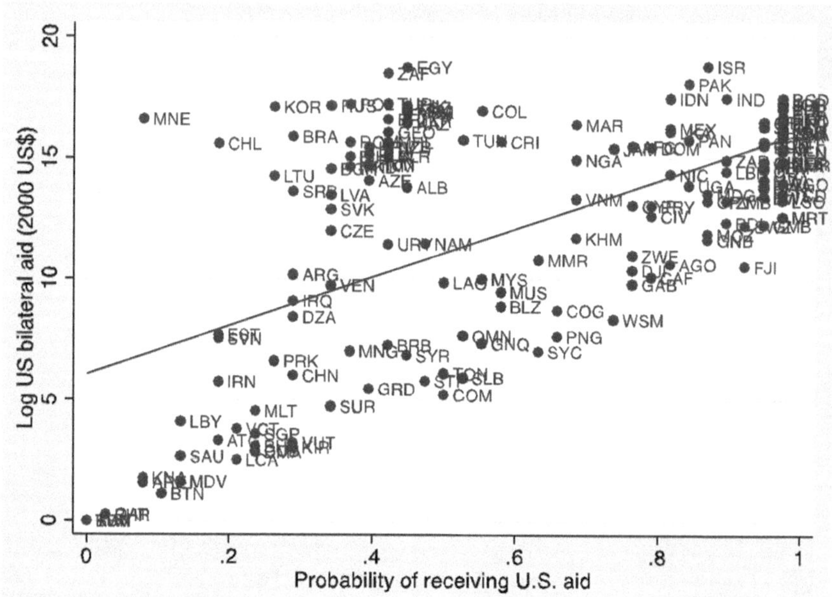

Fig. 9.3 Annual probability of receiving US aid (P_i) and average US bilateral economic aid (2000 US$). (Source: OECD DAC)

out higher amounts of aid to more frequent recipients. This figure plots a country's average receipts of US aid (over the period 1972–2008) against the country's annual probability of receiving any US aid, P_i.[5] For instance, Nigeria has a 68% probability of receiving US aid in any given year, with aid disbursements averaging $31.3 million per annum. In contrast, Algeria receives a substantially lower amount of aid ($41,803 on average per annum) about once every three years. The cross-sectional relationship identified in Fig. 9.3 is analogous to Nunn and Qian's (2014) observation that US bilateral food aid is higher for countries that receive food aid more frequently from the United States.

Interestingly, countries that tend to receive US aid *more* frequently are *less* likely to experience *changes* in their annual aid receipts. Or stated alternatively, more frequent aid recipients tend to have more stable (less variation) aid receipts from year to year. Empirically, this means the interaction of $FRAG_t$ and P_i will be negatively associated with US aid receipts; an effect that the first stage regression in Table 9.1 demonstrates.

Table 9.1 The legislative determinants of US bilateral aid (first stage regression)

	Type of US bilateral aid (in log units, 2000 US$)			
Dependent variable	*Economic*		*Econ. and military*	*Military*
	(1)	*(2)*	*(3)*	*(4)*
$FRAG_t \times P_i$	−0.343 (0.058)***	−0.342 (0.068)***	−0.314 (0.062)***	−0.153 (0.062)**
Recipient characteristics				
Fragmentation ($FRAG_t$)	0.37 (0.052)***			
Prob. of rec. aid (P_i)	40.73 (5.384)			
Log GDP per capita (2000 US$)	−0.099 (0.285)	−1.412 (0.801)*	−0.946 (0.709)	1.177 (1.541)
GDP per capita growth (% annual)	0.032 (0.019)	0.023 (0.012)*	0.023 (0.013)*	0.048 (0.020)**
Log population	0.571 (0.171)***	1.638 (1.907)	0.39 (1.913)	−2.684 (3.013)
UNSC member	−0.275 (0.406)	−0.065 (0.329)	0.054 (0.309)	−0.201 (0.476)
US ally	0.111 (0.538)	−0.256 (0.534)	1.279 (0.419)***	0.872 (0.651)
Log US exports (2000 US$)	0.153 (0.065)**	0.1 (0.064)	0.165 (0.065)**	0.118 (0.086)
Constant	−36.978 (5.229)***	20.62 (30.008)	34.132 (30.118)	53.779 (54.008)
Country fixed effects	N	Y	Y	Y
Year fixed effects	N	Y	Y	Y
R-squared	0.44	0.66	0.65	0.57
Number of observations	3853	3853	3853	3853
Number of countries	151	151	151	151
F-statistic on instrument	35.14	25.32	25.39	6.13

Notes: Estimation via OLS. Robust standard errors, clustered by country reported in parentheses. *, **, *** = significant at 10%, 5%, and 1% respectively

Source: Data is from OECD DAC, World Development Indicators, Correlates of War, and the United Nations

"Identifying" the Causal Effect of US Aid

I exploit these sources of variation in US aid disbursements to construct a powerful cross-national and time-varying instrumental variable (Z) for US aid. The basic idea is to use the instrument (Z) to predict some of the variation in the potentially endogenous variable, foreign aid. One can then use this "predicted variation" from an exogenous variable (Z) to evaluate the effect of foreign aid on the main outcome variable, political rights. This identification strategy is valid if two conditions hold: Z is a "strong" predictor of US aid and Z is uncorrelated with the outcome variable, political rights.

The discussion in the previous section suggests that the legislative fragmentation of the US House of Representatives and P_i may be helpful in explaining some of the variation in US aid disbursements and these two terms are unlikely to be correlated with political rights in developing countries. Thus, I interact the legislative fragmentation of the US House of Representatives ($FRAG_t$) with the probability a country receives US aid in any year (P_i) as an instrumental variable for US aid.

This instrument ($Z_{it} = FRAG_t \times P_i$), which is constructed by interacting a plausibly exogenous term ($FRAG_t$) with one that is potentially endogenous (P_i) can be interpreted as exogenous since the first stage and second stage regressions control for main effect of the endogenous variable (see equations below). Specifically, the identifying assumption is that the "endogenous" variable and the outcome of interest are jointly independent of the "exogenous" variable. Such an identification strategy underlies existing research examining the effect of foreign aid on politics (e.g., Nunn and Qian 2014; Ahmed and Werker 2015).

Armed with this instrumental variable, the 2SLS setup is:

$$\text{First Stage}: \text{AID}_{\text{it}} = \alpha + \beta\left(\text{FRAG}_{\text{t}}\ \text{x}\ \text{P}_{\text{i}}\right) + \gamma \text{X}_{\text{it}} + \text{Y}_{\text{t}} + \text{C}_{\text{i}} + \varepsilon_{\text{it.}}$$

$$\text{Second stage}: \text{RIGHTS}_{\text{it}} = \text{a} + \mathbf{b} * \text{AID}_{\text{it}} + \text{c} * \text{X}_{\text{it}} + \text{Y}_{\text{t}} + \text{C}_{\text{i}} + \text{u}_{\text{it.}}$$

Where i refers to the country, t indexes the year, X_{it} is a vector of controls, and C_i and Υ_t are dummies for countries and years respectively. The inclusion of country fixed effects implies the estimated coefficients will evaluate each aid recipient's within-country variation in $RIGHTS_{it}$. To account for serial correlation, the standard errors are conservatively clustered by country.

In the first stage regression, AID_{it} is each country's annual receipts of US bilateral economic aid, measured in logarithmic units (i.e, $\log(1+AID_{it})$). In the second stage regression, $RIGHTS_{it}$ is an increasing measure of political rights (where higher values imply *greater* political repression). *This means that if US aid harms political rights, the coefficient on AID_{it} (b) should be positive and statistically significant.*

In the second stage regression, $RIGHTS_{it}$ is Freedom House's *POLITICAL RIGHTS* index. Based on the opinions of experts, this index measures the ability for "people to participate freely in the political process, which is the system by which the polity chooses authoritative policy makers and attempts to make binding decisions affecting the national, regional, or local community" (e.g., the right to vote, the capacity of elected officials to have decisive votes on public policies). This index has been used in similar studies and has the largest country (~150) and temporal coverage (1973 onwards) compared to related measures, such as those from POLITY and CIRI Human Rights Project.

POLITICAL RIGHTS lies on a seven-point (1–7) scale, where *higher* values of *POLITICAL RIGHTS* (e.g., 6 or 7) correspond to *less* freedom. Turning to the instrument, $FRAG_t$ is equal to $\left(1-\frac{|DEMOCRAT_t - REPUBLICAN_t|}{435}\right)\times 100$; where a higher value (i.e., closer to 100) implies greater legislative fragmentation in the House of Representatives. The tendency for a country (i) to receive any aid is given by $P_i = \frac{1}{38}\sum_{t=1972}^{2009} P_{i,t}$ where $P_{i,t}$ is equal to 1 if that country receives any aid in year t and zero otherwise. Observe, the vector of country fixed effects absorbs this probability since P_i is specific to each country (i) and time-invariant. The inclusion of year fixed effects subsumes the main effect corresponding to legislative fragmentation since $FRAG_t$ changes from year to year, but remains the same across all aid recipients. Year fixed effects also account for any constant time trend in the independent and dependent variables.

In both stages, I control for a parsimonious set of covariates (X_{it}) that affects both the allocation of aid in the first stage regression and $RIGHTS_{it}$ in the second stage regression: log GDP per capita ("need") and economic growth ("merit").[6] I also control for a country's population size since smaller countries tend to receive disproportionately higher amounts of aid and the "cost" of political repression often varies by country size (Alesina and Dollar 2000). These control variables also serve to account for the main channels through which "modernization theories" can foster political liberalization (e.g., Finkel et al. 2007). Finally, to account for the United States' geopolitical motives in allocating its economic aid, I control for a recipient's annual consumption of US exports, its membership on the UNSC, and its alliance status with the United States (for further discussion of these geopolitical motives, see Ahmed 2016). The economic and demographic controls are drawn from the World Development Indicators. UN Security Council membership is available from the United Nations, alliances from the Correlates of War data set, and US exports from the International Monetary Fund.

US Aid Represses

This section presents the main results evaluating the effect of US foreign aid on repression. I first show that the instrumental variable is a robust and valid determinant of annual disbursements of US bilateral economic aid. I then move to the second stage regression and show that instrumented aid deteriorates political rights in recipient countries. The section ends by showing that US foreign aid harms political rights by lowering a government's "tax effort", thus weakening its incentives to be accountable to its population.

Determinants of US Bilateral Aid

Table 9.1 shows that the instrumental variable ($FRAG_t$ x P_i) is a robust determinant of annual bilateral disbursements of US aid to about 150 recipient countries. Column 1 presents a specification without any fixed effects. Consistent with Fig. 9.2, greater legislative fragmentation raises US aid disbursements (coefficient = 0.37). And consistent with Fig. 9.3, more frequent aid recipients receive higher amounts of aid (coefficient = 40.73). The coefficient on the instrumental variable is –0.34 and is highly statistically significant (p-value = 0.00). This negative coefficient is consistent with the claim that *more* frequent aid recipients tend to experience *less variation* change in annual US aid receipts. The corresponding F-statistic (=35.14) means the instrument is "strong" (since it exceeds the threshold of 9.6 suggested by Stock et al. 2002) and implies the second stage estimates can be interpreted as causal.

Column 2 shows that the instrument is a strong predictor of bilateral economic aid in a specification with country and year fixed effects. Note that this specification excludes $FRAG_t$ and P_i since they are subsumed by year and country fixed effects respectively. Column 3 shows that the instrumental variable is also a strong predictor of bilateral disbursements of US economic *and* military aid. Yet the instrument is a poor predictor of military aid by itself (column 4). In this regression, the coefficient estimate is much smaller in magnitude and the corresponding F-statistic (=6.13) is smaller than that associated with economic aid only. This drop in coefficient size and statistical precision is expected since Congress has less influence over the allocation of US military aid and therefore, movements in $FRAG_t$ should *not* affect these disbursements.

Given the strong predictive power of the instrument for economic aid from these first stage regressions, I therefore gauge the causal impact of US bilateral economic aid on repression in the second stage (although, as Table 9.2 shows instrumented US economic and military aid and instrumented military aid also harm political rights). Finally, in the first stage regressions, the control variables have their expected effects. In general, richer countries tend to receive lower amounts of aid, while those experiencing economic growth are "rewarded" with more aid. The time-varying geostrategic measures tend to have very little effect on US aid.

The Impact of US Aid on Political Rights

Table 9.2 evaluates the effect of US aid on political rights. Column 1 shows that in a "naïve" OLS specification, US economic aid has no impact on political rights. This effect is unsurprising and wholly consistent with the weak (or null) effects found in existing studies of aid on political rights. In contrast, column 2 shows that instrumented US aid *causes* a deterioration of political rights: a unit increase in log US economic aid raises *POLITICAL RIGHTS* by 0.15 index point. This effect is highly statistically significant (p-value < 0.01) and substantively meaningful: moving from the 10 percentile of aid receipts to merely the 50 percentile corresponds to around a 2.5 index point rise in *POLITICAL RIGHTS*. Such a jump corresponds to a 1.25 standard deviation increase in the *POLITICAL RIGHTS* index and is equivalent to moving from a less repressive country like Peru to a more repressive country like Sudan or Vietnam. This 2SLS

Table 9.2 US aid harms political rights (second stage regression)

Dependent variable	*Political rights*				
	(1)	*(2)*	*(3)*	*(4)*	*(5)*
Method of estimation	OLS	2SLS	2SLS	2SLS	2SLS
Economic aid	−0.01 (0.010)	0.149 (0.069)**	0.157 (0.059)***		
Econ. and military aid				0.171 (0.064)***	
Military aid					0.351 (0.191)*
Controls					
Fragmentation ($FRAG_t$)		−0.048 (0.010)***			
Prob. of rec. aid (P_i)		−2.13 (1.012)**			
Recip. characteristics	Yes	Yes	Yes	Yes	Yes
Country fixed effects	Yes	No	Yes	Yes	Yes
Year fixed effects	Yes	No	Yes	Yes	Yes
R-squared	0.73	0.003	0.64	0.64	0.07
Number of observations	3853	3853	3853	3853	3853
Number of countries	151	151	151	151	151
F-stat on instrument		35.14	25.32	25.39	6.13

Notes: Robust standard errors, clustered by country reported in parentheses. *, **, *** = significant at 10%, 5%, and 1% respectively. Economic aid is US bilateral economic aid (2000 US$, log units). Military aid is US bilateral military aid (2000 US$, log units). Recipient characteristics include log GDP per capita, GDP per capita growth, log population, UNSC member, US ally, and US exports. These coefficients, country fixed and year fixed effects, and a constant are not reported.

Source: Data is from OECD DAC, World Development Indicators, Correlates of War, and the United Nations

estimate and those with fixed effects are larger than the OLS estimates, suggesting that they adjust for the tendency of US aid to be directed to countries with higher quality of democratic governance.[7] The control variables (not reported) are consistent with existing findings. For example, richer countries (i.e., higher GDP per capita) are less repressive.

Instrumented US economic and military aid also harms political rights (column 4), as does military aid separately (column 5). US economic aid harms political rights when controlling for military aid separately, as well in specifications that lag aid by one, two, and five years. As expected, the effect of lagged aid on *POLITICAL RIGHTS* is smaller than contemporaneous aid. The results also hold with data averaged over two- and five-year periods. Finally, to allay concerns that controlling for time-varying recipient characteristics (e.g., level of economic development), may introduce potential "post-treatment bias", instrumented US economic aid continues to damage political rights in a specification without these controls.[8]

Robustness

The core results in Table 9.2 are robust to an exhaustive list of other potential concerns, such as: country and temporal outliers (e.g., exclusion of frequent aid recipients, restriction of samples to the post-Cold War and pre-2001 periods); spatial diffusion; the inclusion of additional controls (e.g., political institutions, oil exports, arms imports, overall trade openness); conflict; percentage of foreign-born population; alternate instruments (e.g., using fragmentation in the Senate); alternate specifications (e.g., controlling for lags and leads of aid, time-varying measures of P_i); alternate clustering of the errors (e.g., by region, year, two-way clustering); the "crowding-out" of aid from other donors; regional trends (e.g., differential effects for Africa); and region- and country-specific trends that vary across the Cold War and post-Cold War period. The core results also hold for alternate measures of the main second stage dependent variable. For example, US aid harms other forms of human rights: civil liberties (Freedom House 2011); political participation (Marshall and Jaggers 2010); and freedoms associated with religious, empowerment rights, and imprisonment (Cingranelli and Richards 2008).[9]

US Aid Reduces Tax Effort

Why might US aid harm political rights? As described earlier, one such channel follows from a model of government insularity.[10] In particular, as a source of nontax income, foreign aid inflows can empower governments to reduce their tax effort, thus permitting them to be less accountable to their population (i.e., more repressive). Empirically, this suggests that the amount of taxes collected from citizens (as a share of total government revenues) should be negatively correlated with aid inflows. To test this mechanism, I regress a state's collection of taxes from income, profits, and capital gains (as a percent of government revenue) on US bilateral aid disbursements plus the baseline controls. A reduction in this dependent variable implies a government exerts less tax effort because it is able to derive a larger share of its revenue from nontax sources.

Table 9.3 US aid lowers tax effort

Dependent variable	*Income tax (share of government revenue)*		
	(1)	*(2)*	*(3)*
Method of estimation	OLS	2SLS	2SLS
Log US aid	−0.324	−1.864	−1.938
	(0.200)*	(1.045)*	(1.023)**
Political rights			−0.050
			(0.556)
Number of observations	925	925	915
Number of countries	113	113	111
R-squared	0.83	0.7	0.69

Notes: Robust standard errors, clustered by country reported in parentheses. *, ** = significant at 10% and 5% respectively. All specifications control for recipient characteristics (i.e., log GDP per capita, GDP per capita growth, log population, UNSC member, US ally, and US exports), country, and year fixed effects. These coefficients and a constant are not reported.

Source: Data is from OECD DAC, World Development Indicators, Correlates of War, and the United Nations

Table 9.3 presents compelling evidence that US aid reduces tax effort. In a naïve OLS regression, US aid is negatively associated with tax effort (column 1). In column 2, instrumented US aid has a much larger and statistically significant effect on tax effort. Moreover, controlling for the potential mediating effect of repression does not attenuate the negative effect of instrumented US aid on tax effort (column 3). Instrumented aid also exhibits a negative effect on the level (in dollars and log units) of taxes collected (not reported). Together, the results in Table 9.3 suggest that US aid harms political rights by reducing a government's tax effort.

Conclusion

Since its inception, the US government—like many other governments—has employed foreign aid as an important component of its foreign economic policy. As an instrument of American economic statecraft, the United States claims to use its bilateral economic aid to promote its national interest by expanding democracy and free markets, while improving the lives of citizens in developing countries. This chapter presents evidence to cast doubt on this assertion. US aid can empower recipient governments to repress their populations, thus weakening an important feature of democracy.

This finding refutes some recent empirical findings that aid may improve political rights in countries that have exhibited a commitment—both instrumental and normative—to political liberalization. Indeed, while policymakers and practitioners hope that foreign aid promotes greater democratic governance, merely examining the correlation between US aid and measures of democracy can be problematic. For instance, if the US government "rewards" countries that undertake democratic reforms, it is unclear whether additional US aid necessarily helps these governments on their reform trajectory. It is quite plausible that these countries would have continued with their reforms *without* additional US aid. Overcoming this concern requires "identifying" a plausibly exogenous of variation in US aid that is uncorrelated with politics in recipient countries. This chapter uses an instrumental variable to better evaluate the causal effect of US aid on an important dimension of democracy: political rights.

Indeed, the evidence in this chapter provides evidence of a channel through which US aid fosters political repression in recipient countries. US aid can actually weaken a government's tax effort, thus reducing its incentive to be democratically accountable to its population. Consequently, to the extent that political liberalization is an important conduit for growth, the article's findings suggest that US aid may also reduce economic development. Future research could investigate this, potentially through the lenses of aid's impact on other dimensions domestic politics in recipient countries (e.g., levels of corruption, constraints on government leaders and so on).

Notes

1. See http://www.state.gov/j/drl/hr/index.htm (Accessed: April 2016).
2. An instrumental variable (Z) can help mitigate concerns with endogeneity bias, such as reverse causality. For instance, if a country's political rights (Y) influence a country's receipts of foreign aid (X) then estimating the causal effect of X on Y will be biased. A valid instrument Z can help overcome this issue if Z is a strong predictor of variation in X but is uncorrelated with the main outcome variable, Y.
3. This section presents an abridged discussion on the discussion through which aid can affect political liberalization. For more detailed discussions, see Finkel et al. (2007), Wright (2009), and Ahmed (2016).
4. In contrast, House members from more right-leaning districts favor *military aid* than do members from less right-leaning district.

5. P_i is based on the proportion of years between 1972 and 2008 a country receives any US aid.
6. Hoeffler and Outram (2011) discuss the "need" and "merit" based determinants of foreign aid.
7. In general, more frequent US aid recipients (who also receive larger amounts of assistance) tend to be democratic. On average, P_i is negatively correlated with *POLITICAL RIGHTS* (see Table 2, column 2).
8. These results are available in Ahmed (2016), Table 2 columns 6–10.
9. These robustness checks are discussed and presented in Ahmed (2016) and its accompanying appendices.
10. Ahmed (2016) shows that US aid does not foster repression via the rent-seeking mechanism.

References

Ahmed, Faisal Z. 2016. "Does foreign aid harm political rights? Evidence from U.S. aid", Quarterly Journal of Political Science, 11(2): 183–217.

Ahmed, Faisal Z. and Eric D. Werker. 2015. "Aid and the Rise and Fall of Conflict in the Muslim World", Quarterly Journal of Political Science, 10(2): 155–186.

Alesina, Alberto and David Dollar. 2000. "Who gives aid to whom and why?", Journal of Economic Growth, 5 (1): 33–63.

Alesina, Alberto and Guido Tabellini. 1990. "A Positive Theory of Fiscal Deficits and Government Debt", Review of Economic Studies, 57(July): 403–414.

Alesina, Alberto and Howard Rosenthal. 1995. Partisan Politics, Divided Government and the Economy, New York, NY: Cambridge University Press.

Bermeo, Sarah. 2011. "Foreign aid and regime change: A role for donor intent", World Development, 39(11): 2021–2031.

Besley, Timothy and Torsten Persson. 2011. "The Logic of Political Violence", Quarterly Journal of Economics, 126: 1411–1445.

Cingranelli, David L. and David L. Richards. 2008. "The Cingranelli-Richards (CIRI) Human Rights Data Project Coding Manual Version 2008.3.13." http://ciri.binghamton.edu/documentation/ciri_coding_guide.pdf

Dunning, Thad. 2004. "Conditioning the Effects of Aid: Cold War Politics, Donor Credibility, and Democracy in Africa", International Organization, 58(Spring): 409–423.

Finkel, Steven E., Anibal Perez-Linan, and Mitchell A. Seligson. 2007. "The Effects of U.S. Foreign Assistance on Democracy Building, 1990–2003", World Politics, 59 (April): 404–439.

Fleck, Robert K. and Christopher Kilby. 2006. "How Do Political Changes Influence U.S. bilateral Aid Allocations?: Evidence from Panel Data", Review of Development Economics, 10(2): 210–223.

Freedom House. 2011. "Freedom in the World Comparative and Historical Data", Available: http://www.freedomhouse.org/report-types/freedom-world

Hoeffler, Anke and Verity Outram. 2011. "Need, Merit or Self-Interest – What Determines the Allocation of Aid?", Review of Development Economics, 15(2): 237–250.

Lancaster, Carol. 2000. Transforming Foreign Aid: United States Assistance in the 21st Century, Washington D.C.: Peterson Institute.

Nunn, Nathan and Nancy Qian. 2014. "Aiding Conflict: The impact of U.S. Food Aid on Civil War", American Economic Review, 104(6): 1630–66.

Marshall, Monty G. and Keith Jaggers. 2010. *Polity IV Data set*, College Park, MD: Center for International Development and Conflict Management, University of Maryland.

Milner, Helen V. and Dustin H. Tingley. 2010. "The Political Economy of US Foreign Aid: American Legislators and the Domestic Politics of Aid", Economics and Politics, 22(2): 200–232.

Moore, Mick. 1998. "Death without Taxes: Democracy, State Capacity, and Aid Dependence in the Fourth World." In The Democratic Developmental State: Politics and Institutional Design, ed. Mark Robinson and Gordon White. Oxford: Oxford University Press.

Roubini, Nouriel and Jeffrey Sachs. 1989. "Political and Economic Determinants of Budget Deficits in the Industrial Economies", European Economic Review, 33: 903–938.

Stock, James H., Jonathan H. Wright, and Motohiro Yogo. 2002. "A Survey of Weak Instruments and Weak Identification in Generalized Method of Moments", Journal of Business and Statistics, 20(4): 518–529.

Tilly, Charles. 1992. Coercion, Capital, and European States, AD 990–1992. Cambridge MA: Blackwell.

World Bank. 2010. *World Development Indicators, 2010.* Washington D.C.: World Bank.

Wright, Joseph. 2009. "How can foreign aid foster democratization in authoritarian regimes", American Journal of Political Science, 53(3): 552–571.

CHAPTER 10

Can Foreign Aid Promote Political and Economic Freedom?

Nabamita Dutta, Michael A. Fakutiju, and Claudia R. Williamson

Introduction

Political and economic freedom are seen as values in themselves, are associated with increases in quality of life across many dimensions, and are often espoused by donors as a goal for foreign aid. An extensive literature exists examining foreign aid's effect on institutional quality; however, robust evidence regarding these associations are mixed. No conclusive answer is reached as to whether foreign aid promotes or degrades political or economic institutions. Various authors claim that aid has a positive impact on recipients' institutions, while others show that it actually has a negative impact. Another interesting perspective is that aid's impact on institutional quality is conditional on existing institutions.

N. Dutta (✉)
University of Wisconsin-La Crosse, La Crosse, WI, USA
e-mail: ndutta@uwlax.edu

M. A. Fakutiju • C. R. Williamson
Mississippi State University, Mississippi, MS, USA
e-mail: maf536@msstate.edu; claudia.williamson@msstate.edu

N. Dutta, C. R. Williamson (eds.), *Lessons on Foreign Aid and Economic Development*, https://doi.org/10.1007/978-3-030-22121-8_10

With higher aid inflows, recipient nations benefit not only from financial resources but also from knowledge, expertise, and technical assistance provided by the donor staff. This knowledge may include how to achieve political or economic freedom. In addition, aid can compensate politically powerful groups in the short run that might otherwise lose out by the adoption of democratic, market-oriented policies, improving the likelihood of reform. As a result, aid can positively influence political and economic transformation toward more freedoms (Heckelman and Knack 2008). Thus, foreign aid can influence institutional quality via three main channels: direct monetary transfer, conditionality, and knowledge transfer (Dreher and Gehring 2012).

Alternatively, aid can degrade institutional quality by expending the role of the state, promoting government over private investment, and entrenching inefficient and corrupt regimes (Dutta and Williamson 2016a, b). As early as 1957, Friedman warned that foreign aid may hurt a recipient country's political institutions and civil liberties. For one thing, aid increases the size of the government (Boone 1996). By providing an alternate source of revenue, aid can disincentivize governments to create efficient institutions (Devarajan et al. 2001, chapter 1). Since aid dollars typically go to the recipient government, political leaders may take up inefficient investment projects and subsidize state-owned enterprises (Heckelman and Knack 2008). In addition, as pointed out by Collier (1997), foreign aid can have unintended consequences such as increased tax revenues and greater trade taxes based on donor advice. Aid is also linked to increases in rent seeking and centralization of power, leading to a deterioration of institutional quality (Djankov et al. 2008).

Recently, scholars have advanced the conditionality hypothesis: aid's impact on institutional quality depends on the pre-existing level of institutions (both political and economic). For example, democratically constrained governments will be more likely to utilize aid in a manner that promotes more freedom. Democratic checks minimize the ability for recipient governments to misappropriate aid funds and increase the likelihood that conditions are met. As a result, aid may be channeled to beneficial uses including positive political and economic reforms.

Theoretically, the prediction of aid's ability to buy political and economic freedoms is ambiguous. Empirical studies also find conflicting evidence. A large literature concludes that aid does not increase institutional quality and may decrease it. For example, Djankov et al. (2008) conclude that aid is a "curse" for institutional quality in a recipient country. Windfalls of foreign aid "may result in the same rent-seeking behavior as documented in the 'curse of natural resources' literature" (Djankov et al. 2008, p. 169). Knack (2004) demonstrates that aid undermines institutional quality by not promoting democracy or increasing the probability of reform toward a democratic regime.

In addition, several studies show that aid can decrease economic freedom (Knack 2001; Young and Sheehan 2014). Heckelman and Knack (2008) find that aid decreases freedom in the 1980s, but aid does not significantly impact economic freedom in the 1990s. In a follow-up study, Heckelman and Knack (2009) conclude that aid has no significant effect on economic institutions. Dreher and Rupprecht (2007) and Knedlik and Kronthaler (2007) focus on changes in economic freedom and find that IMF involvement reduces economic freedom.

However, Bearce and Tirone (2010) show that aid has no effect on economic freedom before the 1990s but has a positive effect after the Cold War. Boockmann and Dreher (2003) document that the number of World Bank projects increases economic freedom. Similarly, Askarov and Doucouliagos (2015) find that aid positively affects democratization in transition countries.

Empirically, others highlight that aid effectiveness is conditional on recipients' pre-existing institutions. As pointed out by Kono and Montinola (2009), Wright (2009), and Dutta et al. (2013) the ability of foreign aid to influence a country's level of democracy is conditional on the existing political institutional infrastructure including the level of democracy and age of the regime. Similarly, Kalyvitis and Vlachaki (2012) show that the probability of reform toward a democratic regime depends on prior economic liberalization. Dutta and Williamson (2016a, b) establish that aid's impact on economic freedom depends on the recipient nations' quality of political institutions. For democratic countries, aid may improve economic freedom; but it may decrease it in autocracies.

This chapter summarizes recent theoretical arguments and empirical evidence examining the associations between foreign aid and political and economic institutional quality. We focus on more recent works; thus, our chapter is not a comprehensive review of the literature. Our summary highlights the ambiguity that exists and believes more research is needed to understand how aid affects institutions. Collectively, this literature suggests that aid responds differently depending on the institutional context, and these results depend on the identification strategy, including estimation selection and choice of instrumental variable(s). Thus, our summary supports the lack of robustness across previous studies and highlights the difficulty in drawing strong policy conclusions.

Aid and Political Institutions

Theoretical Arguments

An optimistic view of foreign aid thinks aid has the ability to make dictatorships into democracies. Aid may directly influence political institutions as it can "release governments from… revenue constraints" (Bräutigam and Knack 2004, p. 255) and enhance the accountability of political institutions.

Knack (2004) highlights several channels through which aid can promote political freedom. First, technical assistance and other support can strengthen opposing branches of government in autocratic regimes. If so, aid can check the executive's power, diminishing autocratic control. Foreign aid specific to organizing democratic elections and supporting election infrastructure, such as providing security at voting locations, monitoring election-day activities, and providing external observers who can certify the legitimacy of electoral outcomes, may also increase political rights and freedoms. Similarly, if targeted aid can strengthen the rule of law by improving the criminal justice system, it could also improve recipients' political institutions. Supporting this view, Bräutigam and Knack (2004) state that aid can serve as a source of revenue to government, enabling leaders to strengthen domestic institutions. It can also provide training and technical assistance which help boost efficiency and effectiveness of governance in recipient countries.

Second, foreign aid may enhance democracy in recipient nations by improving education and income. Research suggests that richer and more educated individuals demand more political freedom. If this is true, and aid has the power to increase education and income among recipients, aid can promote democracy in autocratic countries. Thus, aid may have a positive unintended, indirect effect on governance (Dijkstra 2018).

Third, foreign aid may increase political freedom through conditionality. Donors can require that recipients increase democratization as a condition of continued assistance, compelling aid recipients to allow more political freedom.

Foreign aid's effect on governance can be unanticipated and unintended. A pessimistic view of foreign aid believes aid will directly turn democracies into dictatorships. Foreign aid gives untrustworthy leaders resources that can be used to repress their populations, corroding democratic institutions needed for economic growth, national wellbeing, and self-determination. Bauer (2000) argues that foreign aid suffers from an important asymmetry: foreign aid is only a small percentage of a recipients' national income but a large percentage of developing countries' discretionary government spending. This gives aid substantial power to increase corrupt rulers' control over resources, allowing them to further concentrate political power, which in turn leads to greater dictatorship.

Similar to Bauer, Dijkstra (2018) contends that large flows of aid weaken domestic accountability, and often increase corruption in recipient countries because governments are no longer dependent on the consent of governing bodies or that of the population (Moyo 2009; Moss et al. 2008). Moreover, aid may strengthen authoritarian regimes by providing them with resources for increasing repression or for buying off (potential) opposition (Dijkstra 2018). Likewise, countries that depend largely on external rents, for example, oil profits or foreign aid, are less accountable to civil society than are governments that must rely on tax revenue (Ross 2001).

Erbeznik (2011) highlights that monetary transfers have negative unintended consequences on the incentives to reform in recipient countries. For example, aid has failed to promote rule of law reform because an influx of aid money provides few incentives for political elites to commit themselves to the sacrifices needed for real reform and democratic accountability. The additional funds enable the elites to remain in power without any institutional reform. In addition, the presence of many donors can have unintended negative effects on governance. The many different projects with different implementation and reporting requirements distract the attention of government officers from their regular planning and implementation activities and weaken state capacities. Therefore, aid, much like oil, tends to hinder political freedom resulting in a political foreign aid resource curse (Easterly 2006; Djankov et al. 2008; Deaton 2013).

On the contrary, Altincekic and Bearce (2014) argue that there is no political foreign aid resource curse. They contend that aid is not oil. Oil has certain key properties: fungibility, no conditionality, and relatively constant. Aid is less fungible (it is more sector specific), more conditional (donors demand that their aid be spent on particular public goods), and aid is less constant compared to state oil revenue. This makes it difficult for recipient governments to use aid to fund either repression or appeasement as they would with oil rent. Thus aid should not hinder democracy.

Dutta, Leeson, and Williamson (2013) offer a third theoretical view about aid's impact on recipient countries' political institutions called the "amplification effect." According to this hypothesis, foreign aid neither causes democracies to become more dictatorial nor causes dictatorships to become more democratic. It only amplifies recipients' existing political institutional orientations. Aid makes dictatorships more dictatorial and democracies more democratic.

Foreign aid provided to corrupt dictators will only amplify their political paths as aid resources intended for democratization are likely to be appropriated and used by autocrats to strengthen their control. By the same logic, democratic recipient countries can use aid to strengthen democratic rights. They have stronger separations of power and more effective checks on executive power, which help to safeguard against misappropriation of aid dollars. Democratic governments can use foreign aid to help solidify political rights and freedoms. This view is similar to Morrison (2007, 2009), Kono and Montinola (2009), Wright (2009), and Bueno de Mesquita and Smith (2010) who highlight aid's institutionally stabilizing effects.

Empirical Evidence

Empirical works support both the optimistic and pessimistic aid perspective. For example, for a subset of African countries, Goldsmith (2001) finds that more aid is associated with more political freedom, civil liberties, and economic freedom. More recently, a sizeable number of authors have reported positive effects of aid on political institutions. In examining aggregate unintended effects of aid, Dijkstra (2018) reviews the empirical evidence of aid on good governance. He argues that the negative impacts of aid on governance are much exaggerated, and that the total effect of aid on democracy is more positive post-Cold War (Dunning 2004). Likewise, its impact on government capacity and to reduce corruption has improved overtime with more studies showing a positive effect of aid on political stability.

More recent empirical works do not support an aid resource curse argument. For example, Bermeo (2016) empirically demonstrates that aid does not have the same negative effect on government as oil, providing a counter to Djankov et al. (2008). In the same light, Altincekic and Bearce (2014) used Ordinary Least Squares (OLS) and an error correction model specification on aid recipients from 1961 to 2006 to show that aid does not produce a political curse.

Heckelman (2010) relates aid to changes in a democracy index for 26 transition nations in Eastern Europe and former Soviet republics from 1997 to 2007. Using OLS, he finds that an increase in aid per capita is beneficial to democratic reforms. Foreign aid helped transition nations in Eastern Europe improve their governance and judicial framework. Askarov and Doucouliagos (2015) also find that aid positively affects democratization in transition countries.

Jones and Tarp (2016) utilize advanced estimation techniques, including random effects, system Generalized Method of Moments (GMM), and bias corrected fixed effects, on a large panel dataset of 104 countries from 1983 to 2010. They find a small positive net effect of aid on political institutions, concluding that aid has not had a systematic negative effect on political institutions. Altunbas and Thornton (2014) also use advanced estimation methodologies, including instrumenting for aid and system GMM, to examine the impact of foreign aid on democracy in 93 developing countries over the period 1971–2010. They concluded that foreign aid promotes democracy. In the same vein, Kersting and Kilby (2014) examine the long run association between aid and democracy with interval regressions on a cross-section of 122 countries from 1972 to 2011. The authors find a significant positive correlation between aid and democracy, indicating that over the long run aid can promote democratization of recipient countries.

Other authors reporting aid's positive impact on political institutions stress conditionality. For instance, Gibson, Hoffman, and Jablonski (2015) used OLS, Ordered Probit, and GMM estimators on Sub-Saharan African countries from 1980 to 2000. Their results show that targeted aid via technical assistance helps to explain the timing and extent of Africa's democratization. Unless economic liberalization has already occurred, Kalyvitis and Vlachaki (2012) suggest that aid decreases the probability of reform toward a democratic regime. Thus, aid's ability to promote political freedom is conditional on economic freedom.

Similarly, Dunning (2004) explains his findings due to post-Cold War conditionalities imposed by donors. Using OLS and two-stage least squares (2SLS) estimation methods, he finds no statistical significant relation between aid and democracy from 1975 to 1986. However, over the 1987–1997 period, the relation between foreign aid and democracy turns positive and statistically significant. This was due to donors' threats to make the disbursement of further aid contingent on the adoption of domestic political reforms.

Testing the amplification effect, Dutta, Leeson, and Williamson (2013) empirically demonstrate that foreign aid's effect on political reform is conditional on a recipient country's pre-existing political institution. Using panel data that covers 124 developing countries from 1960 to 2009, they find that foreign aid increases political freedom in democracies but decreases it among dictatorial countries. They conclude that aid does not alter recipient countries' institutional paths—it amplifies their existing ones.

Not all papers report a positive effect of aid on political institutions. Evidence exist suggesting negative or at best neutral effects of aid on political institutions. Knack (2004) concludes that aid does not promote democracy. For example, Bräutigam and Knack (2004), using OLS, Ordered Logit, and 2SLS methods from 1982 to 1997 for 32 African countries, find evidence that higher aid levels are associated with larger declines in the quality of governance. This has led to lower accountability of the government to its people.

Jablonski (2014) shows that aid distribution can increase incumbent vote share, suggesting that aid may entrench democratic leaders. In the same vein, Asongu (2012) uses 2SLS and system GMM on 52 African countries for the period 1996–2010. He finds a positive relation between aid and corruption. Djankov, Montalvo, and Reynal-Querol (2008) lend support to Bauer's hypothesis. They empirically show that aid weakens recipients' democracy and does so more than natural resource richness does via the resource curse. Rajan and Subramanian (2007), Smith (2008), Kalyvitis and Vlachaki (2012), and Bueno de Mesquita and Smith (2009) provide additional support for the idea that aid may have a corrosive effect on recipients' political institutions.

Aid may also encourage political instability and coup (Grossman 1992). In some extreme situations, aid may even increase violent civil conflicts. Maren (1997) finds evidence that food aid causes Somalia's civil war. Nielsen et al. (2011) suggest that sudden decreasing aid will cause more conflicts, hence donor countries need to gradually decrease aid to prevent conflicts from happening. Nunn and Qian (2014) find that increasing US food aid would increase civil conflicts in recipient countries, in terms of both incidence and duration, but not on interstate or onset of conflicts.

Aid and Economic Institutions

Theoretical Evidence

As with political institutions, theoretical arguments exist for both sides as to whether foreign aid can positively influence a recipient country's economic institutions. Dreher and Gehring (2012) summarize three main arguments to explain how aid can influence economic freedom. First, direct monetary transfers provide funding for public investments and public goods without the need to raise taxes (Vasquez 1998). This in effect raises economic freedom since no additional taxes were collected. Aid dollars can also provide financing to build economic infrastructure in resource constrained countries, which can allow for more business formation. In addition, foreign aid can promote economic freedom by directly investing in entrepreneurs and by reducing arbitrary business regulations that hamper competition.

Second, recipient nations can also benefit from knowledge, expertise, and technical assistance provided by the donor staff. This knowledge can include promoting market-oriented economic reforms, a prime reason that led to the Washington Consensus—foreign aid should promote free trade, sound money, and property rights. Foreign aid donors can explicitly state that the role of aid is to promote free market economic policies with the aim of limiting economic activities by government (Heckelman and Knack 2005). That is, foreign aid is intended by donors to improve the policy environment for private sector development in recipient nations by encouraging market liberalization, and donor staff expertise is available to help transition toward economic freedom.

Third, donors can shift a recipient country's economic institutions by allocating aid conditional on improving the economic policy environment. Practically speaking, aid be used to compensate politically powerful groups in the short run that might otherwise lose out by the adoption of market-oriented policies, improving the likelihood of reform. Thus, aid may positively influence economic transformation toward economic freedom (Heckelman and Knack 2008).

Similarly, Heckelman and Knack (2005) state that aid can affect policies in several ways: (1) it can create opportunities for donor staff to offer policy advice informally or in the form of technical cooperation; and (2) aid can be allocated on the principle of selectivity—favoring recipients with a more favorable policy environment. Like conditionality, selectivity can incentivize recipient governments to implement market-oriented reforms in order to increase their aid allocation.

Yet, on the other hand, by providing an alternate source of revenue, aid can disincentivize governments to create efficient economic institutions (Devarajan et al. 2001, chapter 1). Since aid goes to the recipient government, political leaders may take up inefficient pet projects and subsidize state-owned enterprises (Heckelman and Knack 2008). In addition, as pointed out by Collier (1997) foreign aid can lead to increased tax revenues and greater trade taxes based on donor advice.

Aid can also increase in rent seeking and centralization of power, leading to a deterioration of institutional quality (Djankov et al. 2008). By strengthening government at the expense of the private sector, aid can reduce pressure on government to maintain an environment favorable to private enterprise. The state becomes larger relative to the private sector, contributing to increased central planning, collectivization, and public takeovers of foreign enterprises. Ultimately, these unintended consequences reduce private entrepreneurship. The money available to governments can also deteriorate the quality of economic regulation by making rent seeking more attractive and increasing corruption (Svensson 1999).

Policy conditionality sounds good in theory, but it is noted that it might backfire. Countries that are persuaded to reform also have an incentive to implement minimum reforms necessary to trigger the release of aid funds, but then reverse the reforms with the promise of future reform in exchange for additional foreign aid (Collier 1997).

Another form of conditionality is the existence of democracy to protect against misappropriation of funds. Dutta and Williamson (2016a, b) emphasize the importance of democratic checks on the impact of aid, as democracies can minimize the ability of recipient governments to misappropriate aid funds. Recipient governments may be willing to liberalize economic institutions if donors provide financial incentives to do so, and democratic checks exist to channel aid dollars to the intended goal. In the same vein, aid's impact on economic freedom might be negative in autocratic countries due to misaligned incentives, corruption, lack of monitoring, and accountability.

Empirical Evidence

Theoretically, aid's impact on economic institutions is ambiguous. Empirical studies also find conflicting evidence. Morrissey (2015) reviews recent evidence on effects of aid on government spending and tax effort in recipient countries. He concludes that aid finances government spending but there is no systematic effect of aid on taxes. Supporting this last conclusion, Crivelli and Gupta (2016) argue that revenue conditionality by IMF has been effective in offsetting the potential negative effect of aid on tax revenue.

Others document a direct positive link between aid and economic freedom. Bearce and Tirone (2010) show that aid has no effect on economic freedom before the 1990s but has a positive effect after the Cold War. Boockmann and Dreher (2003) document that the number of World Bank projects increases economic freedom.

Other authors are less convinced that aid has positive impact on economic institutions. Powell and Ryan (2005) find that from 1970 to 2000 foreign aid decreases economic freedom. They also document that as economic freedom increases, foreign aid decreases. This highlights that more free countries typically do not need aid, but it also suggests that political leaders might choose to not liberalize in order to continue receiving more aid dollars.

Using OLS and Granger-causality tests over the 1980–2000 period on 76 developing countries, Heckelman and Knack (2005) find that aid discourages and slows market-oriented policy and institutional reform. They specifically show that aid harms growth through slowing reform in property rights and sound money—which are major areas of market-oriented policy and institutional reform. Heckelman and Knack (2008) find that aid decreases freedom in the 1980s, but aid does not significantly impact economic freedom in the 1990s. In a follow-up study, Heckelman and Knack (2009) conclude that aid has no significant effect on economic institutions.

Using OLS and two-stage least square estimations on a panel of 166 countries from 1970 to 2010, Young and Sheehan (2014) examine the effects of foreign aid flows on variety of measures of institutional quality. They find that aid flows have a negative impact on both political and economic institutions. Dreher and Rupprecht (2007) and Knedlik and Kronthaler (2007) focus on changes in economic freedom and find that IMF involvement reduces economic freedom.

Related, Alesina and Weder (2002) do not find evidence that aid may reduce the level of corruption. In addition, aid may also be linked to cronyism and patrimonialism (Buss and Gardner 2005), weak governance

(Rajan and Subramanian 2007), and more government interventions (Easterly 2014).

Dutta and Williamson (2016a, b) test foreign aid's impact on economic freedom by employing five estimators, including OLS, instrumental variable (IV) estimation, two-way fixed effects, IV fixed effects, and system GMM on a panel of 108 countries from 1971 to 2010. They establish that aid's impact on economic freedom depends on the recipient nations' quality of political institutions. For democratic countries, aid may improve economic freedom; but it may decrease it in autocracies. Collectively, the results suggest that aid may improve economic freedom when given to wealthier, economically free, and mature democracies. This suggests that aid responds differently depending on the macroeconomic and institutional context. They warn, however, that the results are highly sensitive to model selection, identification strategies, choice of controls, time period sample, and measurement of aid. As such, it is difficult to draw a definitive conclusion regarding foreign aid's influence on economic institutions. Donors and policymakers should be cautious when attempting to influence economic institutional quality given that aid's impact is highly context specific.

In a similar exercise, Dutta and Williamson (2016a, b) test foreign aid's effect on press freedom, a subset of economic freedom. Using 2SLS analysis with IV estimation on a panel of up to 106 aid recipient countries from 1994 to 2010, they find that aid only has a positive and significant effect on press freedom when given to democratic countries; however, the size of the effect is relatively small. Meanwhile, in most cases, aid has no impact on press freedom in autocracies.

Another group of studies relates aid to specific aspects of economic freedom. Remmer (2004) finds that bilateral aid increases government spending. Ear (2007) finds that ODA reduces property rights and increases regulations, but Kilby (2005) shows that aid decreases regulations. Cali and te Velde (2011) find that aid specific to trade reduces trading costs. Dreher (2005) finds a connection between IMF projects and lower inflation rates.

Conclusion

Previous findings are often inconclusive and contradictory. It is difficult to draw generalizations summarizing if foreign aid positively or negatively affects institutional quality. The evidence seems to be more mixed for political institutions with authors finding that aid increases democracy under certain circumstances, but it may also lead to more autocracy. The amplification effect helps to resolve this ambiguity where aid does not alter the paths of political institutions; it only amplifies a country's political path. The evidence regarding economic institutions is more supportive that aid decreases economic institutional quality. Conditionality also matters for economic institutional quality where aid may increase economic freedom in wealthier, democratic countries.

Collectively, this literature suggests that aid responds differently depending on the institutional context, and these results depend on the identification strategy. Thus, our summary supports the lack of robustness across previous studies and highlights the difficulty in drawing strong policy conclusions. This suggests that donors should be cautious when attempting to influence institutions. Aid may lead to marginal improvements under the right conditions, but it may not be capable of major institutional shifts. In addition, most countries that "need" aid do not have high-quality, democratic institutions; thus, any positive improvement in institutional quality attributed to foreign aid is not likely to happen in most aid receiving countries. Overall, this highlights the sensitive nature of finding a top-down, one size fits all solution to institutional improvements.

We believe this highlights the need for additional work in order to understand how aid can alter a country's institutions and when it might do so. In order to draw any conclusions, a common empirical framework should be adopted. This includes how to address endogeneity concerns.

References

Alesina, Alberto, and Beatrice Weder. 2002. Do Corrupt Governments Receive Less Foreign Aid? American Economic Review, 92 (4): 1126–1137.

Altincekic, C., and D. H. Bearce. 2014. Why there should be No Political Foreign Aid Curse. World Development, 64, 18–32.

Altunbas, Y., and J. Thornton. 2014. The (small) blessing of foreign aid: further evidence on aid's impact on democracy. Applied Economics, 46(32), 3922–3930.

Askarov, Z., and H. Doucouliagos. 2015. Aid and institutions in transition economies. European Journal of Political Economy, 38, 55–70.

Asongu, S. A. 2012. On the effect of foreign aid on corruption. African Governance and Development Institute Working Paper, WP/12/031.

Bauer, Peter T. 2000. From Subsistence to Exchange and Other Essays. Princeton: Princeton University Press.

Bearce, D.H., and D. C. Tirone. 2010. Foreign Aid Effectiveness and the Strategic Goals of Donor Governments. The Journal of Politics, 72, 3, 837–851.

Bermeo, S. B. 2016. Aid Is Not Oil: Donor Utility, Heterogeneous Aid, and the Aid Democratization Relationship. International Organization, 70(1), 1–32.

Boockmann, B., and A. Dreher. 2003. The Contribution of the IMF and the World Bank to Economic Freedom. European Journal of Political Economy, 19(3), 633–649.

Boone, P. 1996. Politics and the Effectiveness of Foreign Aid. European Economic Review, 40: 289–329.

Bräutigam, D. A., and S. Knack. 2004. Foreign Aid, Institutions, and Governance in Sub-Saharan Africa. Economic Development and Cultural Change, 52(2), 225.

Bueno de Mesquita, Bruce, and Alastair Smith. 2009. Political Survival and Endogenous Institutional Change. Comparative Political Studies, 42: 167–197.

Bueno de Mesquita, Bruce, and Alastair Smith. 2010. Leader Survival, Revolutions, and the Nature of Government Finance. American Journal of Political Science. 54(4), 936–950.

Buss, Terry F., and Adam Gardner. 2005. Why Foreign Aid to Haiti Failed – And How to Do It Better Next Time. Foreign Aid and Foreign Policy: Lessons for The Next Half-Century: 173.

Cali, M., and D. W. te Velde. 2011. Does Aid for Trade Really Improve Trade Performance? World Development, 39(5),725–740.

Collier, P. 1997. The Failure of Conditionality. in C. Gwin and J. Nelson, eds., Perspectives on Aid and Development, Washington, DC: Overseas Development Council.

Crivelli, E., and S. Gupta. 2016. Does Conditionality Mitigate the Potential Negative Effect of Aid on Revenues? IMF Working Papers 16/142.

Deaton, A. 2013. The great escape: Health, wealth, and the origins of inequality. Princeton, NJ: Princeton University Press.

Devarajan, S., D. Dollar, and T. Holmgren. 2001. Aid and Reform in Africa. Washington, D.C.: World Bank.

Dijkstra, G. 2018. Aid and good governance; Examining aggregate unintended effects of aid. Evaluation and Program Planning, 68, 225–232.

Djankov, S., J. G. Montalvo, and M. Reynal-Querol. 2008. The curse of aid. Journal of Economic Growth, 13, 169–194.

Dreher, A. 2005. Does the IMF Influence Fiscal and Monetary Policy? The Journal of Policy Reform, 8(3), 225–238.

Dreher, A., and K. Gehring. 2012. Does Aid Buy (Economic) Freedom? Economic Freedom of the World: 2012. Annual Report, Fraser Institute, Chapter 5.

Dreher, A., and S. Rupprecht 2007. IMF Programs and Reforms—Inhibition or Encouragement? Economics Letters, 95(3): 320–326.

Dunning, T. 2004. Conditioning the Effects of Aid: Cold War Politics, Donor Credibility, and Democracy in Africa. International Organization, 58: 409–423.

Dutta, N. D., P. T. Leeson, and C. R. Williamson. 2013. The Amplification Effect: Foreign Aid's Impact on Political Institutions. Kyklos, 66(2), 208–228.

Dutta, N., and C. R. Williamson. 2016a. Aiding economic freedom: Exploring the role of political institutions. European Journal of Political Economy, 45, 24–38.

Dutta, N., and C. R. Williamson. 2016b. Can foreign aid free the press? Journal of Institutional Economics, 12(03), 603–621.

Ear, S. 2007. Does Aid Dependence Worsen Governance? International Public Management Journal, 10(3), 259–286.

Easterly, W. 2006. White man's burden: Why the west's efforts to aid the rest have done so much ill and so little good. New York: Penguin Press.

Easterly, William. 2014. The Tyranny of Experts: How the Fight Against Global Poverty Suppressed Individual Rights. New York: Perseus Books Group.

Erbeznik, K. 2011. Money Can't Buy You Law: The Effects of Foreign Aid on the Rule of Law in Developing Countries. Indiana Journal of Global Legal Studies, 18(2).

Friedman, M. 1957. Foreign Economic Aid: Means and Objectives. Yale Review, 47(4), 500–516.

Gibson, C. C., B. D. Hoffman, and R. S. Jablonski. 2015. Did Aid Promote Democracy in Africa? The Role of Technical Assistance in Africa's Transitions. World Development, 68, 323–335.

Goldsmith, A. 2001. Foreign Aid and Statehood in Africa. International Organization, 55, 123–148.

Grossman, H. I. 1992. Foreign Aid and Insurrection. Defense and Peace Economics, 3(4): 275–288.

Heckelman, J. C. 2010. Aid and Democratization in the Transition Economies. Kyklos, (4), 558–579.

Heckelman, J., and S. Knack. 2005. Foreign Aid and Market-Liberalizing Reform. World Bank Policy Research Working Paper 3557.

Heckelman, J. C., and S. Knack. 2008. Foreign Aid and Market-Liberalizing Reform. Economica, 75, 524–548.

Heckelman, J. C., and S. Knack. 2009. Aid economic freedom and growth. Contemporary Economic Policy, 27, 46–53.

Jablonski, R. S. 2014. How aid targets votes: the impact of electoral incentives on foreign aid distribution. World Politics, 66(2), 293–330.

Jones, S., and F. Tarp. 2016. Does foreign aid harm political institutions? Journal of Development Economics, 118, 266–281.

Kalyvitis, Sarantis, and Irene Vlachaki. 2012. When Does More Aid Imply Less Democracy? An Empirical Examination. European Journal of Political Economy, 28(1): 132–146.

Kersting, E., and C. Kilby. 2014. Aid and democracy redux. European Economic Review, 67, 125–143.

Kilby, C. 2005. Aid and Regulation. Quarterly Review of Economics and Finance, 45, 325–345.

Knack, S. 2001. Aid Dependence and the Quality of Governance: Cross-Country Empirical Tests. Southern Economic Journal, 68(2), 310–329.

Knack, S. 2004. Does Foreign Aid Promote Democracy? International Studies Quarterly, 48: 251–266.

Knedlik, T., and F. Kronthaler. 2007. Aid and Economic Freedom: An Empirical Investigation Using the Heritage Index. Journal of Development Perspectives, 3(1): 116–135.

Kono, Daniel, Yuichi, and Gabriella R. Montinola. 2009. Does Foreign Aid Support Autocrats, Democrats, or Both? Journal of Politics. 71: 704–718.

Maren, Michael. 1997. The Road to Hell: The Ravaging Effect of Foreign Aid and International Charity. New York: The Free Press.

Morrison, Kevin M. 2007. Natural Resources, Aid, and Democratization: A Best Case Scenario. Public Choice, 131: 365–386.

Morrison, Kevin M. 2009. Oil, Nontax Revenue, and the Redistributional Foundations of Regime Stability. International Organization, 63: 107–138.

Morrissey, O. 2015. Aid and government fiscal behavior: What does the evidence say? World Development, 69, 98–105.

Moss, T., G. Petterson, and N. Van de Walle. 2008. Ad aid-institution paradox? A review essay on aid dependency and state building in Sub-Saharan Africa. (i. W. 255–281, Ed.) Cambridge, MA: MIT Press.

Moyo, D. 2009. Dead aid: Why aid is not working and how there is another way for Africa. London/New York: Allan Lane/Penguin Books.

Nielsen, Richard A., Michael G. Findley, Zachary S. Davis, Tara Candland, and Daniel L. Nielson. 2011. Foreign Aid Shocks as A Cause of Violent Armed Conflict. American Journal of Political Science, 55(2): 219–232.

Nunn, Nathan, and Nancy Qian. 2014. US Food Aid and Civil Conflict. American Economic Review, 104(6): 1630–66.

Powell, B., and M. Ryan. 2005. Development Aid and Economic Freedom: Are They Related? Independent Institute Working Paper, (60).

Rajan, Raghuram G., and Arvind Subramanian. 2007. Does Aid Affect Governance? American Economic Review, 97: 322–327.

Remmer, K. L. 2004. Does Foreign Aid Promote the Expansion of Government? Political Science, 48(1), 77–92.

Ross, L. M. 2001. Does Oil Hinder Democracy? World Politics, 53(3), 325–361.

Smith, Alastair. 2008. The Perils of Unearned Income. Journal of Politics, 70: 780–793.

Svensson, Jakob. 1999. Aid, Growth and Democracy. Economics and Politics, 11: 275–297. University Press.

Vasquez, I. 1998. Official Assistance, Economic Freedom, and Policy Change: Is Foreign Aid like Champagne? Cato Journal, 18, 2: 275–286.

Wright, J. 2009. How Foreign Aid Can Foster Democratization in Authoritarian Regimes. American Journal of Political Science, 53, 552–571.

Young, A.T., and K. M. Sheehan. 2014. Foreign Aid, Institutional Quality, and Growth. European Journal of Political Economy, 36, 195–208.

SECTION IV

The Political Economy of Privately Provided Aid

CHAPTER 11

Potential Pitfalls in Private Aid: A Cautionary Note for Non-Governmental Assistance

Thomas K. Duncan

Introduction

Since the turn of the century, there has been a shift in the approach to economic development taken by the Western world. Once it became "obvious that earlier public policy models of economic development and poverty reduction were less effective than desired…international institutions, devoted to promoting development throughout the world, began a reassessment of their aid programs and the general mode of thinking about the problem of underdevelopment" (Boettke 2005: 235). After repeated failures to generate economic growth and prosperity through top-down technocratic approaches (Easterly 2009, 2015), military means (Coyne 2005a, b, 2006, 2008), and top-down humanitarian efforts (Coyne 2013; Duncan and Coyne 2015b), there has been pressure from the economic literature to focus on institutional and cultural change in the developing world (North 1990; Boettke 1998; Boettke and Fink 2011). This reassessment is still an ongoing process, but along with a shift in thinking over the issues of development there has also been a shift in the nature of foreign aid delivery and financing that reflect the acknowledgment

T. K. Duncan (✉)
Radford University, Radford, VA, USA
e-mail: tduncan13@radford.edu

N. Dutta, C. R. Williamson (eds.), *Lessons on Foreign Aid and Economic Development*, https://doi.org/10.1007/978-3-030-22121-8_11

of the need for change. With "official aid channels…facing sustained criticism for favoring political ends rather than development concerns in the allocation of funds across countries, and for failing to deliver results in many cases…Citizens in rich countries are increasingly looking to channel their funds through private organizations, rather than through governments" (Kharas 2007: 4).

The landscape of economic development has seen a continued shift away from a predominance of Official Development Aid (ODA) toward reliance on more private means. Since 2000, "All types of international financing to developing countries have grown" with "private flows (remittances) [having] grown the fastest (242% over 2000–2016, compared to 113% of commercial flows and 101% of official flows)" (Development Initiatives 2018: 3). While remittances have been the fastest growing type of financing and is likely underestimated due to the inability of official statistics measuring informal remittances (Sy and Rakotondrazaka 2015: 3), commercial, or private capital flows, remain the dominant form of financial flows to the developing world (The Index of Global Philanthropy and Remittances 2016: 6; Development Initiatives 2018: 3). As of 2014, "private financial flows of capital investment, remittances, and philanthropy was $801 billion…of which $764 billion came from DAC donors, and $37 billion from the non-DAC donors measured by CGP. Government aid totaled $147 billion with $137 billion from DAC donors and $10 billion from the 11 non-DAC donors measured" (The Index of Global Philanthropy and Remittances 2016: 5).

While private development assistance (or private philanthropy)[1] remains fourth in dollars spent behind commercial (or private capital) flows,[2] remittances,[3] and official government aid for the world (The Index of Global Philanthropy and Remittances 2016: 6), the swing toward privatization of flows has led private philanthropy in the US to now exceed ODA (Adelman 2009: 25; The Index of Global Philanthropy and Remittances 2016: 9). This shift in balance has a dramatic effect on development efforts as more than "two thirds of all private development assistance comes from private sources in the United States…[where] the US is an even more significant contributor of private development assistance (providing 69% of the total in 2013) than of ODA (17% of the total in 2013)" (Development Initiatives 2016: 2). The US provides approximately nine times the private philanthropy as the UK, which is the next closest contributor (The Index of Global Philanthropy and Remittances 2016: 10). Private aid, then, is of particular interest to scholars who want to study the impact that the US has on the international aid community.

In any study of private aid effectiveness, however, it is necessary to distinguish the overall appeal of private development assistance in relation to Official Development Aid. While it is possible for private aid to perform more effectively than ODA, those who see it as a cure-all may assume too much. Private aid must also overcome a number of obstacles that are similar in nature to those faced by official assistance. In order to highlight these potential pitfalls, the remainder of this chapter will proceed as follows. Section "The Appeal of Private Aid" will discuss the issues faced by ODA and discuss the theoretical appeal of private assistance. Section "NGOs and Aid" will provide an overview of non-governmental organizations (NGOs) to illustrate the particular challenges that private aid still must overcome. Section "Implications and Conclusion" will conclude.

The Appeal of Private Aid

Issues arise with the utilization of ODA for development purposes for a number of reasons, all of which are not resolved by the shift toward private philanthropy. The traditional framework for analyzing official aid is fairly straightforward. As described by Kharas (2007: 3):

> Citizens in rich countries pay taxes to their governments, some of which are used for development assistance. These rich country governments on-lend or grant money to poor country governments, who in turn implement programs and policies designed to accelerate development and reduce poverty. The framework works well when the public in rich countries is willing to have tax revenues spent on aid, when rich country governments have confidence in poor country governments to develop appropriate projects and programs and when poor country governments have the capacity to implement these programs so as to generate the desired developmental results.

The neat box of this framework begins to break down once certain dubious assumptions prove to be problematic, and each assumption made above is accompanied by a measure of dubiousness. The ability or willingness of poor country governments to develop or implement those projects and programs is not guaranteed (Easterly 2006, 2009, 2015; Guest 2010; Coyne 2013). There are inconsistent results regarding the ability or willingness of rich country governments to select poor country governments based on their confidence that development will arise (Coyne and Mathers 2010; Coyne 2013; Easterly 2015; Duncan and Coyne 2015b). Questions arise regarding the willingness of citizens in rich countries to have their tax dollars spent on aid, in what quantities, and for what purposes (Smith 1990; Milner and Tingley 2013; Stoianova 2013) as well as the willingness of citizens in poor countries to accept aid, in what quantities, and for what purposes (Duncan and Coyne 2015b; Milner et al. 2016). Simply put, the concept of "desired developmental results" omits discussion of the level of decision-making on what those results may be.

The idea that there is confusion between desire and results along the official aid path from citizens in rich countries to citizens in poor should not be shocking. Rather than utilizing market mechanisms for determining the allocation of resources, the tax and spend model of aid distribution remains a top-down undertaking (Kapur and Whittle 2010: 1150), and the budgetary process itself creates separation between outcomes and "the private sacrifices required for its operation. Assessing the personal distributions of benefits and costs associated with the various programs is impractical, and likely to remain so" (Brubaker 1997: 355). Rich country citizens do not have a direct link between liability and the subsequent value-creation of aid projects as it is "the tax system in place, along with its various exemptions and exclusions that determines the liability" (Wagner 2012: 43) and the "ends to be served by the fiscal system are determined by political decisions" (Buchanan 1949: 504). With the link between giver and taker severed, the incentive structure is not one that generates concern for current revenue stream-to-value calculations (Coyne and Duncan 2019). In short, the ODA channels provide numerous places for which the principle-agent problem can be exacerbated.

Ostensibly, private aid is better adapted to close this separation. Private donations are voluntary in nature, implying that private aid donors can be more selective about the programs they support (Kharas 2007: 5) in both amount of support and what types of outcomes they are attempting to achieve. Private aid also has the potential to circumvent the state apparatuses of both the rich country government and the poor country government (Smith 1990; Kragelund 2004; Knack 2014),[4] implying that private aid can operate more quickly and efficiently than its official counterpart. Private aid may also provide a direct link between the rich country donors and the poor country recipients as it may allow funds to go directly to organizations working within recipient countries who are more in touch with the individuals therein (Bebbington 2005; Peterson 2014). While these are all potential implied reason for the idea that private aid is more capable of success than official aid, there is still the question of whether or not these implications hold under scrutiny. If private aid is to actually be more successful, it must better answer the fundamental questions than official aid does: (1) are rich country citizens (donors) satisfied, (2) do private organizations make better decisions than rich country governments, (3) do private organizations make better decisions than poor country governments, and (4) are poor country citizens (recipients) satisfied? Each of these questions does have significant overlap with the others. To put the question succinctly: can private aid arrangements solve the principal-agent problems better than official aid arrangements?

A surface-level discussion of private aid would suggest that the answer to that question is "yes" given the reasoning above. The switch to a voluntary basis for aid rather than a process of generalized taxation and spending should provide private actors with the ability to better signal their discontent. In private charity, unlike official aid, there is the idea that "the giver is giving directly to the intended recipient...through churches, religious institutions, not for profit organizations, NGOs, and other approved entities that are accountable to report to their respective government...Here, the giver gives something tangible and of value to an intermediary institution that then either uses those funds to help address needs or provides a conduit for those funds to get to the intended recipient" (PovertyCure.org n.d.). However, a deeper analysis may indicate a more nuanced approach is necessary. The calculation of private philanthropy typically includes contribution numbers from foundations, corporations, private and voluntary organizations, individual volunteer time, religious organizations, and universities and colleges. Not all private aid works the same way, suggesting that there may be varying degrees of success depending upon the way that the aid is transferred from rich countries to poor countries. More importantly, the lack of success may not be the worst outcome of private philanthropy as "Even the most altruistic giving, with the best of intentions, does not necessarily achieve the desired end. As with government-to-government foreign aid, sometimes charitable giving may actually do harm" (PovertyCure.org n.d.). Also, it should be noted that not all private aid is completely private. Each of the listed types of philanthropic activities may have differing objectives and functionalities, however the significant utilization of non-government organizations cannot be ignored. Though differing activities will face challenges that are unique to their specific structures and implementations, the analysis of non-government organizations provides useful examples of the types of issues that private philanthropy may face and, subsequently, must overcome.

NGOs and Aid

Non-government organizations, or NGOs, are the main channel and mobilizers for private support (Stoianova 2013). According to Development Initiatives (2016: 4), more than "half of private development assistance comes from NGOs" with corporations providing approximately 20% and foundations providing 16%. It is also estimated, incompletely, that "there are somewhere between 6000 and 30,000 national NGOs in developing countries" (Kharas 2007: 4). While those numbers include data from the OECD it is worth noting that if two-thirds of world funding comes from the US and over one half of world private philanthropy funding comes from NGOs, the implication is that US-based NGOs are major factors in the distribution of private aid. Beyond just the dollar amounts, "NGOs are widely perceived to have set many of the global public policy agendas..., including issues like unsustainable debt, environmental degradation, human rights law, landmine removal, and corporate social responsibility" (Jordan and Van Tuijl 2006: 4). Given such importance, the nature of the NGO must be discussed in detail.

The Structure of NGOs

The appeal of NGOs mirrors and highlights the general appeal of private aid. These organizations are typically "self-governing, private, not-for-profit" (Jordan and Van Tuijl 2006: 8) and are "seen as having the capacity to react more quickly and impartially than government institutions in bringing aid" (Smith 1990: 3). While there is a rational basis for this idea, NGOs do tend to have a number of structural designs in place that mimic governmental structures. It is not and should not be surprising that this structural overlap exists. Both fundamentally operate outside of a market context, implying that the decentralized decision-making processes will be weak or not available. The similarities in the problems faced for both lead to similarities in organizational structure. In both instances, those attempting to shape the world through aid must rely on a top-down, bureaucratic system for implementing their goals.

With governmental interventions, including the use of official aid, the goal is to "alleviate potential or existing human suffering and to improve the human condition" (Coyne 2013: 18). Given this objective, official aid and its implementation in the poorer country is "an attempt to produce a more beneficial allocation of resources, planned and implemented by the intervening state" (Duncan and Coyne 2015b: 686). A major issue that arises with this attempt is that efficient resource allocation is not determined a priori, but rather is the outcome of the process of market activity (Mises [1920] 1990, [1922] 1981, [1949] 2007; Hayek 1945; Kirzner 1973). Absent the "higgling and bargaining of the market" (Smith [1776] 1991: 37) with its feedback mechanisms of monetary prices, profit and loss, the knowledge of individual preferences and resource valuations is "not given to anyone in its totality" (Hayek 1945: 520). The channels of official aid, utilizing rich country governments and poor country governments, almost by definition are intended to circumvent the market process. However, resources must still be allocated in some way, leading aid channels to rely on a non-market method of allocation. Rather than utilizing the decentralized information network of market activity, purveyors of official aid default to administrative decision-making that involves the reliance upon a combination of bureaucratic structures and humanitarian "experts" (Easterly 2015; Duncan and Coyne 2015b).

In providing private aid, non-government organizations are similarly attempting to reallocate resources without the use of market mechanisms. Though they are private and non-governmental by design, their not-for-profit status and mission to alleviate human suffering and improve the human condition are reminiscent of state-led agencies and organizations. It should not be overly shocking, then, that the NGO organizational structure is one that also moves toward administrative decision-making and bureaucratic mechanisms relying upon expert advice.[5] This shift toward non-market allocation and its structural impact creates a series of unintended consequences, namely revolving around changes in the incentive-compatibility of the organization. Firstly, while NGOs "can bring expertise and local knowledge to the need being addressed...there is no guarantee of this" (PovertyCure.org n.d.) as "outside of the market context there is no way for experts to determine the true opportunity cost of resources. Due to the lack of market feedback, the technological experts will remain, regardless of years of experience and the level of their expertise, unable to actually fulfill their informational role" (Duncan and Coyne 2015a: 400). Secondly, but related to the first, once administrative decision-making becomes the source of allocation, "administrative determinations, based on the intervener's [or expert's] preference for resource distribution, take precedent over the determinations of those who consume the resources" (Duncan and Coyne 2015b: 687; see also Hoff 1949; de Soto 2010). The combination of these phenomena may lead to a further series of missteps and unforeseen issues in the process of private aid distribution.

Unintended Consequences of Expert Information: Solving the Planner's Problem

The overall point is that whether it is official aid or private aid, if there is not a price system providing the information necessary for the allocation of resources, then someone other than the "buyer" must make decisions regarding where resources go, which resources go, and how much go. Kapur and Whittle (2010: 1149–1150) describe the typical flow of information for aid projects as flowing from Service Providers to Intermediaries to Principals (or Funders), a line that does not include the actual beneficiaries of the programs. Rather, the authors note (Kapur and Whittle: 1150) that "the preferences of beneficiaries and their reactions to aid projects have often been inferred" for "a variety of reasons, including the cost of communications, long distances, language, and attitudes." In order to be a more efficient source of aid than official agencies, private organizations and NGOs must show that they are better able to overcome these reasons or provide more accurate inferences. To illustrate effectiveness in solving the informational feedback problem, NGOs should demonstrate some capacity for sending aid to where it is most needed or provides the most benefit, as well as showing an increased capacity for solving the problems it is intended to solve.

The evidence for whether NGOs perform more admirably is mixed at best. Büthe, Major, and Souza (2012) show that "humanitarian need" is a predictor of where NGOs allocate private aid, but that there does not seem to be a correlation between where private flows go and the expected "bang for the buck."[6] Other studies have found less correlation between need and distribution of aid. Fruttero and Gauri (2005) discuss how indicators of poverty are not the only or necessarily the most important determinant of aid target locations. Barr, Fafchamps, and Owens (2005: 673) also find that aid tends not to get to the poorest parts of poor countries, and that even when NGOs attempt to solve the informational problem by increasing the involvement of the target population, the methods of identifying the actual target population may be suspect. Or as Kapur and

Whittle (2010: 1153) note, "there is no clear evidence that private foreign aid programs achieve their intended goals."

In order to illustrate the difficulty in administrative resource allocation, it may be useful to consider a humanitarian scenario where donors generously donated medical devices to the Mulago National Referral Hospital and the Bwindi Community Hospital in Uganda as described in Duncan and Coyne (2015b: 688–689; see also Miesen 2013). The hospitals were able to receive the devices, including incubators for Mulago's Neonatal Intensive Care Unit and an anesthesia machine for Bwindi. Yet in both cases, the medical devices have become more of a burden on the local hospitals than a boon. Though Mulago received 20 incubators, 13 are broken and 1 had instructions delivered that were in Dutch, a language not spoken in the region. The anesthesia machine in Bwindi served for one patient before it stopped working (Duncan and Coyne 2015b: 688).

A system in which prices, profit, and loss were providing information through the market would allow for feedback mechanisms to "signal a demand for staff, technicians, repair people, spare parts, etc., but under the administrative context, these complements and adjustments to changing circumstances must be recognized and accounted for within the plan" (Duncan and Coyne 2015b: 688). The absence of the market feedback when giving donations leads the administrative decision-maker with the full responsibility for planning for the array of complementary goods to keep the devices functioning. Creating that system of support a priori is a herculean task that borders on the impossible. Without that system, "the medical devices now litter wings in both hospitals, taking up space rather than providing actual humanitarian benefits" (Duncan and Coyne 2015b: 688–689).

Lest one think this example too specific, it can be noted that this is not the only case in which administrative decision-makers and experts show an inability to grasp the difficulty of economic coordination absent price systems. The knowledge problem is a well-known phenomenon in economics (Hayek 1945), but Easterly has been very clear in his examples of the planners versus searchers issue (Easterly 2006) and the problems that arise with heavy reliance upon experts for a solution (Easterly 2015). Moving from the international aid scene to a more local issue, Smith and Sutter (2013: 177) note that in the aftermath of the 2011 tornado in Joplin, Missouri, the relief effort saw "excessive and unnecessary donations" including an overabundance of bottled water and donated clothing to the point the useless donations were referred to as "the disaster after the disaster." That does not imply that in this instance the private relief aid was more harmful than beneficial, but the relief process was aided by the coordination of local individuals, retailers, and organizations that had local knowledge of the crisis. Even with the localized knowledge and cultural similarities between the donors and donation recipients, Joplin still received an inefficient mix of donations. The local knowledge sources and cultural similarities are often lacking for international private aid, leading to an even greater separation between the efficient and the actual outcome (Bell and Carens 2004).

The Producers Are Consumers

The idea that NGOs and private aid may fail to address the needs of the proposed beneficiaries is not a new concept. As Kapur and Whittle (2010: 150) note, the information flow is from Service Providers to Intermediaries to Funders, but the delegation flow runs the reverse: Funders to Intermediaries to Service Providers. The informational channel, then, is not necessarily intended to provide the most benefit to the poorest, but rather to provide the most perceived benefit to the funding source. Part of Fruttero and Gauri's (2005) explanation for aid locations not being fully determined by "charitable inclinations alone" is that the need to secure donor funding is also a large determinant in where aid and aid projects are targeted. The incentive structure of NGOs is not difficult to surmise. Even for those organizations that truly desire to provide aid to those in need, they "like any organization, have to meet payroll, and they face the constant temptation of becoming primarily focused on doing what best allows them to meet that goal" (PovertyCure.Org n.d.).

The drive to attract donors in order to sustain the organization does have effects on the populations that NGOs will target. As stated above, there are between 6000 and 30,000 NGOs operating in the developing world. Each of these organizations must compete in this crowded landscape. Burger and Owens (2011) find that NGO survival is dependent upon the ability to attract foreign or international grants. This situation creates a fierce competition for donors, leading organizations to spend resources for both outright lobbying and advertising (Cooley and Ron 2002: 17; Coyne 2013: 97). In the race to create financial viability for the organization itself, "many are put in the position of having to choose between actual aid for those in need and finding convenient ways to signal that the organizations are operating where they are needed and that the money is being well-spent" (Duncan 2014: 137).

The competition for funding and the need to visibly signal leads NGOs toward selecting high-profile locations in which to operate. Since the target audience is the international community (Burger and Owens 2011), greater media visibility or "media saturation" is an important component to being noticed in a crowded field (Cooley and Ron 2002). The example of Goma, Democratic Republic of Congo after the 1994 Rwandan Genocide crisis illustrates the effect that media saturation can have on the motives of NGOs (Cooley and Ron 2002; Terry 2002; Mills 2005; Duncan 2014). Given the attention received by the genocide and cholera epidemic that followed in the refugee camps, Goma became a must-go place for aid organizations lest they miss out both the short-term funding for the crisis and the long-term funding that such a public crisis would provide. While the crisis was severe and an appropriate response would have been beneficial to the refugees, the lack of coordination amongst responding NGOs led to a massive influx of between 150 and 200 organizations bringing roughly $1 billion to the area in a single year (Cooley and Ron 2002; Buscher and Vlassenroot 2010). With a mix of the best of intentions and a desire to be seen as responding in order to attract donations, this influx may very well have been the "disaster after the disaster." The scale of this intervention into the region shifted the nature of regional economic activity. During this period, Goma became a city based on NGOs with a local population increasingly dependent on the organizations themselves as the chief labor market (Buscher and Vlassenroot 2010; Duncan 2014). While dependency on aid is not an unknown problem (Easterly 2002, 2006), the magnitude of this disruption reoriented the labor market, the housing market, and altered any healthy economic growth path that the area may have formed in the absence of the organizational influx.[7]

The Goma influx illustrates how the drive for donors can influence the decision of where NGOs undertake their activities, as well as illustrating the unintended consequences when a large number of organizations respond to the same incentive. This same desire to attract funds also results in the utilization of government sources.[8]

Non-Government But Government Funded

The overlap between private organizations and government funding is also not a new phenomenon (Smith 1990; Najam 2000; Coyne 2008). During World War II, the US government provided select private organizations with funding to achieve policy goals that matched the war effort; a greater number of organizations were allowed to access federal funds (Smith 1990).[9] Given the flow of federal money allocated to private organizations during the war effort, the organizations' leadership had every incentive to continue the relationship into the post-war and Cold War periods. The attachment of NGOs to military engagements also did not end following World War II. During the Korean War, "all voluntary cash contributions were channeled through the Department of State" and then distributed to private organizations who "proved to be useful instruments in the accomplishment of U.S. government goals abroad" (Smith 1990: 51). This trend of entangling military and NGO activities has continued in varying degrees through more recent engagements, such as the war in Afghanistan.

While the perceived militarization of humanitarian aid does cause tension between the aid community and the military, the utilization of NGOs is viewed as a strategic tool by the military (Coyne 2013: 139). Though the NGOs do not operate as active combatants, they do help to ease the burden of relief projects so the military can focus on combat activities. The aid and relief projects also increase the legitimization of military exercises in foreign arenas (Hechter and Vidal-Aparicio 2011). The NGOs in Afghanistan, for example, may "place primary emphasis on gaining community buy-in and investing in quality projects," these efforts overlap with the military's attempt to win the hearts and minds of the local populations (Coyne 2013: 139).

The example of the military ties with NGO activity is a very specific example, yet it illustrates an important point. While not all the organizations involved in Afghanistan may be federally funded, many were still utilized for ends not their own. Najam (2000: 388–389) describes such scenarios as co-optive relationships "when governmental and nongovernmental organizations share similar strategies but prefer different goals," where the relationships "are likely to be unstable, and one or both parties will attempt to change the goals of the other. The relationship could linger into mutual manipulation, turn into outright confrontation, or convince one party that their ends are a subset of the other party." The co-optive relationship and goal manipulation may become more prominent, and less likely to end favorably for the NGO, when the power structure is shifted in such a way as to make the NGO dependent upon government as a source of funding.

As governmental funding flows through the private organizations, their very identity as "non-government organizations" may be called into question (The Economist 2000; Coyne 2013: 37). The NGOs' shift in stance does not necessarily have to be paired with military engagement as in the example provided. However, given that NGOs are credited with helping to establish numerous global public policy agendas (Jordan and Van Tuijl 2006: 4), concerns arise regarding potential biases that may emerge.[10] If the problem with official aid channels is their "favoring political ends rather than development concerns" as Kharas (2007: 4) suggests, then to the extent that NGOs respond to the will of the governmental donors and press toward political ends, the "privatization" of aid may not actually resolve the issue. Even Kharas's choice of development concerns is an interesting one. Though not a complete proof of the politicization bias, it is worth noting that many NGOs identify as developmental rather than relief even though private donations are far more likely to expand during times of disasters (Smith 1990: 7; Stoianova 2013: 1). This correlation may imply that attracting private donors, who appear more interested in relief than development, may not be the primary focus of many NGOs.

Avoid the Toxic Partnerships

A final issue to discuss regarding NGOs is their use or non-use of partnerships with poor country governments. Again, if the idea of private aid is to avoid the involvement of governments who lack the desire or capacity for desired projects, then NGOs must show that they fair better on this margin than official aid. In this aspect, NGOs may have the advantage over the official aid channels (Bebbington 2005; Peterson 2014; Knack 2014). The 2005 Paris Declaration on Aid Effectiveness stressed an international desire for greater private aid cooperation "to ensure the effective delivery of development assistance by placing responsibility on partner governments and donors" and improve "donor performance and developing country government systems" through "the joint delivery and management of aid" (Harmer and Ray 2009: 5). While there has been this push for NGOs and other private flows of aid to involve the poor country governments, there has also been an understanding that "the Paris Declaration is only applicable beyond a specific threshold in state capacity, legitimacy and accountability. If these elements are weak or under threat the Paris Declaration cannot be applied to development cooperation" (Harmer and Ray 2009: 5). Knack (2014) shows empirically that donors have taken this mixed approach seriously, utilizing poor country governments where corruption and institutional issues are less prevalent but relying upon their own systems in places where there is greater prevalence.

Implications and Conclusion

Ultimately, there is still a great appeal in the use of NGOs and private aid generally. There are margins on which the privatization of aid appears to be more effective than the official aid channels. However, the use of private aid should not be viewed as a cure-all for the important issues that surround foreign aid in either the humanitarian or the development area. Private organizations face many of the same concerns that governmental agencies do and must continue to develop appropriate feedback mechanisms to strengthen the chain of information. Without these feedback mechanisms, there may remain an inherent "tension between accountability to the foundation giving [the NGO] financial support and allegiance to the intended beneficiaries who may see the world differently than the foundation's grant officer" (Charnovitz 2006: 33). Potentially, some incentive issues may be mitigated by shifting the focus of accountability toward measures of performance (Charnovitz 2006), including additional stakeholders in the discussion regarding aid projects (Okwaare and Chapman 2006), or generally experimenting with other forms of information pathways (Jordan and Van Tuijl 2006). However, even should the incentive problem be resolved through changes in the accountability processes, these feedback mechanisms must also form a resolution of the knowledge problem regarding resource distribution. The channels of private aid, NGOs or otherwise, who are able to avoid these pitfalls to a greater extent will perform more admirably.

Notes

1. Private philanthropy here includes giving from foundations, corporations, private and voluntary organizations (PVOs), universities and colleges, and religious organizations (Adelman 2009: 25; The Index of Global Philanthropy and Remittances 2016: 9). Per Development Initiatives (2016: 1), "Private development assistance includes all international concessional resource flows voluntarily transferred from private sources for international development. These flows are the private finance channelled through NGOs, foundations and corporate philanthropic activities. Other

terms used interchangeably with private development assistance include international private giving, international philanthropy, voluntary giving, private development aid, and private development cooperation."

2. Commercial, or private capital flows, include resource items such as foreign direct investment, commercial long-term debt, short-term debt, and portfolio equity rather than money given specifically as philanthropic assistance. According to Development Initiatives (2018: 3), "commercial long-term debt was the largest single resource flow in 2016" signifying that these types of flows often come in the form of loans to developing countries.
3. Remittances are treated separately from private philanthropy as "the World Bank and other studies are clear that the funds sent back by migrants to their families and to community development projects are one of the strongest poverty reduction forces in poor countries" (Adelman 2009: 23).
4. It should be noted that private aid research often has qualifying statements regarding both the ability to circumvent governments and achieve efficiency gains, some of which will be discussed below. For example, the donors' use or non-use of poor country government mechanisms is in part determined by the quality of those mechanisms (Knack 2014).
5. Add to this effect the legal need for NGOs to report to official channels and agencies, who operate in an administrative and bureaucratic manner, and the shift toward mimicry of bureaucracy becomes even more pronounced (Bebbington 2005: 939).
6. The aid effectiveness is generally difficult to measure for private or official aid. If aid goes to where it is "most effective" the effectiveness may also be a function of capability for resolving the issue, growth or humanitarian, that the country already possessed (Flores and Nooruddin 2009).
7. The lack of coordination, and its subsequent lack of communication, also led to NGOs unknowingly funding the rearmament of aggressors that perpetrated the original refugee crisis (Chandler 2001; Cooley and Ron 2002; Terry 2002).
8. For example, a 2016 report by NGO Monitor shows that for 27 NGOs it sampled between 2012 and 2014, 65% of funding came directly or indirectly form government sources, 34% came from private sources, and for 1% the source remained unclear (NGO Monitor 2016). Stoianova (2013: 16) similarly notes: "On average, 98% of ICRC [The International Committee of the Red Cross] financing comes from institutional donors and a mere 2% is raised from private donors" though that relationship does flip in favor of private funding for the International Federation of Red Cross and Red Crescent Societies (Stoianova 2013: 14) and the American Red Cross (Kapur and Whittle 2010: 1145).
9. According to Smith (1990: 48), one of the early non-military funding programs was used to send surplus agricultural products overseas to keep farm prices high, culminating officially in the Agricultural Act of 1949.

10. As an interesting example of organizations avoiding this bias, consider Doctors Without Borders (*Médecins sans Frontières*), an NGO that is "explicit in their mission and principles that they are funded independently, and operate independently…and the fact that they are not funded by any governments" (Peterson 2014: 90).

References

Adelman, Carol. 2009. Global Philanthropy and Remittances: Reinventing Foreign Aid. Brown Journal of World Affairs, 15(2): 23–33.

Barr, Abigail, Marcel Fafchamps, and Trudy Owens. 2005. The Governance of Non-Governmental Organizations in Uganda. World Development, 33(4): 657–679.

Bebbington, Anthony. 2005. Donor-NGO Relations and Representations of Livelihood in Nongovernmental Aid Chains. World Development, 33(6): 937–950.

Bell, Daniel A., and Joseph H. Carens. 2004. The Ethical Dilemmas of International Human Rights and Humanitarian NGOs: Relections on a Dialogue Between Practitioners and Theorists. Human Rights Quarterly, 26(2): 300–329.

Boettke, Peter J. 1998. Why Culture Matters: Economics, Politics, and the Imprint of History. Journal of the LSE Hayek Society, 2(1): 9–16.

Boettke, Peter J. 2005. Introduction-Forum Series on the Role of Institutions in Promoting Economic Growth. The Review of Austrian Economics, 18(3/4): 235–240.

Boettke, Peter J., and Alexander Fink. 2011. Institutions First. Journal of Institutional Economics, 7(4): 499–504.

Brubaker, Earl R. 1997. The Tragedy of the Public Budgetary Commons. The Independent Review, 1(3): 353–370.

Buchanan, James M. 1949. The Pure Theory of Government Finance: A Suggested Approach. Journal of Political Economy, 57(6): 496–505.

Burger, Ronelle, and Trudy Owens 2011. Receive Grants or Perish? The Survival Prospects of African Nongovernmental Organizations. Credit Research Paper No. 11/07: Centre for Research in Economic Development and International Trade.

Buscher, Karen, and Koen Vlassenroot. 2010. Humanitarian presence and urban development: new opportunities and contrasts in Goma, DRC. Disasters, 34(S2): S256–S273.

Büthe, Tim, Solomon Major, and André de Mello e Souza. 2012. The Politics of Private Foreign Aid: Humanitarian Principles, Economic Development Objectives, and Organizational Interests in NGO Private Aid Allocation. International Organization, 66(4): 571–607.

Chandler, David G. 2001. The Road to Military Humanitarianism: How the Human Rights NGOs Shaped a New Humanitarian Agenda. Human Rights Quarterly, 23(3): 678–700.

Charnovitz, Steve. 2006. Accountability of Non-Government Organizations in Global Governance. In Accountability: Politics, Principles & Innovations, edited by Lisa Jordon and Peter Van Tuijl. London: Earthscan.

Cooley, Alexander, and James Ron. 2002. The NGO Scramble: Organizational Insecurity and the Political Economy of Transnational Action. International Security, 27(1): 5–39.

Coyne, Christopher J. 2005a. The Institutional Prerequisites for Post-Conflict Reconstruction. The Review of Austrian Economics, 18(3/4): 325–342.

Coyne, Christopher J. 2005b. Postwar Reconstruction: Some Insights from Public Choice and Institutional Economics. Constitutional Political Economy, 16: 31–48.

Coyne, Christopher J. 2006. Reconstructing Weak and Failed States: Foreign Intervention and the Nirvana Fallacy. Foreign Policy Analysis, 2: 343–360.

Coyne, Christopher J. 2008. After War: The Political Economy of Exporting Democracy. Stanford: Stanford University Press.

Coyne, Christopher J. 2013. Doing Bad by Doing Good: Why Humanitarian Action Fails. Stanford: Stanford University Press.

Coyne, Christopher J., and Rachel L. Mathers. 2010. The Fatal Conceit of Foreign Intervention. Advances in Austrian Economics, 14: 225–250.

Coyne, Christopher J., and Thomas K. Duncan. 2019. The Unproductive Protective State: The U.S. Defense Sector As a Fiscal Commons. In James M. Buchanan: A Theorist of Political Economy and Social Philosophy, edited by Richard E. Wagner. New York: Palgrave Macmillan.

De Soto, Jesus Huerta. 2010. Socialism, Economic Calculation, and Entrepreneurship: New Thinking in Political Economy. UK: Edward Elgar Publishing Limited.

Development Initiatives. 2016. Private development assistance: key facts and global estimates. Bristol: Development Initiatives Poverty Research Ltd. Retrieved August 3, 2018: http://devinit.org/post/private-development-assistance-key-facts-and-global-estimates

Development Initiatives. 2018. Understanding ODA in the mix of international resources. Bristol: Development Initiatives Poverty Research Ltd.

Duncan, Thomas K. 2014. Doing Bad by Doing Good in Goma. Studies in Emergent Order, 7: 135–143.

Duncan, Thomas K., and Christopher J. Coyne. 2015a. The Revolving Door and the Entrenchment of the Permanent War Economy. Peace Economics, Peace Science & Public Policy, 21(3): 391–413.

Duncan, Thomas K., and Christopher J. Coyne. 2015b. The Political Economy of Foreign Intervention. In The Oxford Handbook of Austrian Economics, edited by Peter J. Boettke and Christopher J. Coyne. Oxford: Oxford University Press.

Easterly, William. 2002. The Elusive Quest for Growth: Economists' Adventures and Misadventures in the Tropics. Cambridge: The MIT Press.

Easterly, William. 2006. The White Man's Burden: Why the West's Efforts to Aid the Rest Have Done So Much Ill and So Little Good.

Easterly, William. 2009. Can the West Save Africa? Journal of Economic Literature, 47(2): 373–447.

Easterly, William. 2015. The Tyranny of Experts: Economists, Dictators, and the Forgotten Rights of the Poor. New York: Basic Books.

Flores, Thomas E., and Irfan Nooruddin. 2009. Financing the peace: Evaluating World Bank post-conflict assistance programs. Review of International Organizations, 4(1): 1–27.

Fruttero, Anna, and Varun Gauri. 2005. The Strategic Choices of NGOs: Location Decisions in Rural Bangladesh. The Journal of Development Studies, 41(5): 759–787.

Guest, Robert. 2010. The Shackled Continent: Power, Corruption, and African Lives. London: Smithsonian Books.

Harmer, Adele, and Deepayan Basu Ray. 2009. Study on the relevance and applicability of the Paris Declaration on Aid Effectiveness in Humanitarian Assistance. Humanitarian Policy Group Working Paper Series, London: Overseas Development Institute.

Hayek, Friedrich A. 1945. The Use of Knowledge in Society. The American Economic Review, 35(4): 519–530.

Hechter, Michael, and Oriol Vidal-Aparicio. 2011. Dynamics of military occupations. In The Handbook on the Political Economy of War, edited by Christopher J. Coyne and Rachel L. Mathers. Cheltenham: Edward Elgar.

Hoff, Trygve J. B. 1949. Economic Calculation in the Socialist Society. London: William Hodge and Company.

Jordan, Lisa, and Peter Van Tuijl. 2006. Rights and Responsibilities in the Political Landscape of NGO Accountability: An Introduction and Overview. In Accountability: Politics, Principles & Innovations, edited by Lisa Jordon and Peter Van Tuijl. London: Earthscan.

Kapur, Devesh, and Dennis Whittle. 2010. Can the Privatization of Foreign Aid Enhance Accountability? International Law and Politics, 42: 1143–1180.

Kharas, Homi. 2007. Trends and Issues in Development Aid. Wolfensohn Center for Development Working Paper No. 1. Washington D.C.: Brookings Institution.

Kirzner, Israel M. 1973. Competition and Entrepreneurship. Chicago: The University of Chicago Press.

Knack, Stephen. 2014. Building or Bypassing Recipient Country Systems: Are Donors Defying the Paris Declaration? The Journal of Development Studies, 50(6): 839–854.

Kragelund, Peter. 2004. The Embedded Recipient and the Disembedded Donor: Private-Sector Development Aid in Ghana. Forum for Development Studies, 31(2): 307–335.

Miesen, Mike. 2013. The Inadequacy of Donating Medical Devices to Africa. *The Atlantic*, September 20. Retrieved November 1, 2018: http://www.theatlantic.com/international/print/2013/09/the-inadequacy-of-donating-medical-devices-to-africa/279855/

Mills, Kurt. 2005. Neo-Humanitarianism: The Role of International Humanitarian Norms and Organizations in Contemporary Conflict. Global Governance, 11(2): 161–183.

Milner, Helen V., and Dustin Tingley. 2013. Public Opinion and Foreign Aid: A Review Essay. International Interactions, 39(3): 389–401.

Milner, Helen V., Daniel L. Nielson, and Michael G. Findley. 2016. Citizen Preferences and Public Goods: Comparing Preferences for Foreign Aid and Government Programs in Uganda. Review of International Organizations 11(2): 219–245.

Mises, Ludwig Von. [1920] 1990. Economic Calculation in the Socialist Commonwealth, Auburn: Mises Institute.

Mises, Ludwig Von. [1922] 1981. Socialism: An Economic and Sociological Analysis, Indianapolis: Liberty Fund, Inc.

Mises, Ludwig Von. [1949] 2007. Human Action: A Treatise on Economics, Indianapolis: Liberty Fund, Inc.

Najam, Adil. 2000. The Four-C's of Third Sector-Government Relations: Cooperation, Confrontation, Complementarity, and Co-Optation. Nonprofit Management & Leadership, 10(4): 375–396.

NGO Monitor. 2016. New Comprehensive NGO Funding Database. Retrieved October 31st, 2018: https://www.ngo-monitor.org/press-releases/new-comprehensivengo-funding-data-base/

North, Douglass C. 1990. Institutions, Institutional Change, and Economic Performance: Political Economy of Institutions and Decisions. Cambridge: Cambridge University Press.

Okwaare, Sarah, and Jennifer Chapman. 2006. Chameleons and Accountability: Linking Learning with Increasing Accountability in ActionAid International Uganda and the Ugandan Land Alliance. In Accountability: Politics, Principles & Innovations, edited by Lisa Jordon and Peter Van Tuijl. London: Earthscan.

PovertyCure.org. n.d. Charitable Giving. Retrieved October 12th, 2018: http://www.povertycure.org/learn/issues/charity-hurts/charitable-giving

Peterson, Lindsey. 2014. A Gift You Can't Refuse? Foreign Aid, INGOs and Development in the World Polity. Studies in Emergent Order, 7: 81–102.

Smith, Adam. [1776] 1991. Wealth of Nations. New York: Prometheus Books.

Smith, Brian H. 1990. More than altruism: the politics of private foreign aid. Princeton: Princeton University Press.

Smith, Daniel J., and Daniel Sutter. 2013. Response and Recovery After the Joplin Tornado: Lessons Applied and Lessons Learned. The Independent Review, 18(2): 165–188.

Stoianova, Velina. 2013. Private funding for humanitarian assistance. Bristol: Global Humanitarian Assistance A Development Initiative.

Sy, Amadou, and Fenohasina M. Rakotondrazaka. 2015. Private Capital Flows, Official Development Assistance, and Remittances to Africa: Who Gets What? Global Economy and Development Policy Paper No. 2015-02. Washington D.C.: Brookings Institution.

Terry, Fiona. 2002. Condemned to Repeat? The Paradox of Humanitarian Action. Ithaca: Cornell University Press.

The Economist. 2000. Sins of the Secular Missionaries. Retrieved October 31st, 2018: https://www.economist.com/special/2000/01/27/sins-of-the-secular-missionaries

The Index of Global Philanthropy and Remittances. 2016. The Index of Global Philanthropy and Remittances 2016. Washington D.C.: Hudson Institute.

Wagner, Richard E. 2012. Deficits, Debt, and Democracy: Wrestling with Tragedy on the Fiscal Commons. Cheltenham: Edward Elgar.

CHAPTER 12

Remittances and FDI As Privately Provided International Aid

Olga Nicoara and Scott A. Burns

Introduction

Foreign aid to the world's poor has been a point of contention since the reconstruction period post-World War II. The battle of ideas and the world race for economic and geopolitical power led to the division of the world into "the West" or the "First World," represented by the capitalist economies; "the East" or "the Second World," represented by the communist economies, including Soviet Union; and "the Rest" or the "Third World" (Bauer 2004). For the dominant leaders of the world at the time, the Third World became grounds for experimentation with two economic systems: capitalist versus communist. The question was: which economic system leads to the greatest economic performance in time? With the fall of communism in Central and Eastern Europe (C&EE) (1989), and the collapse of the Soviet Union (1991), experts in Western nations assumed the task of prescribing solutions for the poor. The first Washington Consensus (1990) contained a list ten prescriptions for development in three target areas of the world: Latin America, Sub-

O. Nicoara (✉) • S. A. Burns
Ursinus College, Collegeville, PA, USA
e-mail: onicoara@ursinus.edu; sburns@ursinus.edu

N. Dutta, C. R. Williamson (eds.), *Lessons on Foreign Aid and Economic Development*, https://doi.org/10.1007/978-3-030-22121-8_12

Saharan Africa, and Eastern Europe. The focus was to privatize, liberalize, and stabilize the economies of the formerly called Second and Third Worlds undergoing transition from predominantly socialist systems to predominantly capitalist systems, from centrally planned to market-based economies, from poverty to prosperity. The three Western intergovernmental organizations established in the post-War period to plan and implement reconstruction and development programs, the IMF, the World Bank, and the United Nations have faced at best moderate success in their initiatives to help the poor.

Concomitant with the elaborate development programs designed by "the West" to fix "the Rest," migrant workers from developing nations earning honest incomes abroad have been sending remittances home, contributing to economic growth and development in a more direct and sustainable way. Indeed, the contribution of remittances to global is so stark that the United Nations have come to recognize them as "an untapped engine for sustainable development" (United Nations 2018).

In this chapter, we argue that despite elaborate prescriptions and corresponding programs for development implemented by international aid organizations, personal remittances and Foreign Direct Investments (FDIs) helped poor nations overcome their initial condition more. Indirectly, increased global economic freedom, including the openness of rich nations to receiving immigrants and migrant workers, along with innovative payment technologies that bridge the gap between givers and recipients, helped the discovery and exploitation of entrepreneurial opportunities, fostering mutually beneficial gains from trade.

We define "private international aid" as any monetary or in-kind contribution or transfer made by a private individual or a private organization engaged in the private sector of an economy of origin to a private individual or organization located in the receiving country. Our definition includes transfers by private individuals at large, making it broader than the profit-oriented definition advanced by the Organisation for Economic Co-operation and Development's (OECD) Development Assistance Committee (DAC).

The Framework for Understanding Privately Provided Aid

Why is the private sector better equipped to provide aid than governments and state-funded entities? Economists who study the political economy of foreign aid generally argue that this is because of two related factors (Williamson 2010). First, private agents are more likely to possess local *knowledge* about a specific culture or region that makes them better suited to determine the best means for providing aid than foreign officials or agencies from afar. To the extent they operate in a market setting, they also have access to market prices and profit and loss signals that government agencies might not. Second, they are more likely to have an incentive to achieve the desired goal and to do so in a cost-effective manner since it is often their money (or their donors') and their firm's reputation that is on the line.

In his book *Doing Bad by Doing Good* (2013), Christopher J. Coyne explains why foreign aid so often fails to meet its stated objectives using insights from the Austrian and public choice schools of economics on these twin problems of inadequate knowledge and poorly aligned incentives. During the socialist calculation debate, Austrian scholars Ludwig Mises (1920 [2012]) and F.A. Hayek (1945) argued that in the absence of private property and market-generated prices it would be impossible for centrally planned economies to engage in rational economic calculation (Boettke 1998). As Coyne puts it, the same "planner's problem" that socialist leaders encounter when trying to plan for an economy in general also applies to the more specific case of foreign aid programs directed by governments or government-affiliated nonprofits. Namely, without access to market-generated price signals, planners would in effect be operating "in the dark," unable to calculate with any precision how effective whatever means they might have at their disposal would be at achieving their desired ends.

The knowledge problem outlined by Austrian scholars provides compelling evidence that foreign aid is likely to fail even if we grant the generous assumption that those who are responsible for administering it have the best of intentions. But even if we turn this assumption on its head and assume that planners could somehow access the sort of knowledge that would be required to efficiently marshal resources, public choice economics explains why the bureaucracies responsible for administering aid programs would still likely fail due to perverse incentives. Bureaucrats don't just suffer from a lack of profit and loss signals, as Austrians stress. As Gordon Tullock (1965 [2005]) observed, they also often face an incentive structure that is fundamentally different than that of market actors.[1] Since their revenue is derived not from sales to the public but from government appropriations, their success or failure cannot be measured by profits or losses which, in a market context, reflect how well they met their customers' needs. It is instead most often gauged by factors like how effectively they were able to increase their budget and expand the scope of their operations rather than achieve their stated goal. This goal to maximize their budget often leads bureaucrats to engage in "mission creep," expanding the scope of their duties to justify additional funding. It also leads them to engage in wasteful spending to deplete their budget and justify asking for more funding.

Although foreign aid and government planning played a major role in many post-war neoclassical growth models, their failure has led many economists today to conclude that the private sector—and, in particular, private *entrepreneurs*—are the primary drivers of sustainable economic growth (Powell 2008; Kasper et al. 2013). The emphasis on entrepreneurship has accelerated dramatically in recent years (Minniti 2007). As noted earlier, private entrepreneurs are far more likely to have access to the sort of local knowledge required to achieve a specific objective. They are also more likely than bureaucrats to have an incentive to marshal their scarce resources in a cost-effective manner. This is why over the past few decades economists' focus has shifted away from the potential benefits of foreign aid and toward the question: what policies do the best job of creating an enabling environment for private entrepreneurship?

In his classic article, William Baumol (1990) argued that the total supply of entrepreneurs exhibits relatively little variation across place and time.[2] Since the supply of entrepreneurship is relatively constant across time and place, Baumol's central thesis is that the degree to which entrepreneurial activity contributes to economic growth ultimately depended on its allocation between productive activities, such as innovation, unproductive activities, such as lobbying and rent-seeking, and destructive activities such as theft. "This allocation," he concluded, "is heavily influenced by the relative payoffs societies offers to such activities," and these payoffs are ultimately determined by the institutional rules that govern a society (Baumol 1990, 893).

Baumol's emphasis on the role that institutions play in directing entrepreneurial activity dovetails nicely with the work of Douglass North and others in the New Institutional School. According to these scholars, institutions are the formal and informal rules of the game that govern a society (North 1986). By establishing clearly defined rules of association, institutions lower transaction costs, facilitate exchange, reduce uncertainty, and help economic actors coordinate their actions over time (North 1990). In short, the institutional rules that govern a society serve as a filter for entrepreneurial activity. They can either steer entrepreneurs toward or away from productive activities.[3]

What specific policies do the best job of promoting productive entrepreneurship? A deep empirical literature has emerged in recent years on the close connection between entrepreneurship and economic freedom. The results show that economic freedom as defined by well-defined property rights, a freely functioning price system, low taxes, and a relatively simple tax code, competition (most notably in the form of low legal barriers to entry into any particular sector), and stable governance under the rule of law plays a critical role in encouraging entrepreneurs to engage in productive, wealth-generating activities (Gwartney et al. 1999; Faria and Montesinos 2009). These findings are wholly consistent with Adam Smith's observation centuries earlier that "Little else is requisite to carry a state to the highest degree of opulence from the lowest barbarism but peace, easy taxes, and a tolerable administration of justice" (Smith 1776 [2008], xliii). They are also consistent with Bauer's (2004) work on the fundamental institutional building blocks that help usher an economy "from subsistence to exchange," Easterly's (2006) discussion of the importance of relying on "searchers" (i.e. market entrepreneurs) over "planners" (politicians and bureaucrats) and their often misguided foreign aid and planning efforts, and Olson's (1996) discussion of the type of institutional rules that erase the wide variety of unexploited gains from trade that are prevalent in the developing world.

What does all of this imply about the efficacy of foreign aid? First, although foreign aid might be able to achieve some limited success in meeting short-run humanitarian goals like providing clean water or vaccinations, private actors are far more likely to possess the sort of local knowledge and properly aligned incentives that are required for meeting these goals (Williamson and Coyne 2014). Second, and most important, foreign aid and government planning are not capable of solving the more fundamental, long-term economic problems that are required to lift large numbers of people out of poverty. Ultimately, the best way to promote sustainable economic development is not to expand foreign aid or cede more resources and authority to politicians and bureaucrats. It is to adopt market-friendly policies that make it easier for entrepreneurs and private donors to find innovative ways to solve complex problems. Development planners and foreign aid advocates often fall prey to the temptation to believe that the developing world can only be saved through "big solutions" orchestrated in a top-down fashion. But as research on the connection between institutions and entrepreneurship illustrates, the only real way to achieve these ambitious goals is by embracing a humbler approach—one that recognizes the importance of the entrepreneur and limitations of foreign aid and top-down planning.[4] Minniti (2007, 787) aptly summarizes this "bottom-up" approach to aid:

> In the long run, governments can only provide an underlying environment conducive to the emergence of productive rather than unproductive entrepreneurship. Thus, government should endeavor to create enabling environments conducive to the division of labor, the commercialization of invention, and exchange.

Remittances and Development

In a globalized world, one major form of private international aid, we argue, is represented by personal remittances. A remittance takes place whenever an individual earning an income in a foreign country sends money to a recipient, typically family members and/or friends, in the home country. Remittances are an important source of external income for many poor nations in the world. Table 12.1 shows the top 30 African countries sorted according to the total personal remittances received in 2000 and 2017. On the African continent, Nigerians abroad sent the most remittances home, totaling 29 billion of US dollars, or 154 US dollars per person in 2017. The per capita impact of remittances is even greater in low-income African economies, like Senegal, with 169 US dollars received per person in 2017 (See Table 12.1). In the low-income economies of Comoros and Gambia remittances accounted for approximately 21% of their respective GDPs in 2017, followed by Liberia (19%), and the lower-middle-income economies of Lesotho (15%), Senegal (14%), Cabo Verde (12%), Togo (8%), and Ghana (7%). Similarly, Table 12.2 shows personal remittances received in a group of 30 formerly socialist countries in Europe and Central Asia in 2000 and 2017. Among the former socialist economies of Europe and Central Asia, remittances sent by Ukrainians abroad

Table 12.1 Remittances received in Africa, 2000 and 2017 (all absolute figures are in constant 2015 US dollar)

2000				2017			
Country	*Billions*	*Per capita*	*% of GDP*	*Country*	*Billions*	*Per capita*	*% of GDP*
Nigeria	5.15	42.11	3.00	Nigeria	29.40	154.00	5.85
Sudan	1.94	71.23	6.51	Ghana	4.26	147.77	7.47
Kenya	1.21	38.45	4.23	Senegal	2.68	168.98	13.67
Lesotho	0.97	516.67	53.83	Kenya	1.66	33.38	2.62
South Africa	0.69	15.15	0.24	Uganda	1.49	34.80	4.79
Senegal	0.47	47.71	4.99	Congo, DR.	1.24	15.26	3.42
Uganda	0.42	17.28	3.84	South Africa	1.16	20.50	0.25
Mauritius	0.28	234.16	3.86	Mali	1.05	56.53	6.80
Cote d'Ivoire	0.27	16.22	1.11	Ethiopia	0.64	6.07	1.01
Benin	0.17	25.24	3.33	Lesotho	0.52	233.41	15.19
Cabo Verde	0.17	395.66	16.65	Burkina Faso	0.50	25.91	3.45
Mali	0.16	14.95	2.48	Tanzania	0.46	7.96	0.81
Burkina Faso	0.14	12.14	2.56	Togo	0.41	52.60	8.36
Ghana	0.13	6.87	0.65	Cote d'Ivoire	0.41	16.72	0.94
Eswatini	0.11	105.22	3.27	Mozambique	0.35	11.83	2.09
Ethiopia	0.09	1.38	0.64	Madagascar	0.35	13.71	2.98
Togo	0.07	14.87	2.65	Liberia	0.34	71.81	18.70
Cameroon	0.04	2.78	0.22	Cameroon	0.31	13.09	0.80
Mozambique	0.04	2.05	0.73	Benin	0.30	26.93	2.87
Niger	0.03	2.82	0.80	Gambia, The	0.26	123.81	21.25
Botswana	0.03	17.30	0.32	Cabo Verde	0.25	463.17	12.01
Congo, Rep.	0.03	8.29	0.32	Rwanda	0.24	19.66	2.36
Madagascar	0.02	1.36	0.29	Niger	0.23	10.51	2.44
Namibia	0.02	9.57	0.23	Eswatini	0.19	139.69	3.27
Sierra Leone	0.02	3.71	1.12	Sudan	0.16	3.87	0.18
Gabon	0.02	13.20	0.12	Comoros	0.15	179.03	21.33
Guinea-Bissau	0.02	12.58	2.17	Zambia	0.11	6.51	0.36
Tanzania	0.01	0.41	0.08	Mauritania	0.10	21.86	1.54
Rwanda	0.01	1.36	0.38	Guinea-Bissau	0.09	50.68	7.69
Eritrea	0.01	2.90	0.47	Namibia	0.08	30.09	0.47

Source: World Bank, World Development Indicators; accessed December 19, 2018; sorted according to the billions of remittances received (from high to low) in each year

reached a total of approximately 15 billion US dollars, or about 334 US dollars per person in 2017, followed by Russians (10 billion), and the Poles (8.5 billion). Remittances reached approximately 33% of GDP in 2017 in Kyrgyzstan, followed by Tajikistan (32%), Moldova (20%),

Table 12.2 Remittances received in former socialist economies, 2000 and 2017 (all absolute figures are in constant 2015 US dollars)

2000				*2017*			
Country	*Billions*	*Per capita*	*% of GDP*	*Country*	*Billions*	*Per capita*	*% of GDP*
Bosnia & Herzegovina	3.54	940.08	28.71	Ukraine	14.99	334.38	10.25
Poland	3.10	80.91	0.87	Russia	9.56	66.18	0.53
Russia	2.00	13.62	0.19	Poland	8.54	224.94	1.31
Croatia	1.91	432.43	3.75	Hungary	5.56	568.68	3.33
Ukraine	1.31	26.57	1.34	Romania	4.74	241.94	2.03
Albania	1.30	419.56	16.46	Czech Republic	4.38	413.24	1.66
Czech Republic	0.79	76.98	0.48	Serbia	3.97	565.65	8.66
Latvia	0.57	240.21	3.18	Tajikistan	3.12	349.47	31.56
Hungary	0.54	53.31	0.47	Croatia	3.10	751.42	4.53
Moldova	0.53	145.51	13.78	Slovak Republic	2.66	489.75	2.26
Georgia	0.47	105.52	6.74	Bulgaria	2.49	351.66	3.88
Armenia	0.45	145.91	9.53	Kyrgyz Rep	2.38	383.47	32.86
Slovenia	0.40	201.36	0.99	Bosnia & Herzegovina	2.36	673.04	11.10
Romania	0.31	13.73	0.26	Georgia	2.06	553.55	11.83
Belarus	0.27	27.46	0.90	Armenia	1.80	613.60	13.34
Kazakhstan	0.27	18.06	0.37	Azerbaijan	1.74	176.05	2.78
Macedonia	0.16	80.65	2.14	Moldova	1.69	476.20	20.17
Bulgaria	0.16	19.09	0.44	Albania	1.53	533.61	10.05
Azerbaijan	0.16	19.30	1.08	Belarus	1.52	160.10	2.30
Lithuania	0.11	32.72	0.43	Lithuania	1.43	505.29	2.76
Slovak Republic	0.04	6.86	0.06	Latvia	1.38	708.88	4.18
Estonia	0.01	7.86	0.07	Kosovo	1.27	691.49	15.59
Kyrgyz Rep.	0.01	1.17	0.16	Montenegro	0.58	931.51	10.94

Source: World Bank, World Development Indicators; accessed December 19, 2018; sorted according to the billions of remittances received (from high to low) in each year

Armenia (13%), and Georgia (12%) (see Table 12.2). The large shares of remittances in developing nations' GDPs confirm the UN's acknowledgment of remittances as an overlooked factor for sustainable growth.

Not all remittances sent/received are recorded or reported, however. Some of the incomes earned abroad may find their way to the home country through informal channels, rather than through established financial institutions, like banks, or popular money transfer and payment intermediaries, like Western Union or MoneyGram, to name a few. In

2010, the World Bank estimated the amount of unrecorded remittances at about 50% of the true total remittances (World Bank 2010). Data on personal remittances is available through the World Bank's Data Bank. In IMF's Balance of Payments Manual, personal remittances are comprised of personal transfers, compensation of employees, and capital transfer between households. Personal transfers consist of "all current transfers in cash or in kind made or received by resident households to or from non-resident households," and compensation of employees consists of "income of border, seasonal, and other short-term workers who are employed in an economy where they are not resident and of residents employed by nonresident entities." Remittances come either from immigrants settled in a new country or from migrant workers sending funds to relatives left behind.

Figure 12.1 illustrates the flows of per capita *personal remittances received by* five main geographical regions of the world, while Fig. 12.2 illustrates the same flows by income groups, as classified by the World Bank in both cases.

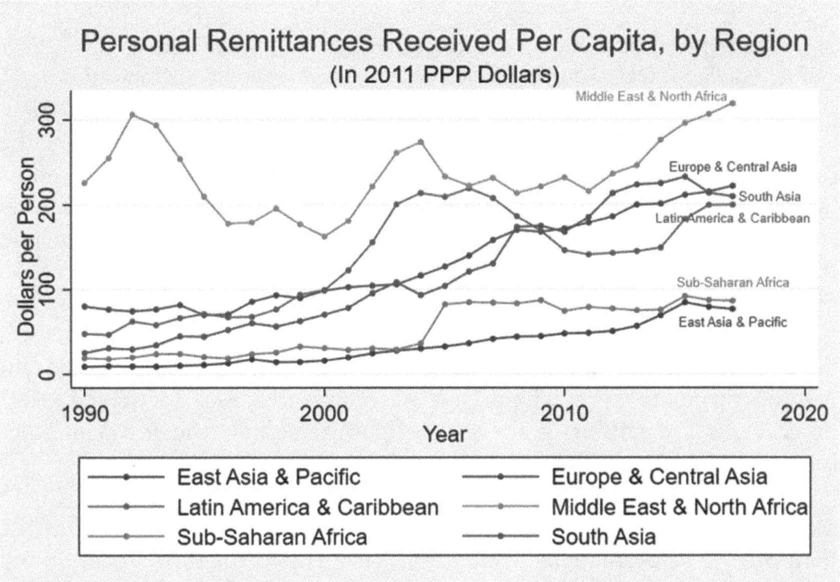

Fig. 12.1 Personal remittances received, per capita, by region, in 2011 PPP US dollars. (Source: World Bank, World Development Indicators)

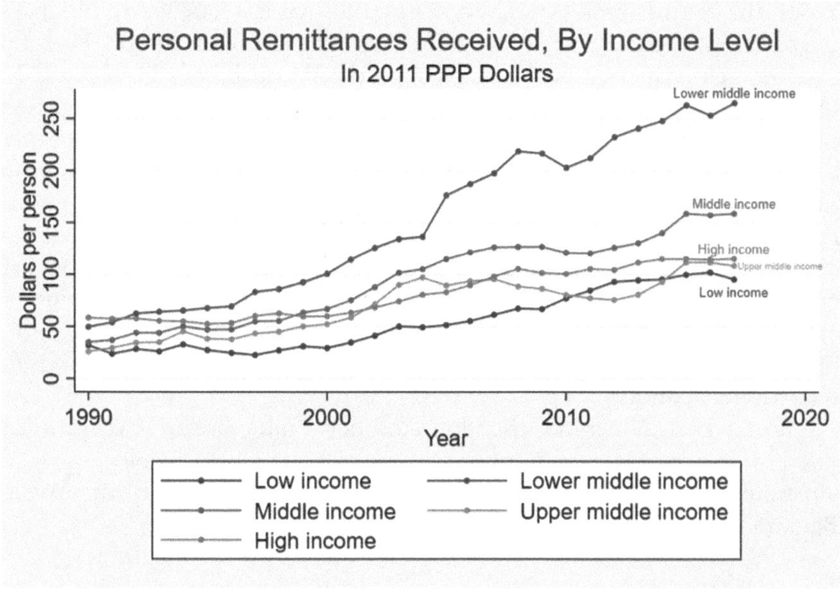

Fig. 12.2 Personal remittances received, per capita, by income level, in 2011 PPP US dollars. (Date Source: World Bank, World Development Indicators)

Going back to 1990 to date, Middle East and North Africa are the regions that received the highest level of real per capita personal remittances of all other regions in the world, followed by Europe and Central Asia, South Asia, Latin America and the Caribbean, and lastly Sub-Saharan Africa, and East Asia and Pacific. By income levels, as illustrated in Fig. 12.2, most flows of personal remittances go to lower-middle income and middle-income countries, where the vast majority of the population lives, including the countries where most immigrants and/or migrant workers originate from. The impact of remittances, as a fraction of GDP, however, is the largest in the group of low-income and lower-middle-income countries, as illustrated in Fig. 12.3.

Remittances, as compiled by the International Monetary Fund (IMF),[5] are "household income from foreign economies arising mainly from the temporary or permanent movement of people to those economies. Remittances include cash and noncash items that flow through formal channels, such as via electronic wire, or through informal channels, such as

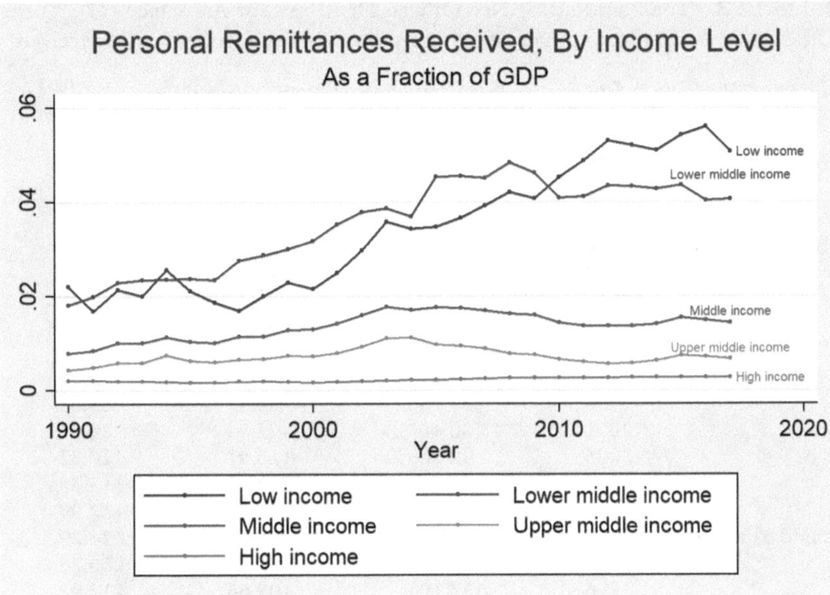

Fig. 12.3 Personal remittances received, % of GDP, by income level, 1990–2020. (Date Source: World Bank, World Development Indicators)

money or goods carried across borders." For many households in developing and transitioning economies, remittances are one of the most important sources of income, and the only way out of poverty. In low-income countries, as Table 12.1 shows, the flows of remittances almost match the flows of Net Official Development Assistance and Official Aid in recent years, growing in magnitude as more low-income countries become more integrated into the global economy thanks to the innovative mobile payment technologies lowering long-distance transaction costs. Remittances engage the local markets and contribute to capital accumulation and real economic growth, often directed into real investments, including reconstruction of personal homes, community roads, and religious venues.

As shown in Table 12.3, in both lower-middle and middle-income groups of countries, in particular, the flows of personal remittances are approximately five to six times the flows of official aid funds received over the recent years. Remittances exceed FDI particularly in lower-middle- and middle-income groups, showing that as a form of private aid personal remittances prevail in poorer countries compared to wealthier countries.

Table 12.3 Total amount of Net Official Development Assistance (ODA) and Official Aid (OA) received, personal remittances received, and net FDI received

Income group	*Year*	*Net ODA and OA received*	*Personal remittances received*	*Net FDI received*
Low income	1986	14.08	1.89	−0.07
	1991	15.45	3.61	1.28
	1996	11.78	4.26	1.42
	2001	14.52	6.75	5.52
	2006	22.76	12.27	8.19
	2011	33.96	21.38	17.69
	2016	33.65	30.38	16.95
Lower middle income	1986	30.77	27.91	6.14
	1991	38.21	38.99	13.16
	1996	26.13	54.55	38.64
	2001	30.46	97.54	29.03
	2006	42.20	173.81	110.52
	2011	37.52	212.27	113.38
	2016	53.27	271.31	122.99
Middle income	1986	39.34	58.55	26.29
	1991	50.77	75.59	66.20
	1996	37.10	103.66	213.91
	2001	42.96	175.49	341.21
	2006	63.82	298.14	585.78
	2011	53.64	311.74	690.00
	2016	71.72	425.51	598.96
Upper middle income	1986	8.20	24.28	20.03
	1991	12.26	34.60	53.15
	1996	10.45	47.28	175.84
	2001	11.94	76.12	313.66
	2006	20.64	124.42	475.24
	2011	14.85	105.95	574.72
	2016	17.26	157.36	475.86
High income	1986	6.02	49.01	170.08
	1991	4.42	65.45	194.33
	1996	5.10	62.70	362.53
	2001	1.87	76.81	993.22
	2006	0.30	111.38	2159.40
	2011	0.25	134.00	1611.88
	2016	0.22	149.94	2107.13

Source: World Bank, World Development Indicators. Figures for personal remittances and net FDI were originally in current US dollars and were converted to constant 2015 US dollars using the GDP deflator; accessed December 19, 2018; all figures are in billions of constant 2015 US dollars

Advantages of Remittances As a Form of Private Aid

Remittances impact the lives of the poor and their families directly, increasing their standard of living. For example, on average a member of a Tajik family earned about 1100 US dollars (about 3 US dollars per day) in 2016, with remittances adding an additional 349 US dollars per year (about 1 extra dollar per day). Remittances, therefore, directly increase a family's disposable income, mitigating various unmet necessities, including consumption purchases, payment of medical bills, financing schooling, offsetting debt, paying the costs of starting small businesses, and making small investments in the local communities.

As a source of external funding, remittances (i.e. personal transfers and compensation of migrant employees working abroad) are more stable than Official Development Assistance and Official Aid combined. The flows of remittances are also more stable than the flows of FDI, over longer periods of time, in relation to fluctuations in the business cycles at home or abroad.

A key feature of personal remittances as a form of private international aid is their decentralized, market-based, voluntary nature. As decentralized, market-based, voluntary sources of funding, remittances are a sustainable solution to development, because the possibilities of mutually beneficial exchanges are virtually limitless in increasingly globalized, open, and competitive world markets.

The allocation of private funds through remittances transferred among private individuals is less likely to suffer from the prevalent knowledge and the incentives problems known to plague official aid giving organizations (Easterly 2006; Moyo and Ferguson 2010). As privately directed funds, remittances reach the intended beneficiaries without the informational asymmetries and incentive problems that typically plague the more centralized forms of aid.

Sending remittances to poor family members abroad is based on trust and a shared understanding of a family's priorities, and the purpose of the funds in a family's expenditure plans. As a direct form of private aid, remittances eliminate the "who plans for who?" problem in development intervention, giving the senders and/or the recipients autonomy to plan the allocation of their own budgets toward subjective goals.

In many developing nations, known to suffer from institutional deficiencies, remittances surpass in magnitude the net ODA and OA, FDI, and other forms of aid (see Table 12.3). Where local institutions and international aid organizations fail the poor, remittances provide a reliable source of financial relief.

Remittances as private aid are simple to achieve. All that is required for remittances, as a source of private, external aid, to increase and reach the target beneficiaries, is freedom to trade on open and competitive global markets, achieved through open border policies. Open borders enable employers and employees to engage in discovering and exploring mutually beneficial gains from trade.

As a solution to help the poor, remittances pay for themselves, that is, they are costless to taxpayers in developed nations. By contrast, net ODA funds require explicit taxation for the purpose of supporting intergovernmental, official aid programs. Freeing labor migration policies benefits businesses employing competitive migrant workers in the developed nation, reducing production costs, and the price to consumers. Remittances aid the poor in an organic, dignifying way, eliminating the problem of complacency and dependency associated with official development aid and assistance (Easterly 2006; Moyo and Ferguson 2010).

Remittances may positively interact with the existing policies and institutions in the recipient nations over time in at least two ways. First, when channeled toward subsidizing travel to rich nations, remittances will allow more individuals in poor nations to compare and contrast institutions abroad with institutions at home, potentially demanding change. With globalization, remittances may facilitate cultural and, ultimately, institutional integration between developed and developing nations. To demand positive institutional change, people in weak institutional contexts must become aware and appreciative of the benefits and opportunities in the higher quality contexts. This integration may lead to cultural synergies, promoting reductions in institutional differentials over time. Assuming functional political institutions, institutional change through the democratic process is possible. Second, the worse the institutions in poor nations, the greater the "brain drain" phenomenon over time, acting as a natural corrective mechanism for governments or political elites. It may prompt political elites to contemplate the tradeoff of too much control of the economy taking measures toward achieving the optimal or the "efficient institutions" (Djankov et al. 2003). Losing highly skilled, knowledgeable, and talented constituents may provide bad governments with enough incentives to make better institutional choices at home to regain the lost talent over time, and to prevent further "brain drain."

Lastly, remittances attract FDI. The enhanced financial possibilities of the poor increase the capacity to spend on consumer goods and services. Foreign direct investors thrive in developing, emerging economies, with relatively stable and credible institutions.

Limitations of Remittances As a Form of Private Aid

The channeling of remittances toward productive activities in the local economy is limited by the quality of the recipient economy's prevalent institutions in two ways. First, unless the institutional environment at home allows for an open and competitive entrepreneurial environment, free of political privilege and cronyism, we can expect remittances to be eventually captured by rent-seeking groups, particularly groups with monopoly power over key resources, markets, and decision-making in society. This is a limitation in the sense that cronyism and monopolized markets reduce the full extent of remittances as a form of private aid. Several of the economies emerging out of the collapse of the Soviet Union, including Moldova, Ukraine, Kyrgyzstan, Belarus, and Russia, are dominated by state monopolies, oligarchies, and crony politicians. In captive markets, where producers have the power to restrict the quantity of goods or services supplied, the increased flow of external funds only exacerbates the increase in local prices of consumer goods compared to the level of the prices of the same goods and services in an open and competitive economy.

Second, in a restrictive institutional environment, remittances lead to "brain drain" or the phenomenon where the highly educated and highly skilled leave the country in pursuit of better opportunities available abroad. For example, working parents often send remittances home to support their children's educational ambitions, including paying for college tuition, and other professional development programs. Equipped with higher knowledge and sophisticated skills, yet trapped in closed environments, lacking opportunities commensurate with their expertise and talents, the children have no other option but to immigrate to countries with competitive job markets and entrepreneurial environments.

Foreign Direct Investment and Development

Advantages of FDI As a Form of Private Aid

Like remittances, private aid through FDI suffers from fewer knowledge problems, and fewer incentive problems, being guided by the competitive market process. Provided a market-enhancing institutional environment, the profit and loss mechanism of the entrepreneurial market process ensures the funds are allocated toward the entrepreneurial projects with the lowest opportunity cost. Investors incur loses when the investment decision turns out an entrepreneurial error, enough to motivate them to correct their calculations in the future. Foreign investors-entrepreneurs will choose to expand their operations in economies with a growing demand for their products or services in countries with reliable economic, financial, and legal institutions.

The emerging economies of Eastern and Central Europe, Russia, and Central Asia provided foreign investors with ideal consumer-oriented, growing markets after the collapse of communism. Table 12.4 shows the total amount of personal remittances received in 30 former socialist economies mirrored by the amount of net FDI received in 2007, and 2016, respectively. With the exception of war-torn countries like Ukraine, as the flows of remittances from Eastern European migrant workers earning wages in Western Europe and other parts of the world increased, the flows of FDI similarly increased (Table 12.4).

The presence of remittances opens up the set of entrepreneurial opportunities discoverable and exploitable by foreign entrepreneurs. Remittances provide the incentive and the confidence for foreign entrepreneurs to increase investments. Remittances stimulate the local economy not only directly by expanding the economic activity of local businesses, but also indirectly by attracting foreign investors employing the local labor force, bringing new ideas, products, services, and technologies.

Limitations of FDI As a Form of Private Aid

When Robert E. Lucas Jr. famously asked "Why does capital not flow from rich countries to poor countries?" (Lucas 1990), the role of the institutions governing the environments within which foreign investors may want to operate became key. In practice, we know that the quality of institutional contexts across countries, particularly the quality of economic,

Table 12.4 Total amount of personal remittances received and net FDI received in former socialist economies

2016			*2007*		
Country	*Personal remittances received*	*Net FDI received*	*Country*	*Personal remittances received*	*Net FDI received*
Ukraine	13.73	4.99	Poland	11.48	27.45
Russia	9.39	45.69	Ukraine	6.05	11.66
Poland	8.88	22.18	Russia	5.89	70.50
Hungary	5.94	89.05	Serbia	3.92	4.60
Romania	4.06	7.27	Bosnia & Herzegovina	3.09	2.12
Czech Rep.	4.04	14.01	Uzbekistan	2.55	1.06
Serbia	3.77	2.77	Hungary	2.48	76.02
Croatia	2.84	2.42	Tajikistan	2.34	0.50
Slovak Rep.	2.69	4.51	Czech Rep.	2.18	16.52
Uzbekistan	2.52	0.14	Croatia	2.16	5.32
Tajikistan	2.48	0.32	Bulgaria	2.03	16.65
Bosnia & Herzegovina	2.25	0.35	Moldova	1.98	0.71
Kyrgyz Rep.	2.03	0.63	Armenia	1.92	0.78
Bulgaria	1.94	1.93	Slovak Rep.	1.79	5.45
Georgia	1.75	1.83	Azerbaijan	1.74	6.31
Moldova	1.73	0.11	Romania	1.69	10.54
Armenia	1.64	0.40	Lithuania	1.64	2.63
Albania	1.61	1.29	Albania	1.60	0.71
Lithuania	1.49	1.12	Kosovo	1.10	0.72
Latvia	1.40	0.28	Georgia	1.05	2.24
Belarus	1.32	1.69	Kyrgyz Rep.	0.87	0.26
Kosovo	1.14	0.28	Latvia	0.58	2.87
Azerbaijan	1.06	7.41	Estonia	0.48	3.97
Montenegro	0.56	0.26	Macedonia	0.39	0.83
Estonia	0.54	1.04	Slovenia	0.36	2.13
Slovenia	0.50	1.78	Belarus	0.33	2.09
Kazakhstan	0.41	25.10	Montenegro	0.23	1.11
Macedonia	0.32	0.61	Kazakhstan	0.20	16.43
Turkmenistan	0.01	2.67	Turkmenistan	0.04	1.25

Source: World Bank, World Development Indicators; accessed December 19, 2018; sorted according to the personal remittances received; all figures are in billions of constant 2015 US dollars

monetary, legal, and political institutions varies considerably (Gwartney et al. 2017), and their complexity should not be taken for granted in development economics (Boettke et al. 2008). The stark differences in the economic performance of the socialist economies of C&EE, Russia, and

Central Asia, in particular, suggests that both the underlying differences in local institutions, and the leaders behind positive institutional reforms matter (Boettke and Nicoara 2015).

Like flows of remittances, the most productive channeling of the flows of FDI in a recipient economy Y is limited by the prevalent institutional context in Y. FDI flows can increase an economy's growth, so long as investors feel confident in the safety of their investment over a longer-term horizon. The answer to Robert Lucas's famous question of why does capital not flow from rich to poor countries became obvious during the post-communist transition. Legal institutions are fundamental for a credible investment climate, yet legal reforms were only partially successful across C&EE, and failed particularly in transition economies closer to Moscow (Boettke and Nicoara 2015). Although, soon after the fall of communism, FDI flows to formerly centrally planned economies of C&EE increased substantially from 1996 to 2010 (Gwartney and Montesinos 2018), as investors expected high returns, given the promising institutional and policy changes guided by Western experts, the FDI flows slowed down in recent years in response to weak legal system. Strong legal systems and policies open to FDI are a precondition for attracting and allocating foreign capital into the most productive and innovative way in a developing economy.

The Role of Institutions and Technologies in Channeling Remittances and FDI

Personal remittances are flows of savings from immigrants and migrant workers in rich countries to their beneficiaries, typically families, left behind, in poor countries. The funds received are typically absorbed by the local economy, being used for either consumption and/or real investment purposes. The subsistence level once surpassed, more of the funds can be used for investment, capital accumulation, and ultimately growth. For productive entrepreneurship, growth, and development, it is the local institutions that ultimately provide the incentives for individuals to choose to focus on the long run, restrain from consumption, and save and invest, or by contrary, indulge in present consumption.

One of the best examples of how better institutional rules can encourage entrepreneurial innovations that provide higher quality aid and lift people out of poverty is the mobile money revolution that has taken place over the past decade in Africa. For decades, policymakers in Africa have attempted to reduce financial exclusion (i.e. the percent of a nation's population that lacks access to a bank account or formal financial services) after numerous reports showed that lack of access to basic financial services like savings accounts and affordable credit was one of the greatest barriers to escaping extreme poverty (World Bank 2008). For the past half century, many policy advisors assumed that private banks were unable to profitably provide financial services to the poor. This was especially believed to be the case in remote regions where the low revenues banks could earn on the local population's meager savings made it economically infeasible for them to establish rural branches. The market's perceived inability to profitably extend financial services to the poor provided the theoretical rationale for a variety of foreign aid projects and state-led interventions into the financial sector (Demirguc-Kunt 2008).

Nowhere were these policies tried more extensively than in Sub-Saharan Africa in the early post-independence era. In the 1960s and 1970s, many governments cited their high rates of financial exclusion and underdeveloped banking systems as a justification for nationalizing private banks (particularly foreign-owned banks), requiring these state-controlled banks to target more services to the local unbanked population, establishing extensive interest rate controls, and forcing private banks to allocate credit at artificially low interest rates to "priority" sectors and, in particular, segments of the community that had been excluded for formal financial services (Brownbridge and Harvey 1998, 3–5).

The abysmal failure of these state-led financial development initiatives has been well documented (Beck and Cull 2013; Easterly and Levine 1997; Eilu and Auma 2017).[6] After decades of failed interventions, Sub-Saharan Africa still suffered from the lowest rates of financial inclusion in the developing world, with less than 20% of the adult population having access to bank accounts and formal financial services (Ondiege 2015; KPMG 2014; Beck and Cull 2013). This failure combined with the increased focus on financial inclusion as a critical step in escaping poverty, however, led some policymakers to shift their focus away from state-led solutions and toward more market-oriented ones (World Bank 2008). Many policy advisors began placing greater emphasis on promoting institutional reforms that would make it easier for private firms, entrepreneurs, and charities to use their localized knowledge to develop innovative products that would be better tailed to the needs of specific communities (Demirguc-Kunt and Cihak 2015).

The rise of mobile money in Kenya is the best case study in this "market-led" approach to achieving inclusive financial development (Burns 2018). Like many other African nations, Kenya suffered from very low rates of financial inclusion after years of failed state interventions. But thanks to the telecom deregulations of the 1990s, it boasted some of the highest rates of cell phone access in Africa. By the mid-2000s, cell phone ownership was nearly universal in Kenya—even in remote rural areas (GSMA 2015).

This combination of high financial exclusion rates and near-universal cell phone access created a unique opportunity for private aid organizations to work with private banks and telecom providers to develop mobile banking-related products that would allow unbanked citizens to access basic financial services. In 2006, the Kenyan telecom firm Safaricom partnered with the local microfinance group Faulu Kenya and the Commercial Bank of Kenya to launch a pilot version of M-Pesa (Hughes and Lonie 2007). The initial goal of M-Pesa was to provide a cheap, easy-to-use mobile payment platform that would to allow microfinance borrowers to more easily receive and repay microcredit and microfinance lenders to offer lower loan rates. Once it was introduced, developers discovered that customers were using M-Pesa to for a wide variety of purposes they hadn't anticipated such as sending money and airtime to family members, making payments to businesses, and even as a more secure repository for small-scale savings. In short, M-Pesa was filling the "financing gap" that policymakers had sought to eliminate for decades by giving customers in even remote areas access to proto-banking accounts.

After the enormous success of the pilot project, Safaricom and its partners wanted to introduce M-Pesa to the entire nation. Unfortunately, know-your-customer and anti-money laundering (KYC-AML) laws in Kenya and other African nations strictly banned non-banks like Safaricom from entering the market for financial services. Luckily, the Kenyan government recognized that M-Pesa might help them achieve their Millennium Development Goal of achieving universal financial access. In February 2007, the Central Bank of Kenya (CBK) issued Safaricom a "letter of no objection" exempting them from the onerous regulations that for decades had served as barriers to entry into the financial services sector. Perhaps most importantly, they also allowed Safaricom to use its vast network of retail branches across the country as mini-banks and exempted these "agent banks" from regulations that had for decades made it virtually impossible for traditional brick-and-mortal banks to profitably offer products to poor, unbanked customers (Burns 2018). Agents were permitted to open accounts under significantly relaxed KYC-AML requirements that were "proportionate" to their size and risk (Di Castri 2013, 22). In effect, M-Pesa was permitted to operate on a relatively unregulated basis as part of the CBK's "test and learn" approach to figuring out how it could monitor mobile money without stifling it at the outset with excessive regulation and red tape (Muthiora 2015).

The success of this "light-touch" approach to regulation has been well documented (GSMA 2015, 19).[7] By 2009, M-Pesa had reached 10 million customers. By 2011, the M-Pesa system in Kenya alone handled more transactions than Western Union did globally (Kendall 2011, 3). More than 95% of small business in Kenya reported that they accepted mobile money in exchange for goods and service and to pay their workers (Gikenye 2011). Today, Kenya has achieved near-universal financial access. As of 2017, there were more than 30 million mobile money accounts in Kenya issued by Safaricom and other telecom operators in partnership with private banks and microfinance firms and more than 150,000 agents branches located throughout the country (GSMA 2018). Moreover, mobile money now plays an essential role in virtually every sector of the Kenyan economy (Islam et al. 2016).

The pervasive reach of mobile money has had a transformative impact on the Kenyan economy. Most notably from the standpoint of providing private aid, it has paved the way for hundreds of new startup companies and private aid organizations who thanks to mobile money technology are now able to cheaply (and, in the case of private firms, profitably) offer their services. In 2011, private banks began partnering with mobile money providers to offer formal micro-savings and -credit accounts. The Commercial Bank of Africa's mobile banking app "M-Shwari" alone has connected more than 18 million Kenyans to interest-earning savings accounts; it has also issued $73.7 million in microloans per month in partnership with charities and microfinance organization (Cook and McKay 2015; Ngugi 2017). These secured mobile accounts have especially helped women by closing the long-acknowledged "gender gap" in access to financial services in the developing world (Chamlee-Wright 2005). Mobile banking apps have helped women become financially independent from their husbands. It has also helped increase their access to small-business loans, which has contributed to the sharp rise in women-owned business in Kenya (Colvile 2017). The new mobile money ecosystem has also caused a proliferation of micro-insurance products that directly cater to the needs of the poor. The most common is life insurance, but mobile health insurance, agriculture insurance, and auto insurance are beginning to gain traction. Bima Mkononi, for instance, allows Kenyans to open mobile life insurance accounts for as little as $0.15 a week. Micro-health startups like Changamka provide cheap mobile health insurance for customers who can't afford traditional healthcare packages and grant them access to health services at local hospitals and clinics (Nishtar et al. 2010). Kilimo Slama provides crop insurance to Kenyan farmers to help them hedge risk in case of a drought. Other popular apps like Lipa Kara help parents pay their children's tuition and other education-related expenses in small monthly installments (Haas and Nagarajan 2011).

All told, mobile money technology and the wide variety of privately provided services that it has helped spawn have done more to reduce poverty than decades of failed government initiatives and billions of dollars of foreign and international aid. Between 2007 and 2014 alone, Suri and Jack (2016) estimate that M-Pesa alone has lifted 194,000 Kenyan households (roughly 2% of the Kenyan population) out of poverty. The success of M-Pesa also has attracted the attention of dozens of private international aid organizations. Over the past few years, the Bill & Melinda Gates Foundation has poured millions of dollars into the Financial Services for the Poor initiative, partnering with telecoms and a variety of other private for-profit and not-for-profit aid organizations like GiveDirectly to expand the reach of mobile money and other digital financial services (Gates Foundation 2018). The Gates Foundation has also lobbied policymakers on behalf of these groups to adopt relaxed regulatory standards that make it easier for new firms and entrepreneurs to enter the mobile money space and launch innovative products.[8]

What's even more promising for proponents of entrepreneurial-led development is that the success of M-Pesa has led many other African nations to emulate Kenya's "enabling regulatory environment" (Burns 2018; Muthiora 2015). In much of the continent, regulators followed the CBK's lead by allowing non-bank payment services to enter the market and exempting them from burdensome KYC-AML requirements and other costly regulations. According to GSMA (2018), Sub-Saharan Africa is home to more than half of the mobile money accounts in the world. Africa leads world in mobile financial accounts, with 24,652 per 100,000 adults versus a world average of only 4361. There are 19 markets in Africa alone that have more mobile money accounts than bank accounts. The World Bank (2014) reported that thanks in large part to mobile money the overall share of adults in Africa with a financial account jumped from 24% in 2011 to 38% in 2017 (World Bank 2018). As of 2017, there have been 276 different mobile money deployments in 90 countries serving 690 million people (GSMA 2018).

The mobile money revolution is a prime example of how, in the right institutional setting, the private sector is more than capable of achieving development goals. These results were achieved not due to foreign aid or expansive state intervention. They resulted from policymakers taking a step back and creating an enabling regulatory environment that was conducive to "permissionless innovation" (Thierer 2014). These enabling policies succeed precisely because they enlisted and utilize the superior knowledge and incentives of private sector actors in the greater development effort. Local entrepreneurs and private aid groups were able to craft innovative products that were economically viable and a better "cultural fit" for their community (Chamlee-Wright 1993). The results in terms of financial inclusion and poverty reduction have been extraordinary.

Conclusion

Social scientists, policy experts, political leaders, NGOs, and even celebrities have all tried different solutions to help the poor, with at best mixed results. For example, foreign aid through Official Development Assistance suffers from pervasive knowledge and incentive problems. Concomitantly with deliberate aid programs and initiatives run for many decades, private individuals and for-profit organizations have been able to prove that remittances and FDIs are a more effective form of international aid. Open borders and strong legal systems, in particular, can help promote growth opportunities for the poor within their developing economies. One feature of personal remittances as a form of private aid is their decentralized nature. Additionally, as a source of funding, remittances may not only surpass in magnitude the net ODA or other forms of giving, but also privately directed funds reach the intended beneficiaries without the informational asymmetries that typically plague more centralized forms. The for-profit nature of FDI, combined with functional market institutions and a strong legal-institutional environment, may lead to the discovery and exploitation of previously untapped opportunities for economic expansion and dynamism in a low-income area (where private saving is lacking or inadequate), including the creation of new jobs, investments in R&D, and the development of financial institutions.

In this chapter, we argue in favor of the role of personal remittances and Foreign Direct Investment (FDI) as the forms of international private aid most compatible with sustainable economic growth and development. We argue that remittances and FDIs may be not only the most prevalent forms of private aid, but also the most effective forms at improving standards of living, market complexity, and the institutional prospects in poor nations. Globalization led to increased flow of remittances and FDI from developed to developing economies. The increased flow of funds across borders helped stimulate the emergence of alternative payment technologies and microfinance institutions more in line with the extent of the local markets and the needs of the poor. Lastly, remittances may positively interact with the existing policies and economic and political institutions in the recipient nations, over time.

Notes

1. North (1994, 359) similarly notes that neoclassical growth theorists largely failed to predict the demise of their own development planning initiatives because they "ignored the incentive structure embodied in institutions."
2. As Mises argued 40 years earlier, entrepreneurship is a universal aspect of human action that can be found in all societies. He (1949 [1996], 251–252) explained:

   > In any real and living economy, every actor is always an entrepreneur and speculator ... Economics, in speaking of entrepreneurs, has in view not men, but a definite function. This function is not [a] feature of a particular special group or class of men; it is inherent in every action and burdens every actor.

3. As Boettke and Coyne (2009, 138) argue:

   > In general, institutions shape entrepreneurial opportunities which have real effects on the ability of the economic system to realize the gains from social cooperation under the division of labor. Where institutions produce a net benefit to productive opportunities (e.g., arbitrage and innovation) entrepreneurs will exploit those opportunities resulting in the creation of wealth. Likewise, when there is a relatively high benefit to engaging in unproductive activities (e.g., rent-seeking and crime), entrepreneurs will take advantage of those opportunities.

4. Coyne (2013) contrasts the "constrained view" of what policymakers can achieve given the economic reality of scarcity and limited knowledge and the political economy reality of perverse incentives and unintended consequences

with the "unconstrained view" of foreign aid advocates like Paul Collier and Jeffrey Sachs. This constrained view is aptly summarized by Hayek's (1988) quote: "The curious task of economics is to demonstrate to men how little they really know about what they imagine they can design."

5. The International Monetary Fund's (IMF) Balance of Payment Manual (BPM6 2013).
6. Brownbridge and Harvey (1998, 1) summarized their findings on post-colonial era banking in Africa: "Government interventions … in the post-independence period, were at best ineffective; at worst, they had very damaging consequences for banks, and for the whole economy." They further concluded that "the countries which had experienced the most extensive government interventions suffered the worst damage" (ibid., 203).
7. Chandy, Dervis, and Rocker (2012, 13) argued that Kenya's approach of "allowing regulation to follow innovation" through the "limited regulation of M-PESA's network of agents" was absolutely critical to its success. As Donovan (2012, 65) concluded, "Kenya's initial success with mobile money" stemmed from "a virtual *absence* of regulations." Ndemo (2017, 356) likewise observed that "M-PESA is a classic case where innovation preceded policy."
8. According to the strategy statement at the Financial Services for the Poor webpage: "For DFS to realize its full potential, policymakers and business leaders will need to invest in the right payment infrastructure, regulatory standards, and customer activation strategies to ensure continued progress toward the promise of financial inclusion."

References

Bauer, Peter T. 2004. *From Subsistence to Exchange and Other Essays.* Princeton, NJ: Princeton University Press.

Baumol, William J. 1990. "Entrepreneurship: Productive, Unproductive, and Destructive." *Journal of Political Economy* 98 (5): 893–921.

Beck, Thorsten, and Robert Cull. 2013. "Banking in Africa." *CSAE Working Paper* (Center for the Study of African Economies).

Boettke, Peter J. 1998. "Economic Calculation: The Austrian Contribution to Political Economy." *Advances in Austrian Economics* 5: 131–158.

Boettke, Peter J., and Christopher J. Coyne. 2009. "Context Matters: Institutions and Entrepreneurship." *Foundations and Trends in Entrepreneurship* 5 (3): 135–209.

Boettke, Peter, and Olga Nicoara. 2015. "What Have We Learned from the Collapse of Communism?" In *The Austrian Handbook of Austrian Economics.* Oxford University Press.

Boettke, Peter J., Christopher J. Coyne, Peter T. Leeson. 2008. Institutional Stickiness and the New Development Economics. *American Journal of Economics and Sociology* 67 (2): 331–358.

Brownbridge, Martin, and Charles Harvey. 1998. *Banking in Africa: the impact of financial sector reform since independence.* Kampala: Fountain Publishers.

Burns, Scott. 2018. "M-Pesa and the Market-Led Approach to Financial Inclusion." *Economic Affairs* 33 (2): 406–421.

Chamlee-Wright, Emily. 2005. *Fostering Sustainable Complexity in the Microfinance Industry.* Oxford: Blackwell Publishing.

Chamlee-Wright, Emily. 1993. "Indigenous African Institutions and Economic Development." *Cato Journal* 13 (1): 79–104.

Chandy, Laurence, Kemal Dervis, and Steven Rocker. 2012. *Clicks into Bricks, Technology into Transformation, and the Fight Against Poverty.* Brookings Blum Roundtable 2012, Washington, D.C.: Brookings Institute.

Colvile, Robert. 2017. *Mobile Phones Are Anti-Poverty Devices.* February 27. https://fee.org/articles/mobile-phones-are-anti-poverty-devices/

Cook, Tamara, and Claudia McKay. 2015. *How M-Shwari Works: The Story So Far.* Washington, D.C.: CGAP.

Coyne, Christopher J. 2013. *Doing Bad by Doing Good: Why Humanitarian Action Fails.* Stanford University Press.

Demirguc-Kunt, Asli. 2008. *Finance and Economic Development: The Role of Government.* Washington, D.C.: World Bank.

Demirguc-Kunt, Asli, and Martin Cihak. 2015. "Revisiting the State's Role in Finance and Development." In *The Oxford Handbook of Banking, Second Edition*, by Allen N. Berger, Philip Molyneux and John O. S. Wilson. Oxford: Oxford University Press.

Di Castri, Simone. 2013. *Mobile Money: Enabling Regulatory Solutions.* GSMA.

Djankov, Simeon, Edward Glaeser, Rafael La Porta, Florencio Lopez-de-Silanes, Andrei Shleifer. 2003. The new comparative economics. *Journal of Comparative Economics* 31 (4): 595–619.

Donovan, K. 2012. Mobile money for financial inclusion. *Information and Communications for Development* 61 (1): 61–73.

Easterly, William. 2006. *The White Man's Burden: why the West's efforts to aid the rest have done so much ill and so little good.* Penguin Press.

Easterly, William, and Ross Levine. 1997. "Africa's Growth Tragedy: policies and ethnic divisions." *The Quarterly Journal of Economics* 1203–1250.

Eilu, Emmanuel, and Theresa Odur Auma. 2017. "Mobile Money Services As a Panacea to Financial Inclusion in Sub-Saharan Africa: The Case of Uganda." *International Journal of Technology Diffusion* 8 (4): 77–87.

Faria, Hugo J, and Hugo M Montesinos. 2009. "Does Economic Freedom Cause Prosperity? An IV Approach." *Public Choice* 103–127.

Gates Foundation. 2018. *Financial Services for the Poor: Strategy Overview.* November 12. https://www.gatesfoundation.org/What-We-Do/Global-Growth-and-Opportunity/Financial-Services-for-the-Poor

Gikenye, Wakari. 2011. "The Diffusion of Mobile Phones for Business and Information Management in Kenya." *2nd International Conference on Information Management and Evaluation*. 511–520.

GSMA. 2015. *2015 State of the Industry Report: Mobile Money.* GSMA.

GSMA. 2018. *2017 State of the Industry Report on Mobile Money.* GSMA.

Gwartney, James D, and Hugo M Montesinos. 2018. "Former Centrally Planned Economies 25 Years After the Fall of Communism." *Cato Journal* 285–309.

Gwartney, James, Robert Lawson, and Joshua Hall. 2017. "Economic Freedom of the World. 2017 Annual Report." Fraser Institute.

Gwartney, James, Robert Lawson, and Randall Holcombe. 1999. "Economic freedom and the environment for economic growth." *Journal of Institutional and Theoretical Economics* 155 (1): 643–663.

Haas, Sherri, and Geetha Nagarajan. 2011. *Going to School with M-PESA.* November. Accessed December 12, 2014. http://www.fsassessment.umd.edu/notes/education-through-mpesa.html

Hayek, Friedrich A. 1988. *The Fatal Conceit: The Errors of Socialism.* London: Routledge.

Hayek, Friedrich A. 1945. "The Use of Knowledge in Society." *American Economic Review* 35 (4): 519–30.

Hughes, Nick, and Susie Lonie. 2007. "M-PESA: mobile money for the "unbanked" turning cellphones into 24-hour tellers in Kenya." *Innovations* 63–81.

Islam, Asif, Silvia Muzi, and Jorge Luis Rodriguez Meza. 2016. "Does mobile money use increase firms' investment? Evidence from Enterprise Surveys in Kenya, Uganda, and Tanzania." *Small Business Economics* 1–22.

Kasper, Wolfgang, Manfred E. Streit, and Peter J. Boettke. 2013. *Institutional Economics: Property, Competition, Policies.* 2nd Edition. Cheltenham: Edward Elgar.

Kendall, Jake. 2011. "An Emerging Platform: From Money Transfer System to Mobile Money Ecosystem." (UC Irvine School of Law).

KPMG. 2014. *Banking in Africa.* KPMG.

Lucas, Robert E. 1990. "Why Doesn't Capital Flow from Rich to Poor Countries?" *The American Economic Review* 80 (2): 92–96.

Minniti, Maria, ed. 2007. *Entrepreneurship: The Engine of Growth.* Vol. 1. 3 vols. Westport, CT: Praeger Perspectives.

Mises, Ludwig. 1920 [2012]. *Economic Calculation in the Socialist Commonwealth.* Auburn, AL: Ludwig von Mises Institute.

———. 1949 [1996]. *Human Action: A Treatise on Economics.* San Francisco: Fox & Wilkes.

Moyo, Dambisa, and Niall Ferguson. 2010. *Dead Aid: Why Aid Is Not Working and How There Is a Better Way for Africa*. Reprint edition. Farrar, Straus and Giroux.

Muthiora, Brian. 2015. *Enabling Mobile Money Policies in Kenya: Fostering a Digital Financial Revolution*. Nairobi: GSMA and the Bill and Melinda Gates Foundation.

Ndemo, Bitange. 2017. "Inside a Policymaker's Mind: An Entrepreneurial Approach to Policy Development and Implementation." In *Digital Kenya*, by Weiss T. Ndemo B., 339–367. London: Palgrave Studies of Entrepreneurship in Africa.

Ngugi, Brian. 2017. *CBA celebrates five years of M-Shwari as clients cross 18m mark*. December 5. https://www.businessdailyafrica.com/corporate/companies/CBA-celebrates-five-years-of-M-Shwari/4003102-4216138-xadd35z/index.html

Nishtar, Sania, and et al. 2010. "Protecting the poor against health impoverishment in Pakistan: Proof of concept of the potential within innovative web and mobile phone technologies." *World Health Report*.

North, Douglass C. 1994. "Economic Performance Through Time." *American Economic Review* 359–368.

———. 1990. *Institutions, Institutional Change and Economic Performance*. Cambridge, MA: Cambridge University Press.

North, Douglass C. 1986. "The New Institutional Economics." *Journal of Institutional and Theoretical Economics* 230–237.

Olson, Mancur. 1996. "Big Bills Left on the Sidewalk: Why Some Nations Are Rich and Others Poor." *Journal of Economic Perspectives* 10 (1): 3–24.

Ondiege, Peter O. 2015. *Regulatory Impact on Mobile Money and Financial Inclusion in African Countries – Kenya, Nigeria, Tanzania, and Uganda*. Nairobi: Center for Global Development.

Powell, Benjamin. 2008. *Making poor nations rich: Entrepreneurship and the process of economic development*. Stanford, CA: Stanford University Press.

Smith, Adam. 1776 [2008]. *An Inquiry into the nature and causes of the Wealth of Nations*. Hamburg: Management Laboratory Press.

Suri, Tavneet, and William Jack. 2016. "The long-run poverty and gender impacts of mobile money." *Science* 354 (6317): 1288–1292.

Thierer, Adam. 2014. *Permissionless Innovation: The Continuing Case for Comprehensive Technological Freedom*. Arlington, Virginia: Mercatus Center at George Mason University.

Tullock, Godon. 1965 [2005]. "The Politics of Bureaucracy." In *The Selected Works of Gordon Tullock, Volume 6*, by Charles Rowley (ed), 13–235. Indianapolis, IN: Liberty Fund.

United Nations Department of Economic and Social Affairs. 2018. "Remittances – an Untapped Engine for Sustainable Development | UN DESA |." n.d.

Accessed June 27, 2019. https://www.un.org/development/desa/en/news/population/remittances-engine-for-sustdev.html.

Williamson, Claudia R. 2010. "Exploring the failure of foreign aid: The role of incentives and information." *Review of Austrian Economics* 23 (1): 17–33.

Williamson, Claudia R., and Christopher J. Coyne. 2014. "Can International Aid Improve Health?" In *The Handbook of Global Health Policy*, by Garrett, Yamey, Gavin, Wamala, Sarah Brown. Wiley-Blackwell.

World Bank. 2008. *Finance for All?: Policies and Pitfalls in Expanding Access.* Washington, DC: World Bank.

World Bank. 2018. *Global Financial Development Report 2017/2018: Bankers Without Borders.* Washington, D.C.: World Bank Group.

World Bank. 2010. "Outlook for Remittance Flows 2010–2011." In *Migration and Development Brief.*

World Bank. 2014. Global Financial Inclusion Database. Retrieved December 8, 2015, from http://databank.worldbank.org/data/reports.aspx?source=global-findex

CHAPTER 13

The Role of Entrepreneurs in Facilitating Remittances in Cuba

Stefanie Haeffele and Anne Lynn Hobson

> We are not in war here in Cuba, but remittances are like a humanitarian help. Cuba is a place of disasters. We don't have earthquakes or volcanoes, but we have a chaotic economic system that makes us living in a constant state of alert due to any upcoming crisis. We can have two or three months of higher income for something that happened, but we always worry that in any moment the situation can turn around and then you have to figure things out. (Alejandro)[1]

Introduction

In times of crises—whether economic or political, natural or man-made—individuals seek to help those in need. Such aid may be given directly to family and friends or through charities and government-led initiatives, and may be targeted to those in need in one's own community, in their current or home country, or across the globe. The characteristics and consequences of the crisis, and the individual needs of those impacted by crisis, is context-specific and plagued with uncertainty. In this complex environ-

S. Haeffele (✉) • A. L. Hobson
George Mason University, Arlington, VA, USA
e-mail: shaeffele@mercatus.gmu.edu; ahobson@mercatus.gmu.edu

N. Dutta, C. R. Williamson (eds.), *Lessons on Foreign Aid and Economic Development*, https://doi.org/10.1007/978-3-030-22121-8_13

ment, aid is likely to be most effective when (1) the local needs and circumstances are understood by the aid providers, (2) the aid is provided directly to those in need (rather than being filtered and altered through middlemen, political processes, etc.) and (3) the aid, and systems used to provide it, is flexible in order to adapt to changing needs and circumstances.[2] We argue that remittances—a form of private aid of money or in-kind goods sent from workers to their home countries—serve as an effective source of aid that is more likely to be provided by individuals with knowledge of the needs and circumstances to those directly in need, and is adaptable when circumstances change. Indeed, remittances now outpace public aid flows (Kpodar and Le Goff 2011), and remittances account for 23.6 percent of global foreign aid spending (Hudson Institute 2016).

The decentralized method of providing remittances works because both the providers and receivers can act entrepreneurially about how to best deliver and use the aid. Specifically, we examine the use of remittances in Cuba and find that entrepreneurs, by relying on creativity and alertness to opportunities, overcome the costs—such as transaction fees, logistical difficulties, and regulatory barriers—associated with delivering aid to intended recipients.

Cuban President Fidel Castro legalized possession of the US dollar in 1993, after the dissolution of the Soviet Union in 1989 and the subsequent economic recession (known as the "special period"). At the time of the dissolution of the Soviet Union, trade between Cuba and Soviet countries amounted to 85 percent of the island's commerce (Eckstein 2010). In the four years following the dissolution, Cuba's economy contracted by over 30 percent even after receiving new aid assistance from Venezuela and China (ibid.). Castro allowed remittance transfers from the US as a way to acquire hard currency to finance investment and imports and serve as a supplemental source of development capital (ibid.). For several years after the collapse of the Soviet Union, the US tried to restrict aid to put pressure on the regime, capping the amount of annual remittances and limiting it to immediate family. However, rising economic need, demand for remittance services by the diaspora, and decreased political pressure paved the way for the US to grant Western Union, a money transfer service, a license to do business in Cuba (Western Union 2016a). At that time, the amount of remittances allowed by US policy was capped at $300 in any three-month period and was restricted to immediate family only (OFAC 2009). The 2009 amendment to the Cuban Assets Control Regulations permitted unlimited remittances at whatever amount and frequency to "close relatives." The amendment also removed travel restrictions for family members, expanded the list of goods Cuban-Americans can send to their families—most notably to include personal hygiene items, clothing, and fishing gear—and permitted American telecommunications companies to operate in Cuba. In 2011, another amendment to the regulations allowed US citizens to send remittances to nonfamily members in Cuba (Sullivan 2016). These changes resulted in increased remittance flows and lower charges for wiring money (Western Union 2016a).

Using remittance practices between the US and Cuba as a case study, this chapter will highlight the critical role of entrepreneurs in identifying need for remittances, connecting suppliers of remittance aid with demanders, and sustaining social networks in the aftermath of economic crises. This chapter utilizes qualitative interviews with 17 Cuban nationals completed in 2016 to demonstrate the key role entrepreneurs play in facilitating remittance flows as a form of private aid.[3] These interviews, used in conjunction with data on remittances and previous literature, helps to provide insight into the individual circumstances and narratives of the entrepreneurs that drive these flows. Given that the role of local entrepreneurs in post-disaster aid is underplayed on the global scene and local efforts are often crowded out by a more bureaucratic provision of aid through NGO's or federal governments, this approach provides insight into the consequences of favoring certain forms of aid over others.

The History of Remittances in Cuba

Remittances are direct transfers between donors and recipients and constitute one of the most robust poverty reduction efforts for poor countries (Adelman 2009). These peer-to-peer transfers are a key source of private aid for countries recovering from crises and have significant economic and social effects in the countries where they are received. For example, in El Salvador, remittances make up a large part of the country's income, accounting for 20.4 percent of GDP in 2017 (World Bank 2017). In Haiti, Nepal, Tajikistan, Tonga, and Kyrgyzstan, the remittances account for roughly one third of GDP. An estimated $564 billion in remittances was sent by migrants to their home countries in 2016, down slightly from $581 billion in 2015 (World Bank 2018).

A Hudson Institute index of 39 donor countries found that private aid was five times greater than government aid for donations to the developing world from 1992 to 2014 (Hudson Institute 2016). It is important to note that in the 1950s and 1960s the dichotomy was flipped—with public flows amounting for the majority of US engagement with poor countries (Adelman 2009). By 2014, remittances constituted the second largest financial flow ($224 billion) to developing countries, behind private capital flows of $513 billion.[4] Notably, these numbers included only official remittance flows, not informal transfers. Moreover, while the index did include countries representing 82 percent of the world's population and 89 percent of the world's GDP, it did not include Cuba. Likewise, the IMF, World Bank and Inter-American Development Bank lack remittance statistics for Cuba. Cuba remains an understudied area due to the lack of official data on flows, an inability to capture informal transfers, and a variety of unique policy constraints and institutional constraints.

The most accurate assessment was calculated by the Havana Consulting Group of Miami, Florida, based on its own estimates and statistics released by the Oficina Nacional de Estadísticas e Información in Havana. Cubans received $6.85 billion in total remittances in 2015, up from $2.6 billion in 2012 (Morales 2016). In addition, in-kind remittances in 2015 were estimated at more than $3.5 billion (ibid.). In-kind remittances in Cuba commonly include medicine, appliances, clothes, electronics, and cell phone minutes. Annual remittances per person now amount to over three times the annual amount paid to state employees in Cuba (Morales 2013).

Technological advancement, such as Western Union's mobile money transfer service, has lowered the cost of sending remittances worldwide. The average cost of sending remittances—estimated at 7.7 percent for $200 worldwide—declined to 6 percent in Latin America and the Caribbean region due to technological advancement such as online and mobile transfer options. Nevertheless, mobile transfer remains inaccessible in Cuba. The cost of sending remittances from the US to Cuba is the second highest in Latin America at 12.43 percent of the total amount sent (Orozco 2010). This includes a 10 percent tax, instituted in 2004, as a response to the strengthening of US sanctions. Despite these taxes, remittance flows are a major source of income for Cubans. Remittances reached more than 62 percent of Cuban households in 2016 (Western Union 2016b). The average amount sent from the US to Cuba in 2010 was $150 (Orozco 2010).

The literature on global remittance flows suggests that remittances reduce poverty through direct aid to those in need as well as reduce inequality, increase investment and growth, and help countries adjust to external shocks (see Fajnzylber and López 2008). In a cross-cultural econometric approach for 69 countries, researchers identified that remittances improve primary and secondary school attainment, increase life expectancy, and reduce infant mortality (Zhunio et al. 2012). In Latin America as a whole, studies conducted using surveys and econometric models showed how remittances increase growth and lower poverty levels, yet only modestly (Acosta et al. 2007, 2008). Remittance flows strengthen economic and societal relations, generate demand for migrant tourism, increase business competition, and are associated with diversification of export economies in Central America (Eckstein 2002; Orozco 2010).

Interviews with Cuban citizens revealed that remittances in Cuba are primarily used for immediate consumption such as purchasing food including chicken, cooking oil, coffee, salt, or powdered milk. Cubans also reported using money remittances for medicines, clothing, home, and car repair, special events, and fixing appliances such as fans or refrigerators. This suggests that Cubans use remittances to first reduce immediate need by purchasing perishable food items (living at subsistence levels) and then, second, to repair or invest in more nonperishable goods that can improve the livelihood. The interviews also show that as Cubans are able to alleviate their most pressing needs through the assistance of remittances, they then may turn to investing resources into more long-term plans. The goal of remittances is often to provide immediate relief to those in need, provided by those who can easily understand and deliver on their needs.

Further, remittances in Cuba operate in a unique societal and institutional environment in which there is an innate tension between the interests of the state and the interests of the Cuban people in receiving remittances (Eckstein 2010). The Cuban government benefits by taxing remittance flows and gaining access to hard currency (Eckstein 2004). Yet by encouraging remittance flows, the Cuban government unintentionally set into motion liberalizing dynamics that authorities can no longer control (Eckstein 2002).[5] She argues that cross-border social and economic ties not only raise the standard of living of Cubans, but expose them to a different set of values that can undermine state control (Eckstein 2010, 1054). Eckstein cautions, however, that while remittances likely reduce the control of the Cuban state on its citizens, remittances also exacerbate urban-rural inequalities and race-based income inequality between whites and non-whites (ibid., 1053).

The individuals who coordinate the sending of remittances, those that provide services through which to send them, and the aid recipients themselves play an entrepreneurial role in overcoming constraints associated with transferring money and in-kind remittances. Further, access to these resources allow for poverty reductions as well as a broadening of the network and ideas that Cubans have access to and, potentially, can lead to liberalizing reforms.

The Role of Entrepreneurs in Facilitating Remittance Flows

In times of crisis, the environment is characterized by uncertainty and change. For instance, after a hurricane or major storm, there is widespread physical damage and, in many cases, utilities and telecommunication is hampered. Survivors must try to locate others, determine if their homes and jobs still exist, and plan to return and rebuild or to start fresh somewhere new. Their decisions will be impacted by the formal response from government and charity, the decisions of their family, neighbors, and coworkers, as well as the opportunities available both at home and elsewhere. In the case of prolonged economic and political crises, such as the contemporary experience in Cuba, daily life is impacted by the lack of resources, access to broader networks, and the changing political landscape. Time, energy, and resources are spent finding creative ways to stretch income, food supplies, and other goods. Uncertainty about the future hinders innovation.

In these circumstances, coordination is costly and difficult. Those seeking to help, whether from within or abroad, must be able to (1) identify the issues and needs of the effected population, (2) provide targeted solutions to those in need, and (3) be able to adjust when their first attempts fail or circumstances change.[6] Entrepreneurs play a critical role in the provision, distribution, and use of remittances as private aid because they are more likely to achieve the criteria of knowledge, application, and adaptability. They act as the "man on the spot," who sees issues on the ground and who also may recognize opportunities to fix them, especially in situations characterized by uncertainty and imperfect knowledge (see Hayek 1945; Kirzner 1997, 1999). Furthermore, entrepreneurs are bold visionaries who disrupt the status quo by providing a new service, creating a new market or employing a new method of acquiring or providing resources (Schumpeter 1962).

In crisis, when uncertainty abounds and information is lacking, the entrepreneur can push recovery or progress forward by acting on possibilities that others may not foresee. Indeed, Storr, Haeffele-Balch, and Grube

(2015) find that entrepreneurs (who can be individuals on or connected to those on the ground) play a critical role in disaster recovery by finding and providing resources, creating or leveraging existing social networks, and connecting aid suppliers with demanders. Entrepreneurs in this sense are individuals, from all aspects of life (not just economic but social, ideological, and political entrepreneurs as well) that employ local knowledge and creativity to facilitate aid.

The role of entrepreneurs in the provision of aid has been well documented in the context of Hurricane Katrina in the US. Local church leaders and small business owners anticipated the needs of their community members by providing food, shelter, health services, and other resources and by connecting people together to overcome challenges—either by assisting in rescue missions, traveling to visit evacuees, or providing a space where residents can swap information, collaborate their efforts, and learn each other's mistakes (Storr et al. 2015). Even large-scale retailers empowered their local managers to act entrepreneurially. For instance, managers of local Wal-Mart stores in Louisiana opened their doors for residents to take any remaining supplies free of charge and delivered water to a local retirement home (Horwitz 2009). Further, government officials even acted entrepreneurially to provide for their community. For instance, Doris Voitier, a school superintendent knew that families would not be able to return to St. Bernard Parish unless there was schooling for their children and promised to reopen her schools as quickly as possible. Despite pushback and red-tape from the Federal Emergency Management Agency (FEMA) and other federal agencies, she purchased equipment and supplies needed to reopen the schools (essentially asking for forgiveness instead of permission) (Chamlee-Wright 2010; Storr et al. 2015). Furthermore, entrepreneurs leveraged their social networks to "serve as informal insurance and promote mutual assistance after a disaster" as well as coordinate invaluable diffuse information and resources (Aldrich 2012, 149–150).

In the context of coordinating aid, three types of knowledge are critical—identifying the extent of the crisis, determining what aid is needed, and evaluating on-going aid efforts (Sobel and Leeson 2007; Storr and Haeffele-Balch 2012). Entrepreneurs drive such coordination by making use of this dispersed and imperfect knowledge, resources, and networks in creative ways. In short, entrepreneurs are both change agents alert to opportunities to help those in need as well as innovators that challenge existing conventions and limitations on the ground.

An Analysis of Entrepreneurship in the Provision of Remittances for Private Aid in Cuba

Entrepreneurs facilitate remittance flows in Cuba by anticipating the local needs of Cubans, connecting aid suppliers with aid demanders, and sustaining social networks. For example, remittance senders who understand the needs of Cubans will ensure remittances are more likely to be used and help those in need. Understanding that Cubans want money to purchase food, medicine, or essential items for themselves and their kids or that they need particular goods like cellphones will allow remittance senders to better address their needs than donating other new or used goods that may or may not be of use. Furthermore, entrepreneurs form informal networks of travelers to the island to ensure the delivery of in-kind remittances (rather than risk them getting intercepted) or to evade the tax on formal money remittances (lowering the cost of remittances and increasing the amount received by Cubans directly). Cubans also create or sustain their social networks with remittance senders, maintaining social ties and distribution channels.

These roles for entrepreneurs are crucial for assisting Cubans. Indeed, interviewees agreed that for a majority of recipients in Cuba, remittances fulfill basic economic needs in a country that is still in a state of economic crisis. For example, Nalda summarized that

> The Cuban society, or better yet, Cuba's economy, is an economy that has been in crisis for many years. Even before 1993. ... When [mines and plantations] were nationalized starting in the year 1961, which was one of the greatest mistakes of the Revolution, nationalizing everything. What happened? The economy went into a crisis. The country did not develop. ... So, we started depending entirely on the former Soviet Union and of the former Eastern Bloc countries. ... And Cuba's production never increased. It was as if the Cuban state thought that we would never stop depending on those countries. Of course, they never thought that the socialist countries would stop being socialist. That never crossed Fidel's mind. So of course, since we were so dependent, when the socialist countries fell, we barely had any production because we had not developed any production. ... Then we started becoming dependent on Venezuela. But Venezuela is a country that is also in crisis. That dependency is not as big as it was before though. So, Cuba has been developing a little in some sectors, but it is still an economy that is in crisis.

The sense of pervasive and persistent economic need was ubiquitous. In the face of such necessity, it became apparent that remittances are a source of relief and comfort. All 17 interviewees recounted a period of time where food was scarce and many noted the role remittances still play in food security: "Without remittances, we would all starve" (Francisco).

Remittance recipients recounted feeling pride and gratitude as well as diminished stress and worry. However, the process of receiving remittances can be strenuous due to taxes, fees, delays, uncertainty, confiscation, a lack of banking infrastructure, and policies restricting the amount of remittances or the weight of items that can be sent.

Of the 11 interviewees (out of 17) who received remittances, 10 relied primarily on Western Union. Western Union remains the quickest and most popular method of direct money transfer, despite the Cuban government taxing the service. Esmeralda states that,

> Western Union is very practical. Someone sends the money and two hours later, at the latest, you can retrieve your money in any Western Union office. There are a lot of offices. You get a number, and you just call the office, give them the number and your name. You receive the given amount in CUC. [The remittance sender] pays the difference [in taxes] when they deposit.

Money transfers from other countries besides the US are not as simple because money is routed through the Cuban state-owned bank network, a process which can take several months and requires intermittently braving a long line to get information about the status of the transfer. For instance, Teresa noted that, "The lines at the bank are huge. Just to take out 4 pesos, it'll take you a whole day." And while Cuban banks do offer a stored-value debit card, it can take weeks to receive one and requires a minimum of 50 Cuban convertible Peso (CUC) to open one (for comparison, the average monthly pension in Cuba is 200 Cuban Peso (CUP), which is around 8 CUC or $8). Furthermore, there are limits on withdrawal amounts. Francisco observes that,

> Say I have my bank account and I have to travel tomorrow to the U.S., and I have 5,000 dollars and I need it, I won't get it. To get it out of the bank account, I need to get out 100 CUC per day. 100 in one location, 100 in another location, and so on. When you have to take it out you have to fill out a form stating what you're using it for … So, it's a hassle to get money out of your account, especially if it's in big amounts. And the line kills you. You lose time and money—and it's your money.

Cubans can legally send in-kind remittances through DHL international shipping services, via Copa Airlines or through regular mail, and the United States Postal Service resumed service to Cuba in 2016. Three interviewees had received mail through traditional mail services. However, the Cuban customs process is notorious for lengthy delays, broken cargo, or packages with replaced items, lost, or stolen items. Francisco recalled waiting for a package with coffee and razors, and only the razors ultimately arrived. He also told us, "I had some friends that went to China to buy winter clothes. By the time they got it out of customs it was summer." As Teresa recounted:

> about three years ago, a relative of mine sent from England some products, and all of the products were replaced. At the end, what is sent from there is not what you receive here. Most of the products are changed here to the ones that they sell in the markets. For example, someone sent me an iron, and the iron that I got was the one that they have in the store here. The beers were Bucaneros, the ones that are made in Cuba.

Luggage coming from the US to Cuba also faces weight restrictions and customs fees. Those traveling with large quantities of single items such as a razors or cell phones may have items confiscated. Alberto explains the process:

> A Cuban that has the possibility to travel and work, as you might have noticed, comes back with several suitcases for their family. When they get to customs they can't enter more than a certain amount of kilograms and they have to pay for each extra kilo that they bring. They charge it at the airport in the U.S., and then they charge it again at the airport here. The things that you were able to bring end up costing you a whole lot of money, like if you would have bought them in the most expensive store in the world. But in a certain way, that also helps people here because you can't find things.

Given the lack of goods being produced or imported into Cuba, remittances (both money and in-kind goods) play a large role in sustaining daily life in Cuba. And the complexity of the situation and the process of aid provision highlight the need for enterprising individuals to help overcome these limitations, create new methods of providing remittances, and leverage social networks to act as agents of positive change. We find that entrepreneurship exists among the providers of remittance services as well as by individual remittance senders and receivers.

Entrepreneurship Among Providers of Remittance Services

The most trusted method for the transport of in-kind remittances is private agencies that arrange trips from the US to Cuba as well as the delivery of goods once they arrive in Cuba. Cubans use this service to mitigate the danger of broken or stolen goods, customs fees, and delays. Six of our interviewees had received packages this way. The individuals who work for these agencies are sometimes called "Mulas" or mules because their primary role is to carry money and goods into Cuba. Francisco stated,

> It is the safest way for you to receive a package. … If you send a television through that agency, you receive it. A pair of shoes, you get them. I worked for that agency. With my car I helped deliver packages. And we were super-efficient. I would pick it up at the airport with a name and address, and I would distribute them throughout the whole city and some other areas. And nothing ever got lost, because we worked private enterprises. But according to the state, [using Mulas] is illegal.

Agency staff members exhibit Schumpeterian entrepreneurship by cultivating a disruptive new market for their services and distributing resources in a novel way. The agencies also aid in maintaining social ties and leverage social networks to facilitate the flow of money remittances and goods through their services. Landa noted that,

> [Agencies] hire two or three people, buy them plane tickets for Cuba and the company sends things with them. Generally, it's people that don't have the money to come to Cuba and see their family, and through these companies they get a free flight to Cuba and [in return] they only have to use their luggage to bring packages to other people.

Such agencies have found ways to reduce the costs of individual remittance transfers and effectively utilize a broad network of remittance senders and receivers as well as people looking for cheaper ways to travel back home.

Entrepreneurship Among Remittance Senders

Interviewees reported that remittance senders held jobs in construction, manufacturing, and food service in the US, working not just to improve their own lot in life but also to save money and send it back home. Often, senders rely on their local knowledge of their family's situation to anticipate their specific needs and help them when they face new challenges. Veronica noted that, "Remittances help you solve problems. Food problems, hygiene problems, housing problems, clothing problems, every kind of problem."

There are also certain types of goods that cannot be consistently found or purchased in Cuba, including car parts, bikes, most electronics, clothes and specialty or quality food items. Having connections outside of Cuba that can acquire and send these items improves the lives of Cubans.

Remittance senders have found various ways to expedite money transfers and in-kind deliveries. They often rely on loose social networks to find out when friends, relatives, or mere acquaintances are traveling to Cuba from the US in order to send packages or money along with them. A majority of our interviewees relied on this method to receive remittances. Coordinating with travelers allows for senders to avoid certain fees or avoid waiting to send goods until they can travel back to Cuba themselves.

Remittance senders may also convert US dollars into Euros because Euros face a more favorable exchange rate in Cuba. And, rather than sending money (which can incur taxes and fees), they find other ways to provide funds that still provide value. For example, they purchase cell phone minutes for Cubans through online services in the US. Cell phone ownership was legalized in Cuba in 2007, and about 70 percent of the cell phones in use on the island are paid for by Cubans living abroad (Morales 2013). While cell phone minutes are less fluid than cash, they provide access to networks and resources that would be restricted otherwise.

Remittance senders are experts at identifying and determining what aid is needed within their social network, as well as finding creative ways to send remittances to ensure delivery to those directly in need.

Entrepreneurship Among Remittance Recipients

A dominant narrative among interviewees was the idea of the Cuban as a survivor and an inventor. "Cubans are inventors," said Oleda, "we always come up with solutions. We are always creating and we always come up strong." Cubans find creative ways to create or utilize existing social ties abroad in order to facilitate remittance flows. Families create an extended network by sending a family member abroad to be able to work and send money back home. Carlos notes that,

> [Sending a family member abroad] has become a kind of family business. Sometimes they sacrifice the youngest member of the family and make them leave the family home. They send them in boats or through marriages or with a job offer and they stay. That is a way [for families] to survive economically.

While this establishes a stream of resources, interviewees also noted that splitting up families is a large cost to pay in order to survive as a family.

Cubans also have had to be inventive about how they exchange remitted dollars for their local currency. Before the dollar was legalized, Cubans leveraged social networks to find foreigners to exchange the money for them. More recently, in order to avoid the high taxes associated with exchanging dollars, Cubans have devised other solutions. For instance, Javier recalls that,

> We could exchange dollars, as many of us did, with someone who was about to travel to the U.S. and needed dollars. They would give us a lower rate. The majority of Cubans do that. When we exchange our dollars in a bank it's because we have no other option left.

This inventiveness also manifests in the entrepreneurial uses of remittance money. While interviewees revealed that a majority of remittances are used for consumption, recent legalization of some private enterprise in Cuba have opened up new avenues for investment facilitated by private remittance flows. "Before, they only sent the money for one to eat" said Francisco, age 51, "now they send it so you can open a business." In 2013, the government authorized 201 legal occupations for *cuentapropistas* or entrepreneurs. This list includes taxi drivers, food vendors, café and restaurant owners, and repair shop owners. Thus, remittances are also linked to the rise of the *cuentapropista*. Nalda observes that,

> Most private businesses, are being set up with the money that people send to their families here. People who live in a foreign country and are doing financially well send money here so that their relatives can have their own business and income. It's not my situation, but I know of people that use remittances to help them start a business or set up a cafeteria, a clothing store.

Entrepreneurs anticipate needs, provide new services, and use resources in new ways. For example, private Cuban restaurants—or *paladars*—dominate the food scene in Cuba. Cubans use excess space to run small eateries, reconfiguring apartments and other small spaces so as not to run afoul of regulations on business size or the numbers of customers that can be served. They also develop new informal supply chains with individuals abroad in order to get around Cuban import restrictions on food items.

Nevertheless, the challenges persist and so too does the demand for entrepreneurial solutions. As Nalda posits,

> I think that the changes will come as long as there is a greater openness and as long as there are more people with new projects and new ideas that can spread. That is what I think. But we still need a lot of changes. … A lot of people have lost faith and have left. They have tried to do things here, and Cuba always imposes a new law that doesn't let them move forward. … Cubans ask if the private sector works, well, it does. Because when you have a business and you make it profitable with your efforts and by sacrificing things, and you see that it's slowly improving, then you'll take care of it. When things don't belong to someone, people don't take care of them.

Echoing Eckstein's findings about the ability of transnational ties to disrupting government control over Cuban citizens, Nalda's comment reveals that there is a sense that entrepreneurship will beget more entrepreneurial activity both in the provision of aid and in the development of local private businesses. Cubans take pride in their inventiveness, whether they use these skills to find new ways to send or use remittances, provide an informal service to circumvent constraints, or create or maintain ties to remittance senders. Increased access to global networks around Cuba may spur entrepreneurial activity within Cuba. As resources continue to enter the country and expand business opportunities, the liberalism that can come along with remittances may impact Cuban society as well.

Interviews with individuals on the ground demonstrate that entrepreneurs identify needs, provide targeted solutions, and adjust their methods when the aid environment changes. For example, recipients interviewed were in regular communication with their remittance senders often via cell phone (a service often paid for remotely by remittance senders), relaying their need for specific items or for funding when appliances break or unexpected circumstances arise. Remittance senders and recipients have knowledge of local shortages in items such as toilet paper or coffee cups, as well as items that are not available on the island. Individuals who are about to travel to Cuba will ask what family and friends need and fill their suitcases with the demanded products. Finally, remittance senders will leverage their social ties to send care packages with people who are about to travel to Cuba.

Additionally, Cubans invent targeted solutions to economic need. Agencies coordinate diffuse information and resources to provide a more trustworthy service than traditional mail to Cuba. Recipients and senders alike use their social networks to find ways to circumvent taxes and fees by sending money and goods directly with friends and family or agencies traveling to Cuba. Cubans circumvented untrustworthy institutions, such as Cuban banks and customs, in order to ensure the delivery of goods and money.

Individuals also adapt to complex situations by adjusting their processes and practices over time. Before the dollar was legalized, Cubans found creative ways to exchange illicit dollars for local currency, such as leveraging their social networks to find a foreigner who could help exchange it for them. They also traded dollars with the local currency of other Cubans who were about to travel abroad. When Western Union entered Cuba, senders and recipients embraced the change as a fast and secure way to receive money. Nevertheless, Cubans continue to adapt to changes in taxes and fees by employing their inventiveness in using remittance agencies or other informal methods of remittance provision.

Coordinating remittance flows is costly and challenging. Entrepreneurs play a critical role by leveraging local knowledge, using social ties to connect aid recipients and senders with services, and facilitating adaption to new rules and regulations. Remittances reinforce this cycle of entrepreneurship that may serve to erode state control and facilitate the exchange of ideas as well as goods and money. While policy changes permitting the flow of more people and money remittances to Cuba have improved the process of remittance provision, there is still room for improvement.

Conclusion

Entrepreneurs play a central role in identifying local need for remittances, connecting potential remittance senders with recipients, and sustaining the networks that facilitate the provision of aid. Remittance senders, recipients, and service providers exhibit entrepreneurial qualities such as alertness to economic opportunities, inventiveness, and adaptability. Entrepreneurs facilitate aid and use local knowledge and social networks to establish services and navigate complex, dynamic environments characterized by institutional and policy-driven constraints on economic activity in the US and Cuba.

This chapter helps highlight that while data and research on remittances in Cuba is lacking, the Cuban experience is similar to that of developing countries in the rest of the literature on the effects of private aid. Remittances help people survive and allow individuals to have access to things they otherwise would not have (whether immediate, perishable items or nonperishable goods meant for investment and a more sustained and improved quality of life). They also help grow private businesses and spread wealth. Remittances serve as a form of private aid to Cubans who live in a prolonged economic crisis. That said, further research is needed to study the direct and indirect effects of private aid on social ties, economic growth, and liberalization in Cuba.

The economic development literature is dominated by discussion on aid provision by governments, public-private partnerships, and non-governmental organizations (NGOs). The goals of this sort of foreign aid are to influence broad, macro indicators such as increasing GDP with hopes that such efforts will trickle down to those in need and reduce poverty, improve health, and increase opportunities. However, such top-down approaches have not led to substantial improvements in growth or wellbeing. Remittances and other bottom-up approaches to aid are first concerned with providing immediate assistance to those in need. Such private aid is primarily focused on improving wellbeing, with evidence of moderate impacts on growth (or a trickle up effect). This contrast in goals and effectiveness is worth exploring and has implications for how best to deliver aid and impact wellbeing of those in need.

This chapter demonstrates that it is valuable to pay attention to the social and economic effects associated with remittances and other forms of donor-recipient transfers, especially in areas where data and traditional aid may be lacking. The narratives explored in this chapter suggest that targeted private remittance flows, driven by entrepreneurs, are best equipped to accommodate local priorities and needs. More research in private and informal aid is needed to better understand the capabilities of assistance and long-term progress.

Notes

1. Quotation from a Cuban citizen from interviews conducted in the summer of 2016 (see note 3 for more information on the interviews).

2. See Coyne (2013) for a systematic approach to the limitations of humanitarian aid. For a discussion on how local knowledge and buy-in from individuals on the ground is important for the effectiveness of development reforms and aid (and the barriers that impede reforms), see Boettke, Coyne, and Leeson (2008). On the role of decentralized and bottom-up solutions to disaster recovery, see Storr and Haeffele-Balch (2012).
3. In-person interviews with 17 Cuba citizens and residents of Havana were conducted in the summer of 2016. The average age of interviewees was 53 and included 7 males and 10 females. The interviews averaged 54 minutes. Interviews were conducted using hub-and-spoke methodology in which the first round of interviewees introduced us to the second round of interviewees, which helped us establish trust while still interviewing a diverse selection of individuals. To protect their identity, pseudonyms are used for all individuals that are quoted in this chapter.
4. Private capital flows are defined as capital investment from non-government sources. The Hudson Institute study also measures private philanthropy spending, which includes donations to foundations and non-profit organizations, volunteering, and corporate giving. By contrast, remittances are defined as monetary flows sent from individuals abroad to recipients in their home countries. For the purposes of this chapter, we also include the discussion of in-kind remittances, or physical goods sent from abroad to an individual's home country.
5. A competing hypothesis suggests that foreign aid has an "amplification effect" on the country's existing political-institutional orientation, and would thus make dictatorships more dictatorial (Dutta et al. 2013). In the context of foreign aid flows from rich to poor countries in the Middle East, Ahmed (2012, 2013) found that an increase in remittances was associated with an increase in corruption of political institutions as well as longer duration of autocratic regimes.
6. For a similar framework applied to U.S. disaster management, see Sobel and Leeson (2007), and applied to community-based disaster recovery, see Storr and Haeffele-Balch (2012) and Storr, Haeffele-Balch, and Grube (2015).

References

Acosta, Pablo A., Cesar Calderón, Pablo Fajnzylber, and Humberto López. 2008. What Is the Impact of International Remittances on Poverty and Inequality in Latin America? World Development, 36(1): 89–114.

Acosta, Pablo A., Pablo Fajnzylber, and Humberto López. 2007. The Impact of Remittances on Poverty and Human Capital: Evidence from Latin American Household Surveys. World Bank Policy Research Working Paper. Washington, DC: World Bank.

Adelman, Carol. 2009. Global Philanthropy and Remittances: Reinventing Foreign Aid. The Brown Journal of World Affairs, Spring: 23–33.

Ahmed, Faisal Z. 2013. Remittances Deteriorate Governance. The Review of Economics and Statistics. 95(4): 1166–1182.

Ahmed, Faisal Z. 2012. The Perils of Unearned Foreign Income: Aid, Remittances, and Government Survival. American Political Science Review. 106 (1): 146–165.

Aldrich, Daniel P. 2012. Building Resilience. Chicago: University of Chicago Press.

Boettke, Peter J., Christopher J. Coyne, and Peter T. Leeson. 2008. Institutional Stickiness and the New Development Economics. American Journal of Economics and Sociology, 67(2): 331–358.

Chamlee-Wright, Emily. 2010. The Cultural and Political Economy of Recovery: Social Learning in a Post-Disaster Environment. London: Routledge.

Coyne, Christopher J. 2013. Doing Bad by Doing Good: Why Humanitarian Action Fails. California: Stanford University Press.

Dutta, Nabamita, Peter T. Leeson, and Claudia R. Williamson. 2013. The Amplification Effect: Foreign Aid's Impact on Political Institutions. KYKLOS, 66(2): 208–228.

Eckstein, Susan. 2002. Grounding Immigrant Generations in History: Cuban Americans and Their Transnational Ties. The International Migration Review, 36(3): 799–837.

Eckstein, Susan. 2004. Dollarization and Its Discontents: Remittances and the Remaking of Cuba in the Post-Soviet Era. Comparative Politics, 36(3): 313–30.

Eckstein, Susan. 2010. Remittances and Their Unintended Consequences in Cuba. World Development, 38(7): 1047–55.

Fajnzylber, Pablo, and J. Humberto López. 2008. The Development Impact of Remittances in Latin America. In Remittances and Development: Lessons from Latin America, edited by P. Fajnzylber and J. H. López. Washington, DC: World Bank, 1–19.

Kpodar, Kangni, and Maelan Le Goff. 2011. Do Remittances Reduce Aid Dependency? St. Louis: Federal Reserve Bank of St Louis.

Hayek, F. A. 1945. The Use of Knowledge in Society. The American Economic Review, 35(4), 519–530.

Horwitz, Steven. 2009. Wal-Mart to the Rescue: Private Enterprise's Response to Hurricane Katrina. The Independent Review, 13(4): 511–528.

Hudson Institute. 2016. The Index of Global Philanthropy and Remittances. Washington, DC: The Center for Global Prosperity, Hudson Institute, 1–44.

Morales, Emilio. 2013. Cuba: $2.6 Billion in Remittances in 2012. Havana Times, June 11, 2013. Access here: http://www.havanatimes.org/?p=94444

Morales, Emilio. 2016. Cuba: The Fastest Growing Remittance Market in Latin America. The Havana Consulting Group, June 23, 2016. Access here: http://www.thehavanaconsultinggroup.com/en-/Articles/Article/20

Office of Foreign Assets Control. 2009. Cuban Assets Control Regulations. Federal Register, 31 CFR Part 515, 74 (172): 46000–07. Access here: http://www.treasury.gov/resource-center/sanctions/Documents/CACR_Amendments_09032009.pdf

Orozco, Manuel. 2010. The Future Trends and Patterns of Remittances to Latin America. Report. Washington, DC: Inter-American Development Bank.

Kirzner, Israel. 1997. Entrepreneurial Discovery and the Competitive Market Process: An Austrian Approach. Journal of Economic Literature, 35(1): 60–85.

Kirzner, Israel. 1999. Creativity and/or Alertness: A Reconsideration of the Schumpeterian Entrepreneur. The Review of Austrian Economics, 11: 5–17.

Schumpeter, Joseph A. 1962. Capitalism, Socialism, and Democracy. New York: Harper & Row.

Sobel, Russell, and Peter T. Leeson. 2007. The Use of Knowledge in Natural Disaster Relief Management. The Independent Review, 11(4): 519–532.

Storr, Virgil Henry, and Stefanie Haeffele-Balch. 2012. "Post-disaster Community Recovery in Heterogeneous, Loosely Connected Communities." Review of Social Economy, 70(3): 295–314.

Storr, Virgil Henry, Stefanie Haeffele-Balch, and Laura E. Grube. 2015. Community Revival in the Wake of Disaster. New York: Palgrave Macmillan.

Sullivan, Mark P. 2016. Cuba: US Restrictions on Travel and Remittances. CRS report RL31139. Washington, DC: Congressional Research Service. Access here: https://www.hsdl.org/?view&did=796908

Western Union Company. 2016a. Western Union Expands in Cuba: Connects the World. Press Release, March 21, 2016. Access here: http://ir.westernunion.com/news/archived-press-releases/press-release-details/2016/Western-Union-Expands-in-Cuba-Connects-the-World/default.aspx

Western Union Company. 2016b. Western Union Pioneers Digital Money Transfer to Cuba. Press Release, June 7, 2016. Access here: http://ir.westernunion.com/news/archived-press-releases/press-release-details/2016/Western-Union-Pioneers-Digital-Money-Transfer-to-Cuba/default.aspx

World Bank. 2018. World Bank 2016 Bilateral Remittance Matrix. Annual Remittance Data, April 2018. Washington, DC: World Bank. Access here: http://www.worldbank.org/en/topic/migrationremittancesdiasporaissues/brief/migration-remittances-data

World Bank. 2017. Personal Remittances Received (% of GDP). Washington, DC: World Bank. Access here: https://data.worldbank.org/indicator/bx.trf.pwkr.dt.gd.zs

Zhunio, Maria Cristina, Sharmila Vishwasrao, and Eric P. Chang. 2012. The Influence of Remittances on Education and Health Outcomes: A Cross-Country Study. Applied Economics, 44(35): 4605–16.

Index[1]

[1] Note: Page numbers followed by 'n' refer to notes.

N. Dutta, C. R. Williamson (eds.), *Lessons on Foreign Aid and Economic Development*, https://doi.org/10.1007/978-3-030-22121-8

FSC
www.fsc.org
MIX
Papier | Fördert
gute Waldnutzung
FSC® C083411

Kolibri 360 GmbH
Ferdinand-Jühlke-Straße 7
99095 Erfurt, Deutschland
produktsicherheit@kolibri360.de